ENVIRONMENTAL POLITICS AND POLICY

ENVIRONMENTAL POLITICS AND POLICY

JOHN McCORMICK

macmillan education palgrave

© John McCormick 2018

All rights reserved. No reproduction, copy or transmission of this publication may be made without written permission.

No portion of this publication may be reproduced, copied or transmitted save with written permission or in accordance with the provisions of the Copyright, Designs and Patents Act 1988, or under the terms of any licence permitting limited copying issued by the Copyright Licensing Agency, Saffron House, 6–10 Kirby Street, London EC1N 8TS.

Any person who does any unauthorized act in relation to this publication may be liable to criminal prosecution and civil claims for damages.

The author has asserted his right to be identified as the author of this work in accordance with the Copyright, Designs and Patents Act 1988.

First published 2018 by
PALGRAVE

Palgrave in the UK is an imprint of Macmillan Publishers Limited, registered in England, company number 785998, of 4 Crinan Street, London, N1 9XW.

Palgrave® and Macmillan® are registered trademarks in the United States, the United Kingdom, Europe and other countries.

ISBN 978–1–137–60400–2 hardback
ISBN 978–1–137–60399–9 paperback

A catalogue record for this book is available from the British Library.

A catalog record for this book is available from the Library of Congress.

Contents

Illustrations and Features	viii
About the Author	xi
Acknowledgements	xii
Abbreviations	xiii
Introduction	xiv

1 Understanding Key Concepts — 1
Defining the environment — 3
Politics and policy — 6
Environmentalism — 10
Evolution of the environmental debate — 15

2 Perspectives on the Environment — 23
Science and the environment — 25
Economics and the environment — 28
Business and the environment — 32
Philosophy and the environment — 36
Security and the environment — 40

3 The Dynamics of Environmental policy — 45
Evolving approaches to environmental policy — 47
The policy cycle — 49
Policy at the state level — 52
Policy at the international level — 55
Environmental policy instruments — 61

4 Actors at the State Level — 68
Understanding environmental governance — 70
Government institutions — 75
Parties and interest groups — 78
Policy diffusion and convergence — 82
Environment and development — 85

5 Actors at the International Level — 91
Understanding international environmental governance — 93
States and the international system — 96
Intergovernmental organizations — 99
Treaty secretariats — 103
International non-governmental organizations — 106

6 Air Pollution: Few Sources, Many Effects — 112
Defining the problem — 114
The major air pollutants — 119
Two encouraging stories: Leaded fuel and the ozone layer — 124
Acid pollution: A mix of success and concern — 130

7 Water: Quantity vs. Quality — 135
Managing water supply — 137
Managing water quality — 141
Shaping water policy — 148
Water and ecology: The case of wetlands — 153

8 Natural Resources: Forests, Oceans, and Fisheries — 157
Defining the problem — 159
Forests: Domestic or global resources? — 162
Oceans: A classic common pool resource problem — 168
Fisheries: Free-for-all on the high seas — 173

9 Waste: A Failure of Consumer Society — 179
Defining the problem — 181
Shaping waste policy — 186
Toxic and hazardous wastes — 194
Exporting and dumping waste — 197

10 Biodiversity: Species, Genes, and Ecology — 202
Defining the problem — 204
The major threats to biodiversity — 207
Shaping biodiversity policy — 215
The case of protected areas — 218

11 Energy: The Slow Road to Renewables — 224
Defining the problem — 226
The prospects for renewable energy — 234
Shaping energy policy — 238

12 Climate Change: The Ultimate Global Test **246**
    Defining the problem 248
    Shaping climate change policy 254
    The climate change convention 258
    To Paris and beyond 262

Glossary 269

References 278

Index 299

Illustrations and Features

Boxes

1.1	The reaction against environmentalism	12
1.2	The environment and globalization	20
2.1	Nature: Boundless or unforgiving?	31
2.2	Religion and the environment	37
3.1	Accidents, disasters, and policy	56
3.2	Regulations – The case of the US Clean Air Act	63
4.1	Environmental citizenship	74
4.2	The resource curse and the environment	88
5.1	The unusual case of the European Union	103
5.2	The role of multinational corporations	108
6.1	Indoor pollution	122
6.2	Thomas Midgley: The one-man wrecking crew	125
7.1	The problem of dams	140
7.2	The dubious benefits of bottled water	147
8.1	The plight of tropical rainforests	165
8.2	Saving the whales	172
9.1	Waste and the consumer society	183
9.2	The problem of radioactive waste	196
10.1	The special place of wilderness	211
10.2	The dominance of charismatic megafauna	216
11.1	The energy-transport nexus	233
11.2	Europe leads the way on energy	242
12.1	Climate change doubters and deniers	253
12.2	The Intergovernmental Panel on Climate Change	259

Figures

1.1	Commoner's four laws of ecology	6
1.2	Reformist and radical approaches to environmentalism	11
1.3	Circles of sustainability	14
3.1	The public policy cycle	50
3.2	Stages in the development of an international treaty	59
3.3	Environmental policy instruments	62
4.1	Political regimes	71
4.2	Four dimensions of the environmental state	73
4.3	The four pillars of Green politics	79
4.4	Environmental Performance Index	85
5.1	Approaches to international environmental governance	94
5.2	Competing theories of international relations	96
6.1	The world's most polluted cities	116
6.2	Electricity generation in the European Union	117
6.3	Electricity generation in India	117
6.4	Comparative sulphur dioxide emissions	132
7.1	Access to improved sources of drinking water	144
7.2	Access to improved sanitation facilities	146
7.3	Top ten consumers of bottled water	147
8.1	Regional trends in forest cover	163
8.2	Global fish catch	174
9.1	Municipal waste production by region	184
9.2	Municipal waste production in the OECD	185
9.3	Comparative municipal waste production	185
9.4	Municipal waste recovery and disposal	190
10.1	Key terms in the biodiversity debate	207
10.2	Threats to biodiversity	208
10.3	Area of protected land	219
11.1	The global energy picture	227
11.2	The world's biggest oil consumers	231
12.1	Changes in CO_2 concentrations and global temperature	250
12.2	The ten warmest years on record	251
12.3	Public opinion on climate change	254
12.4	The ten biggest producers of carbon dioxide	257
12.5	Carbon dioxide emission trends among the five biggest producers	265

Tables

1.1	Key environmental concerns	5
1.2	Four dimensions of environmental problems	9
2.1	The tensions between policy and science	27
2.2	Types of goods	29
2.3	Voluntary environmental practices	34
3.1	Evolving approaches to environmental policy	48
3.2	Examples of environmental accidents and disasters	57
3.3	Examples of international environmental treaties	58
3.4	Examples of international environmental conferences	61
3.5	Carbon tax: Benefits and costs	65
4.1	Ideology and the environment	72
4.2	Government environment departments	76
4.3	The techniques of environmental NGOs	81
5.1	Intergovernmental organizations with environmental interests	100
5.2	Examples of environmental treaty secretariats	105
5.3	Examples of international environmental NGOs	109
6.1	Major air pollutants	120
6.2	The ozone layer and climate change: Political responses compared	129
7.1	A dozen different uses for water	137
7.2	Sources of water pollution	141
7.3	Comparing air and water policy	148
8.1	Types of natural resources	160
8.2	Maritime zones under international law	169
8.3	International treaties on marine pollution	171
9.1	Waste policy options	187
9.2	Incinerators: Benefits and costs	193
9.3	Toxic and hazardous substances	194
10.1	Number of species identified	205
10.2	The megadiverse countries	205
10.3	International treaties on biodiversity	217
10.4	Protected areas: Benefits and costs	221
11.1	The major sources of energy	229
11.2	Renewable sources of energy: Benefits and costs	236
11.3	The place of energy policy in national government	239
12.1	Greenhouse gases	249
12.2	Key events in the climate change debate	260
12.3	Key articles in the 2015 Paris climate change accord	263

About the Author

John McCormick is Professor of Political Science at the Indianapolis campus of Indiana University in the United States. His academic interests lie in the fields of comparative politics, environmental policy, and the politics and policies of the European Union. Before entering academia he worked for two London-based environmental groups, the World Wildlife Fund and the International Institute for Environment and Development. He is the author of more than a dozen books, including *The Global Environmental Movement* (John Wiley) and *Environmental Policy in the European Union* (Palgrave).

Acknowledgements

As ever, I'd like to begin my acknowledgements by expressing my heartfelt thanks to the staff at Palgrave for their usual professional, flexible, and good-humoured work – they are the ideal publishers in every way. I particularly thank Lloyd Langman for guiding the work on this book from start to finish, and Chloe Osborne for her assistance. I'd also like to thank the six anonymous reviewers (from the United Kingdom, the United States, and the Netherlands) for their helpful comments on the original proposal for the book, and the two anonymous reviewers from the United Kingdom for their more detailed comments on the finished manuscript. Finally, my love to Leanne, Ian, and Stuart – my sons have been too young to take much interest in my books so far, but I am hoping this will be the first one they try out.

Abbreviations

CBD	Convention on Biological Diversity
CFCs	chlorofluorocarbons
CITES	Convention on International Trade in Endangered Species of Wild Fauna and Flora
CSR	corporate social responsibility
EEZ	exclusive economic zone
EC	European Community
EPA	US Environmental Protection Agency
EU	European Union
FAO	Food and Agriculture Organization of the UN
GHG	greenhouse gases
IGO	intergovernmental organization
IMO	International Maritime Organization
INGO	international non-governmental organization
IPCC	Intergovernmental Panel on Climate Change
IUCN	International Union for Conservation of Nature
MNC	multinational corporation
MSY	maximum sustained yield
NGO	non-governmental organization
NIMBY	not in my back yard
ODSs	ozone-depleting substances
OECD	Organization for Economic Cooperation and Development
PM	particulate matter
STS	science and technology studies
TEL	tetraethyl lead
UN	United Nations
UNCLOS	UN Convention on the Law of the Sea
UNEP	United Nations Environment Programme
VOCs	volatile organic compounds
WHO	World Health Organization

Introduction

In the northern summer of 2016, hundreds of reindeer in the Arctic region of Russia were brought down by a mysterious disease. Soon afterwards, nomadic herders in the region began to fall sick, and a 12-year-old boy died after becoming ill with a fever, stomach pains, diarrhoea, and vomiting. The problem was soon identified as anthrax, a bacterial infection that had not been seen in the region for 75 years. The source? Abnormally high temperatures that led to a thaw in the permafrost, releasing anthrax bacteria that can survive in human and animal remains for hundreds of years. When nomads bury their dead, they cannot dig too deeply because of the hardness of the permafrost, so with a thawing in the wake of temperatures reaching as high as 35°C (95°F), the river banks where many of the dead were buried began to erode, releasing the bacteria into the air and the water (Luhn, 2016).

While this was an isolated incident, it was symptomatic of the broader fallout from human-induced climate change. Global temperatures have been rising in the wake of higher concentrations of greenhouse gases, weather patterns have been changing, there have been more extreme examples of tropical storms and natural disasters, polar ice caps and mountain glaciers are melting, sea levels are rising, coastal erosion is worsening, crop-growing patterns are changing, and landscapes are being transformed as a result of alterations in temperatures and patterns of rainfall. More people are becoming aware of the problems and the potential effects, and are changing the way they live in response, but governments and industries have been slow to respond, and there are still some people who argue that climate change is not a serious problem, and even that it is not a problem at all – that it may just be an elaborate hoax.

Climate change is just one of a litany of environmental problems that have followed in the wake of the Industrial Revolution, and have accelerated the widespread changes wrought by human activity on nature. So substantial have been those changes that we may even be living through a distinctive geological epoch known as the **Anthropocene**. This follows the Holocene, dated from the end of the last ice age 10,000 years ago, and is a label proposed as early as the 1870s but popularized by the Nobel laureate Paul Crutzen (2002) to illustrate the extent to which human activity has changed global ecological systems. Mankind, he suggests, is likely to remain 'a major environmental force for many millennia', a force already reflected in the size of the human population, the spread of human settlements to almost every corner of the earth, widespread and massive changes to landscapes, the rise in levels of airborne and waterborne pollutants, and the sharp increase in the number of species extinctions (Zalasiewicz et al. 2010).

This is a book about the political and policy response to these problems. It is designed to introduce students to the key concepts in the field, to survey the major debates, and to assess the multiple dimensions of the environment as a political and policy problem. As well as looking at the underlying character and dynamics of the problem, it assesses the policy record in a selection of key areas, ranging from air and water pollution to biodiversity and climate change. Each of these cases raises a separate set of challenges, helping illustrate the multidimensional nature of the environment as a political and policy matter.

In the chapters that follow, you will:

- Learn about the relationship between humans and their environment.
- Review the character of the environment as both a political and a policy issue, and its relationship to science, economics, ethics, law, development, and security.
- See how the political debate over environmental issues has evolved, and be introduced to the contrasting influences over that debate in different situations.
- Gain insight into the work of the national and international actors involved in making and implementing policy: who they are, what they do, the sources of their authority, the barriers they face, and their levels of efficacy.
- Better understand the national and international policy responses to environmental needs and problems: how they are shaped, who shapes them, and the key influences that come to bear on the policy process.
- Learn about the major environmental problems we face, their causes, and how we have responded.

The main task faced by the authors of textbooks can be summed up in one word: synthesis. The purpose of a book like this is to take large bodies of data, research, and knowledge and boil them down to their essentials, offering students a good idea of the state of understanding of a given topic, and pointing the direction to possibilities for more detailed research. It does this by using three complementary sets of approaches.

First, the book is not exclusively about environmental politics or policy, but is instead a combination of the two: it looks at the political factors and pressures that come to bear on the environmental debate, and at the policies that result. The underlying logic is that understanding one cannot be achieved without also understanding the other; a book on environmental policy must inevitably look at politics and government, while a book on environmental politics must inevitably look at the policies that result from the work of governments and their interaction with industry, agriculture, interest groups, and consumers.

Second, the book combines two sub-fields in the study of political science: comparative politics and international relations. The first focuses on domestic politics and policy, and compares approaches in different states and different types of states; the chapters quote from a variety of cases, with a particular focus on four of the biggest global actors: the European Union, the United States, China, and India, but with references also to many other countries, using examples chosen to offer a wide and representative geographical, political, economic, and environmental range. While there are always dangers in generalization, the terms *North* and *South* are used to distinguish the wealthier and post-industrial states of Europe, North America, East Asia, and Australasia from the poorer and/or industrializing states of Asia, Latin America, and Africa.

For its part, the study of international relations focuses on the dynamics of the relationship among states. Trade, globalization, the transboundary nature of many environmental problems, and the growing reach of international organizations and international law have combined to mean that states cannot entirely function in isolation, and much of what passes as domestic law and policy is actually a result of law and policy made and shaped at the international level. Hence the book looks at the work of international organizations, and the mixed record in achieving international agreement on key environmental problems.

Finally, and unlike any other textbook on the topic, this one goes beyond a study of the broad principles underlying environmental politics and policy, and applies them through a detailed assessment of seven different cases: air, water, natural resources, waste, biodiversity, energy, and climate change. Just as we cannot fully understand the broad principles without looking at how they work in specific cases, so we cannot fully understand those cases without looking at the broad principles. The first five chapters look at the bigger picture, while the last seven chapters look at how politics and policy has worked (or has not worked) in a more detailed fashion.

This combination of politics and policy, of comparative politics and international relations, and of broad principles and more detailed cases, has resulted in a book that is designed to meet the needs of students in a variety of different settings and countries, and who are looking for a survey of this critically important subject, which impacts everyone and in which everyone has a direct interest. The environment is a multifaceted subject, the politics of decisions on environmental problems spilling over into science, economics, business, philosophy, and security. These problems relate to the quality of the air we breathe and the water we drink, how we manage essential natural resources, how we dispose of waste, our sources of energy, the way we relate to nature, and – most critical of all – what we are doing to the planet, and how our actions affect us.

Chapter summaries

Chapter 1 opens the book with a discussion of some of the key concepts at the foundation of environmental politics and policy. It begins with a discussion of the meaning of the terms *environment*, *politics*, and *policy*, and then looks at the competing arguments about how best to address environmental challenges, ranging from reforms to existing political, economic and social structures, to the more radical view that we need fundamental change and entirely new approaches to both economic growth and environmental protection. It ends with a brief review of the evolution of approaches to environmental policy, focusing on developments since the 1960s.

Chapter 2 reviews five of the most important perspectives on environmental politics and policy: the importance of objective and verifiable scientific understanding, the economic challenges of giving a value to different courses of action, the choices made by business and consumers, the different ethical dimensions of the environmental debate, and the relationship between environmental and security problems. Each of them has its own sets of problems and possibilities, the outcome and the results depending on the balance of political support for opting for one approach over another.

Chapter 3 focuses on the character and dynamics of environmental policy: how it is made, the pressures that shape its development and implementation, the differences between approaches at the state and the international level, and the different instruments or tools available to policymakers. It begins by reviewing four different phases in approaches to the environment, then looks at the policy cycle as a means for understanding a process that often disorderly. It then compares approaches to environmental policy at the state level, contrasting them with approaches at the international level, before ending with an assessment of the different tools used in policy, ranging from regulatory command-and-control approaches to market-based options.

Chapter 4 examines the way in which states have approached environmental problems, beginning with making a distinction between the approaches of democracies vs. authoritarian states, and of wealthy countries vs. poor countries. It considers the role of ideology and the meaning of environmental citizenship, then reviews the problem of administrative fragmentation in the structure of government institutions. It then contrasts the role of parties and interest groups, before assessing the dynamics of policy diffusion and convergence, ending with a discussion about the relationship in developing countries between environmental management and economic development.

Chapter 5 uses the perspectives of international relations to assess the actors, influences, and politics involved in the shaping and implementation of environmental policy at the international level. It begins with an assessment of the meaning of international environmental governance, and offers four different ways of understanding how such governance works. It then reviews competing views about the place of states in the international system, before looking – in turn – at the structure, interests, and impact on environmental politics and policy of intergovernmental organizations, treaty secretariats, international non-governmental organizations, and multinational corporations.

Chapter 6 offers the first of the issue cases, focusing on air quality. It begins with a review of the problem, looking at the reasons behind the decline in air quality, the major sources and effects of pollution and the major pollutants, and the action so far taken (or not) at the local, national, and international levels to address air pollution. It then looks at two relatively successful cases – the efforts made to remove lead from petrol and to stop production of the chemicals that created a thinning of the earth's ozone layer – before assessing the mixed policy record on acid pollution.

Chapter 7 shifts the focus to water, which poses challenges both of quality and of quantity. The chapter opens with a review of the different forms in which water is found and the many uses to which it is put, and looks at the options available for addressing problems with supply. It goes on to look at the multiple threats to water quality, and at the record in achieving improved sources of drinking water and improved sanitation facilities. It then assesses the shaping of water policy, explaining the emphasis on local and national responses, and the modesty of international responses. It ends with a review of the relationship between water and ecology, using a case study of wetlands.

Chapter 8 assesses the qualities of natural resources, and the political tensions between approaches that vary according to whether resources are renewable or non-renewable, finite or infinite, global or local, and private, public, or common pool goods. The chapter takes an example of a private resource (forests) and two common pool resources (the oceans and fisheries), and compares and contrasts the record in developing workable policies. National and international responses have had mixed results, for sometimes different reasons, while regional responses have often been more successful.

Chapter 9 focuses on a prime symbol of the failure of the consumer society: waste. It begins with an outline of the problem, defining the meaning of the term before looking at the different forms taken by waste, and trends in production. It then looks at the shaping of waste policy, reviewing the varied record with prevention, recovery, and disposal. The chapter goes on to look at the particular challenges posed by dealing with toxic, hazardous, and radioactive waste, and ends with a review of the dynamics of the international export and dumping of waste, and the mixed record of the international waste regime.

Chapter 10 focuses on biodiversity, beginning with a discussion of the difficulties of measuring the breadth and the depth of the problem. The chapter reviews the five major threats to biodiversity: habitat loss, invasive species, and pressures from human population, pollution, and overexploitation, including the particular problem of trade in endangered species. It ends with a discussion of the directions so far taken in addressing the threats to biodiversity, including the ethical, ecological, and practical arguments involved, and the unbalanced interest in so-called charismatic megafauna. It also looks at the development of protected areas, weighing up their advantages and disadvantages.

Chapter 11 looks at energy, beginning with a review of the major sources, at the trends taking place in each sector, and at the resulting environmental problems. It then assesses the changing prospects for renewable energy, which will inevitably play an ever bigger role as technology changes and market forces accelerate the move away from fossil fuels. The chapter ends with an assessment of energy policy. Few states have a clear set of policy goals (beyond the security of supply), there is little in the way of an international energy regime, and it has mainly been left to the private sector to take the lead on change.

Chapter 12 is about climate change, the ultimate global test for environmental policy. It begins with an outline of the science of the issue, discussing the key greenhouse gases and their sources, trends in emissions, the effects of climate change, and the dynamics of public opinion. It then reviews the political response, contrasting the opposing positions of key players in the debate, and assessing the different steps in the political debate leading up to the conclusion of the 2015 Paris accord. It ends with an analysis of the results achieved so far with climate policy, including several potential explanations for the evolution of that policy.

Features of the Book

Key arguments and chapter overviews Each chapter begins with a set of key summary arguments and an overview of what the chapter is about and how it is structured.

Boxes Each chapter contains two boxes focusing on a topic or concept related to the nearby text.

Tables and figures The text is dotted with tables and figures that present key data or that try to express some of the more complex ideas in visual form. Most are based on the latest data available from the websites of key national and international organizations.

Discussion questions Each chapter ends with a set of open-ended and occasionally provocative questions designed to help students think about some of the critical issues raised in the book, and to suggest subjects for further research.

Key concepts Each chapter ends with a list of the key terms introduced in that chapter, all of which are highlighted and defined within the relevant chapter and brought together in a Glossary and the end of the book including more than 170 definitions.

Further reading Each chapter ends with a short list of books chosen to provide more detailed and current information and to act as resources for research assignments.

1 Understanding Key Concepts

Key arguments

- The environment consists of the physical surroundings in which humans, animals, plants, insects, bacteria, and other organisms exist.
- As a policy and political issue, the environment is hard to compartmentalize; it overlaps with almost all other policy issues.
- Politics and policy are different but related terms; one is a process of decision-making, the other is a course of action (or inaction).
- Environmental politics are distinguished from most other arenas of politics by varieties of scale, which range from the local community to the entire earth. The environment may be the only political issue that has truly global dimensions.
- Environmentalism seeks political and economic change, but there are competing views about how this can be achieved, ranging from change within the existing capitalist system to an entire rejection of that system.
- Environmentalism emerged in different places and for different reasons, was influenced at first by events and thinking in the West in the 1960s, and later included the concerns of poorer parts of the world.

Chapter overview

While concerns about the deteriorating relationship between humans and their environment date back at least to the Industrial Revolution, the political response was late arriving. The earliest efforts to change policy date back to the late 1800s, but the environment has been a regular feature of the public policy agenda only since the 1960s, and while we now understand much more about the sources and effects of environmental needs and problems, the record on addressing them has been mixed at best. They vary by time and place, there is disagreement on their implications, government and industry often disagree on the best and most practical responses, the economic implications are not always clear, and the science behind many environmental problems is still debatable. The environment must also compete for public and political attention with other needs that most people regard as more immediate: climate change may be the greatest threat ever faced by humanity, but it has moved only slowly up the policy agenda, and the threats posed by terrorism, poverty, unemployment, and by war and civil conflict in many parts of the world can often seem more immediate.

The key to understanding any subject is to understand the concepts that form the foundation of that subject, so this opening chapter introduces some of the key concepts at the foundation of environmental politics and policy. Unfortunately, this is not always as easy as it might seem. Unlike the natural sciences, which are guided by laws and replicable experimentation, the social sciences – because they focus on the study of human society – revolve around concepts whose meanings are softer, are often a matter of interpretation, and are both debatable and widely debated. It is usual to see scholars and politicians defining the same terms differently, or using different terms to describe the same thing, or using terms without defining them on the assumption that their meaning is understood.

But we should not forget the admonition credited to Plato or Socrates that 'the beginning of wisdom is the definition of terms', and no analysis of environmental politics and policy can be either focused or complete unless the parameters of the topic are understood. The meanings of words are also important in legal terms, because of their role in establishing the scope of policy, law, and the work of political organizations. Sands et al. (2012: 16) quote the example of the failure of the 1946 Convention for the Regulation of Whaling to define a 'whale', leading – among other things – to a debate about whether or not the work of the International Whaling Commission should include dolphins.

This chapter begins with a discussion of the meaning of the terms *environment*, *politics*, and *policy*. Environmental matters are often difficult to clearly distinguish from other areas of politics and policy, and are made more complex by their multifaceted nature and by a scale that ranges from the local to the global. Environmentalists have long been divided over the question of whether radical and fundamental change is needed, for example, or whether it is enough to reform existing political and economic structures through ideas such as sustainable development and ecological modernization. They must also address the doubts of anti-environmentalists, many of which are built on the challenges of reaching agreement on the science of environmental problems. The chapter ends with a brief review of the evolution of approaches to environmental policy, focusing on the formative events of the 1960s, the influence of the landmark 1972 Stockholm conference, the emergence of green politics, the competing views of industrialized and emerging countries, the rise of global perspectives, and the arguments of post-environmentalism.

Defining the environment

It is unwise to write a book about a particular subject without a clear definition of the terms involved, and yet much of the research in the social sciences suffers from just such a problem. It is usual to introduce a term, to comment on the many different ways in which it has been defined, to point out that definitions change by time and place, to quote multiple competing definitions, and then to avoid taking a particular stand on its meaning. The noun ***environment*** suffers from just such a problem, exacerbated by its relatively recent use as a political concept. It only began to appear in relation to nature and ecosystems in the 1960s, having until then been used only in the context of the home or work environment (Dauvergne, 2009: xii). It continues to be conditioned even today by multiple adjectives, such as *political, economic, social,* and *cultural,* but has been surprisingly rarely defined in its political and policy sense. As a result, it shares the problem that Caldwell (1990: 197) once ascribed to the term *development*: it has become 'a term that everyone understands and no one is able satisfactorily to define'.

For our purposes, the term *environment* is defined simply as the physical surroundings in which humans, animals, plants, insects, bacteria, and other organisms exist. For the purposes of politics and policy, it comes in three main varieties:

- The *natural environment* consists of those parts of the earth – living or non-living – that are not a product of human activity. This includes living organisms, ecosystems, climate, weather, minerals, soil, air, and water. The implication, of course, is that humans are not part of the natural system, which is clearly wrong; but it is reasonable to distinguish natural from man-made change. Such a distinction, however, is increasingly artificial; Wapner (2014) argues that humans and nature cannot be considered as two separate domains, while Purdy (2015) argues that the world in which we live is one we have made, and that we should think of it as a post-natural world.

- The *built environment* consists of everything constructed by humans, including buildings, towns, cities, roads, infrastructure, water and energy supply systems, and perhaps even cultivated forests, urban parks, botanic gardens, and reservoirs. The quality and density of construction has environmental effects (for example, dams disrupt rivers, fisheries, natural habitats, and groundwater levels – see Box 7.1), while indoor pollution has its own distinctive set of problems and policy needs.
- The *human environment* is a combination of the two, emphasizing the place of humans within their natural and built surroundings. It was significant that the landmark 1972 Stockholm conference (see later in this chapter) was titled the United Nations Conference on the Human Environment. The implication here is that understanding the environment means not just understanding its natural dimension but also its political, economic, and social dimensions.

In a sense, trying to outline the parameters of the environment as a policy matter is an exercise in futility, because environmental issues cannot be housed in neat boxes (Dryzek, 2013: 9). Almost every activity in which humans take part and for which governments have a policy responsibility has an environmental dimension, and it could be argued that there is almost no distinct area of public policy that is *not* linked in some way to the environment. Conversely, many environmental problems have multiple policy dimensions; in order to address climate change, for example, we must rethink our approaches to transport, energy, industry, agriculture, forestry, urban and rural planning, health care, and tourism, at a minimum. Furthermore, environmental problems are interdependent, often stemming from common roots; so when we address the problem of waste, we also need to address air and water pollution, and vice versa. Instead of thinking about environmental policy as a distinct field, then, we should perhaps be thinking about the environmental dimensions of all policy activities. The European Union has recognized this with its efforts to integrate environmental protection into the definition and implementation of its other policy areas (McCormick, 2001: 63).

Another way to define the environment as a political or policy matter is to consider the kinds of issues that are usually defined as 'environmental'. Some – such as air and water pollution – might be

Table **1.1 Key environmental concerns**

Category	Problems
Air quality	Urban pollution, industrial and vehicle emissions, acid pollution, threats to the ozone layer, climate change, and indoor air quality.
Water quality	Urban and agricultural run-off, algal growth (eutrophication), siltation, oil spills, management of fisheries, and water-based ecosystems. Also includes the management of water for recreation, transportation, and energy generation, and the overuse or contamination of groundwater.
Chemicals	Impact on air and water quality, ecosystems, and living organisms.
Waste	Production, shipment, disposal, and dumping. Distinctions must be made between human, domestic, municipal, agricultural, industrial, biomedical, and radioactive waste. The impact of disposal through landfill or incineration.
Natural resources	Forests, fisheries, soils (erosion, loss of fertility, contamination), crops and arable land (loss to urban spread, desertification, overgrazing, contamination by chemical fertilizers, herbicides, insecticides).
Energy	Different sources (fossil fuels vs. renewables), how energy is generated and used, nuclear power, fracking, energy efficiency, overuse of fuelwood and biomass.
Biodiversity	Nature and natural ecosystems, endangered/threatened species, trade in wildlife, protection of natural habitats (wetlands, forests, marshes, mangroves, and coral reefs), wild genetic resources, genetic modification, and invasive species.

thought of as 'traditional' elements of the environmental debate, but others overlap uneasily with other sectors of policy. For example, should we consider organic farming and genetically modified organisms as environmental issues, agricultural issues, health issues, or all three? Similarly, the European Union has expended a significant amount of political energy on drafting and agreeing laws and policies targeting noise pollution (encouraging the manufacture of quieter road vehicles, construction equipment, aircraft, and domestic appliances), but is noise an environmental issue? In the United States, meanwhile, environmental politics almost uniquely includes concerns for the management of public lands (land owned and managed by the federal government). And while the production of air pollution from the burning of fossil fuels is clearly an environmental issue, to what extent should energy policy be treated separately from environmental policy? In order to help provide some focus, Table 1.1 lists the kinds of concern that most often appear in debates about environmental policy.

A related concept that deserves mention is **ecology**. Developed by the German biologist Ernst Haeckel in the 1850s, it describes the branch of biology that studies the relationships among organisms

Figure **1.1** **Commoner's four laws of ecology**

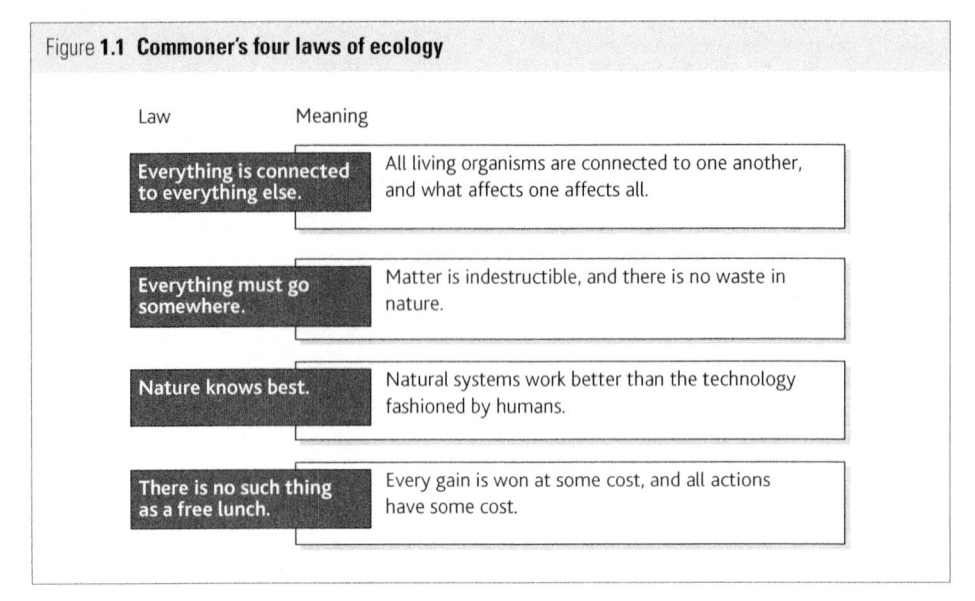

Law	Meaning
Everything is connected to everything else.	All living organisms are connected to one another, and what affects one affects all.
Everything must go somewhere.	Matter is indestructible, and there is no waste in nature.
Nature knows best.	Natural systems work better than the technology fashioned by humans.
There is no such thing as a free lunch.	Every gain is won at some cost, and all actions have some cost.

Source: Commoner (1971)

and between organisms and their physical surroundings, and we will see in Chapter 2 that there is a close relationship between science and policy when dealing with environmental issues. Ecology has been co-opted by some as a synonym for *environment* (so that we sometimes see reference to the ecology movement rather than the environmental movement), and it has also been used in other senses. For example, **political ecology** (another term that has defied agreed definition) can be understood as an interdisciplinary field of study interested in the relationships among politics, economics, society, culture, and the environment (see Robbins, 2012). The overlap between ecology, politics, economics, and technology is succinctly illustrated in the four informal 'laws' of ecology developed by the American biologist Barry Commoner (see Figure 1.1).

Politics and policy

When it comes to understanding the term ***politics***, it is relatively easy to identify examples of political activity, but less so to outline the boundaries of that activity. Politics can be broadly understood as the process by which people decide collectively how to manage and share the resources of the society in which they live. These resources include money, land, minerals, education, jobs, health care, and consumer goods. When citizens vote at elections, when national leaders negotiate with their counterparts in other countries, when corporations or interest groups lobby legislatures, or when masses of citizens hold public demonstrations for or against the actions of government, there is political activity at play. But is politics simply about making and implementing decisions, does it also include efforts to reconcile differences, is it fundamentally about persuasion (see Goodin et al., 2006: 5–7), or is it a competitive struggle for power among people seeking to promote their own interests?

Taken literally, any relationship involving two or more people can be considered political, because it involves shared decision-making, even if one person dictates terms to the others. But the kind of politics that interests us is that of the broader communal kind, involving the making of decisions by those in positions of power (whether legitimately or illegitimately), and that involves significant numbers of people, ranging from local communities to the populations of cities and states, and – in some instances – the entire global population. This begs the question of the meaning of two more terms: power and authority.

Power is another one of those concepts that we think we understand but that we sometimes struggle to define, mainly because it comes in different forms, and can be defined according to different channels, such as the power *to do* something as distinct from the power *over* someone or something. In essence, power means the capacity to control in the sense of being able to bring about change or to resist pressures to change. If power is the capacity to act, then **authority** is the acknowledged right to act. A person pointing a loaded gun at someone else has the power to make the second person bend to their will, but only has authority if they have the right to own and use the gun as – for example – members of the police or the military engaged in their legitimate work.

In legal and constitutional terms, power and authority are more clearly delineated at the national level than at the international level. We live in a world of sovereign states, and in Chapter 4 we will look at the structure and powers of those states and at the dynamics of the authority they hold to take environmental decisions within their jurisdiction. In Chapter 5 we will look at how politics and policy function at the international level, and will find that the environment cannot be neatly delineated by state boundaries: the air and the oceans are both global resources, for example, while rivers often flow through multiple states, and pollution from one country can easily find its way to others. The result is that much environmental policy is made as a result of international cooperation and political pressure involving governments.

If we define **government** as the institutions and offices through which societies are governed, it exists in a meaningful form only at and below the level of states. There is no multinational or world government, so we must instead think of international administration as a process of **governance**, referring to the broader process by which public decisions are made, with or without the input of formal institutions, and with or without formal mechanisms. At the international level, governance typically involves the development of policy via a mixture of governmental and non-governmental forces, and is reflected in the membership of international organizations and the agreement of declarations and treaties.

The politics of the environment are complex and multifaceted. Decisions must often be shaped by communities and economic sectors with conflicting interests and needs, and that might seek to protect their environmentally unfriendly habits out of fear that reform would be expensive. Addressing air pollution, for example, means potentially treading on the toes of the oil, mining, electricity-supply and vehicle manufacturing industries, all of which often have powerful political lobbies. Environmental politics are also distinguished from most other arenas of politics by the varieties of scale, which range from the local community to the entire earth. Indeed, the environment may be the only political issue that can be said to include truly global dimensions. There are many political activities that are common to large parts of the world's population, or even all of it (we almost all have a vested interest in trade, security, health, and economic growth, for example), but they are all an accumulation of multiple local, national, or regional interests. Of all the political challenges that we face, climate change is the most truly universal and fundamentally existential – everyone is impacted to some degree, no matter where they live, and nothing less than the continued welfare of all life on earth is at stake.

Politics, in turn, is the driving force behind **public policy**, which can be defined as whatever actions those in positions of authority take – or deliberately avoid taking – in order to achieve public goals (see Knill and Tosun, 2012: 3–7; Kraft and Furlong, 2015: 3–4). The details of policy can be found in the positions adopted by leaders, the speeches they make, the platforms they publish, the laws they support and pass, and the steps they take (or deliberately fail to take) as they seek to pursue their political objectives. Policies exist at almost every level of human activity, but those that interest us here are public policies, or those that impact large sectors of society. Politics is the lifeblood of policy in the sense that policies are defined, developed, and implemented through political competition, the review of alternative strategies, and the influence brought to bear by interested parties, of which there are often many. Environmental policy is shaped not just by elected officials, but by individual citizens, interest groups, corporations, international organizations, banks and other financial institutions, and economic sectors ranging from farming to transport, energy, and manufacturing. In poorer regions or states, it is poverty rather than wealth that forms the basis of the policy debates that surround most environmental issues.

It is important to make a distinction between policy decisions arising out of the harmful effects of human activity on the environment (placing us in a repair or cure mode), and policy decisions arising out of a need to more efficiently manage the environment and natural resources (placing us in a maintenance or prevention mode). The former are based on recognizing a problem only after it has emerged, a process that is all too often sparked by crisis and disaster: oil spills, the poisoning of water supplies, floods caused by soil erosion, industrial accidents, and so on. An emergency arises, news headlines are generated, governments must respond, and it is debatable how much is learned and how much is changed in order to prevent similar future crises. By contrast, being in a maintenance mode means taking a broader and longer-term approach, gathering accurate data, understanding natural processes, assessing demand for resources, identifying emerging threats, and managing sensibly. Prevention is always better than cure, but it also runs counter to the way that most humans intuitively think.

Policymakers must also wrestle with the different spatial dimensions of environmental problems. Where once such problems might have been seen as localized difficulties impacting relatively few people and demanding mainly local responses, many have become broader in scope, and demand either a cooperative multinational approach or – at the very least – a sharing of policy ideas and experience. They can be broadly placed in one of four types: global, shared, international, and local (see Table 1.2).

Environmental policy is not only influenced by space, but also by time. One of the challenges to making good policy is that most

Table **1.2 Four dimensions of environmental problems**

Type	Features	Examples
Global	Affect almost everyone (not necessarily equally), and demand a global response. Relatively rare, but also relatively serious.	Climate change, threats to the ozone layer.
Shared	Common to multiple parts of the world and often cross national borders, but may have different sources, affect people differently, and require international or national responses.	Air and water pollution, threats to biodiversity.
International	Involve two or more states, and best resolved by affected states working together.	Acid pollution, management of shared rivers, lakes, fisheries.
Local	Problems with local roots, demanding local responses. Similar problems may be found in multiple locations around the world, but they are the responsibility of local communities and authorities.	Waste removal and processing.

environmental problems take years or even decades to emerge, and remedial action can take many more years or decades to be felt. Thus, for example, it took about 40–50 years for science to identify the threat posed to the ozone layer by synthetic chemicals such as chlorofluorocarbons, and another 20 years for agreement to be reached on a solution. And even though the key international ozone layer agreement came into force in 1989, the ozone layer is not expected to recover until at least 2035, and possibly as late as 2050 (see Chapter 6). While effective environmental management demands a long-term view, the industries often involved in creating (and thus addressing) environmental problems are looking mainly to annual profit and loss statements, while elected officials are mainly planning ahead only as far as the next election. It does not help that many environmental problems are not directly observable, or – at best – that they take many years to become observable.

Environmentalism

Environmentalism is a term that is used interchangeably to describe a philosophy, a theory, or an ideology that promotes deeper understanding of the threats faced by the environment, and of the means to developing improved management and protection (see Peterson del Mar, 2012). Environmentalists support a view of the world shaped by the argument that the natural environment is threatened by human action, that humans are ethically responsible for earth's ecological integrity, and that efforts are needed to rebalance the relationship between humans and their environment. These efforts include changes in individual behaviour, but environmentalism is also an example of a social movement: one emerging from society and aimed at pursuing broad goals, by orthodox and/or unorthodox means, usually driven by traditional outsiders challenging existing elites, and seeking to change public policy without becoming part of government. In this sense, environmentalism is usually – if not entirely accurately – equated with activism. It has also been criticized (at least in industrialized Western societies) for portraying humans as somehow separate from nature, to which the counter-argument is made that humans should be seen as an integral part of nature (Foss, 2009).

As a social movement, environmentalism seeks political and economic change, but there are competing views about how this can be achieved, ranging from change within the existing capitalist system to an entire rejection of that system. Different authors have used different terms to distinguish a bifurcated movement (see Figure 1.2), but while they would argue that the terms they use have different meanings, it has become usual (see Young, 1993; Hayward, 1994) to distinguish between **reformist** and

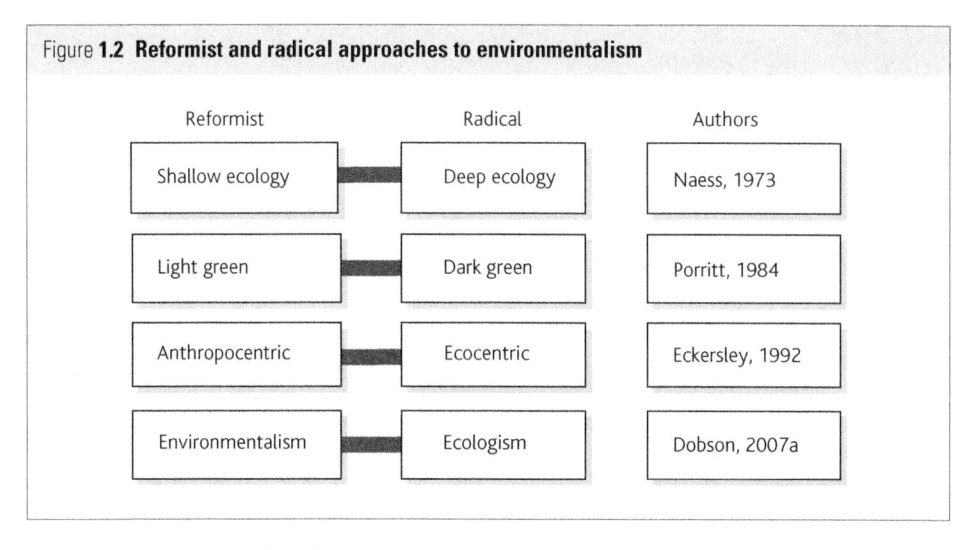

Figure 1.2 **Reformist and radical approaches to environmentalism**

Reformist	Radical	Authors
Shallow ecology	Deep ecology	Naess, 1973
Light green	Dark green	Porritt, 1984
Anthropocentric	Ecocentric	Eckersley, 1992
Environmentalism	Ecologism	Dobson, 2007a

radical environmentalism. The former supports human-centred change within existing political, economic, and social structures, and argues that economic growth and environmental protection can be compatible. For its part, radical environmentalism – which emerged in the 1980s out of disillusion with the failures of reformism (Carter, 2007: 157–60) – argues that we face urgent dangers that cannot be resolved within existing structures, and that we need fundamental change and entirely new approaches to both economic growth and environmental protection. These perspectives are reflected in the distinction made by the Norwegian philosopher Arne Naess (1973) between shallow and **deep ecology**; where the former is an anthropocentric (human-centred) concern for the environment based on how environmental damage will impact humans, the latter is ecocentric (nature-centred) in that it is focused on a concern for the environment for its own sake (see Chapter 2).

Radicals argue that economic growth and material consumption are incompatible with sound environmental management, an argument that traces its heritage back to the publication in 1972 of *The Limits to Growth* (Meadows et al., 1972). This was a report sponsored by an informal association of scientists and politicians known as the Club of Rome, and that used computer modelling to predict future trends using variables such as population growth and resource demand. Given existing trends, the study concluded, the limits to growth on the planet would be reached within a century, although catastrophe could be averted by reductions in population growth and in industrial and agricultural investment. The pessimism of this argument was attacked from many quarters, as was the assumption that economic growth and environmental protection were incompatible, and that a focus on one would necessarily compromise the other.

> **Box 1.1** *The reaction against environmentalism*
>
> Ranged against both reformist and radical environmentalism in its different forms is the phenomenon of **anti-environmentalism**, whose adherents argue that the problems we face are not as serious – nor the earth as fragile - as environmentalists suggest. At one end of the scale, the Danish scholar Bjørn Lomborg caused a stir with his book *The Sceptical Environmentalist* (2001) in which he questioned the view that environmental problems were becoming worse, charged that environmental activists used data selectively to make their case, and pointed to examples indicating that the state of the environment had improved. At the other end of the scale, we find more broad-based resistance to environmentalism as anti-growth and anti-development, and even suggestions that the problems we supposedly face are just part of an elaborate hoax – see Box 12.2.
>
> In the wake of the rising number and influence of environmental groups, of the creation of government environment departments, and of the passage of environmental regulations, informal movements have arisen in several countries to challenge the arguments of environmentalists. Focused on promoting private property rights and the multiple use of resources, and on opposing environmental regulation, they include the Wise Use Movement in the United States and the Share Movement in Canada. Meanwhile, businesses opposed to environmental regulation – finding that they could no longer rely simply on trying to influence government – have instead worked to build internal alliances and coalitions, to fund research, and to launch advertising and public relations campaigns designed to improve their image and to promote their views (Rowell, 1996; Layzer, 2012). The deliberate effort to give the false impression that a company's products or aims are environmentally friendly is known as **greenwashing**. This phenomenon has generated efforts by interest groups and research bodies to offer fact-checking services designed to offer counter-points.

It is helpful here to understand the dynamics of a **paradigm**, meaning a widely shared pattern or set of values, beliefs, and ideas that guides action. Capitalism has been the dominant economic paradigm since the Industrial Revolution, based on the argument that the free market is the best way of maximizing social welfare, and that there is an infinite supply both of natural resources and of sinks into which to dispose of waste. But radical environmentalists in particular argue that this approach is unsustainable, and that it is time for a paradigm shift. The potential for such a shift lies in three related fields:

- Politics, involving a move away from power relations based on the control of resources towards the accessibility of knowledge and information outside conventional political institutions.
- Economics, involving a move way from large, industrial and bureaucratic organizations focused on the mass production of cheap products towards a new digital economy in which

products and services can be provided on a smaller and more human scale.
- Society, involving a move away from centralized and hierarchically controlled arrangements towards a more decentralized, bottom-up approach.

One alternative paradigm – which opposes the arguments of the radicals – is **sustainable development** (see Sachs, 2016), an idea associated with the report of the 1987 UN-sponsored World Commission on Environment and Development (often named the Brundtland report after the chair of the commission, Norwegian prime minister Gro Harlem Brundtland). The report defined sustainable development as 'development that meets the needs of the present without compromising the ability of future generations to meet their own needs' (Brundtland et al., 1987: 43). Like so much that is 'new' in the social sciences, it was not actually a new idea at all, having been reflected – for example – in the almost identical philosophy of **conservation** that was at the foundation of the creation in 1905 of the US Forest Service, and which was defined by its first chief (Gifford Pinchot) as 'the greatest good of the greatest number for the longest time' (Miller, 2013).

The argument underlying sustainable development is that the uncontrolled free market does not work, that resources are not unlimited, and that while they can be used and exploited, this should be done only in such a way as to ensure indefinite supply. While it has been at the heart of environmental debates since the late 1980s, it has been criticized as a concept on several fronts: it is so vague as to have different meanings for different people; some ask whether it applies only (or mainly) to environmental issues or whether it has broader applications; it has tended to be associated mainly with the debate over environment and development in poorer countries; and questions have been asked about how much it has gone beyond the stage of political discourse and been reflected in real change (Happaerts and Bruyninckx, 2014). The lack of such change has combined with the global economic downturn since 2007 and a widespread reaction against global governance (notably in the wake of the immigration crises in Europe and the United States) to reduce interest in the concept in recent years. (But some feel it still has much to offer; for example, see Sachs, 2016).

Sustainable development is related to two other concepts that often appear in discussions about environmental policy. The first of these is **green growth**, a process that builds on sustainable development by achieving growth based on economic, social, and environmental sustainability (see OECD, 2011), a relationship that is often illustrated in the kind of Venn diagram shown in Figure 1.3. The current reality is that the economic circle is bigger and given more emphasis, while the environmental circle is much smaller. The ideal

Figure **1.3 Circles of sustainability**

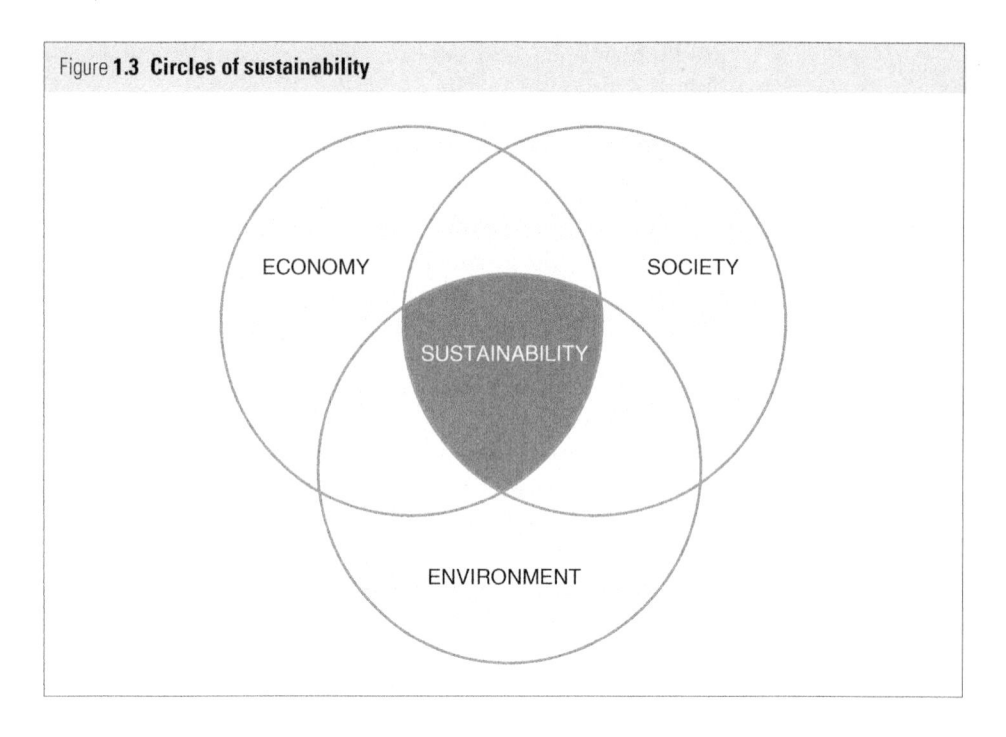

A Venn diagram with three overlapping circles labeled ECONOMY, SOCIETY, and ENVIRONMENT, with SUSTAINABILITY at the center intersection.

is that all three circles should be the same size and should be given equal attention (see Adams, 2006). Meanwhile, a **green economy** is one that generates growth in a manner consistent with sustainable development, simultaneously advancing economic, social, and environmental well-being (Pearce et al., 1989). It stands in contrast to the conventional emphasis placed on growing gross domestic product at almost any cost. Although no country has yet achieved a green economy, there are many examples of green growth in contained areas, such as efforts in major cities to reduce congestion, and investments in renewable sources of energy.

While sustainable development began as an effort to encourage developing states not to make the same environmental mistakes as industrialized states, the related concept of **ecological modernization** is based on the argument that reform is possible within existing economic systems, and that there is no need for a radical revision of conventional economic ideas. This term emerged in Western Europe in the 1980s, and was meant to suggest that the efficient use of natural resources – and the development of new clean technologies – could be a means to achieving economic growth, and even to addressing the environmental costs of globalization. It was at first based on the idea of changing technology, then evolved into an emphasis on the reform of institutions, and then focused on the transformation of patterns of consumption. The overall idea has been to produce a new form of 'sustainable capitalism', a goal that not everyone thinks is possible (for more details, see Mol et al., 2009).

Evolution of the environmental debate

Although the politicization of the environment dates back only a few decades, awareness of the effects of human activity on the environment date back centuries. Just how that awareness evolved into political action, though, is a matter of debate. Science has clearly played a critical role, providing us with new information about the quality of air and water, and about declines in the acreage of forests, the productivity of fisheries, and the numbers of endangered species. Our own eyes, noses, and taste buds have also told us a great deal; the evidence of environmental decline can often be seen, smelled, and tasted. Finally, awareness of environmental decline has grown alongside awareness of other political, social, and economic threats to the new-found affluence of the global middle classes, encouraging a change in values. While the poor and the marginalized often have neither the time nor the political influence always to protect their interests, and are more focused on material demands and subsistence, the middle classes and the wealthy – whose numbers have grown since the Industrial Revolution – have the time, the education, and the resources to identify threats and to organize responses.

The definition of environmental problems – and the underlying ideas behind the debate over those problems – is heavily influenced by Western ideas, in large part because developments in the West (primarily Europe) created many of those problems, and have since been behind the shaping of the responses. Many of these problems have a long history, as in the case of air pollution in London; the burning of coal there was already enough a problem in the 1600s as to encourage the naturalist and diarist John Evelyn to campaign for a response to the 'Hellish and dismall Cloud' which made the city resemble 'the suburbs of hell' (see Lodge, 1969). The scale of the damage accelerated and broadened with the Industrial Revolution, such that London became infamous for its smogs (a combination of smoke and fog), inspiring Charles Dickens to write in his 1841 novel *The Old Curiosity Shop* about factories and chimneys that 'poured out their plague of smoke, obscured the light, and made foul the melancholy air'. One of the effects of urban pollution was to inspire the creation of an amenity movement in Britain that would give people respite from polluted cities in unspoiled countryside. It also inspired the passage of the 1863 Alkali Act (the world's first national law aimed at controlling air pollution) and the creation of the Alkali Inspectorate (the world's first national environmental agency).

In the United States, meanwhile, environmental thinking was influenced by a distinction between **preservation** and conservation. The former – exemplified by John Muir, founder in 1892 of the Sierra Club – was focused on protecting wilderness in the face of westward expansion (a movement that had led to the creation of the world's first national park at Yellowstone in 1872), while the latter was focused on efforts to manage resources sustainably, a view that was behind the creation in 1905 of the US Forest Service. In the 1930s, the problem of land mismanagement was exemplified by the Dust Bowl, when more than half a century of ill-advised agricultural practices produced a flurry of regional dust storms, eroding nearly 1.3 million square kilometres of land in 16 American states. The result was the development of more careful and informed approaches to land management, in the United States and elsewhere.

If there was a single event that could be identified as a turning point in environmental thinking it was the publication in 1962 of the book *Silent Spring* by Rachel Carson, an American marine biologist. The book warned of the effects of DDT and other pesticides and insecticides on agriculture, and more broadly called into question 'the paradigm of scientific progress that defined postwar American culture' (Lytle, 2007: 166–67). It became an international bestseller, and made the effect of chemicals on the environment a public issue for the first time.

Other and broader pressures were also at work that promoted changing habits and new levels of public and political awareness:

- The decades after World War II saw the burgeoning of international cooperation spearheaded by the United Nations (UN). Among the items on the new international agenda was how to improve the management and supply of food and water, with UN agencies such as the Food and Agriculture Organization and the UN Educational, Scientific and Cultural Organization (UNESCO) encouraging discussions, funding research, and hosting conferences.
- A series of major incidents and accidents drew wider public attention to environmental threats. These included smogs in London, the concerns over radioactive fallout from atmospheric nuclear tests that led to the signing in 1962 of the Partial Test Ban Treaty, news that the dumping of mercury in Minamata Bay in Japan was implicated in birth defects, and the first oil disaster to attract world headlines: the grounding of the tanker *Torrey Canyon* off the coast of England in 1967.
- Advances in scientific knowledge drew more attention to the state of the natural environment. The publication in 1966 of the first photographs of Earth taken from space showed the planet alone in space and made people more aware of the vulnerability of humanity.

- New levels of dissatisfaction with politics as usual were behind a counter-culture that spawned mass movements and demonstrations based around nuclear disarmament, feminism, civil rights, opposition to the war in Vietnam, and concerns about environmental problems.

There was also a brief and lively debate about the carrying capacity of the earth, and the relative threats of population growth and flawed technology. Even though the world's population stood at barely 4 billion in the late 1960s (it is today 7.5 billion, and projected to reach 9 billion by 2042), there was much worried talk of the 'population bomb', a phrase popularized by the title of a 1968 book by the American biologist Paul Ehrlich. Ehrlich warned that – unless action was taken to control growth – the limits of human capability to produce food by conventional means would be reached, millions faced the threat of starvation, and the only solution lay in a change in human attitudes.

His warnings harked back to those made in 1798 by the British classical economist Thomas Malthus, whose *Essay on the Principle Population* argued that the natural rate of population growth was exponential, while that of food production was arithmetical. Unless population growth was checked, the population would outstrip the available food supply and there would be widespread famine (Malthus, 1798). Ehrlich's arguments were quickly challenged and refuted by Barry Commoner (1971), who argued that the problem was not so much the growth in population and economic activity as the qualitative problem of 'flawed technology': it was not so much that more goods were being produced and consumed, but that their production and disposal was more costly in environmental terms, undermining 'the finely sculptured fit between life and its surroundings'.

The rising political pressure to address environmental problems was behind the convening in 1972 of the UN Conference on the Human Environment, otherwise known as the Stockholm conference, the first event at which governments (113 in all) had sat down and discussed the state of the environment and the potential political response. Where environmental problems had been discussed in the 1950s and 1960s mainly as a localized problem in rich countries, the perspective of poor countries now entered the debate, and there was a new emphasis on taking the global view. Stockholm encouraged the creation of new national environmental protection departments in countries around the world, and led to the founding in 1973 of the UN Environment Programme, headquartered in Nairobi. Citizen initiatives also played a key role, with the work of national environmental interest groups being reinforced by the work of new international groups, including the World Wildlife Fund (founded 1961), Friends of the Earth (1969), and Greenpeace (1971).

For wealthy states, one of the underlying causes of a change in political and public attitudes was the shift towards new values. The term ***post-materialism*** was developed by the American social scientist Ronald Inglehart (1971) to make a distinction between the more traditional materialist interest in economic growth and security and a new focus on quality of life issues such as environmental protection, nuclear disarmament, and gender equality. His thesis was that Westerners born after World War II had grown up during a time of unprecedented prosperity and relative international peace, freed from many of the concerns about security and survival that had influenced earlier generations. This combination of affluence, peace, and security had led to a 'silent revolution' in Western political cultures, in which the priority given to economic achievement had given way to an increased emphasis on the quality of life: 'the disciplined, self-denying and achievement-oriented norms of industrial society are giving way to the choices over lifestyle which characterize post-industrial economies' (Inglehart, 1997: 28).

One of the consequences of post-materialism was the birth of **green politics** in countries feeling the long-term effects of industrialization. Although green views are most readily associated with a concern for the environment, they are much broader in their reach: Greens seek to build a sustainable society rooted in ecological wisdom, social justice, nonviolence, diversity, and grassroots democracy, their views overlapping with those of feminists and peace activists (see Dobson, 2007a). Green economics is critical of globalization and of business as usual, while green politics emphasizes the importance of decentralization and participatory democracy (for more details, see Chapter 4).

The world's first environmental political party was probably the Values Party, founded in New Zealand in 1972 and which contested the general election that year on a predominantly environmental platform (see McCormick, 1995, ch. 9). The first Green party in Europe was founded in Britain in 1973 under the name People, later becoming the Ecology Party and then – in 1985 – the Green Party. The Belgian greens were the first to win national legislative seats, in 1981, and they were followed by Green parties in Germany and most other Western European countries, followed later by similar parties in most Eastern European countries and in wealthier emerging countries such as Brazil and Mexico. The first greens to enter government as part of a governing coalition were those in Finland in 1995.

Meanwhile, the definition of environmental threats changed post-Stockholm as the focus on the problems of wealthy industrialized countries (often known collectively, if not entirely accurately, as the North) was joined by a new focus on the problems of poor countries (collectively known as the South). In the former it was mainly a problem of unsustainable development, growing out of the industrialization that came earliest to Western Europe and North America, and then later to Russia and Japan. In the latter (most of Africa, Asia, and Latin America) the problems stemmed mainly from unplanned development of the kind that had been seen in the early decades of industrialization in the North; while environmental problems in wealthy countries tended to be a consequence of affluence, in poorer countries they tended to be a consequence of poverty. But the common view of governments in the South was that efforts to encourage improved environmental management would slow down their economic development, placing them at a disadvantage relative to wealthy countries. Why, they asked, should they have to tread more carefully when wealthy countries had not, and had clearly benefited in economic terms from uncontrolled exploitation of resources? But it was also clear that citizens of developing countries lived more closely with nature than was the case in wealthy countries, which had a larger stock of skills, capital resources, and technological capabilities, and that environmental degradation could have a more immediate and more rapid impact on economic development in poorer countries. The result was a redefinition of the causes of environmental problems and of the best responses.

Another of the effects of Stockholm was the emergence of a new global view of environmental problems. Until then, the only problem seen in global terms was the radioactive fallout created by several hundred atmospheric nuclear tests carried out during the late 1940s and 1950s. This was resolved by the 1962 ban on above-ground tests. The new post-Stockholm global sensitivity was soon illustrated by problems that had been decades in the making: the regional threats posed to the natural environment and human health by acid pollution, and the thinning of the earth's ozone layer as a consequence of the use of synthetic chemicals in aerosol propellants, refrigerants, coolants, sterilizers, and solvents. Both were the subject of intense international debate that resulted in international agreements that have since greatly reduced the emissions of the chemicals involved (see Chapter 6). But even as they ceased to draw less public attention, new concerns were generated by what is undoubtedly the greatest and most truly global of all environmental threats: climate change (see Chapter 12).

The debate about environmental politics and policy – particularly at the international level – was given additional focus by the convening of the 1992 UN Conference on Environment and Development, held in Rio de Janeiro and usually known as the Rio Earth Summit. The goal was to give new momentum to the changes sparked 20 years earlier at Stockholm, but while the conference resulted in the publication of the Rio Declaration on Environment

20 | Environmental Politics and Policy

> **Box 1.2** *The environment and globalization*
>
> At the heart of recent debates about the authority of states and the changing nature of the international system – as well as debates about the definition and perhaps even the creation of environmental problems – has been **globalization**. This describes the process by which the links between people, corporations, and governments in different states have become integrated through trade, investment, and technology. The effect has been to move us away from a world of sovereign states towards political, economic, and social pressures and networks that transcend state boundaries. This process of integration has long been under way, but has reached new levels in recent years as its effects have made themselves felt on the decisions taken by governments, the opportunities pursued by corporations, changes in the workplace, and the choices made by consumers.
>
> Critics of globalization charge that poorer countries have suffered further from economic competition and exploitation, that corporate interests in rich countries have profited, that jobs have been lost in rich countries, and that the environment has suffered as facilities are closed in industrialized countries and moved to those with weaker regulations and cheaper labour. They also point to the creation of resource shortages in poorer countries as a result of demands from consumers in wealthier countries. But supporters argue that globalization has helped promote democracy and free markets, helped promote economic and social equality, contributed to increases in life expectancy, helped promote technological innovation, encouraged modernization, and has promoted higher environmental standards as consumers in wealthy countries demand better quality products from factories in poorer countries (see, for example, Goklany, 2007; Christoff and Eckersley, 2013)

and Development, and the signature of the Convention on Climate Change and the Convention on Biological Diversity, the tangible effects were limited. Two later conferences – the 2002 Johannesburg Earth Summit (otherwise known as Rio+10) and the 2012 Rio Earth Summit (Rio+20) – seemed to achieve even less and seemed indicative of declining levels of attention to environmental problems, although opinions differ on their significance.

One line of thinking that has recently attracted interest (as well as criticism) is that of **post-environmentalism**. The idea derives from a self-published pamphlet titled *The Death of Environmentalism* by Michael Shellenberger and Ted Nordhaus (2004), which argues that mainstream environmentalism is guilty of perpetuating the idea of limits to growth, of using scare tactics to draw attention to climate change, and of arguing that individuals must make personal sacrifices. It also suggests that environmentalists are still fighting the battles of the 1960s without realizing that values have changed, and still sees modernization and technology as the source of environmental problems rather than the solution. Rather than the inevitable hopelessness and despair that will arise from this logic, post-environmentalism calls for new approaches and strategies that would define wealth not in gross economic terms but in terms of overall well-being (Nordhaus and Shellenberger, 2007: 270).

Two notable trends have helped redefine the place of the environment on the policy agenda in recent years. First, the global financial crisis of 2007–10 resulted in a broad economic downturn from which most countries took years to recover, changing the policy priorities of national governments. One of the effects was to place economic matters back at the core of the environmental debate, with a new focus on the green economy. Another of the effects has been to decrease the willingness of national governments to make the changes required under the terms of international agreements, such as the climate change convention. Second, and looking at the international level, the rise of concerns about international terrorism and about immigration in the wake of war and civil unrest has diminished the level of faith in international cooperation, strengthening the appeal of political parties and movements that campaign to strengthen borders and put national interests first.

Discussion questions

- Is it possible or desirable to inject environmental concerns into all other areas of public policy?
- Can environmental problems be addressed through a reform of existing political, economic, and social structures, or are more radical changes needed?
- What kinds of changes would need to be made to bring about the creation of a green economy?
- On balance, has globalization been good or bad for the environment?

Key concepts

Anti-environmentalism	Environmentalism
Authority	Globalization
Conservation	Governance
Deep ecology	Government
Ecological modernization	Green economy
	Green growth
Ecology	Green politics
Environment	

- Greenwashing
- Paradigm
- Political ecology
- Politics
- Post-environmentalism
- Post-materialism
- Power
- Preservation
- Public policy
- Radical environmentalism
- Reformist environmentalism
- Sustainable development

Further reading

Armiero, Marco, and Lise Sedrez (eds) (2014) *A History of Environmentalism: Local Struggles, Global Histories* (Bloomsbury). An edited collection with chapters on the development of environmentalism in different parts of the world.

Dobson, Andrew, and Robyn Eckersley (eds) (2006) *Political Theory and the Ecological Challenge* (Cambridge University Press). An edited collection of studies of the links between environmentalism and key political ideologies and concepts.

Haq, Gary, and Alistair Paul (2011) *Environmentalism since 1945* (Routledge). Offers both a short history of environmentalism and an assessment of the links between the environment and politics, science, economics, and popular culture.

Peterson del Mar, David (2006) *Environmentalism* (Routledge). A history of environmental ideas, with an emphasis on developments since 1945.

Sachs, Jeffrey D. (2016) *The Age of Sustainable Development* (Columbia University Press). An analysis of the way in which sustainable development can help us address environmental problems as well as persistent poverty and political and economic injustice.

2 Perspectives on the Environment

Key arguments

- Environmental politics and policy are multidimensional in nature.
- Science plays a key role in shaping environmental policy, but its value is compromised by scientific uncertainties and by differences in the logic of science and policy.
- Efforts to develop environmental policies that are economically efficient are compromised by the difficulties of accurately calculating the costs and benefits of action and inaction.
- The choices made by businesses and consumers help shape environmental policy, but their interests are often at odds with those of the environment.
- The human relationship with nature raises many troubling ethical, moral, and religious questions, few of which have been answered.
- Environmental problems become a security concern when there is a mismatch between the supply of natural resources and the human demand for those resources.

Chapter overview

Barry Commoner's idea that everything is connected is reflected in the multidimensional nature of environmental politics and policy. Since the environment consists of our entire physical surroundings, it should come as no surprise to find that environmental matters can be related to almost all other facets of human action, and that they can be approached from multiple perspectives (see Cohen, 2014: 3–4, 12). This chapter will make this point by focusing on five of those perspectives:

- *Science* is concerned with objective and verifiable certainty of a kind that can be replicated through experimentation, and with drawing conclusions that are –

ideally – value-free. More than most other areas of policy, the definition and resolution of environmental problems depends on scientific understanding, but we will see that scientists and policymakers have an uncomfortable relationship stemming from different expectations, timetables, and values.
- *Economics* approaches environmental questions with market forces in mind, and is concerned with the environmental impact of production and consumption, and with the relative impact of regulation and market-driven alternatives. Placing a value on a commodity or a course of action, however, is not always as easy as it might seem.
- *Business* can see environmental regulation either as a costly nuisance or as an opportunity. In recent decades there has been a move towards the latter, with the rise of corporate social responsibility and consumer-based approaches to environmental management. But the relationship between government and business has not always been an easy one.
- *Philosophy* sees environmental issues as ethical issues, and deals with the values and worldviews behind environmental problems and the policy responses to those problems. It tries to answer questions about whether humans are part of nature of separate from it, and about how far nature as shaped by humans should be treated differently from nature unaffected by humans.
- *Security* is a factor because environmental issues can pose strategic challenges, revolving either around disputes over access to scarce resources, or around problems created by man-made environmental change, such as global warming. In this regard, environment and security have a close relationship.

This chapter looks in turn at each of these perspectives, showing how they influence the political debates about the environment, as well as giving us greater insight into the way in which policy is shaped. Environmental policymakers are interested in finding sound (or, at least, politically viable) answers to the challenges of environmental management, in designing effective institutions and laws, and in achieving a consensus among competing interests and priorities. But the problems with which they wrestle go beyond political factors; in reaching authoritative decisions,

> environmental policymakers must be sure of the science, must consider the economic implications of the options they face, must take into account the views of business, must address ethical questions, and are often driven by security considerations. These different pressures and influences make environmental policy among the most complex areas of public policy to address and resolve.

Science and the environment

As a policy and political issue, the environment is unusual in the extent to which it relies upon science to identify, measure, and understand the core problems and potential solutions. What we know about air and water pollution, for example, is driven by how much we understand about the chemistry and biology of the interactions between chemicals, air, and water, and the consequences for life on earth. How we fashion our policy response, in turn, must be based on an understanding of that chemistry and biology. The political debate about climate change, meanwhile, hinges on the quality of the evidence that global warming is a result of human activity rather than part of a natural warming cycle.

Unfortunately, the debate about the role played by scientists in shaping policy is unresolved, with social scientists tending to pay it less heed than scholars of science and technology (Keller, 2009: 3). The key issues are scientific certainty and scientific neutrality. The former revolves around the question of whether policy should proceed only on the basis of a certain link between cause and effect, or whether it should proceed on the lesser basis of a high level of risk. The latter revolves around the question of the credibility and legitimacy of scientific research. At one end of the continuum, environmentalists are sometimes charged with using a selective understanding of science to make an alarmist or exaggerated case for the existence or seriousness of a problem. At the other end, those opposed to action (such as big business, or politicians associated with big business) may try to delay change by exploiting uncertainties or ambiguities in the science, and by arguing that more certainty is needed to justify the often substantial costs of action.

Kasperson (2011) notes the gap between science and policy practice, and argues that policy decisions go well beyond issues of science (whose role in those decisions, as a result, is watered down), and that the findings of scientific research are often overlooked because they have been framed to meet the needs of science rather than the needs of policy. He concludes that there needs to be more of a two-way interaction between science and policy so that each learns from, and meets the needs of, the other. But science does not always offer definitive answers to the kinds of questions asked by policymakers, and has three particular characteristics that compromise its value to policy calculations.

First, while policymakers seek a high degree of certainty before making policy, our understanding of natural processes and ecological systems is incomplete. Scientific understanding is always evolving, and we are constantly learning, but numerous holes remain in our knowledge. Taking biodiversity as an example: we cannot be sure of the extent of the threats to biodiversity quite simply because we do not know how many species are in existence. Our best guess is that there are probably about 9 million (+/− 1 million), but estimates of the total run as high as 30 million. We will never know how many species have existed over time, or how many have gone extinct, and we have only an approximate idea how many are threatened or endangered today, or of the population numbers of different species (see Chapter 10). Under these circumstances, it is clearly difficult to make good policy.

In an ideal world, we could use well-considered **risk assessment** as a means of shaping policy; in other words, we could methodically assess the degree and the nature of environmental risks posed by human action. However, the risks posed by chemicals in the environment show how difficult this can be. While we have become more sensitized to the risks involved in our use of chemicals, there are large gaps in our knowledge of their toxicity. In the United States, for example, there are more than 84,000 chemicals used daily in industry, of which about 10,000 have not yet been tested, and there is no legal requirement to test the approximately 700 new chemicals introduced every year into commerce (Rosenbaum, 2014: 245). Even with those chemicals that have been tested, the effects are often open to debate, for several reasons.

- Much of the data we have are based on studying chemicals in a laboratory environment, where they may have different effects than they might have in general circulation.
- A particular chemical by itself might be harmless, but in combination with another it might be dangerous. Since we do not breathe or ingest individual pollutants, it is hard to isolate their effects, to know which is the most dangerous, and to know which combination of pollutants poses the greatest threat.
- Humans are affected differently by pollutants, making it difficult to know where to set the threshold of risk. Infants and small children face greater dangers from lead than adults, for example, and people with respiratory problems face greater dangers than those without. We probably all know or have heard of people who ate well, exercised regularly, and yet died young, while others are in their eighties despite being sedentary, smoking three packs of cigarettes a day, or eating a diet high in fat.

- Many of the toxic effects of chemicals do not show until years or decades after exposure, by which time it may not be clear which chemicals were involved, or at what levels (Rosenbaum, 2014: 137). Asbestos, for example, was used for many years before its effects on human health were isolated and understood.

Given such uncertainties, policymakers can fall back on the **precautionary principle**. While this simply means that prevention is better than cure, there are two competing perspectives on the idea. It can be seen in terms of action, meaning that where there are suspicions that a problem might emerge, it can be agreed to proceed with caution, or perhaps to avoid proceeding at all. It can also be seen in terms of inaction, meaning that where there are suspicions that a problem might emerge, 'lack of full scientific certainty shall not be used as a reason for postponing cost-effective measures to prevent environmental degradation' (Principle 15 of the 1992 Rio Declaration). The principle has proved controversial, because it has never been tightly defined (more than a dozen different definitions have been found in international treaties and declarations (Foster et al., 2000)), there has been no agreement on when it should be triggered, and it is subject to differences of opinion about the extent to which we should take precautionary action, running the gamut from allowing some risks to allowing none at all (Gupta, 2015).

Second, there is a tension between politicians and scientists in terms of the logic of their thinking (see Table 2.1). Elected officials are driven by the limits of their terms in office, and will be looking to make progress before the next election. But scientific research takes time to conduct, and often demands the kind of financial investment that may not be readily available thanks to stretched government budgets or multiple demands on private philanthropy. Taking immediate action on climate change, for example, will have benefits (if any) that will not begin to show for multiple generations, far beyond the political horizons of today's governments or bureaucracies. And against the background of limited funds, there will be political disagreements over how best

Table 2.1 **The tensions between policy and science**

Quality	Policymakers	Scientists
Certainty	Looking for high degree of certainty upon which to base policy decisions.	Understanding of environmental interactions is sometimes incomplete and always evolving.
Timing	Driven by the limits of their terms in office.	Driven by the time and resources needed to conduct research.
Logic	Driven by practical political considerations such as feasibility, credibility, and public opinion.	Driven by the objective search for facts.

to spend them, with officials seeking to achieve the best results as quickly as possible with the smallest expenditure.

Third, scientists and politicians differ in terms of the logic of their thinking: scientists are interested in facts and experimentation, and thus tend to be cautious, while politicians are motivated more by subjective issues such as the political feasibility of pursuing a particular course of action, or whether or not a law or policy will be popular, credible, effective, or constitutional. Public opinion and awareness will also be a factor, with policymakers responding to problems as they move up and down the public agenda and compete for attention. In addition, few elected officials are scientists, as a result of which few will think like scientists or have the kind of technical background needed to understand the finer points of environmental science. Scientists, meanwhile, will be so focused on the search for verifiable data that they might find the uncertainties of politics hard to fathom.

At the same time, there is occasionally some overlap between science and policy in regard to how facts are presented; science is not necessarily neutral or unbiased (Rosenbaum, 2014: 140–41). We sometimes think that it is concerned with facts, when in reality it is concerned with the search for facts. Scientists who seek those facts can be as fallible, inaccurate, and subjective as social scientists, and they can also disagree with each other in how they interpret facts, much like social scientists. They are also sometimes guilty of the falsification of information, or the painting of biased pictures driven by a political agenda, as when research is supported by companies or foundations with such an agenda. The results of research can also be censored or adjusted for political ends, as was the case when the Bush administration in the United States censored a report produced by the US Environmental Protection Agency in 2003; several warnings about the causes and effects of climate change were deleted so as make the report appear non-committal on the topic (Revkin and Seelye, 2003). Similarly, the government of Prime Minister Stephen Harper in Canada (2006–15) developed a record of managing media contacts with Environment Canada so as to control coverage of stories on climate change and the negative effects of industrial development (Linnit, 2013).

Economics and the environment

Policymakers not only face the challenge of developing environmental policies based on sound science, but must also try to achieve economic efficiency, which means quantifying the costs of action and inaction. There is little doubt that remedial action can be expensive: cleaning up toxic waste sites in older industrialized states, for example, is neither cheap nor easy, particularly when it involves legal action. Cleaning the air in the world's biggest and fastest growing cities – notably those in India and China – is also expensive, particularly given the relative poverty of their governments. Regulation has long been the favoured approach employed by governments, but it faces resistance from the economic sectors that are being regulated, and is criticized for being inefficient. In response, several experiments have been conducted in market-based incentives, by which goals are agreed and it is left to the market to achieve the results (see Chapter 3).

At the heart of the environment–economics nexus is the tension between managing natural resources that are **public goods** (provided by nature, government, or business and free for general use) and those that are common goods or **common pool resources** (their size or extent makes it difficult or impossible to prevent individuals from making use of them). They stand in contrast to private or toll goods (see Table 2.2). The common pool qualities of natural resources pose many problems to policymakers as they seek to design and implement policy that works. If the

Table 2.2 Types of goods

	Excludable Those who do not own or pay for them cannot use them.	*Non-excludable* Others cannot be prevented from using them.
Rivalrous Consumption by one user reduces or precludes consumption by others.	**Private goods** Goods or services that must be bought and owned to be consumed, and where use by one person excludes others. Examples: consumer goods, food, privately owned homes or road vehicles, privately owned land, forests, and fisheries.	**Common goods** Size or qualities make it hard or impossible to control access, raising the prospect of over-use and depletion (the tragedy of the commons). Examples: atmosphere, oceans, fisheries, water aquifers, wildlife.
Non-rivalrous Consumption by one user does not reduce or preclude consumption by others.	**Toll goods** Goods or services that must be bought and owned to be consumed, or whose benefits are limited to a specific group, but where use by one person does not exclude others. Examples: subscriptions to services, access to private parks, membership of international organizations.	**Public goods** Goods or services accessible without cost to all members of a society. Examples: clean air, public parks, open spaces, scenic views, national defence, air conditioning and heating in public buildings.

use of such resources is balanced and sustainable, then all is well, but the self-interest of some users might encourage them to draw more than their share (or to use the air and water as a free sink for wastes), so that they benefit while passing on the costs to other users. If all users take this approach then the resource is depleted to the cost of all users, a phenomenon described in an influential 1968 essay by the American ecologist Garrett Hardin (1968) as the '**tragedy of the commons**'.

Prompted mainly by his concerns over growing human population, and drawing on an 1833 essay by the British economist William Forster Lloyd (which had also focused on population growth), Hardin saw the 'tragedy' as the inevitability of the destruction of common pool resources, and the difficulty of legislating temperance. He used the example of a pasture open to all farmers in a locality to use. As long as the numbers of cattle were controlled, all was well. But as soon as each farmer decided to add one more cow to their herd, increasing their benefits at the cost of the others, the problems would start. This was the tragedy, argued Hardin: 'Each man is locked into a system that compels him to increase his herd without limit – in a world that is limited. Ruin is the destination toward which all men rush, each pursuing his own best interest in a society that believes in the freedom of the commons. Freedom in a commons brings ruin to all.'

Hardin has since been criticized for being too pessimistic, and for failing to point out that few common resources are entirely unregulated. The American political scientist Elinor Ostrom was awarded the 2009 Nobel Prize in economics for research that outlined the design principles that could produce the stable use of common pool resources. These include defining clear group boundaries; matching the rules governing the use of common goods to local needs and conditions; ensuring that those affected by the rules can participate in modifying the rules; making sure the rule-making rights of community members are respected by outside authorities; developing a system for effective monitoring; using graduated sanctions for rule violators; and providing accessible means for dispute resolution (Ostrom, 1990).

In their efforts to achieve economic efficiency in environmental management, the baseline option for governments is **cost-benefit analysis**, by which efforts are made to weigh the relative costs and benefits of different courses of action with a view to designing the most economically efficient policies. But while this sounds logical, and can work well at a small scale, it has had mixed results in practice, and the bigger and more complex the problem, the harder it is to develop realistic figures; the costs of remedial or preventive action are usually easier to calculate than the benefits of that action. How, for example, do we quantify the

> **Box 2.1** *Nature: Boundless or unforgiving?*
>
> Economic principles have been at the heart of an ongoing debate about the dimensions of nature and the environmental risks posed by human action. Haas (2002) credits cultural anthropologists with having identified four 'myths of nature' that have driven that debate:
>
> - The Cornucopian approach sees nature as boundless, robust, and benign, and takes a view towards the environment that is 'relaxed, non-interventionist, and laissez-faire' (Jordan and O'Riordan, 1997: 28). The thinking here is that economic growth encourages technological innovation that can be used to address resource scarcity. In short, free-market thinking helps us develop new ideas to offset and adapt to problems that might arise.
> - The Malthusian approach (a name deriving from the eighteenth-century British classical economist Thomas Malthus – see Chapter 1) sees resources as limited and finite, portrays nature as 'precarious and unforgiving, vulnerable and constraining' (Jordan and O'Riordan, 1997), and worries that population growth outstrips the supply of resources, creating dangerous scarcities. The best response is to control population growth and reduce resource use.
> - The sustainable development approach sees nature as manageable provided that its limits are taken into account, and argues that economic development need not be inconsistent with sound environmental management.
> - The radical or post-modern approach sees nature as capricious, and focuses on the unequal access to (and distribution of) resources (Galtung, 1973; Redclift, 1987). It focuses on the importance of redistribution as a means of addressing resource scarcity.
>
> The failure to reach an accommodation between these four approaches illustrates how little politics and economics have been able to agree on firm answers regarding the best approach to environmental management.

health benefits of cleaner air? It is impossible to know exactly how many lives we will save or make better with a particular course of action on clean air. Even if we eliminate one kind of air pollutant, the existence of others may offset the benefits, and the result may be no net improvement in the overall quality of life. How do we place a price on improved quality of life to begin with? And what exactly is 'clean air', how much is it worth, and how do we calculate the role of clean air in a happier and healthier population?

Since it is clear that traditional economics falls short when it comes to placing a value on clean air, pristine wilderness, or sustainable numbers of animal and plant species, one alternative is to use **contingent valuation**. This is an effort to place a price on a commodity that does not have a market value because it is not directly sold. It is typically established through surveys of 'users'; for example, hunters are asked what value they would place on an area of wilderness, hikers on the provision of footpaths, climbers on a hilltop view uninterrupted by smog, and so on. Critics tend to dismiss this as 'junk economics', with Hausman (2012), for example, charging that it is undermined by the frequent overstatement of the value of resources. Studies repeatedly find that people will attach a higher value to a commodity when asked what compensation they would expect in return for giving up that commodity than when asked how much they would be willing to pay for its improvement. Nonetheless, contingent valuation has been the subject of a growing body of studies (see Carson, 2011).

Business and the environment

Business plays a pivotal role in both creating and responding to environmental problems. It makes many of the decisions that determine how energy and natural resources are managed and exploited, and is a key actor in shaping the policy responses that governments adopt to environmental problems. Consumers also play a role, of course, via the choices they make and the manner in which they use and dispose of the goods they purchase, but business has the upper hand because of the collective action problem that limits the effects of consumer choice (see later in this section). Businesses seek to maximize profits, to minimize costs, and to build and protect positive corporate reputations, three goals which are often at odds with each other. This was illustrated by the efforts made after 2000 by British Petroleum, known since the late 1980s as BP, to alter its image by replacing its shield logo with a new green and yellow floral logo and an advertising campaign using the slogan 'Beyond Petroleum' (in spite of remaining fundamentally an oil and gas company). Then came the *Deepwater Horizon* disaster of 2010, when a BP drilling rig exploded in the Gulf of Mexico and millions of gallons of crude oil were released. While BP had been involved in multiple earlier environmental accidents, this latest and biggest event clearly undermined BP's new corporate image, and Greenpeace was prompted to alter the floral logo into a new design that looked like a splash of oil, and published banners bearing the slogan 'British Polluters'.

When new environmental laws and policies first began to be adopted in industrialized countries in the 1960s and 1970s, they were usually met with hostility and suspicion by most corporations (particularly the large ones), which saw environmental and financial goals as mutually exclusive: regulations promised to limit both their options and their profits, and their contributions to environmental policy were mainly restricted and reactive (Falkner, 2008). Encouraged by changes in political and consumer demands, and by the bad publicity attached to a number of disasters tied to careless corporate policy (such as Seveso in 1976, the Ixtoc-I blowout in 1979, and Bhopal in 1985 – see Chapter 3), corporate approaches and expectations began to change in the 1980s. The political response to threats posed to the ozone layer proved to be a turning point: it attracted the support of the industry implicated in the problem, which quickly realized that there were cheaper alternatives available to the chemicals implicated in the problem, and marketing advantages to be gained from greener policies.

Business came to be influenced by the **polluter pays principle**, an approach based on addressing problems by making the polluter (or the producer of a problem) pay the costs of amelioration or clean-up. The point here is not that producers should build the costs into the price of their products and pass them on to consumers, but that they should instead absorb the costs themselves. The principle has been encouraged and endorsed since the 1970s by the Organization for Economic Cooperation and Development (OECD) and by the European Union, and has been built in to several international treaties. The principle has the benefit of promoting economic efficiency by ensuring that the price of goods and services reflects the true price of production rather than being raised to meet the costs of pollution control. But it only works if the polluter is clearly identified (sometimes easier said than done, because much pollution comes from diffuse sources), and if the payment demanded is a fair reflection of the cost of the problem.

Preparations for the 1992 Rio Earth Summit had an important transformative impact on corporate attitudes. In 1990, the Business Council on Sustainable Development was founded to represent business at the summit, and its leader Stephan Schmidheiny promoted the idea of **corporate social responsibility** (CSR) by arguing that companies should place social and environmental issues at the core of their decision-making because it was in their financial interests so to do. Clearly business must obey the law, but CSR goes further by making a virtue out of a necessity, encapsulated in the four questions described by Hay et al. (2005) as 'may they, can they, should they, do they'.

As an idea, CSR dates back to the 1950s (see Bowen, 1953), has never been firmly defined, and is not restricted to environmental matters (it also includes attitudes towards working conditions, gender and racial equity, and human rights, for example), but Schmidheiny brought it into the environmental realm by speaking of 'eco-efficiency'. This implies that companies can cut costs through reducing energy inputs and waste, for example, while building greener images that can help attract customers and create new markets (Schmidheiny, 1992). Many businesses – including General Electric, Walmart, and Xerox – have since made significant efforts to change their practices and to capitalize on claims of their new environmental sensitivity, often using it as a positive marketing tool (see Auld et al., 2008; Crane et al., 2009). For Cannon (2012), CSR has evolved from being *a* vital business issues to being *the* vital business issue. But while this development is seen by some as a genuine sense of social and environmental responsibility on the part of business, it is seen by others as a cynical ploy to exploit changing political and consumer demands.

Corporations are today active in most efforts to rationalize approaches to environmental policy, adding a voluntary and non-regulatory aspect to the kinds of imposed regulations on which policy otherwise relies. Some corporations still act in a reactive and involuntary manner, others try to make as few changes as they can get away with, and yet others make a genuine effort to cooperate with other actors in the making of domestic and international policy. Consumers, shareholders, and local communities have increasingly expected assurances that goods and services meet minimum standards of environmental responsibility, and many corporations and business sectors have accordingly created codes of conduct, certification schemes, and other means of promoting voluntary environmental practices (see Table 2.3). Among them is the ISO I4001

Table 2.3 **Voluntary environmental practices**

Type	Purpose	Examples
Environmental certification	Scheme by which companies agree to comply with environmental objectives or standards.	Carbon Trust Standard aimed at cutting energy and water use, and waste generation.
		Blue Flag Campaign for cleaner beaches and coastal water quality.
		Forest Stewardship Council efforts to promote sustainable forestry.
		Green Globe 21 International Ecotourism Standard.
Code of conduct	Principles that guide behaviour, which may or may not have legal force.	Numerous businesses have adopted such codes, the elements of which range from the broad to the specific.
Eco-labelling	Awarding government- or NGO-sanctioned rights to label consumer products as environmentally friendly.	European Union Ecolabel.
		US Energy Star energy efficiency scheme.
		Marine Stewardship Council scheme for sustainable fisheries.

standard created in 1996 by the International Organization for Standardization (ISO), which sets standards for Environmental Management Systems aimed at improving environmental management, environmental auditing, and environmental labelling.

One approach that has been used with increased frequency since the 1980s is **eco-labelling**, or the practice of awarding government- or NGO-sanctioned rights to label consumer products as environmentally friendly, either because they have been manufactured less wastefully or because they use less energy. Germany introduced the first such scheme in 1978 with its Blue Angel label designed to encourage innovation and recycling. It was followed ten years later by Canada with the Canada's Environmental Choice scheme, followed in turn by similar programmes in Japan, the United States, Scandinavia, Australia, New Zealand, and South Korea (see Tews et al., 2003). The EU launched its Ecolabel scheme in 1992, and it has since been awarded to nearly 45,000 products. Also in 1992, the United States began its Energy Star label for energy-efficient appliances (since adopted by several other countries and by the EU), and the Marine Stewardship Council since 1997 has awarded labels for sustainable fisheries. The achievements of eco-labelling have been mixed, with concerns expressed about ensuring accurate data, charges of misleading claims, resistance from businesses concerned about the imposition of new costs, and concerns that the labels pose a barrier to free trade.

While much of the blame for environmental problems is laid at the door of business, it is important to remember the role of consumers in shaping business practice. In seeking low prices for goods and services, for example, consumers have helped encourage businesses to close factories in industrialized countries and to move them to emerging states with weaker environmental regulations and lower worker costs. Following this logic, it has often been argued that if we cannot expect solutions to environmental problems through system-wide changes, then perhaps we can look to **consumer-led solutions**; the actions of individual consumers – assuming enough take such actions – can change the demand system from below.

While one person cannot make much of a difference, if thousands or millions change their habits, the cumulative effect can be substantial. This means encouraging people to better understand the links between actions and effects, and changing their values and demands so that industry responds. Change is happening, but it remains unusual and unconventional (Shirani et al., 2015), and it is still mainly only a phenomenon among consumers in wealthy countries rather than among the growing middle classes of emerging countries. Consumer-led solutions are also a classic **collective action problem**, meaning that while almost everyone would benefit from making better consumer choices, there are costs involved (such as higher prices for goods and services, or a loss of independence if someone switches from private to public transport), making it less likely that individuals will agree to take the necessary collective action.

Maniates (2001) is not convinced by the merits of consumer-led solutions. He identifies the dilemma of the 'individualization of responsibility' (seeing environmental problems in individual terms), and argues that it threatens to narrow the collective 'environmental imagination' and to undermine the capacity of society to react effectively to environmental threats by drawing attention away from deeper and broader conversations about consumerism. 'Given our deepening alienation from traditional understandings of active citizenship, together with the growing allure of consumption-as-social-action', he argues, 'it's little wonder that at a time when our capacity to imagine an array of ways to build a just and ecologically resilient future must expand, it is in fact narrowing'. He calls instead for a conversation about the 'consumption problem', which would allow consumers to see that while their individual choices are environmentally important, their control over these choices is 'constrained, shaped, and framed by institutions and political forces that can be remade only through collective citizen action, as opposed to individual consumer behavior'.

Philosophy and the environment

Approaches to environmental policy raise not just political, scientific, and economic questions, but also ethical and philosophical questions, summarized in the definition by Taylor (1986: 3) of **environmental ethics** as those 'concerned with the moral relations that hold between humans and the natural world' and as determining the 'duties, obligations, and responsibilities [of humans] with regard to the Earth's natural environment and all animals and plants that inhabit it'. (For a brief summary of the debates involved, see Brennan and Lo, 2015; for a more detailed version, see James, 2015.) Questions arise about whether the focus should be on nature or the environment, about whether humans are part of nature of separate from it, and about how far nature as shaped by humans should be treated differently than nature unaffected by humans. It is dilemmas of this kind that philosophy seeks to address (Box 2.2).

Although ethical questions have been asked about the human relationship with nature for centuries, environmental ethics

Box 2.2 Religion and the environment

It has been argued that the environmental crisis is ultimately a crisis of values (Nasr, 1975), for which reason it makes sense to consider the impact of religion on the shaping of attitudes towards nature; this is in spite of the claims that are made in modern democracy that there should be a separation of religion and the state. But understanding the impact of religion is not always easy thanks to the contradiction often found within religious teachings. For example, Judeo-Christianity has occasionally been criticized for assuming and encouraging human domination of nature while also being credited for promoting the idea of human stewardship of nature.

It has been suggested by Dasgupta and Ramanathan (2014) that responses to our environmental problems demand not just the engagement of science and politics, but the kind of 'moral leadership that religious institutions are in the position to offer'. They did not offer much in the way of details, but the appeals of religious leaders might play a role. Several modern popes, for example, including Paul VI and John Paul II, expressed concerns about environmental deterioration, while Pope Francis issued an encyclical in May 2015 that acknowledged the 'human causes' of climate change, and criticized the manner in which the earth's resources were being 'plundered because of short-sighted approaches to the economy, commerce and production'.

Such appeals are less likely to work from a religious perspective in most democracies (particularly those in Europe), because people are moving away from organized religion. But the underlying message will still have some resonance there, and the influence of religious leaders – and of religious beliefs – still carries weight in Latin America, Africa, the Middle East, and Asia, where large majorities continue to have strong religious beliefs. One of the questions posed by recent research on the links between religion and the environment is the extent to which global or international approaches to environmental problems can find support among supporters of multiple cultural and religious traditions (see Jenkins and Chapple, 2011).

as a sub-discipline of philosophy dates back only to the turn of the 1960s, when the sense of a worsening environmental crisis led to a debate about the moral source of the crisis and suggestions that a fundamental change of values was in order. In 1967, the historian Lynn White caused a stir by arguing that the Judeo-Christian tradition of humans as 'superior to nature, [and] contemptuous of it' had paved the way for unbridled exploitation of nature by humans (White, 1967). Three years later, the political scientist Lynton Keith Caldwell made a similar point, suggesting that the environmental crisis stemmed from the dominant Western philosophical view that humans ruled over nature and that nature was valuable only to the extent that it was valued by humans, and that it was time to look instead at the intrinsic value of nature (Caldwell, 1970). Soon after that, William Blackstone (1974: 3) argued that the basic causes of the environmental crisis were 'mistaken values and attitudes' and that the resolution of the crisis would require a change of those values. For a while, these ideas spilled over into the emerging feminist movement, spawning the idea of **ecofeminism** that likened men's control and exploitation of women to their control and exploitation of nature.

The debate has since continued, pitting two core views against one another:

- **Anthropocentrism** is human-centred, giving priority to human interests over those of the rest of the natural world, and defining the value of nature not in its intrinsic terms, but extrinsically in terms of its value to humans. Environmental policy, in this view, is driven by the value of nature to human needs and interests. It is associated with the idea of shallow ecology discussed in Chapter 1, which the Norwegian philosopher Arne Naess (1973) described as a fight against pollution and resource depletion whose core objective was 'the health and affluence of people in the developed countries'. It is represented by the views of the Australian philosopher John Passmore (1974), who argued that nature should be valued in terms of what it offered to sentient beings, including humans.
- **Ecocentrism** is nature-centred, arguing that the whole of nature – human and non-human, living and non-living – has intrinsic value, that humans do not represent the pinnacle of evolution, and that humans should not see themselves apart from nature but as part of an interconnected web of relationships (see Eckersley, 1992). These ideas date back to the work of the American writer Aldo Leopold whose landmark book *A Sand County Almanac* (1949: 129, 204) argued that people should learn to 'think like a mountain' and adopt a new ethic that changed the role of humans 'from conqueror of the land-community to plain member and citizen of it'. Ecocentrism is associated with Naess's idea of deep ecology or 'biospheric egalitarianism', and is one of the foundations of green politics.

Environmental ethics (or philosophy – the terms are complimentary) plays a key role in the environmental debate because of the kinds of questions that politics, science, and economics cannot answer. Political scientists can tell us about the dynamics of the political and policy response to climate change, for example, while scientists can tell us about the mechanics of climate change and its effects on ecosystems, and economists can speculate on the financial costs. However, none of these groups can tell us much about our moral obligation to address climate change, assuming such an obligation exists, and nor can they tell us the whole story about why people – whether political leaders, business leaders, or citizens – do what they do, or how they define their place in nature.

A particular ethical question is the one that drives human treatment of animals. Just where this sits in relation to the definition of the environment is debatable, but it is less about questions of sustainability than about questions of exploitation: what responsibilities do we have regarding the way we treat pets, or how animals are treated in entertainment (for example, in circuses) or in sport (as in bull-fighting and fox-hunting), or how far we should allow animals to be used in laboratory testing, or how animals are treated in agriculture or in slaughter-houses? The social and moral questions related to animal rights have been the subject of a substantial political and academic debate (see, for example, Waldau, 2011; Smith, 2012). A classic argument in the field is the 1975 book *Animal Liberation* by the Australian moral philosopher Peter Singer, which argues that the utilitarian idea of 'the greatest good of the greatest number' can be applied to animals as well as humans. He also popularized the term *speciesism*, which describes the way in which humans discriminate against other animals. Meanwhile, Regan (1985) makes the case for animal rights, including the abolition of the use of animals in science, the end of commercial animal agriculture, and the end of commercial and sport hunting and trapping.

Ethical questions are raised not just in discussions about the human relationship with nature and animals, but spill over into questions of social justice and equity: how can we define environmental problems – and develop responses – while also making sure that the costs and the benefits of the solutions are equally borne? **Environmental justice** is a paradigm concerned with ensuring the meaningful involvement and fair treatment of all parties involved in making and implementing environmental policy, regardless of race, wealth, religion, or any other political, social, or economic category (see Walker, 2012). Inequities can be found both within countries and between countries. Justice is not served, for example, when waste dumps or chemical plants are sited nearer poorer communities, or when more effort is made to provide wealthier communities with cleaner water supplies, or when jobs are moved from wealthy countries to poorer countries with weaker environmental laws. The poor are particularly susceptible to environmental injustice because they are often less politically engaged, and too focused on daily existence to focus on longer-term problems. Critics have gone so far as to charge the mainstream environmental movement with being racist and elitist because of its concern with 'wilderness over people' (Sandler and Pezzullo, 2007).

Security and the environment

Environmental management does not end with concerns about scientific certainty, ecological stability, and economic sustainability, but can also spill over into matters of national and international security (see Schnurr and Swatuk, 2012). The question here is less about the threats posed directly to species and ecosystems by environmental decline than it is about **environmental scarcity**: the idea that population growth will lead to increased consumption and production, causing environmental deterioration, encouraging new competition for increasingly scarce resources, and sparking instability or conflict. There may be a problem with supply due to the degradation or depletion of resources, or a problem with demand as populations grow and their needs change or grow, or a problem with both supply and demand stemming from the unequal distribution of a resource (Homer-Dixon, 2001). The result can be new pressures and tensions that become security problems when they generate political and economic instability, or spark conflicts over resources. Three examples, illustrate the problem.

First, the widespread international dependence on fossil fuels gives the Middle East more strategic importance than it might otherwise have, and much of the political instability in that region stems from the long-held desire by foreign powers (and major oil consumers) to ensure stable supplies of oil through political or military intervention. To be sure, the problem here is less one of scarcity than of the abundance of oil in the Middle East. But that abundance, and the cheapness of Middle East oil, is a reflection of relative scarcity in other parts of the world. One of the benefits of a switch to renewable sources of energy would be decreased global reliance on Middle East oil, and – quite possibly – more political stability in the region.

Second, a combination of terrestrial pollution, waste dumping at sea, and overfishing in the coastal waters off the Horn of Africa was one of the causes of an outbreak of piracy off the coast of Somalia between 2005 and 2013. Scarcity caused by misuse and overuse encouraged people in the region to turn to a new source of income that involved violence or the threat of violence. In response, the international community had to wrestle with how to respond, with major naval powers sending warships into the region, helping to reduce the number of pirate attacks. It is a case, argues Panjabi (2009), which clearly illustrates the nexus between poverty and environmental degradation, and between environmental degradation and criminal action against international targets.

Third, **environmental refugees** (or environmental migrants) are people forced to leave their home as a result of human-made environmental changes such as soil erosion, desertification, or flooding that undermines their livelihood (Brown et al., 1976). A famous example was the Dust Bowl of the 1930s in the United States, when a combination of soil mismanagement and drought forced tens of thousands of people to abandon their farms. Today, climate change is seen as a major actual or potential cause of displacement. The number of 'climate refugees' is contested, but there is little question that rising sea levels, more extreme weather events, and changing patterns of crop production will lead over the long term to movements of population. A comprehensive study published in 2013 in the journal *Science* (Hsiang et al., 2013) concluded that there was 'strong causal evidence linking climatic events to human conflict across a range of spatial and temporal scales and across all major regions of the world'.

Concerns about the links between the environment and security are far from new, but they have taken time to attract broader attention. Writing as long ago as 1977, for example, Lester Brown of the Worldwatch Institute was warning that threats to security could begin to 'arise less from the relationship of nation to nation and more from the relationship of man to nature' (Brown, 1977). In 1989, Jessica Tuchman Mathews of the World Resources Institute sparked broader debate with an article in which she argued that global developments demanded a broadening of the definition of national security to include resource and environmental issues. 'Environmental strains that transcend national borders are already beginning to break down the sacred boundaries of national sovereignty', she warned (Mathews, 1989). Homer-Dixon (2001) developed these ideas, arguing that environmental scarcity would contribute indirectly to insurrections, ethnic clashes, urban unrest, and other forms of civil violence, especially in the developing world. (For a review of the evolution in thinking, see Campbell and Parthemore, 2008.)

History is replete with examples of conflicts over resources, Hitler's rise to power being in part due to a fight over 'living space' for the German people, resources being part of the motivation behind wars of independence in Algeria and the Congo, and Israel's need to guarantee access to water in Palestinian territory being one reason why the Arab-Israeli conflict has yet to be resolved. The idea 'that wars are associated with resources is probably as old as war itself', concludes Le Billon (2012).

But not everyone agrees that environmental scarcity necessarily leads to conflict. Using the logic of supply and demand, it could be argued that scarcity can sometimes be a good thing, leading to an increase in prices that can encourage reduced demand or a switch to greener alternatives; hence, for example, the increased use of bicycles in many European cities in the wake not just of traffic congestion but of the cost of owning and maintaining private vehicles. Haas (2002) is one of the sceptics, noting the long list of problems cited by those writing about environmental security, but going on to argue that 'the empirical record of wars fought over resources is quite meager', that 'virtually no one has been killed in direct international conflicts over water or any other resource', and that natural resources 'are seldom issues over which nations will go to war, either directly … or even indirectly because of the stresses generated from resource scarcity'.

For his part, Curwin (2015) notes that many recent wars, notably in Africa, have been fought in countries with a wealth of resources, not a scarcity. 'High-value resources such as oil, gas or minerals', he suggests, 'can support secessionist movements and other nonstate groups that seek to control and develop a regional economy', and he points to the examples of Guatemala, Nepal, Sierra Leone, Yemen, and South Sudan as states where access to land or other resources has been a grievance leading to conflict. Meanwhile, there have been many examples – including ozone depletion, threats to biodiversity, acid pollution, and fisheries management – where environmental scarcity and degradation have provided an impetus for cooperation and negotiation between states (Dinar, 2011). Research into **environmental peacebuilding** looks at ways in which the management of natural resources can be integrated into conflict prevention or mitigation, with equitable access to land, forests, minerals, oil, water, and other resources removing the pressures that lead to environmental mismanagement as well as conflicts arising from scarcity (see Bruch et al., 2016).

The focus of the debate should not be so much on environmental scarcity as on environmental security: the efforts made by states to guarantee continuing supplies of resources to feed growing industries and populations. Few countries have gone so far in this direction in recent decades as China, its most assertive actions being in the East and South China Seas. According to the terms of the UN Convention on the Law of the Sea (see Chapter 8) it must take its place alongside Japan, Vietnam, the Philippines, Malaysia, and Brunei in terms of zones of maritime control in the area. But the seas are rich in oil and natural gas, the South China Sea has two chains of islands (the Paracels and the Spratlys) that several countries claim, and China has gone so far as to build artificial islands to strengthen its claims. Meanwhile, further north, Russia has been extending its claims over the Arctic region, with an interest in its potential oil and mineral supplies; ironically, the region has become more accessible and useful as a result of climate change leading to a retreat of the winter ice pack.

Discussion questions

- When it comes to making decisions on environmental laws and policies, how much risk can or should we tolerate?
- Given the limitations of cost-benefit analysis, how much does contingent valuation have to offer as a means of helping us make economic decisions on the environment?
- Does individual action have a useful part to play in addressing environmental problems, or must we rely instead on collective action?
- Should environmental policymaking be based on giving human interests priority over those of the rest of the natural world, or vice versa? Is giving the natural world priority – or even equal ranking – practicable?

Key concepts

Anthropocentrism

Collective action problem

Common pool resources

Consumer-led solutions

Contingent valuation

Corporate social responsibility

Cost-benefit analysis

Ecocentrism

Ecofeminism

Eco-labelling

Environmental ethics

Environmental justice

Environmental peacekeeping

Environmental refugees

Environmental scarcity

Polluter pays principle

Precautionary principle

Public goods

Risk assessment

Further reading

Cannon, Tom (2012) *Corporate Responsibility: Governance, Compliance and Ethics in a Sustainable Environment*, 2nd edn (Pearson). A review of the evolving debate over corporate social responsibility in regard to environmental matters.

Dinar, Shlomi (ed) (2011) *Beyond Resource Wars: Scarcity, Environmental Degradation, and International Cooperation* (MIT Press). An edited collection which acknowledges that environmental scarcity and degradation can spark conflict, but can also provide an impetus for cooperation and negotiation between states.

James, Simon P. (2015) *Environmental Philosophy: An Introduction* (Polity Press). An accessible survey of the questions and issues that arise in philosophical and ethical debates about nature and the environment.

Keller, Ann Campbell (2009) *Science in Environmental Policy: The Politics of Objective Advice* (MIT Press). A study of the impact of scientists on the environmental policy process, using acid pollution and climate change as cases, and concluding that their neutrality and objectivity strengthens in the later stages of the process.

Tietenberg, Tom, and Lynne Lewis (2016) *Environmental and Natural Resource Economics*, 10th edn (Routledge). A survey of the economic questions that arise in environmental policy-making.

3 The Dynamics of Environmental Policy

Key arguments

- There have been four phases in the evolution of environmental policy, the fourth – since the 1980s – being more strategic, integrative, creative, preventative, and international in nature.
- Studies of the often disorderly and unpredictable character of public policy are made more manageable by thinking of policy-making and implementation in terms of a cycle.
- States are the key players in making policy, and yet their work on the environmental front is often overlooked.
- In the absence of a system of global government, the international response to environmental problems relies for its substance on international treaties.
- There are several instruments available upon which to base environmental policy, most of which take the form of either a stick, a carrot, or a sermon.
- Often overlooked in discussions about environmental politics and policy is the role of the marketplace in leading to changes in approach.

Chapter overview

As we saw in Chapter 1, public policy can be defined as the actions that those in positions of authority take – or deliberately avoid taking – in order to achieve public goals or address public problems. It encapsulates objectives, the means applied to achieving them, the informational basis of policy, the underlying principles that drive policy, decisions and sets of decisions, and overall styles of governing. Public policy is shaped by a combination of laws, regulations, constitutional obligations, political ideology, available budgets, carefully targeted objectives, opportunism, crises and emergencies, and a combination of good fortune and misfortune.

In an ideal world, a problem or a need would be identified, alternative approaches would be studied and weighed, goals and schedules would be agreed, the preferred approach would be implemented, and the problem would be solved, or the need met. But this **rational policy model** is little more than an ideal, because life is not that simple. There is rarely agreement on the dimensions of a problem or need, or on the best solution, the costs and benefits of the available policy options are hard to pin down, and problems are rarely solved so much as mitigated or ameliorated. Governments face multiple demands from multiple interests driven by multiple objectives, political difference offer diversions, and items move up or down the public agenda according to the relative amounts of attention, funding, and urgency that are brought to bear. Two alternative policy models have been proposed to more accurately reflect the reality of policy:

- In the **incremental policy model**, a problem or a need is identified, the various stakeholders are consulted, and an effort is made to achieve a consensus on the best way to proceed. This typically involves achieving change by building incrementally on what has come before, and responding less with a comprehensive plan than with a series of minor adjustments in what Lindblom (1979) described as 'the science of muddling through'.
- In the **garbage-can policy model**, the reality of most policy-making is recognized as being partial, fluid, anarchic, incomplete, disorganized, and opportunistic. Cohen et al. (1972) describe this model as 'a collection of choices looking for problems, issues and feelings looking for decision situations in which they might be aired, solutions looking for issues to which they might be the answer, and decision makers looking for work'. Ideas are more important than preferences, problems and needs must wait their turn, and action is taken as much on the basis of pressing need as on the basis of clear policy goals.

This chapter begins with an assessment of the changing approaches to environmental policy, showing how the bulk of policy has been a response to the effects of industrialization. The policy cycle is then discussed, explaining how an effort is made to impose some order and logic on a disorderly and often illogical system. The chapter

> then looks at the environmental policy process from the perspective both of states working in isolation and of those working within the international system, and ends with a review of the key tools used in environmental policy, ranging from regulatory command-and-control approaches to market-based options.

Evolving approaches to environmental policy

In looking at how governments and publics have thought (or not thought) about environmental policy, we can identify four distinct phases (Table 3.1). The first lasted until the late eighteenth century, and was marked by the absence either of substantial problems or of a general understanding about the need to develop policies towards nature, natural resources, or the environment. There are numerous examples dating back thousands of years of damage created by human activity, including salinization in the Fertile Crescent of the Middle East, the soil erosion that was implicated in the drought that contributed to the collapse of the Mayan civilization in the eighteenth and nineteenth centuries, and the introduction of invasive species in the wake of the Spanish settlement of the Americas. People lived more directly off and with nature, while natural resources seemed to be boundless, human populations were low, human demands were limited, and the long-term costs of change were not well understood. Under these circumstances, policies rarely emerged.

The second phase began with the advent of the Industrial Revolution in Europe in the late eighteenth century. This brought mechanization and a new reliance on pollutive fossil fuels (first on coal and later oil and natural gas), the rise of the factory system, rapid and often unregulated expansion of new industrial towns and cities, accelerated population growth, and new levels of exploitation of natural resources (see Josephson, 2012). People began to move away from living directly off the land and began to lose much of their sense of association with nature and the natural environment. Advances in scientific understanding helped promote new awareness of some of the environmental costs of industry and urbanization, and limited action was taken to protect nature and human health, but the profit motive prevailed and most environmental initiatives came from individuals and private groups rather than from governments. The focus was on local problems and local solutions.

The third phase, which was sufficiently distinctive and identifiable as to earn itself the label of a policy paradigm, was both short and sharp. It emerged during the 1960s in the wake of new

Table 3.1 **Evolving approaches to environmental policy**

Phase	Dates	Features
1.	Pre-industrial era	Simple technologies and slow population growth meant few major threats to the environment and few incentives to develop policy.
2.	Industrial Revolution, 1760s–1950s	Mechanization, rise of factory system, rise of towns and cities, growth of population, new reliance on fossil fuels, worsening air and water pollution, but little organized government response beyond the local.
3.	1960s–1970s	Heightened political and public awareness of problems, new national institutions and broader legal response, but policies piecemeal rather than strategic.
4.	Since the 1980s	Policies more strategic, better informed, more integrative, based on a wider set of policy tools, more focused on outcomes, more preventative, and more international.

levels of environmental awareness and activism, and was capped by the 1972 Stockholm conference. A broader view was taken during this phase about the causes and effects of environmental problems, but Weale (1992: 10–23) argues that national policies were merely reactive, and reflected the history and circumstance of the countries in which they were developed. Many new environmental laws were adopted, but few governments drew up national plans or took a strategic approach to problems, instead bringing together a cluster of previously disparate responsibilities under the charge of a department of the environment with few substantial powers, and treating the environment as a discrete area of policy. Policy responses were piecemeal, modest, and based on an incomplete understanding of the nature of the problems they addressed. The initial focus was on air and water pollution, which were the most visible effects of environmental mismanagement, and governments relied on traditional regulatory tools borrowed from other areas of policy, failing to follow up with studies of policy implementation. As a cumulative result, not much was achieved in terms of improved environmental conditions.

The fourth phase has been evolving since the 1980s, with several distinct features:

- Governments have been more strategic in trying to better understand the causes of problems, developing long-term solutions, and drawing up national plans of action.
- Policies have been based on an improved scientific understanding of the causes and effects of threats to the environment.
- Policy design has been more integrative in the sense that the environment is no longer seen as a discrete area of policy, but as one that relates to almost all other areas of policy.

- Governments have been more creative in terms of the regulatory tools they have employed, many of the options having been sparked by the particular needs of sound environmental management rather than being adapted from other areas of policy.
- More attention has been paid to outcomes, with more emphasis on implementation and on measuring results.
- There has been a shift away from trying to repair problems and towards changing patterns of production and consumption in order to prevent problems emerging in the first place.
- Policy has become more international, with the realization that many environmental problems are common to multiple countries, or are shared among multiple countries. The views and priorities of poorer emerging countries have joined those of industrialized countries in driving the design of policy.

While approaches to environmental policy have matured during this fourth phase, based on a better understanding of the causes of the problems we face and of the most effective and realistic responses, levels of progress remain mixed. Trends in some areas are positive but in others we are doing little more than treading water, emphasizing not just the ongoing political and economic barriers to meaningful change, but also the realities of policy-making more generally.

The policy cycle

The public policy process is usually anything but orderly or predictable, and is best understood – depending on the problem being studied – as fitting within either the incremental or the garbage-can models. But one approach to making sense of a disorderly system is to see it in terms of a cycle that rarely ends (see Figure 3.1). Fragments of the cycle may be found in most studies of policy, but the purpose of using it is not so much to suggest that real-world policy works in this fashion so much as to help us work through an otherwise complex process. There are six steps in the cycle, illustrated here using the example of acid pollution.

Problem recognition. The first step is to agree that a problem or a need exists, and that it is the responsibility of government to respond. In terms of environmental policy, science plays a critical role in this stage, but new or worsening problems might be identified or promoted by political leaders, interest groups, the media, the advent of a disaster, the release of an official report or a book, the broadcast of a documentary, or a new trend on social media. There is no guarantee of a policy response: ideology, budgets, political priorities, and the competing demands of other policy problems

Figure 3.1 The public policy cycle

Problem recognition
Recognizing that a problem or need exists.

Agenda-setting
Placing the problem on the public agenda.

Formulation
Designing a response.

Adoption
Converting the response into law or policy statements.

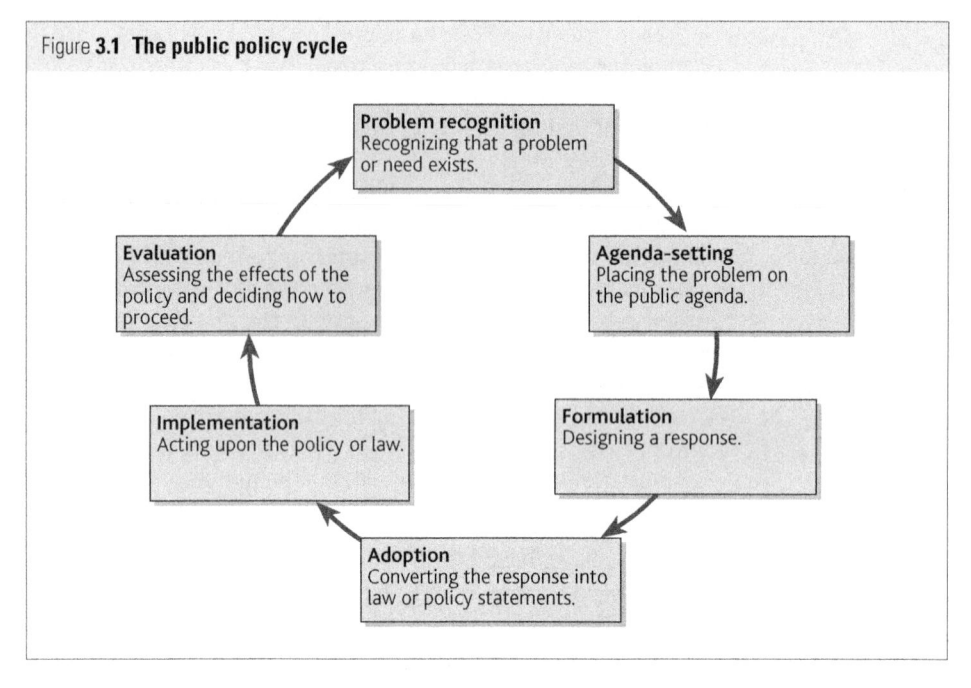

Implementation
Acting upon the policy or law.

Evaluation
Assessing the effects of the policy and deciding how to proceed.

might mean that while a new need or problem is acknowledged, no action will be taken beyond perhaps rhetorical statements. In the case of acid pollution, the science of the problem was first spelled out – very clearly – in 1872 by the Scottish chemist Robert Angus Smith in his book *Air and Rain* (Smith, 1872). Except at the local level, however, it was barely addressed for more than another century, when forests and lakes in areas downwind from major industrial centres in North America and Western Europe began to die from the effects of acidification, and public concerns grew.

Agenda-setting. Recognizing that a problem exists does not necessarily mean that it will work its way onto the public agenda, but it must if a response is to be formulated. With all the demands jostling for public and political attention, not all problems will make it to the higher reaches of the agenda, and the **issue-attention cycle** outlined by Downs (1972) suggests that policy issues go through cycles of attention that are fed by media interest, but may fall back down the agenda once politicians are seen to respond (no matter how unsubstantial the response), or as the costs of action become clear, or as other issues compete for attention. Acid pollution did not earn a prominent place on the public agenda until science and politics pushed it onto that agenda in the 1980s.

Policy formulation. Once a problem or a need is identified, a response needs to be formulated. The earliest approach to acid pollution was to focus on building taller smokestacks at coal-fired power stations in the hope that pollutive sulphur and nitrogen oxides would either stay in the atmosphere and do no one any harm, or would be so diluted as to cease to be a threat; the solution to pollution was dilution, ran the logic. But whatever goes up must come down, and once that was realized and the problem of acidification became clear, there was a change of heart, and new policies began to be developed aimed at addressing the cause rather than passing the effects on to someone else.

Policy adoption. Once a policy response has been designed, it must be adopted as a formal goal of government. At a minimum, this might involve public statements to that effect, but because actions usually speak louder than words, policy adoption means writing and passing new laws and regulations. For Western Europe, the United States, and Canada, the options chosen for dealing with acid pollution focused on fitting scrubbers to factories, power stations, and vehicle exhausts, and liming lakes in order to neutralize the acids they contained. Industrializing states have only relatively recently acknowledged the existence within their borders of the kind of problems identified decades ago in industrialized states, so they are further behind the curve of policy development and adoption.

Policy implementation. Policy serves little purpose unless it is implemented, but this is such a key step that it is often the point where policy fails or succeeds. The financial costs of policy (whether direct or indirect) are routinely underestimated, as is the time needed to implement policy, and as is the resistance to implementation, whether from governments, public opinion, the industries involved, or market forces in general. Policies are also often undermined or compromised because of inter-agency bickering and the defence of political turf by different government departments. Policy will be interpreted differently by the actors involved, and the more complex a problem, the more difficult it will be to ensure implementation by the different actors affected. Regulations may set neat targets and spread them uniformly across industries, but they inevitably face resistance because of the costs and extra work involved in implementation.

Policy evaluation. The final stage is to assess the degree of success or failure of a given policy, law, or regulation. In the example of acid pollution, evaluation has meant reviewing trends in sulphur dioxide and nitrogen oxide emissions, as well as studying the health of forests, lakes, and freshwater fisheries. The results have been encouragingly positive in North America and Europe; the former saw a 60 per cent reduction in sulphur dioxide emissions between 1990 and 2010, while the latter saw a 77 per cent reduction (see Chapter 6). Unfortunately, the results of environmental policy are rarely so rapidly positive or even easily measurable; action was taken to remove threats to the ozone layer in the 1990s, for example, but it was not expected to recover until at least 2035, and perhaps as late as 2070. The results of policy also depend to a large extent on the clarity of the original goals as well as the reporting of governments and of government departments, both of which may exaggerate achievements in order to score political points or – in the case of the latter – to win improved budgets, more authority, and better job security.

Policy at the state level

The key political actors in the world are sovereign states. They not only shape policy and enforce law within their territory, but are the core actors involved in the shaping of international agreements. Although a precise definition of the state has long been contested, most scholars would agree that states have sovereignty in a territory containing a population and marked by borders. States are the legal entities and government is the managing authority; that authority is regarded as both sovereign and legitimate by the citizens of the state and the governments of other states (see Pierson, 2011). Using the membership roster of the United Nations (UN) as a guide, at the time of writing there are currently 193 states in the world, although there are still significant swathes of territory that lack one or more of the key features of a state, and are not members of the UN; these include Kosovo, Palestine, Taiwan, and Western Sahara. It is also important to remember that coastal states have jurisdiction over seas and oceans as far out as the territorial limit of 22 km (12 miles) recognized under the 1982 UN Convention on the Law of the Sea (see Chapter 8).

While states play the major role in making policy for their citizens, and in reaching agreements with other states in addressing shared problems, it is surprising how often their work on the environmental front is overlooked. Most research on environmental policy focuses on either the local level or the international/global level, the general view being that states have either failed to live up to expectations or have often allowed domestic policy to be shaped by the pressures of the international marketplace or international agreements on the environment. Duit (2014) has identified several of the criticisms directed at states, including the following:

- Most environmental problems have global or regional dimensions, and states often have neither the institutional ability nor the political incentive to address them.
- Electoral pressures tend to push the governments of democracies in the direction of promoting economic growth over environmental protection.
- Democratic states have a tendency to prefer short-term over long-term gains, particularly when short-term reductions in well-being are at stake (Underdal, 2010).

- The reliance in many states on command-and-control approaches to environmental management and on hierarchical and expert-dominated political organization falls short of requirements for managing complex and unpredictable ecosystems (Holling and Meffe, 1996) or responding to popular demands for change (Durant et al., 2004).

To this list should be added the weaknesses of poorer and/or authoritarian states in their approaches to environmental policy:

- In poorer states, the urban elite often copies the patterns of material consumption found in capitalist democracies, but without the same levels of regulation.
- The urban poor often live in shanty towns that have grown haphazardly without efforts made to provide clean water, sanitation, waste removal, or clean sources of energy.
- For the rural poor, the struggle simply to subsist often encourages them to pursue inefficient agriculture and to exploit natural resources without much regard to long-term consequences.
- In authoritarian states, the efforts of leaders and elites to remain in power encourages them to focus on short-term gain and resource exploitation, an agenda on which the long-term interests of nature and the environment barely register.

But while states may have structural and political handicaps that have made them less than ideal environmental policy actors, they remain essential. Most of the decisions that have an impact on the environment are made at the state level, and states are collectively responsible for defining international environmental priorities, and for shaping and implementing international environmental agreements. In spite of this, most of the research on environmental politics and policy at the state level has focused on individual states in isolation, and it has only been relatively recently that there has been more focus on comparison, and on trying to identify patterns, similarities, and differences in the way that states approach environmental matters. There are some who argue that so much policy is now made at the international level – and that states have lost their 'authoritative monopoly' on policy – that the cross-national study of environmental policy should be abandoned (Spaargaren and Mol, 2008; Mol, 2016). But most would argue that comparison is an essential means of understanding how politics and policy works in different countries, and therefore in explaining how it is made internationally. There are many benefits to comparison:

- It helps us better describe national political and policy systems.
- It gives us the broader context within which to better understand differences and similarities in national approaches.

We can study environmental politics and policy in depth in the United States, or Germany, or India, or South Africa, but we will always be missing critical contextual understanding so long as we fail to compare the findings with results from other states.
- It helps us draw up rules about environmental politics and policy.
- It helps us better understand why some countries have built stronger records on environmental policy and others have lagged behind.
- It helps us predict policy outcomes by looking at experiences and records in different political situations.
- It helps us make choices by allowing each state to act as a political laboratory from which ideas can be borrowed or adapted.
- It helps us better understand the manner in which international policy is shaped and implemented.

Comparison sheds light on how different states approach similar policy problems; in one form or another, for example, they all experience air and water pollution, the challenge of waste management, and questions about the best sources of energy supply. They also have much in common regarding the environmental policy institutions they create, the laws they pass, the political debates they witness, the adoption of environmental policies by political parties, and the organization of interest groups. But they also have important differences that can be overlooked without comparison. Prime among these are the contrasting roles of wealth and poverty in creating environmental problems and shaping policy responses: publics in wealthier countries tend to be more interested in post-material quality of life issues such as the condition of the environment, and are better placed to bring pressure to bear on government for change, whether through voting choices or through support for interest groups. They must also face often powerful economic interests, such as the energy, automobile, and chemical industries, but they also have a greater capacity to organize themselves politically and to express their views through consumer choices and individual action.

Environmental policy tends to be weaker in poorer states where people have less time to act on their concerns and may be more politically marginalized, while in authoritarian states the definition of policy interests remains primarily in the hands of elites, and rarely includes a concern for the environment. It has been suggested that China offers an example of what has been dubbed **environmental authoritarianism**: its response to climate change is noteworthy for being shaped by a government that has a greater capacity to impose change on industry and consumers than is the case in democratic systems (Beeson, 2016). But Schreurs (2011) argues that while China's leaders have used

China's status as the world's second largest economy to demand a greater voice in international climate negotiations, they have also exploited its status as a society in which millions still live in poverty to resist international demands that China commits itself to reducing greenhouse emissions. Polls also find that climate change is regarded as a serious problem by fewer than one in five Chinese (see Chapter 12).

Comparison also sheds light on the unique problems faced by some states, or the problems that apply only to states that are similarly placed in terms of resources, economic structure, or social development. The concept of protected areas, for example, is quite different in Europe (where almost all land had been settled and reshaped by humans long before it was set aside for protection) than it is in North America or sub-Saharan Africa, where protection was imposed in order to discourage human settlement. Similarly, the challenge of protecting biodiversity in those states considered to be 'megadiverse' by virtue of the sheer number and variety of species to which they are home (see Chapter 10) is quite different from the challenges faced by less well-endowed states. Finally, simple misfortune has often played a role in changing policy, as reflected in the effect of accidents and disasters (see Box 3.1).

Policy at the international level

One of the defining features of the environment as a political and policy issue is its transboundary nature. Where many policy needs can be demarcated by national frontiers and addressed by national policy (even when they are common to multiple countries), the physical and political worlds do not coincide, posing challenges for environmental policy. Among the results:

- A problem might have a source in one country but an effect in another, as when air pollution is emitted in China and blown on the winds to Japan and even across the Pacific to the United States, or when deforestation in Nepal leads to river siltation and flooding downstream in the Ganges delta in India and Bangladesh.
- A problem might be hard or impossible to resolve without the joint action of multiple countries, as in the case of climate change, or the more particular case of protecting wetlands for migratory species of birds.
- North Atlantic fisheries have been pushed to the brink of collapse because of the absence of joint policies on sustainable catches involving fishing fleets from the United States, Canada, and Western Europe.

Box 3.1 Accidents, disasters, and policy

There is a story (sadly, apocryphal) that British Prime Minister Harold Macmillan was once asked by a journalist about what might blow his government off course. 'Events, dear boy, events', was his supposed response. Policy is ideally designed with time and care, but governments must also expect to have to respond to short-term crises and emergencies (see Vallero and Letcher, 2012). Some can be anticipated and planned for, but many cannot; Japan, for example, is well-prepared for earthquakes and tsunamis, but was not expecting a tsunami to wash ashore in 2011 and to cause meltdowns at three reactors in the Fukushima Daiichi nuclear power plant complex. The result was a short-term disaster followed by a longer-term and unanticipated rise of anti-nuclear sentiment in Japan, and moves towards greater reliance on other sources of energy, such as liquefied natural gas and coal (Hindmarsh, 2013). Fukushima Daiichi was the latest in a string of accidents and near misses – ranging from Windscale in Britain to Three Mile Island in the United States and Chernobyl in what was then the Soviet Union – that encouraged improvements in the safety of nuclear power stations and also cast more doubts on nuclear energy.

More than most other areas of public policy, the direction taken by environmental policy has been unusually prone to the effects of dramatic headline-making accidents and disasters (see Table 3.2), which have helped heighten public awareness of environmental threats. But while accidents can be dramatic, many of the problems caused can be resolved relatively quickly, so they may not result in long-term changes in policy, particularly given how quickly they can be replaced in the headlines by other concerns. If serious enough, however, and particularly if they are preceded or followed by many other and perhaps smaller accidents or events, they can lead to changes in policy; London, for example, had experienced decades of unhealthy smogs before the infamous four-day Great Smog of December 1952 that was implicated in the hastened death of an estimated 4,000 people (Bell et al., 2004). It led to the passage of the 1956 Clean Air Act, the first step in a series of changes that led to London smogs becoming a thing of the past. Disasters can also have a global effect on policy, as in the case of oil spills from ever-bigger oil tankers that led to improvements in tanker design and navigation; the *Exxon Valdez* accident in Alaska in 1989 led directly to new US laws encouraging double-hull tankers, although it did little to improve safety in oil drilling, leaving the way clear for the 2010 *Deepwater Horizon* disaster (Busenburg, 2013).

Where the national response to environmental problems is based on the creation of institutions and the passage of laws and regulations (see Chapter 4), the international response – in the absence of a system of global government – relies for its substance on international treaties. A **treaty** is a written agreement under international law between or among states that holds them responsible for meeting specified goals and deadlines. These goals range from the broad to the narrow, they are voluntarily agreed by signatory states, they bring these states together to achieve a consensus on policy goals, and they tie these states into

Table **3.2** **Examples of environmental accidents and disasters**

Year	Location	Details
1957	Windscale, UK	Three-day fire at nuclear plant that spread radioactivity across much of Europe.
1976	Seveso, Italy	Accident at chemical plant leading to death of livestock and preventative slaughter of more than 80,000 animals.
1979	Three Mile Island, Pennsylvania	Partial meltdown at nuclear power station.
1979	Gulf of Mexico	Blowout at Ixtoc I oil well; 3.1 million barrels of oil spilled.
1984	Bhopal, India	Worst industrial accident in history. Leak of toxic gases from Union Carbide plant killed nearly 4,000 people.
1986	Chernobyl, USSR	Explosion at nuclear power station.
1986	Switzerland	Fire at Sandoz agrochemical plant resulting in release of chemicals into the Rhine and destruction of wildlife.
1989	Prince William Sound, Alaska	Tanker *Exxon Valdez* runs aground, creating what was then the second largest oil spill in US history.
2010	Gulf of Mexico	Explosion at *Deepwater Horizon* oil rig; 5 million barrels of oil spilled.
2011	Fukushima, Japan	Explosions and fire at a nuclear plant in the wake of an earthquake and tsunami.

a policy community where action, achievement, and failure are all closely monitored and the results shared among members of the community.

There are tens of thousands of treaties in existence, dealing with many areas of policy. In the environmental field, one database lists nearly 1,600 bilateral agreements and 1,260 multilateral agreements, in addition to nearly 250 other kinds of agreements, for a total of just over 3,100 (Mitchell, 2016); see Table 3.3 for examples. There are several explanations behind these numbers, including greater international cooperation on the environment, a new awareness of problems generated by improved data and scientific understanding, and greater public support for international action. Quantity, however, does not necessarily translate into quality, and many environmental trends remain negative despite the proliferation of treaties designed to address them (UNEP, 2012).

There are several reasons for this, beginning with the long and arduous process that is usually involved in writing, agreeing, and implementing treaties, the different steps depending on the breadth and complexity of the problem being addressed and the number of parties involved (see Figure 3.2). It may take years to achieve recognition that a problem merits being addressed by a

Table 3.3 **Examples of international environmental treaties**

Year signed	Where signed	Topic
1946	Washington DC	Regulation of whaling
1954	London	Prevention of pollution of the sea by oil
1971	Ramsar	Wetlands
1972	London	Prevention of marine pollution by dumping of wastes
1973	Washington DC	International trade in endangered species
1979	Geneva	Long-range transboundary air pollution
1979	Bonn	Conservation of migratory species of wild animals
1980	Canberra	Conservation of Antarctic marine living resources
1982	Montego Bay	UN Convention on the Law of the Sea
1985	Vienna	Protection of the ozone layer
1989	Basel	Control of transboundary movements of hazardous wastes and their disposal
1992	New York	Climate change
1992	Rio de Janeiro	Biological diversity
1994	Paris	Combatting desertification
1994	Geneva	International Tropical Timber Agreement
2001	Stockholm	Persistent organic pollutants

treaty, many more years to reach agreement on the content of the treaty, and still more years for the treaty to be given teeth in the form of meaningful targets. Some are sufficiently controversial that they never achieve enough ratifications to bring them into force, and yet others set targets that are politically difficult to achieve.

Bodansky (2010: 15) argues that international environmental law is 'neither a panacea nor a sham', but that while it can play a constructive role, that is all that can be said about it, and it might best be described as a 'thirty-percent solution'. Selin (2014) suggests that the negotiation and implementation of environmental agreements 'is a process that encourages and enables, but does not require, cooperation. Treaties can play a constructive role in establishing common rules and standards, but they cannot be the sole problem-solving mechanism.' At the same time, he points out that compliance is not the only measure of effectiveness, and that treaties should also be assessed by the extent to which they mitigate a problem, change relevant practices, and shape norms and decisions beyond the confines of the treaty process. Achieving each of these objectives, in turn, is a function of the extent to

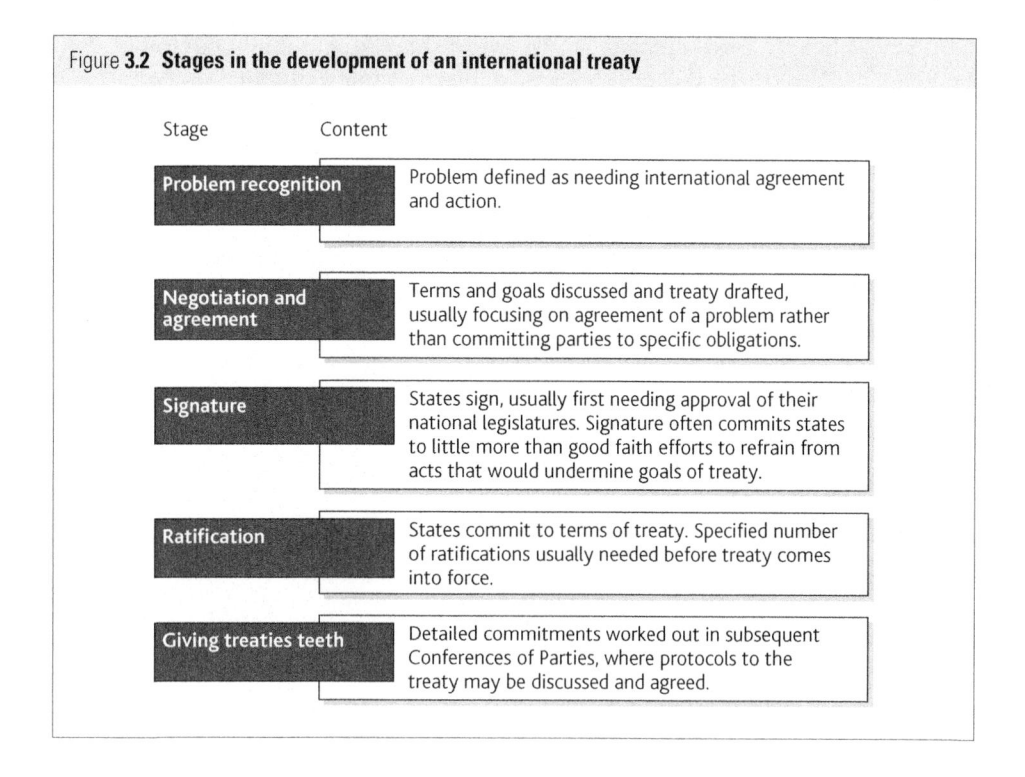

Figure 3.2 Stages in the development of an international treaty

Stage	Content
Problem recognition	Problem defined as needing international agreement and action.
Negotiation and agreement	Terms and goals discussed and treaty drafted, usually focusing on agreement of a problem rather than committing parties to specific obligations.
Signature	States sign, usually first needing approval of their national legislatures. Signature often commits states to little more than good faith efforts to refrain from acts that would undermine goals of treaty.
Ratification	States commit to terms of treaty. Specified number of ratifications usually needed before treaty comes into force.
Giving treaties teeth	Detailed commitments worked out in subsequent Conferences of Parties, where protocols to the treaty may be discussed and agreed.

which treaty secretariats and national signatories can overcome three key handicaps:

1. *Enforcement.* Although treaties are by definition binding agreements, there is no centralized political authority at the global level, so compliance cannot be enforced in the same manner as domestic law. As a result, appeal is made less to the letter of law than to 'playing the game' and shaming those who do not live up to their obligations. An example of this phenomenon at work can be found in efforts made at meetings of the International Whaling Commission to shame Japan into stopping its whaling activities (without much success) (Epstein and Barclay, 2013). There is also an element of quid pro quo involved; a state that does not cooperate cannot expect other states to reciprocate on matters that might be of interest to the recalcitrant state. Generally, the best means of encouraging compliance is through non-judicial mechanisms: regular meetings of parties to a convention (which remind them of the provisions of the treaty), the establishment of treaty secretariats, and regular reporting requirements.
2. *Structure.* As the goals of treaties become more complex, so their contents become less precise and their effectiveness

less predictable. The most successful treaties tend to be those with focused interests and goals, and limited geographical reach. This is part of the reason why topics as all-encompassing as climate change and the protection of biodiversity have proved difficult to address through international treaties.
3. *Translation into national law*. Treaties mean little until their goals are translated into national law, which must then be implemented. Because treaties and conventions are often no more than agreements in principle, they are influenced (and even weakened) by the need to accommodate the different priorities of signatory nations, and there are often large differences between what is agreed during the negotiations behind a treaty and what is subsequently found to be acceptable to national legislatures.

Another means of encouraging an international response to environmental problems is to organize a conference. This may sound like a recipe for talk rather than action, and may not result in specific action, but Haas (2015: ch. 9) points out several of their benefits: they can bring new actors (such as non-governmental organizations) into discussions about the environment, offer a means to building networks and coordinating national campaigns, push debates in new directions, mobilize concern about new problems (or new understanding of old problems), and encourage coordination of national policies. Andresen (2012) is not so sure, arguing that the results of the big global conferences are usually characterized by 'high and vague ambitions' that are hard to realize under real-world conditions.

There have so far been four **mega-conferences** on the environment: Stockholm in 1972, Rio in 1992, Rio+10 (in Johannesburg) in 2002, and Rio+20 (in Rio) in 2012. Stockholm is widely regarded as a landmark event, but the political and policy effects of the mega-conferences later tailed off, reaching a new low at Rio+20, which was attended by relatively few national leaders and resulted only in agreement of a non-binding document titled *The Future We Want*. Numerous additional and more focused conferences have been held along the way, few of which have attracted headlines but some of which have resulted in significant outcomes; the most important have been meetings of the parties to treaties such as the climate change and biodiversity conventions, some of which have given more substance to those treaties. Others – some organized by UN specialized agencies and others by industry – have dealt with issues such as water, recycling, the built environment, environmental justice, environmental statistics, environmental law, and environmental engineering (see Table 3.4).

Table **3.4 Examples of international environmental conferences**

Year	Location	Title
1946	Fontainebleau	World Conservation Congress*
1954	Rome	World Population Conference*
1972	Stockholm	UN Conference on the Human Environment
1974	Rome	World Food Conference*
1976	Vancouver	UN Conference on Human Settlements*
1977	Nairobi	UN Conference on Desertification
1977	Tbilisi	International Conference on Environmental Education*
1979	Geneva	World Climate Conference*
1992	Rio de Janeiro	UN Conference on Environment and Development
2007	Singapore	B4E Business for the Environment*
2015	Barcelona	World Congress and Expo on Recycling*
2017	Madrid	Global Solar Energy Summit

* First of a series

Environmental policy instruments

Governments have different tools or instruments available to them as they shape and implement policy. It might be tempting to think that once a problem is understood, a government can adopt new laws and regulations to address the problem, and spend money to support its legislative goals. On the other hand, some might argue that government intervention is the wrong way to go, and that it is best to leave policy as far as possible to market forces and consumer choice. The core problem with this latter option is that policy is not shaped on a level playing field; those with the loudest voices, the most immediate vested interests, the most money to spend, and the most sophisticated resources will be heard more clearly than those without. Meanwhile, to hope that consumer choices will shape policy outcomes assumes that consumers have all the information they need to make informed choices, are sufficiently interested in all the areas of policy over which they have influence, and will participate in numbers that are large enough to make a difference. In reality, government is usually needed as an arbiter, or – at the very least – as a source of policy alternatives, as well as a source of expertise and as the primary overseer for policy implementation.

Bemelmans-Videc et al. (1998) suggest that policy instruments broadly fall into one of three categories (Figure 3.3):

- The stick approach is the most common, even to the point of being considered 'traditional', and consists of efforts to regulate behaviour through laws, penalties, taxes, bans, or sanctions.

Figure 3.3 **Environmental policy instruments**

Type	Features	Examples
Sticks	Regulating activity, through laws, penalties, taxes, fees, bans, or sanctions	Regulations, command-and-control policies, carbon taxes, market-based incentives - such as emissions trading, fees for the provision of wastewater treatment, and garbage disposal
Carrots	Providing incentives, through financial rewards and benefits	Subsidies, grants and tax exemptions; deposit refund schemes
Sermons	Awareness raising	Public information campaigns, energy efficiency labels

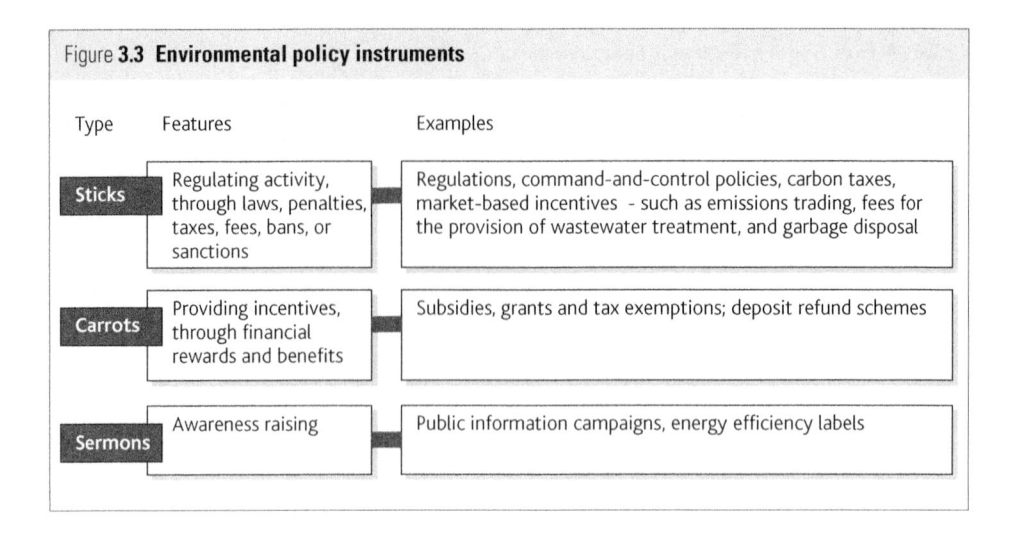

Laws or regulations represent sticks by saying what can and cannot be done, and what penalties will be imposed on those who ignore the stick.

- The carrot approach is based on offering mainly financial incentives, rewards, and benefits, such as subsidies, grants, and tax exemptions. For example, some governments offer homeowners and businesses grants to install solar panels.
- The sermon approach relies on raising awareness through public information and education campaigns, by which the targets of policy (say, consumers or industries) are exhorted to change their behaviour through reasoned arguments and persuasion.

Sticks and carrots can be found to different degrees in the most common tool used by most governments to achieve environmental policy goals: **regulations**. Where statute law is the kind adopted by legislatures and applied by courts and the police system, regulations are rules, standards, or restrictions imposed by executive agencies operating under the authority of legislatures. They have the effect of laws, and often serve to convert the general goals of statute law into more detailed technical standards and requirements, providing details of how the law is to be followed, and often setting goals, standards, and limits (see Baldwin et al., 2013). The website of the US Environmental Protection Agency provides a succinct outline of the difference between laws and regulations: 'The EPA is called a regulatory agency because [the US] Congress authorizes us to write regulations that explain the technical, operational, and legal details necessary to implement laws. Regulations are mandatory requirements that can apply to individuals, businesses, state or local governments, non-profit institutions, or others' (see Box 3.2).

> **Box 3.2** *Regulations – The case of the US Clean Air Act*
>
> An example of the difference between laws and regulations is offered by the federal response in the United States to air pollution. The first step was taken in 1955 with the passage of the Air Pollution Control Act, which provided funds for research. A second step was taken with the passage of the 1963 Clean Air Act (CAA), which did little more than authorize research into the means for monitoring and controlling air pollution – no specific goals were set. Amendments to the CAA in 1970 and 1977 required the setting of National Ambient Air Quality Standards for seven primary pollutants (including lead, sulphur dioxide, and carbon monoxide), as well as the development of implementation plans by all 50 US states. There were more amendments in 1990 which produced regulations in the form of limits on air pollution from factories and power plants, emission standards for road vehicles, and limits for toxic substances in fuel, but were focused particularly on addressing the problem of acid pollution through an emissions trading scheme. The evolving complexity of the clean air programme was reflected in the growing size of the documents involved: the 1970 CAA amendments were 68 pages in length, the 1990 amendments expanded to 788 pages, and the regulations required for their implementation now run to more than 10,000 pages (Rosenbaum, 2014: 18).
>
> By 2011, the CAA legislation was summarized as follows:
>
>> It requires the Environmental Protection Agency to establish minimum national standards for air quality, and assigns primary responsibility to the states to assure compliance with the standards. Areas not meeting the standards, referred to as "non-attainment areas", are required to implement specified air pollution control measures. The Act establishes federal standards for mobile sources of air pollution and their fuels and for sources of 187 hazardous air pollutants, and it establishes a cap-and-trade program for the emissions that cause acid rain. It established a comprehensive permit system for all major sources of air pollution. It also addresses the prevention of pollution in areas with clean air and protection of the stratospheric ozone layer. (US Congressional Research Service, 2011)

As the number of environmental regulations has grown, so they have come under increased criticism from their target industries and from supporters of smaller government. Regulations are variously accused of being economically inefficient, of leading to inflated costs for products and services, of stifling innovation, of encouraging bureaucratic bloat, and of leading to job losses. But supporters argue that the economic costs are more than offset by the health benefits, and suggest that while the coercion implicit in regulation is unfortunate, it is sometimes the only way to oblige polluters to pay heed to the environmental effects of their activities.

The standard approach to pollution control is **command-and-control**, a stick whereby a set of goals is established, quality standards are agreed (for example, permissible levels of air pollutants), emission levels are set with the goal of achieving those standards, the technologies needed to achieve them are sometimes specified, and government is made responsible for enforcement. The 'command' element sets out the standards and targets while the 'control' element involves the sanctions that can be applied in the event of non-compliance (Moosa and Ramiah, 2014: 12). Among the benefits of command-and-control: it is relatively simple, and it allows regulators to respond relatively quickly to developments that do not meet the prescribed standards. However, it offers regulated industry few carrots, it is routinely subject to political and business resistance that can result in watered-down standards, it is often accused of undermining economic competitiveness and of skewing global markets, and it gives environmental agencies new responsibilities that they are often unable to meet unless they have enough staff and large budgets.

An example of a stick can be found in the idea of a **carbon tax**, a fee assessed on the carbon content of fuels, or a tax on carbon dioxide emissions from burning fossil fuels. This is based on placing a fee on goods and services that is proportional to the amount of carbon emitted in their production and consumption. Finland introduced the first carbon tax in 1990, followed by Norway (1991), Sweden (1991), Denmark (1992), and the Netherlands (1992) (Tews et al., 2003). Sweden claims that the tax has helped it reduce carbon dioxide emissions by 20 per cent without a reduction in economic competitiveness. It has also been used in Chile and Ireland, and was introduced in Australia in 2012 but repealed in 2014. Like most policy options, it has both benefits and costs – see Table 3.5.

One alternative to regulation that offers more in the way of carrots is to employ **market-based incentives** by setting goals and standards while leaving it to the marketplace to deliver the results. An example of this is the cap-and-trade or **emissions trading** approach to air pollution (Tietenberg, 2006). Under this arrangement, air quality standards are agreed in a given area, caps are then set on emission levels (the cap later being lowered at a gradual and predictable rate), and permits are issued or auctioned to the affected industries. If a given factory or power station falls below its permitted emissions cap, it can sell its excess 'right to pollute' to a factory or power station that is above the cap, while those above the cap must buy the 'right to pollute' from their peers below the cap, or otherwise face fines. This arrangement – if designed well – sets targets while providing a financial incentive to reduce emissions. The plan is both flexible and predictable, with the added bonus that environmental groups can increase the pressure by buying and retiring credits.

The United States has used an emissions trading scheme since 1990 to address acid pollution in the eastern one-third of the country (see Chapter 6), and one of the effects has been a 60 per cent reduction in sulphur dioxide emissions in the region, without significant economic ill-effects. The European Union (EU) intro-

Table 3.5 **Carbon tax: Benefits and costs**

Benefits	Costs
No recording problems, because we know carbon content of all fuels.	Increases cost of fuel and products, which will be passed on to consumers. (But can be offset by reductions in other taxes made possible by new carbon taxes.)
Encourages alternatives. Natural gas produces the least CO_2, coal the most, so market pressure to move away from coal.	No limits placed on amount of carbon emitted (unlike emissions trading).
Incentive to reduce carbon emissions through conservation, substitution, innovation.	Tax revenues may be wasted on non-environmental spending.
Can be implemented more quickly than emissions trading.	Idea of taxing unpopular with business and government.
New revenue stream that could be used to invest in renewables.	Unless everyone does it at same level, production may shift to 'pollution havens' with no or lower carbon taxes.
Revenue more predictable than with emissions trading.	Higher taxes may encourage industries to hide carbon emissions.
Tax can be collected using existing tax structures.	Consumers do not like new taxes.

duced a similar system in 2005 with a focus on climate change (see Chapter 12), aimed at helping it meet its target of reducing carbon dioxide emissions by 20 per cent by 2020, and by 80 per cent by 2050 (Faure and Peeters, 2008). The EU caps are reduced by just under 2 per cent each year, and since 2013 the allowances have been allocated through auction. By 2013, the scheme had contributed to a 20 per cent reduction in CO_2 emissions in the EU (from a 1990 base).

As for the third kind of policy instrument (the sermon), public information campaigns have an idealistic quality about them. Governments might provide details on the nature of a problem, on the role of different actors in creating and maintaining that problem, on the policy options available to address it, and on the reasons why actions need to be taken. For example, we can be told that it makes sense to recycle household waste, and government will provide us with data on how much we produce along with the costs of disposal and the environmental benefits of recycling. But one of the problems with information is that facts can be manipulated to present pictures of a problem that fit with the goals of an administration and its major supporters. Another problem is that most people do not have the time or the interest to absorb information on all the policy problems that impact them, directly or indirectly, from day to day. By electing governments, they are deferring to elected officials and bureaucrats to represent their interests and to take care of much of the detail of policy.

Sticks, carrots, and sermons are all instruments that involve deliberate efforts to change the behaviour of target groups, whether they are industries, specific business, or individuals. Often overlooked in these calculations are the inherent pressures of the marketplace. For example, as we will see in Chapter 11, much of the pressure for change in energy policy has come not from regulation so much as from the fact that coal is usually dirtier and more expensive to extract and transport that natural gas, and from technological changes in the road vehicle industry, where manufacturers have developed hybrid and electrical vehicles at least in part because of consumer demand and new understanding about how to make more efficient vehicles.

Discussion questions

- Which of the three models of policy – rational, incremental, or garbage-can – do you find most convincing, and why?
- What are the major political and economic barriers to meaningful change in the direction taken by environmental policy?
- To what extent are states still the leaders in making environmental policy, and to what extent do they come under international pressure?
- Which environmental policy instruments are most effective: sticks, carrots, sermons, or markets?

Key concepts

Carbon tax

Command-and-control

Emissions trading

Environmental authoritarianism

Environmental policy instruments

Garbage-can policy model

Incremental policy model

Issue-attention cycle

Market-based incentives

Mega-conferences

Policy cycle

Rational policy model

Regulation

Treaty

Further reading

Cohen, Steven (2014) *Understanding Environmental Policy*, 2nd edn (Columbia University Press). A broad assessment of the development and implementation of environmental policy, illustrated with several case studies, including fracking and climate change.

Crabbé, Ann, and Pieter Leroy (2008) *The Handbook of Environmental Policy Evaluation* (Earthscan). A practical guide to evaluating environmental policy, with a review of general principles and specific methods.

Moosa, Imad A., and Vikash Ramiah (2014) *The Costs and Benefits of Environmental Regulation* (Edward Elgar). An assessment of the origins, types, costs, benefits, and effects of environmental regulation.

Sands, Philippe, Jacqueline Peel, Adriana Fabra, and Ruth MacKenzie (2012) *Principles of International Environmental Law*, 3rd edn (Cambridge University Press). A comprehensive survey of the origins, structure, approaches, and effects of international environmental treaties.

Vallero, Daniel A., and Trevor M. Letcher (2012) *Unraveling Environmental Disasters* (Elsevier). A study of short-term and long-term environmental disasters, their causes, and their policy implications.

4 Actors at the State Level

Key arguments

- Environmental politics and policy at the state level are shaped by a combination of democratic, economic, and ideological differences.
- There are few consistencies in the way national governments approach the definition of responsibilities for environmental management.
- Non-state actors have been influential in making environmental policy, interest groups much more so than political parties.
- Green politics has converted a focused set of policy interests into a party movement in multiple countries.
- National environmental policy is not formed in a vacuum, and states influence each other through policy diffusion and convergence.
- In the South, the links with economic and social development are critical to understanding how environmental politics and policy have evolved.

Chapter overview

We saw in Chapter 3 that states have only in the past few decades begun to take an approach to environmental policy that has been strategic, integrative, creative, and preventative (rather than curative) in terms of the policy tools used. But many environmental problems remain: the record in democracies has been mixed at best, while in poorer and/or authoritarian states it has been weak. Partly as a result, there is a widely held assumption that many environmental problems are better addressed at the international level, which has been the subject of much of the research on environmental politics and policy. While there have been numerous studies of environmental policy in individual states – particularly the United States, Germany, and China – there has been remarkably little comparative study, where states are compared with a view to drawing general conclusions about the domestic pressures that drive environmental politics and policy. This is unfortunate, because – as we have seen – states continue to be the dominant actors in making and implementing policy, and there is no government above the level of states. (There is instead a system of governance, discussed in Chapter 5.)

With these thoughts in mind, this chapter sets out to review the dynamics of environmental politics and policy at the state level. It begins with an assessment of the contrasting characteristics of different political regimes, moving the discussion beyond the kinds of economic factors that often dominate comparative studies of the environmental records of states, and looking also at the differences between democratic and authoritarian regimes. It then looks at the influence of ideological factors before reviewing the features of states where environmental factors have come to influence policy more broadly. Several labels have been developed to describe this phenomenon, including *green states* and *environmental states*.

The chapter then looks at the major state-level actors (governmental and non-governmental) involved in shaping and implementing environmental policy. It begins with a review of the manner in which government departments and bureaucracies work, before looking at the role of legislatures and courts. Their work is contrasted with the mixed response to environmental issues of the major non-state actors: political parties and interest groups. The latter have been particularly important: many were founded decades before states decided to create government institutions, they collectively continue to play an active and creative role in shaping environmental policy and building environmental awareness, and – as a result – scholarly studies of environmental NGOs far outnumber those of government departments and regulatory agencies. This does not mean that the latter do not deserve more attention, though, even if we study them only to give us a better understanding of why so much of the pressure for change and innovation has come from civil society rather than from government.

The chapter goes on to look at the role of policy diffusion and convergence in shaping state responses to environmental needs; diffusion happens when policies spread from one country to another, and convergence when policies become more similar across countries. It ends with an assessment of the particular experiences of developing states (collectively known as the South) and the tensions between the goals of economic and social development on the one hand, and those of sustainable environmental management on the other. It asks how the South can have the same economic opportunities as the industrialized states of the North while also avoiding their environmental mistakes.

Understanding environmental governance

The role of states in making and implementing environmental policy has often been overlooked, a popular view being that most environmental questions are best addressed at the international level. For example, Doyle et al. (2016: 233) suggest that there is sometimes 'a tendency to allow a focus on the global and the forces of global capitalism to convince us that there is no longer much point in studying the roles and practices of nation states in environmental politics'. Barry and Eckersley (2005) long ago challenged this trend, arguing that states needed to be more closely examined as facilitators of progressive environmental change rather than simply as contributors to environmental destruction. More recently, Duit et al. (2016) have argued that states matter because they 'structure political, economic, and social interactions', maintain legal frameworks backed by coercive power, and deploy significant economic and administrative resources, while systems of national regulation continue to provide the foundations for environmental policy. And international organizations and treaties – while important – remain largely dependent on the states that created them. In short, conclude Duit et al., states 'remain the most powerful human mechanism for collective action that can compel obedience and redistribute resources'.

While the state is important, then, it is not monolithic, and different states have had different experiences in the fields of environmental politics and policy. As we saw in Chapter 1, the earliest political initiatives were taken in the industrial states of the North that faced the earliest problems, and it was only later that the distinctive concerns and perspectives of the South (mainly African, Asian, and Latin American states) entered the equation. But in understanding the contrasts, the focus has long been on economic rather than political distinctions, and surprisingly little attention has been paid to understanding the role of different political regimes, ranging from the democratic to the authoritarian, with multiple shades between. Clearly, different levels of economic development are important, but the manner in which political systems are organized plays a critical role in determining how environmental policies are shaped and implemented.

Political science has yet to develop a means for classifying political regimes that has achieved universal acclaim, but the Democracy Index maintained by UK-based Economist Intelligence Unit (see Figure 4.1) is at least as good as any, and divides regimes into two broad types:

- Democracies are the most politically responsive and transparent, with strong links between the rulers and the ruled, complex power relationships, multiple channels through which competing opinions can be expressed, and multiple views heard from individuals, political parties, interest groups, businesses, mass media, and social media. Most democracies are also advanced economies, and will have associated environmental interests, as well as strong international ties based on political associations and economic links. But some democracies – such as India and Mexico – have economies that are still emerging, and whose environmental priorities are different from those of older industrial states such as Germany and Britain.
- Authoritarian states (found mainly in the South) are the least politically responsive and transparent, with weak links between ruling elites and most citizens, more focused power

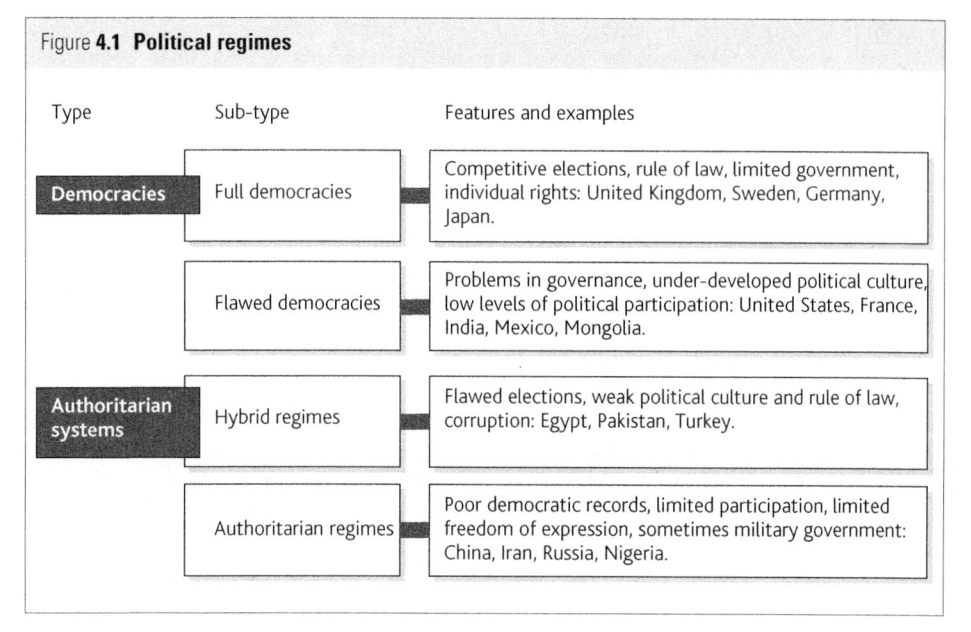

Figure **4.1 Political regimes**

Type	Sub-type	Features and examples
Democracies	Full democracies	Competitive elections, rule of law, limited government, individual rights: United Kingdom, Sweden, Germany, Japan.
	Flawed democracies	Problems in governance, under-developed political culture, low levels of political participation: United States, France, India, Mexico, Mongolia.
Authoritarian systems	Hybrid regimes	Flawed elections, weak political culture and rule of law, corruption: Egypt, Pakistan, Turkey.
	Authoritarian regimes	Poor democratic records, limited participation, limited freedom of expression, sometimes military government: China, Iran, Russia, Nigeria.

Source: Democracy Index (2017).

relationships, few channels through which competing views can be expressed (assuming that they are tolerated at all), and attention paid mainly to the voices of those who are members or supporters of the ruling elite. Most authoritarian states are also less advanced economies, and thus have international political and economic ties that are weaker than their democratic counterparts, and environmental priorities that are different from those of advanced economies.

In addition to democratic and economic differences, environmental policy at the state level is also impacted by ideological differences. Table 4.1 summarizes the links between ideology and environmental policy, moving from right to left on the political spectrum. These distinctions mainly apply to democracies, where ideological variety is supported and encouraged, while varieties of conservatism and liberalism are found in authoritarian regimes. **Neoliberalism** has come to characterize most capitalist democracies since the 1980s, and is viewed by many of its critics as being behind the weakness in the development of sound and effective environmental policies. Monbiot (2014) summarizes neoliberalism as the view that the market can resolve most social, economic, and political problems, that people are best served by the minimum of intervention and spending by the state, and that the general social interest is maximized by the pursuit of

Table **4.1 Ideology and the environment**

Approach	Ideology	Features
Right-wing	Conservative	Favours strong social institutions and takes a pessimistic view of human nature, emphasizing the importance of regulating human behaviour.
	Liberal	Supports a more moderate view of the role of the state, with a greater emphasis on individual rights. Environmental citizenship is important (see Box 4.1).
	Neoliberal	Favours political and economic decentralization, emphasizes personal responsibility, criticizes regulation, and believes that the free market can solve most environmental problems.
Left-wing	Socialism	Favours political and economic centralization, criticizes the free market, and emphasizes the role of community responses to environmental problems.
	Anarchism	Takes a more optimist view of human nature than conservatism, rejects the need for rules, and believes humans and nature can co-exist if left to their own devices.
	Feminism	All humans are equal, domination of nature equated with men's domination of women, and fundamental change is needed in social order so as to produce a just and sustainable society.

Source: Based on Doyle et al. (2016: 54–67).

self-interest. Critics reject this view, worry that market forces play too great a role in driving environmental choices, and argue that capitalist market forces cannot resolve the problems they helped create (see Büscher et al., 2014).

Studies of the state as an environmental actor have often focused on those with a strong record of factoring environmental concerns into politics and economics. These have been variously described as ecological states, ecostates, environmental states, or green states. Eckersley (2004: 2) defines a **green state** as 'a democratic state whose regulatory ideals and democratic procedures are informed by ecological democracy rather than liberal democracy'. (For its part, **ecological democracy** has been defined as a form of democracy based on the elimination of attempts to dominate the natural world, and on efforts to reintegrate humans and nature (Fotopoulos, 2001).) Meanwhile, Christoff (2005: 42) describes a green state as one that includes high levels of environmental capacity, the strong cultural and political institutionalization of ecological values, and a commitment to eco-citizenship (good environmental citizenship).

Duit et al. (2016) opt for the term '**environmental state**', which they define as 'a state that possesses a significant set of institutions and practices dedicated to the management of the environment and societal–environmental interactions'. Elsewhere, Duit (2016) argues that environmental states have four dimensions: as systems of regulation, administration, redistribution, and knowledge (see Figure 4.2). He likens the rise of the environmental state to the rise of the welfare state in the sense that both have had to address

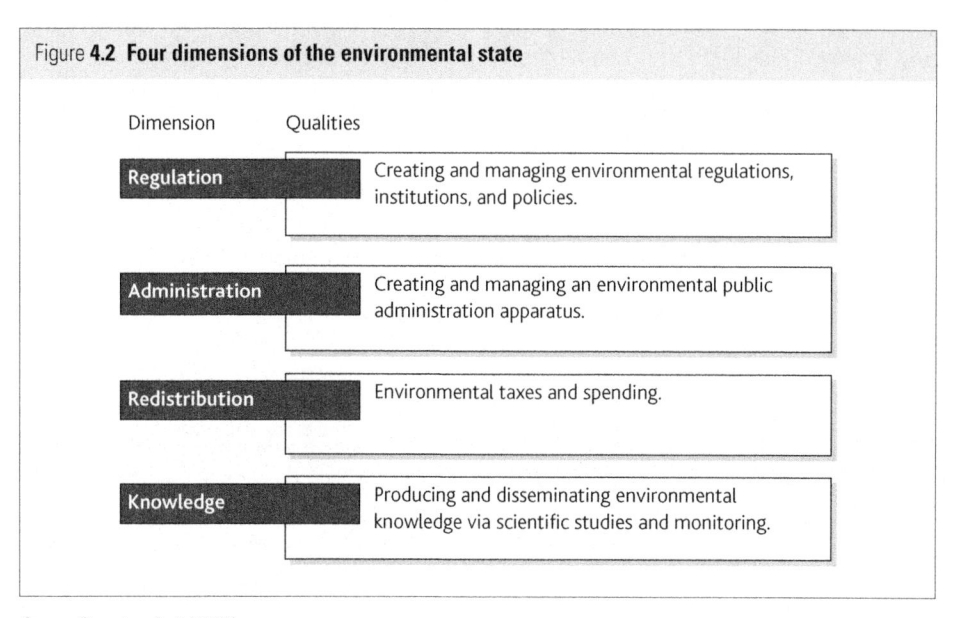

Figure **4.2 Four dimensions of the environmental state**

Dimension	Qualities
Regulation	Creating and managing environmental regulations, institutions, and policies.
Administration	Creating and managing an environmental public administration apparatus.
Redistribution	Environmental taxes and spending.
Knowledge	Producing and disseminating environmental knowledge via scientific studies and monitoring.

Source: Based on Duit (2016).

the negative social and human effects of the marketplace. Just as the welfare state did this through labour laws, family benefits, and social security, the environmental state has done it through environmental regulation aimed at cleaner air and water, the protection of nature, and the sustainable use of natural resources.

Since most states in the North have taken on at least some responsibility for environmental management, they can all be considered to be environmental states, the main distinction being one of degree: Duit (2016) borrows the label *ecological state* (Eckersley, 2004) to describe one in which the prevailing priority of economic concerns over environmental ones has been reversed, and 'the environment takes precedence over the economy in the sense that government regulation and redistribution consistently prioritize environmental sustainability over economic concerns when the two conflict'. But he also concedes that no state has yet

---

Box 4.1 *Environmental citizenship*

The performance of states is only part of the discussion about environmental governance; at least equally important is the performance of the citizens of states. In this regard, we need to understand and measure **environmental citizenship**, or the obligation that individuals have for acting responsibly and positively towards the environment of which they are a part. A good environmental citizen understands this and acts accordingly, while a bad environmental citizen does not. While much can be achieved by top-down government policy and regulation, even more can potentially be achieved by bottom-up changes in individual responsibility. As Dobson and Bell (2005) suggest, it is better for individuals to make personal changes in the interests of achieving sustainability because they believe it is the right thing to do, not because they are compelled to do it by government. Elsewhere, Dobson (2007b) elaborates on the features of environmental citizenship:

- Since self-interested behaviour will not always protect or sustain public goods such as the environment, environmental citizens make a commitment to the common good, knowing that 'their private actions have public implications'.
- It involves the 'recognition that rights and responsibilities transcend national boundaries'.
- 'The duty of the environmental citizen is to live sustainably so that others may live well.'
- Behaviour driven by the considerations of environmental citizenship 'is more likely to last than behaviour driven by financial incentives' (or, it should be added, by government regulation).

Part of the challenge with encouraging environmental citizenship is to assure individuals that there are choices available to them by which they can make a positive contribution, and that individual action in the face of what might seem like collective indifference is worth their investment. This is not easy.

achieved that status, leaving them all as less perfect environmental states in which environmental concerns sometimes trump economic priorities. Using an analysis based on the four dimensions, Duit suggests that environmental states can be ranked as *established*, *emerging*, *partial*, and *weak*, but research in this area is still at an early stage and has focused mainly on wealthier industrialized states with longer histories of environmental regulation. Broadly, the stronger environmental states are mainly Northern states such as the United States, Germany, the United Kingdom, and the Scandinavians, while weaker environmental states are mainly Southern, including most African states.

Government institutions

It might be logical to think that the most important institutions involved in making and implementing environmental policy are those that constitute the governments of states: executives, legislatures, courts, and bureaucracies. It would come as a surprise, then, to see how rarely they are assessed in studies of environmental politics and policy. The wide-ranging reviews of comparative environmental politics found in Steinberg and VanDeveer (2012) and in Duit (2014), for example, make no mention of legislatures or courts, and the former makes only passing mention of government departments. Elsewhere, much of the comparative study of environmental policy tends to focus more on the activities of non-state actors – such as interest groups – than on those of state actors.

To begin with bureaucracies, the institutional centrepiece of state government is the department or the ministry. All major areas of public policy are typically the responsibility of a department that usually has cabinet-level status, meaning that it is headed by a secretary or a minister who is a member of the national cabinet or the council of ministers. This is a position that gives office-holders direct access to the executive; in presidential systems they play an advisory role, while in parliamentary systems they are a central part of the government. There is a pecking order among departments, the most important typically including foreign affairs, the economy, the treasury, and justice. The environment has long been only a middle-range department in most states, its political importance rising or falling according to the relative levels of attention devoted to foreign and economic affairs.

One of the problems faced by governments in designing environmental departments is a reflection of the argument made in Chapter 1: environmental issues cannot be housed in neat boxes. As a policy matter, the environment has so many dimensions that a true environmental department would need to be linked directly

Table **4.2** Government environment departments

Country	Major departments
Australia	Department of Agriculture and Water Resources
	Department of the Environment and Energy
Brazil	Ministry of the Environment
Germany	Federal Ministry for the Environment, Nature Conservation, Building and Nuclear Safety
India	Ministry of Chemicals and Fertilizers
	Ministry of Drinking Water and Sanitation
	Ministry of Environment, Forest and Climate Change
	Ministry of Water Resources, River Development and Ganga Rejuvenation
Japan	Ministry of the Environment
	Ministry of Agriculture, Forestry and Fisheries
Nigeria	Federal Ministry of Agriculture and Natural Resources
	Federal Ministry of the Environment
	Federal Ministry of Water Resources and Rural Development
South Africa	Department of Agriculture, Forestry and Fisheries
	Department of Environmental Affairs
United Kingdom	Department for the Environment, Food and Rural Affairs
United States	Environmental Protection Agency
	Department of the Interior

Source: Government websites of respective countries, accessed March 2017.

with almost every other government department, particularly those dealing with agriculture, energy, fisheries, forestry, industry, trade, transport, and urban and rural planning. This would be unacceptable to other departments protecting their political responsibilities and government budgets, and looking to protect the interests of their constituencies (for example, farmers, oil companies, or vehicle manufacturers). The question then arises of how to divide up responsibilities for policies with an environmental dimension, and – as Table 4.2 indicates – different states have different ways of slicing the cake. In short, the problem of **administrative fragmentation** is one to which environmental policy is particularly prone.

Another type of state institution is the non-departmental public body, which works more distantly from government with limited independence. The number of such bodies has been growing in democracies as efforts have been made to decentralize government and redraw lines of responsibility. The prime example – for environmental interests – is the **regulatory agency**. This is a body set up to exercise autonomous authority over a focused area of policy by implementing government regulations. Examples include the Environment Agency in the United Kingdom, the Umwelt Bundesamt in Germany, the Federal Energy Regulatory

Commission in the United States, and the Nuclear Regulatory Authority in Japan. While all states regulate, regulations are used more often in industrialized than in developing countries, where there has been more emphasis on liberalization and deregulation as a means of encouraging new business and investment from overseas (see Minogue and Cariño, 2006).

In contrast to bureaucracies, the role of national legislatures in the environmental policy process has been modest. In democracies, at least, the purpose of legislatures is to represent voter interests, to provide an arena for the public airing of matters of national importance, to review and vote upon proposals for new law, to authorize spending, and to keep other parts of government accountable. They are not so much governing bodies as they are foundations for both liberal and democratic politics, but this means that they are driven by local considerations rather than national or international considerations, and are also divided along party lines, and dominated by the electoral cycle. In short, they tend to look at a picture focused in time and place rather than on the kind of longer-term factors that matter so much in environmental policy. The example of the US Congress is telling: Rosenbaum (2014: 94) argues that its response to environmental problems has been 'highly volatile, waxing and waning according to changing public moods, emerging environmental crises, economic circumstances, or today's front-page ecological disasters', pulling it easily into a 'pollutant-of-the-year mentality' according to which environmental problems seem most urgent, or seem to have captured the public mood, at a given time.

The opposite has happened within the European Union (EU), where much of the initiative for developing environmental policy has moved from the national to the European level, meaning significant influence for the European Parliament (EP). Keleman (2010) argues that the EP has long had a strong incentive to see a powerful environmental role for the EU, for three main reasons:

- Many national environmental regulations adopted in the 1970s and 1980s threatened to impose restrictions on the building of a single European market.
- The championing of a strong EU environmental policy could serve to increase the popularity of the EU, widely criticized (even today) for protecting business interests rather than public interests.
- Green member states could use the EP to export their stronger environmental standards to member states with weaker standards, addressing the leader–laggard problem (see the section 'Policy diffusion and convergence' below).

In contrast to legislatures, courts have played a more central role in national environmental policy by virtue of their function as arenas for the interpretation of law and for the resolution of disputes. They interpret environmental law (a job that often amounts to making policy) and they rule on the performance of government agencies in carrying out their responsibilities. Environmental groups have often made adept use of courts in bringing cases against governments and business for not fulfilling their obligations, and have relied on courts (not always with justification, given that courts are capable of making political decisions) to stave off challenges to environmental law by business. In this institutional area, at least, courts in the United States and the EU have been more alike: US courts have routinely been involved in making decisions on the meaning of US environmental law, while Lenschow (2016) argues that the case law of the European Court of Justice 'has played a crucial role in establishing the legitimacy of environmental measures at the EU level'. Several countries – including Australia, India, New Zealand, and the Philippines – have gone so far as to establish specialized environmental courts (see Pring and Pring, 2015).

Parties and interest groups

Institutions that are not formally part of the state are also part of the system of governance, particularly in democracies. Prime among these so-called non-state actors are political parties and interest groups: the former seek direct power by running candidates for office and attempting to control government, while the latter seek indirect power by influencing policymakers through various means. Political parties may be the foundation for the formation of governments, but in environmental terms they have been less important than interest groups: they have a wide range of interests, of which the environment is only one, and a relatively late addition at that. Parties in democracies were slow to adopt environmental positions, and the environment still tends to be low down the list of the positions on which most of them campaign, and on which voters make their choices. Support for parties has also been on the decline in recent decades; where once they represented the particular interests of key segments of society, and worked to change the state, they have increasingly become part of the state, and are often seen as being less interested in offering voters alternatives than in promoting their own interests. As voters have become disenchanted with politics and parties, they have moved instead towards social movements, interest groups, and social media.

The exception to the changing role of party politics can be found in Green parties. Although they are interested in more than environmental issues, they offer one of the few modern examples of a focused set of policy interests that has been converted into a party movement in multiple countries. Green parties were first formed in industrialized countries in the early 1970s, and then moved into a more intensive phase of growth in the 1980s, at which point the greening of mainstream political parties became a new factor in party politics (in this sense, green parties are different from Green parties).

Green politics overlaps with **ecologism**, which some argue can be seen as a new political ideology based on the idea that sustainability requires that we make radical changes to our relationship with the natural world, of a kind associated with deep ecology and ecocentrism. The four major pillars of Green politics (see Figure 4.3) trace their roots back to the 1970s and to the kinds of arguments included in Hardin's 'Tragedy of the Commons' (published 1968), *The Limits to Growth* (published 1972), and a book titled *Small is Beautiful: Economics as if People Mattered*, written by the German-born British economist E.F. (Fritz) Schumacher, and published in 1973. Schumacher argued that economies, political units, societies, and industry had lost their human scale, criticized 'the idolatry of giantism' that both suffocated and debilitated human nature, and warned of humanity's desire to dominate rather than to understand (Schumacher, 1973: 72, 156). As an alternative, he supported the idea of restoring a human scale to institutions and processes, and of giving technology 'a human face' (or a scale that was simple, controllable, and non-violent).

Almost every industrialized country has seen the formation of a Green party, and the Greens have been part of governing coalitions (or supporters of minority governments) in Germany, Belgium, Finland, Italy, Sweden, Ireland, and the Czech Republic. The only

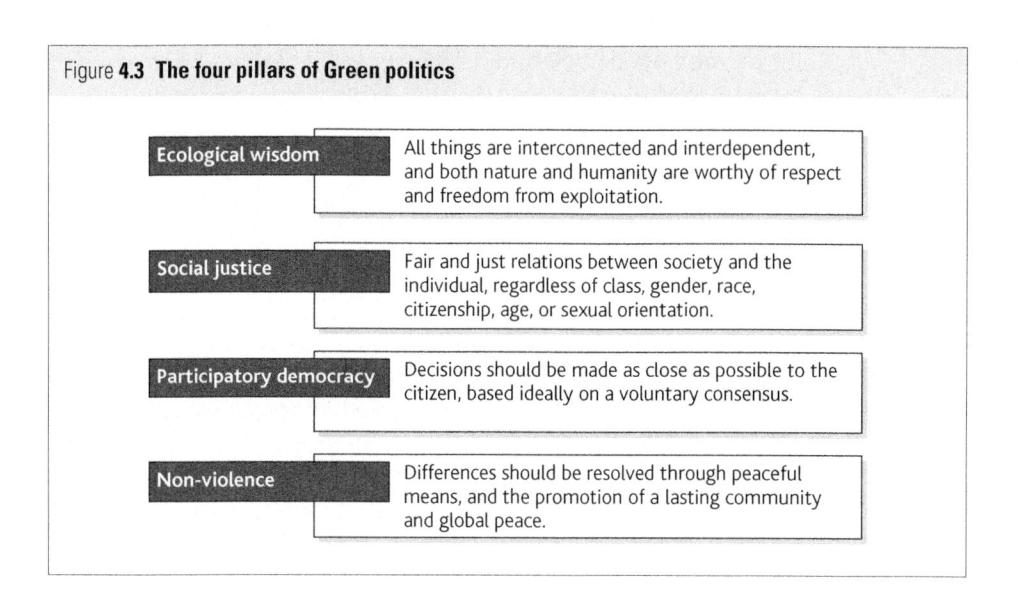

Figure **4.3 The four pillars of Green politics**

Ecological wisdom	All things are interconnected and interdependent, and both nature and humanity are worthy of respect and freedom from exploitation.
Social justice	Fair and just relations between society and the individual, regardless of class, gender, race, citizenship, age, or sexual orientation.
Participatory democracy	Decisions should be made as close as possible to the citizen, based ideally on a voluntary consensus.
Non-violence	Differences should be resolved through peaceful means, and the promotion of a lasting community and global peace.

country that has had a Green head of government to date is Latvia, where Indulis Emsis served nine months as prime minister in 2004 at the head of a coalition government. Greens had a more negative effect on national leadership in 2000 when the Green candidacy of Ralph Nader in the United States almost certainly took away enough votes from Democratic Party candidate Al Gore to deliver the presidency to Republican George W. Bush. Green parties have also been formed in Southern states such as Mexico and Brazil, but have had less political success. A Global Greens international network was created in 2001 to strengthen ties among national parties and to promote a Global Green Charter based on the four pillars of Green thinking.

In contrast to political parties, interest groups – otherwise known as non-governmental organizations, or NGOs – have long played an influential role in initiatives on the environment. In this sense, environmental policy has been driven less by government and business than by **civil society**: the arena outside government in which citizens and interest groups work to promote the common interest and to influence policy. Many environmental NGOs have existed far longer than government institutions, they have often provided the critical pressure for changes in policy, and many still continue to carry out some of the functions that might logically have been assigned to government, including scientific research, the management of protected areas, spending on environmental initiatives, and efforts to change consumer behaviour. In the South, they may be the only significant source of efforts to address environmental questions.

Groups have periodically coalesced into broader social movements focused less on contained issues than on broader structural change; examples include movements against nuclear power, harmful development, and whaling, and in favour of environmental justice, the rights of indigenous societies, and the protection of forests. NGOs and the movements they sometimes spawn operate at the local, national, or international level, vary from a few hundred members to several million, cover the full spectrum of political ideologies, have budgets that range from the small to the substantial, may have one narrow goal in mind (such as opposition to the construction of a new highway or oil pipeline) or a variety of goals, and use multiple techniques to achieve their goals (see Table 4.3).

Markham (2008: 2) describes environmental groups as 'among the most persistent, adaptable, and influential forms of environmental action in Western democracies', while their role in acting as watchdogs of EU environmental policy is well known (Delreux and Happaerts, 2016: 123ff). Their political role dates back decades in many countries: the United States, for example,

Table **4.3 The techniques of environmental NGOs**

Technique	Features
Lobbying	Direct influence on local or national policymakers – or corporations – through personal contact, including the provision of expert advice.
Raising and spending funds	Maintaining paid memberships and/or launching promotions to raise funds to spend in support of their goals.
Forging alliances	Working with other NGOs or with corporations to promote ideas and encourage change.
Membership engagement	Providing facilities for members to experience nature, through visits to parks, hiking, bird-watching, whale-watching, and so on.
Managing protected areas	Buying and maintaining protected terrestrial and marine areas.
Undertaking research	Funding, supporting, and disseminating environmental research.
Public awareness	Running public education programmes, and disseminating information via regular or social media.
Direct action	Organizing days of action, protests, mass demonstrations, boycotts, or engaging in sabotage.

did not create its Environmental Protection Agency until 1970, by which time multiple environmental interest groups had long been at work; the Sierra Club for almost 80 years, for example; and the National Wildlife Federation and the Wilderness Society for almost 35 years. Other groups that long preceded their respective national government agencies include the Royal Society for the Protection of Birds (United Kingdom, founded 1889), Naturschutzbund Deutschland (Germany, 1899), Birds Australia (1901), the Norwegian Society for the Conservation of Nature (1914), and Nature Canada (1939). Meanwhile, environmental think tanks such as the Worldwatch Institute in the United States, the International Institute for Environment and Development in the United Kingdom, and the Energy and Resources Institute in India carry out research that feeds into media coverage of environmental problems, and into government policy.

Environmental NGOs also have a substantial record of providing leadership in the South, where political parties rarely have much interest in addressing environmental issues. A famous example is the Chipko movement that emerged in India in the early 1970s (with roots dating back to the 1700s). This was a rural movement driven mainly by women that worked to draw attention to deforestation by organizing non-violent resistance to commercial logging operations. Chipko's interests spilled over into the problems faced by women and by tribal and marginal societies in India, and inspired similar initiatives in other parts of the world (Guha, 2013: 65–67). Another example from the South is the Green Belt Movement of Kenya, founded in 1977 to encourage rural women to plant trees in the interests of providing new sources of fuelwood, and combatting soil erosion and deforestation. For her efforts, founder Wangari Maathai was awarded the 2004 Nobel Peace Prize.

A contrasting example is offered by China, where the Chinese Communist Party has developed a stronger track record on changing its environmental policy positions than has generally been the case with mainstream parties in democracies, while interest groups (many of them government-organized) have played a relatively modest role. Tang and Zhan (2008) argue that while groups have organized educational campaigns and run specific conservation projects, they have maintained a largely non-oppositional stance in their dealings with government, working to influence policy in more subtle ways.

Just as there is evidence that interest groups can influence the outcome of policy in such as a way as to advance that policy, so there is evidence that they can also act as an impediment. This has particularly been the case in the United States, where environmental scepticism has had a strong tradition. One study (Jacques et al., 2008) of more than 140 environmentally sceptical English-language books published between 1972 and 2005 found that 92 per cent (most published in the United States since 1992) were linked to conservative think tanks. The conclusion of the study was that scepticism was 'a tactic of an elite-driven counter-movement designed to combat environmentalism, and that the successful use of this tactic has contributed to the weakening of US commitment to environmental protection'.

Policy diffusion and convergence

While it is important to understand how policy works at the national level, it is also important to appreciate that states do not work in a policy vacuum, and that much of what they do is determined by the effects of **policy diffusion** and **policy convergence**. The former happens when policies spread from one country to another, as in the case of the eco-labelling schemes discussed in Chapter 2. The latter happens when policies become more similar across countries, as when almost all members of the OECD adopted similar policies during the 1960s on air and water pollution, and on waste management (Tews et al., 2003). It might be logical to think that national policy-makers simply borrow good ideas from their peers in other countries, or learn from their mistakes, but both diffusion and convergence tend to happen for a variety of reasons. One influence, which has been particularly important in the environmental field, has been the **leader–laggard dynamic** by which leader states pull others behind them to more ambitious standards and goals, while the laggard states either follow along later or force compromises that result in more modest goals (Knill et al., 2011).

The United States, Germany, the Scandinavian states, and the Netherlands have long had a reputation for being leaders on environmental policy, while Eastern Europe, Russia, and emerging states have had a reputation for lagging behind. Germany, argues Uekötter (2014), might reasonably lay claim to being the world's greenest state, applauded for its 'strict environmental laws, its world-class green technology firms, its phase-out of nuclear power, and its influential Green Party'. Germans are proud of these achievements, he argues, and environmentalism has become part of the German national identity. Japan, meanwhile, once had a reputation as an environmental leader, but had lost that position by 2000, thanks to a combination of its failure to establish the same kind of influential NGOs found in other states, the weakness of its state Environmental Agency, and the influence of business on the governing Liberal Democratic Party (which, with only two short breaks, has held power in Japan since 1955) (Takao, 2012).

The reasons why some states lead and others lag are many and varied, and include political structure, governing party ideology, voter priorities, and economic circumstances. High-income states in the North have tended to be leaders on the environment because they have had the longest experience of the problems arising from industrialization, their publics have gone through the changes associated with post-materialism, they have the most resources to commit to addressing needs and problems, and they have governments with high levels of responsiveness to voter demands (see Rogers (2003). With low-income and/or authoritarian states in the South, the opposite is usually true.

Among them, Knill and Tosun (2012: 275) and Gilardi (2012: 460–61) have identified five key influences on policy diffusion:

- *Independent problem-solving* occurs when states undergoing similar changes develop similar needs and problems, and respond with similar policies. When industrialization came to Europe, for example, many countries experienced parallel problems with air and water pollution, and responded in a similar way and at a similar time, a pattern that has been repeated more recently with newly industrializing countries such as China and India.
- *Coercion* occurs when sanctions and conditions are threatened or imposed by one state or group of states on another. A large

part of the effort to limit trade in endangered species, for example, has been based on bans on the import of products such as ivory and rhino horn. Attaching strings to the provision of development aid to poorer countries has also been used by wealthier countries and international banks to compel environmental policy change.

- *Competition* plays a role when states seek to keep or attract investment. On the one hand, this can lead to states using weaker environmental standards in order to attract business and investment from states with tighter standards, leading to a 'race to the bottom'. On the other hand, it can lead to states with large and attractive markets, and tighter environmental standards, requiring that businesses from other states seeking to sell to that market ensure that their products meet domestic environmental quality standards, leading to a 'race to the top' (see the discussion on the 'California effect' in the section on 'Environment and development' below.)
- *Learning* involves drawing policy lessons from other countries, whether in regard to good policies that are worth adopting or bad policies that should be avoided. This tends to happen most when existing domestic policies have clearly failed, and countries are most likely to look for ideas in similar or neighbouring countries.
- *Emulation* occurs when countries adopt similar policies because of the overlap in norms among those countries, or the connections that encourage them to move in similar political directions. Eco-labelling, for example, began in a few countries (notably Germany and Canada) in the 1970s and 1980s, and quickly spread to others.

The results of policy diffusion and convergence are reflected in an expanding selection of league tables that rank states on a variety of political and policy features, ranging from democracy to economic freedom, corruption, and environmental performance. The results are debatable because of disagreements about the criteria used and about how to interpret the data, but such indices give us helpful insight into how states compare in terms of their achievements and problems. The Environmental Performance Index, maintained by Yale and Columbia universities, ranks countries out of 100 according to several performance criteria, such as environmental health, levels of air and water pollution, habitat protection, and land use. Created in 1999 as the Environmental Sustainability Index, it was renamed and reformulated in 2006 with the goal of providing a global view of environmental performance (see Figure 4.4). Leader Scandinavian states do best, while laggard African states do worst.

Figure 4.4 Environmental Performance Index

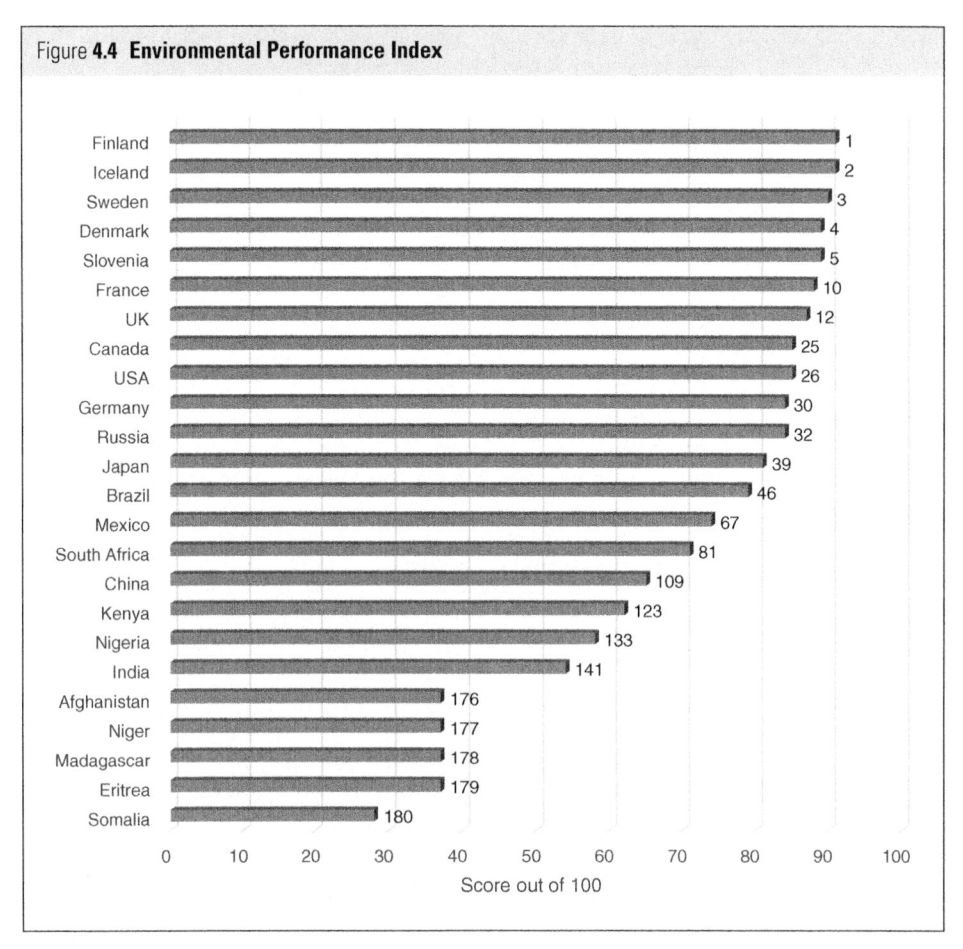

Country	Ranking
Finland	1
Iceland	2
Sweden	3
Denmark	4
Slovenia	5
France	10
UK	12
Canada	25
USA	26
Germany	30
Russia	32
Japan	39
Brazil	46
Mexico	67
South Africa	81
China	109
Kenya	123
Nigeria	133
India	141
Afghanistan	176
Niger	177
Madagascar	178
Eritrea	179
Somalia	180

Score out of 100

Source: Environmental Performance Index 2016 at http://epi.yale.edu (accessed August 2016). Numbers at the end of columns indicate ranking.

Environment and development

Problems such as pollution and waste are among the long-term consequences of the kind of unregulated development and rapid population growth that came to Europe and North America in the eighteenth and nineteenth centuries, and whose effects are still being felt. But where there has been a complex policy response in the North, the same is not always true of regions to which industry came later, such as Russia, Japan, China, or the South. The South has moved more slowly to address its environmental problems, which often come from different sources than those in the North, and its efforts have often been undermined by a problem never much faced by Northern states: an unequal and often disadvantaged placed in the global economic system.

Where many of the environmental problems of the North are associated with the long-term effects of industrialization and consumption, those in the South are associated with a more complex combination of shorter-term economic change and poverty. Nunan (2015) is quick to argue that the idea of a 'vicious circle' in poorer countries (that is, poverty forces the poor to overuse and degrade the environment, thereby making them poorer) does not pay enough attention to other factors, such as governance, institutions, and power relationships. The tensions between environment and development have resulted in three different dynamics:

- In the cities of the South, the rapid rise of the middle class has been at the heart of many environmental problems (see Martine et al., 2008); their demands as consumers mirror those in the North, but against a background of fewer limits from environmental regulation.
- The urban poor in the South outnumber their wealthy neighbours in the North, but use and waste little, occupy less land, rely more heavily on public transport, and have modest energy demands. But they must literally and figuratively live on the margins of rapidly growing cities in squatter areas, suffering overcrowding, traffic congestion, and a widespread failure by urban governments to keep up with demand for homes connected to clean water supplies, dependable energy sources, sewage systems, efficient waste disposal, and good public transport networks.
- In the rural areas of the South, where population is also growing, agriculture might be inefficient and badly planned, and there is often a heavy reliance on wood as a source of fuel. Ironically, the rural poor may have a greater understanding of their natural environment, because they live with it more directly than their wealthier urban neighbours, but poverty encourages them to exploit nature without taking a long-term view. The results include problems such as deforestation (leading to soil erosion and a greater susceptibility to floods), indoor pollution from the use of solid fuels, and increased pressures on natural habitats and biodiversity.

The relationship between environment and development has emerged as a distinct sub-field of policy studies (see Agola and Awange, 2014). The debate has revolved around the question of how to ensure that development can proceed without being restricted by the kinds of environmental regulations that were absent from the North during the Industrial Revolution, while also ensuring that the environment is protected and resources are used wisely. The underlying idea is encapsulated in Principles 3 and 4 of the 1992 Rio Declaration on Environment and Development:

- The right to development must be fulfilled so as to equitably meet developmental and environmental needs of present and future generations.
- In order to achieve sustainable development, environmental protection shall constitute an integral part of the development process and cannot be considered in isolation from it.

The problem, of course, is that such noble goals are often easier outlined than achieved. It is human nature to place immediate needs above longer-term concerns, and the more urgent those needs, the less the focus on the longer-term concerns. If people are adequately housed, fed, and clothed, with enough income to meet their needs, they will have more time and inclination to focus on quality of life concerns. But if they are struggling to maintain a basic quality of life, the incentives to exploit all opportunities that come their way – at whatever long-term cost – begin to grow. Consider the following environmental effects of rural poverty:

- With rhino horn fetching more on the international black market than its equivalent weight in gold (thanks largely to its entirely mythical medicinal properties), the temptation to poach rhinos in eastern and southern Africa is almost irresistible for the unscrupulous.
- The intensified removal of tropical rainforests for cattle pasture or farming, or to build dams and dig mines, dates back to the 1970s. But the roads built by developers in countries such as Brazil have opened rainforest areas up to poor farmers, illegal logging, and land speculation. Improved law enforcement and satellite monitoring have helped reduce the rate of forest clearance in some countries, but in poorer tropical countries it continues unabated.
- In many parts of the world, the rural poor rely mainly on fuelwood as a source of energy for cooking and heating. It is relatively freely available in the form of nearby trees and vegetation, but the uncontrolled gathering of fuelwood leads to deforestation, habitat degradation, and soil erosion.

In the North, citizens mainly have the time and the resources to be concerned about threats to the quality of life, their political structures are complex and responsive to public demands, and the technological base of economies is deep and diverse. In the South, meanwhile, the challenges posed to good environmental policy are often different: the majority of citizens (urban elites excluded) are usually more concerned with immediate challenges such as income, employment, and shelter, while the concern of authoritarian rulers and ruling elites is with retaining and wielding power rather than with ensuring the general welfare of society. Policy tends to be subservient to politics, the economy is usually shallower and narrower, and political decisions are taken by a privileged few.

Several problems found in the South stem from the unequal place of poorer states in the global political and economic system. Prime among these is **dumping**, which involves the export of polluting industries or activities to poorer countries with weaker (or less stringently enforced) environmental regulations and cheaper labour. This allows those industries to manufacture goods more cheaply for export back to their home markets. This '**pollution haven hypothesis**' is controversial because of the difficulties of measuring environmental standards in many of the target countries, and because of doubts about the evidence of a link between investment decisions and environmental regulations (Manderson and Kneller, 2012).

One of the responses in the North to dumping has been to consider the imposition of environmental tariffs on goods imported from countries with weaker standards, but this is done more often out of concern for the unfair advantages that lax regulation gives to manufacturers than out of concern for the quality of the environment in the South. There have also been calls for more pressure to harmonize environmental regulations, bringing the South more in line with the North, but some argue that this is

---

Box 4.2 *The resource curse and the environment*

A policy problem with environmental implications in a more select group of countries in the South is the **resource curse**. This exists when a country is well endowed in a natural resource that is so profitable and valuable that it becomes the target of almost all political and economic attention, and is exploited at almost any cost, including harm to the environment. Among the results: there is little investment in anything else, little is done to study the environmental impact of the exploitation of the dominant resource, little is done to tackle inequality or unemployment outside the one economic sector, and exploitation of the resource takes precedence over sustainable economic or environmental policies. The country suffering the 'curse' often ends up being worse off – environmentally and economically – than its less well-endowed neighbours.

Oil, for example, has become just such a problem for several sub-Saharan African states, such as Angola, Chad, Nigeria, and Sudan, while for other states the 'curse' stems from easily exploitable resources such as forests, minerals such as copper or uranium, or precious gems such as diamonds. The imbalance created not only spurs governments to overlook most other sectors of the economy, but encourages theft and corruption, and prompts governments – in their rush to exploit the resource – to ignore sound environmental management. The Niger delta region of Nigeria has become infamous for the environmental damage caused by the petroleum industry, impacting not just the 20 million people who live in the region, but also the biodiversity contained in its wetlands, lowland rainforests, and mangrove swamps (Steyn, 2014).

unnecessary given what Vogel (1995) calls the '**California effect**': this is an example of policy diffusion, where exporting industries in the South are obliged to meet stronger environmental standards in order to be allowed to export to large markets that require those standards. It is named for California because of the tighter emissions standards for road vehicles adopted there in the 1960s, which led to higher standards being adopted across the United States, which in turn led to higher standards being adopted in Western Europe. (The dynamic has since changed; it now tends to be Germany and the Scandinavians who adopt high standards, which are then adopted more widely across Europe, forcing change in the United States; see the example of chemicals policy in Chapter 9.)

Addressing many environmental problems means having access to the best technologies, including pollution controls and more efficient generators of energy. Many of these technologies were developed in the North but are also needed in the South if environmental goals are to be met. This raises questions about **technology transfer**, or the channels by which advanced technologies might be made available to emerging states. Many international agreements and development aid programmes include some element of technology transfer, which is also funded by the Global Environment Facility (see Chapter 5). But it is not just a question of the expenses and of the intellectual property rights involved; it also raises questions about the capacity of emerging states to absorb and operate advanced technology (Metz et al., 2000). The more complex the problem, as in the case of climate change, the more difficulties are raised in transferring and applying advanced technologies. On the other hand, 'technology leapfrogging' is not unknown, meaning – for example – that developing countries might be able to avoid the mistakes of industrialized countries and build new and more sustainable options into their development (Watson and Sauter, 2011).

Discussion questions

- Is neoliberalism compatible with sound and effective environmental policies?
- To what extent does the country in which you live meet (or fail to meet) the qualities of an ecological, green, or environmental state?
- Which accounts more convincingly for changes in environmental policy at the state level: diffusion or convergence?
- Should developing countries be given free rein to learn from their own environmental mistakes, as did the older industrialized states, or saved from those mistakes by export of the lessons learned in the North?

Key concepts

- Administrative fragmentation
- California effect
- Civil society
- Dumping
- Ecological democracy
- Ecological state
- Ecologism
- Environmental citizenship
- Environmental state
- Green state
- Leader–laggard dynamic
- Neoliberalism
- Policy convergence
- Policy diffusion
- Pollution haven hypothesis
- Regulatory agency
- Resource curse
- Technology transfer

Further reading

Delreux, Tom, and Sander Happaerts (2016) *Environmental Policy and Politics in the European Union* (Palgrave). An assessment of environmental policy in the EU, including the actors involved, the methods used, and the impact on its member states.

Nunan, Fiona (2015) *Understanding Poverty and the Environment: Analytical Frameworks and Approaches* (Routledge). A survey of the debate over the links between poverty and the environment.

Rosenbaum, Walter A. (2014) *Environmental Politics and Policy*, 7th edn (Sage). A textbook review of environmental policy, government institutions, and approaches to key problems in the United States.

Shapiro, Judith (2012) *China's Environmental Challenges* (Polity Press). A study of the environmental problems faced by China, and the dynamics behind state-led and civil society responses.

Steinberg, Paul F., and Stacy D. VanDeveer (eds) (2012) *Comparative Environmental Politics: Theory, Practice, and Prospects* (MIT Press), and Andreas Duit (ed) (2014) *State and Environment: The Comparative Study of Environmental Governance* (MIT Press). Two edited collections offering comparative analyses of environmental governance in developed and developing countries.

5 Actors at the International Level

Key arguments

- There is no global government, but there is a system of global governance, although opinion is divided at least four ways on how best to understand it.
- Opinion is also divided on the place of states in the international system. Realists focus on the self-interest of states, liberals believe in the possibilities of international cooperation, some feel that states are becoming stronger, and others believe they are becoming weaker.
- The environment is on the agenda of a large network of intergovernmental organizations, but there are mixed opinions regarding their efficacy.
- A particular kind of intergovernmental organization is the treaty secretariat, whose numbers have grown in the wake of the signature of more environmental treaties.
- As with their national counterparts, international non-governmental organizations have filled in some of the gaps left by political initiatives on the environment.
- Debates about sustainability have raised troubling questions about patterns of international business in the face of globalization, and of demographic, economic, and social change.

Chapter overview

The previous chapter used the perspectives of comparative politics to assess the manner in which environmental politics evolve – and environmental policy is shaped and implemented – at the state level. This chapter uses the perspectives of international relations to assess the actors, influences, and politics involved in the shaping and implementation of environmental policy at the international level. While such actors are relatively easy to identify – they include states, intergovernmental organizations, treaty secretariats, non-governmental organizations, and multinational corporations – they all function within an international system whose dynamics are both complex and constantly changing, and are subject to competing theoretical analyses.

The challenges faced by efforts to address environmental matters at the international level are threefold:

- The international legal system lacks either the same qualities of accountability or the same mechanisms for enforcement as are found at the state level. There are numerous international treaties, and the European Union has developed its own unique supranational system of regional environmental law, but there are no global authorities responsible for enforcing environmental regulations affecting multiple states. Even in the case of treaties, signature is a voluntary action and there is little that can be done to encourage unwilling states to sign and ratify, or to hold signatories accountable for their obligations. And only in recent years have we seen the development of a set of policy principles that can guide international policy.
- National governments are less motivated to act on transboundary or global issues than on domestic issues because they are not directly answerable to public or consumer opinion outside their own borders, and also find it easier to ignore or transfer the costs of inaction at the international level to other parties.
- Because many environmental problems are either shared by multiple states, or are common to multiple states, there is little motivation for individual states to act unless they are sure that their neighbours and partners will do the same.

This chapter begins with an assessment of the international system of environmental governance, looking at four approaches to understanding how that system works: one based on institutions, a second based on networks of experts, a third based on the meeting of science and policy, and a fourth based on peer networks. It then looks at the role of states in the international system, building on arguments made in Chapter 4 about the nature of domestic politics and policy, and reviewing the debate about the changing power of states, asking whether they are more or less powerful than they have been in the past, or are simply changing form.

The chapter moves on to an assessment of the structure and role of intergovernmental organizations, focusing on the work of the UN Environment Programme, and then looks more specifically at the work of the secretariats that manage and monitor international treaties. Finally, the chapter looks at the role of international non-governmental organizations and multinational corporations, the key non-state transnational actors involved in influencing international environmental politics and policy.

Understanding international environmental governance

In the previous chapter we saw how environmental policies are shaped at the state level, looking at the kinds of institutions involved, and at the political forces that come to bear on those policies. We saw that government consists of institutions and offices charged with reaching and executing decisions for the community over which they have jurisdiction, and that there is direct public accountability, in democracies at least: voters make demands of governments, parties, and elected officials, while governments claim to be responsive to those demands.

Matters are quite different at the international level, not least because there is no global government or electorate. There are institutions, to be sure, but they lack the qualities enjoyed by states, such as authority, legitimacy, or sovereignty. They also lack a direct political relationship with voters. Instead, what we find is a system of governance, as a result of which the term *global governance* has become increasingly popular since the 1990s, even though it is not all that new: the roots of the institutions and processes that we associate today with global governance have been traced back to the end of the Napoleonic wars in 1815 (Murphy, 2015). Even so, its dynamics are still evolving, and it means different things to different people. Biermann (2006), for example, lists three contrasting assessments: it can be seen as 'a rallying call for policy advocates who hail it as panacea for the evils of globalization; a global menace for opponents who fear it as the universal hegemony of the many by the powerful few; and an analytical concept that has given rise to much discussion among scholars of international relations'. The outlines of that discus-

Figure 5.1 Approaches to international environmental governance

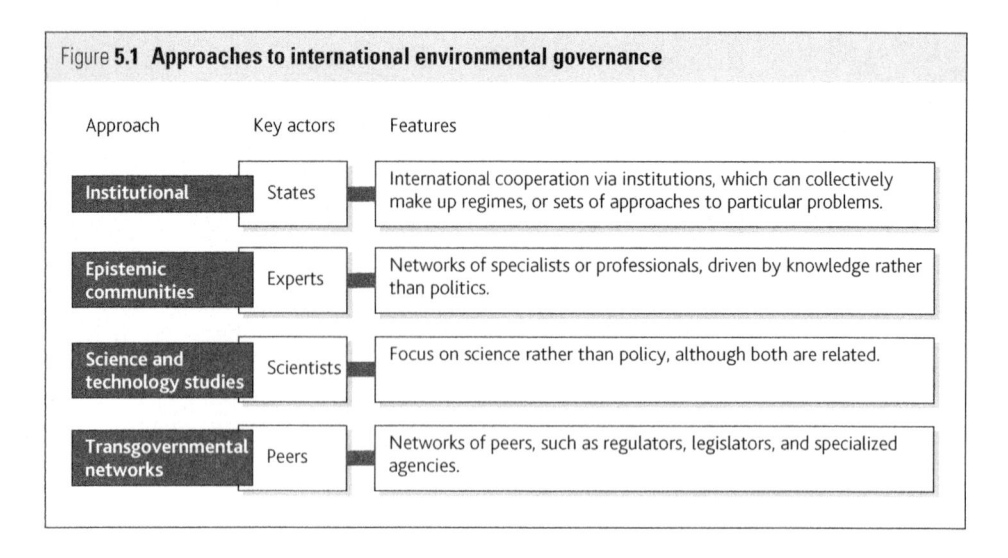

Approach	Key actors	Features
Institutional	States	International cooperation via institutions, which can collectively make up regimes, or sets of approaches to particular problems.
Epistemic communities	Experts	Networks of specialists or professionals, driven by knowledge rather than politics.
Science and technology studies	Scientists	Focus on science rather than policy, although both are related.
Transgovernmental networks	Peers	Networks of peers, such as regulators, legislators, and specialized agencies.

sion are summarized by Lidskog and Sundqvist (2011a: 12–16) who, in their review of changes in air pollution policy, suggest three approaches to understanding international environmental governance.

First, there is the *institutional* approach, which is used most commonly. This begins with states seeing opportunities for mutual benefit, leading to international cooperation and the creation of institutions that result from negotiations among the states, and that are shaped by the tension between the expected political benefits and the costs of achieving those benefits. **Institutions** have been defined by Young (2002: 5) as sets of rules, decision-making procedures, and programmes that define practices, assigning roles to participants in these practices and guiding interaction among those in the different roles. The institutional approach is ultimately about the study of **regimes**, a term which (when applied at the international level) describes the 'principles, norms, rules, and decision-making procedures' around which the expectations of actors converge in a given, structured area of international relations (Krasner, 1983: 2). Hence we find references to the ozone regime (Chapter 6), the tropical timber regime (Chapter 8), the biodiversity regime (Chapter 10), and the climate change regime (Chapter 12).

Regimes do not have to be based on specific international treaties or the creation of dedicated bodies such as the Intergovernmental Panel on Climate Change (IPCC), although it gives a regime more focus if they are. Nor are they exclusively driven by the work of governments; non-governmental organizations, multinational corporations, and mass movements all have a role to play (see Breitmeier et al., 2006). Regimes can also be contrasted with **non-regimes**, where policy is pursued across borders without formal multilateral agreements (Dimitrov et al., 2007: 231). The existence of a regime is not necessarily an indication of progress (as the often-stalled talks on dealing with climate change reveal), although the absence of a regime is usually an indication of a lack of progress; little in the way of identifiable global regimes have yet formed – for example – around forests, fisheries, energy, coral reefs, or deserts, and the global maritime regime discussed in Chapter 8 has not been particularly effective.

Second, Lidskog and Sundqvist write about the ***epistemic community*** approach, which places a greater emphasis on the part played in regimes by science rather than states. An epistemic community is a transnational network of professionals with recognized skills and knowledge in a particular area (Haas, 1992), who share a set of causal beliefs and a set of practices, and whose influence and power lie in their specialist knowledge of the issues being addressed. Where the institutional approach is based on cooperating states, the epistemic community approach is based on a consensus among specialists or experts. States are still important, but the assumption here is that regimes are also driven by the application of scientific understandings about ecosystems to the management of policy. The goals of epistemic communities derive from their knowledge rather than from political, social, or other motives, and this gives them authority and credibility. Many of the studies of such communities have focused on scientists, but they could as well review networks of economists, lawyers, diplomats, or journalists (Cross, 2013). Epistemic communities have been associated with the development of policy on the protection of the ozone layer, whaling, acid pollution, and – above all – climate change.

Finally, the science and technology studies (STS) approach is based on the idea that policy and science – instead of being separate from one another – are two sides of the same coin. It questions the long-held assumption that the more autonomous and independent science is from policy, the greater its potential influence. Lidskog and Sundqvist (2015) argue that the STS community is less interested in developing a framework for understanding international environmental governance than in understanding the role of science in the policy process. The result is that knowledge is something that is 'co-produced' by policy and science in the sense that 'policy influences the production and stabilization of knowledge, while knowledge simultaneously supports and justifies policy'. They quote the example of the IPCC and its role in shaping climate policy as a case of the conditions under which 'science matters'.

Some studies of global environmental governance have moved beyond regimes to take a fourth approach based on the dynamics of **transgovernmental networks**. These are informal horizontal peer-to-peer webs of cooperation that bring together national regulators, legislators, judges, specialized agencies, and other actors, going beyond ad hoc communication but stopping short of the creation of international organizations (Slaughter and Hale, 2011). The European Union has been an active facilitator of such networks on the environmental front, encouraging national environmental agencies in EU member states to work together as something of a 'back door' into achieving more cross-national cooperation on environmental regulation (Martens, 2008). The development of these networks does not stop at the national level, as Kern and Bulkeley (2009) have shown with their study of cooperation on climate change at the municipal level in Europe.

States and the international system

The critical role of states in the international system is undeniable. But while their influence is clear, how they relate to one another is debatable, and has been the subject of a variety of contrasting theoretical approaches (see Figure 5.2). On the one hand, **realism** argues that the state is the key actor, and that just as humans are by nature self-centred and competitive, states are rationally motivated to protect their interests relative to other states and do not always entirely trust long-term cooperation and alliances. Realists talk of an anarchic global system in which there is no authority above the level of states that is capable of helping them manage their interactions with one another, and believe that states must use both conflict and cooperation to ensure their security through a balance of power among states. In this view, global politics is best understood by the study of relations among states: forming alliances, going to war, imposing sanctions, protecting and promoting their individual interests, and pursuing self-interested goals of security, open markets, and autonomy. (For a brief outline of key theories in international relations, see Slaughter, 2011.)

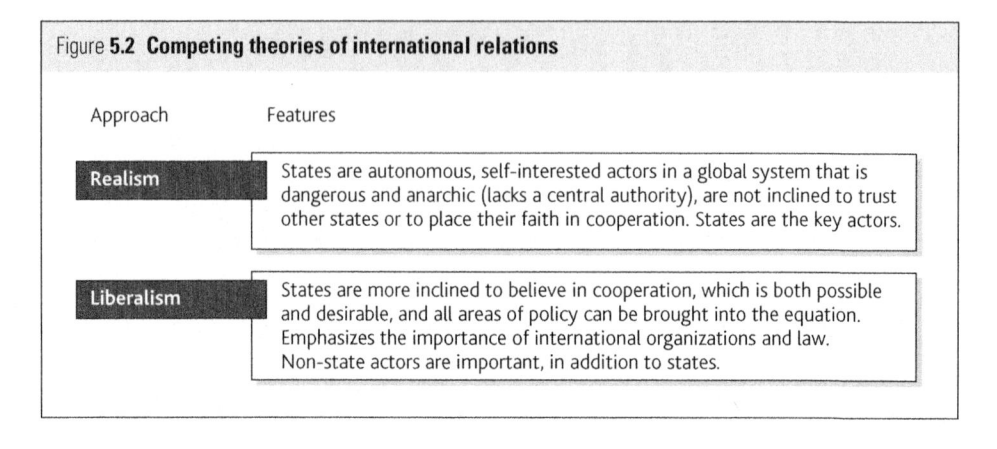

Figure **5.2 Competing theories of international relations**

Approach	Features
Realism	States are autonomous, self-interested actors in a global system that is dangerous and anarchic (lacks a central authority), are not inclined to trust other states or to place their faith in cooperation. States are the key actors.
Liberalism	States are more inclined to believe in cooperation, which is both possible and desirable, and all areas of policy can be brought into the equation. Emphasizes the importance of international organizations and law. Non-state actors are important, in addition to states.

On the other hand, **liberalism** – while also acknowledging the existence of an anarchic international system – believes in the possibility of cooperation to promote change. Liberals argue that war and anarchy are not inevitable, that humans can place higher causes such as environmental protection above self-interest, can pursue ideals in the interests of improving the quality of life, and can thereby work to avoid conflict. In contrast to realist ideas about inter-state rivalry, liberals emphasize the importance of international organizations and international law in understanding and driving relations among states, and believe in the notion of **globalism**, where institutions and ideals other than state citizenship attract the loyalty of humans.

While opinion is divided on how states relate to one another in the international system, it is clear that they are the key actors in shaping and executing international policy on the environment. They make national policies that collectively determine the goals and outcomes of international policy, they collectively set the international policy agenda, they alone have the authority to negotiate treaties of the kind that have been so critical to addressing international environmental problems, and they alone have the authority to implement the terms of such treaties. As we saw in Chapter 4, the positions taken by some states can also have a telling effect – via policy diffusion or convergence – on those taken by other states, whether in the form of providing leadership on policy or in the form of providing a drag on policy.

'Leader' states have long played the most influential role in driving the definition and implementation of environmental policy at the international level, but the balance has changed with the rise of new economic powers, exerting new levels of influence. Dahlman (2012) points to the emerging influence on both the global economy and the global environment of China and India. Their rising presence, he argues, 'is creating frictions in trade, finance, foreign investment, intellectual property rights, and competition for natural resources – not to mention concerns about climate change, global governance, security, and balance of power'. He notes that they are both resource-poor, and that their access to arable land and water is strained, and also notes the impact that their rapid and relatively unregulated economic growth is having on the production of air and water pollution, and specifically on climate change: between them they are responsible for about one-third of the global production of carbon dioxide.

The rise of China and India is part of the continuing body of evidence pointing to the constant changes in the place of states in the international system, although opinion is divided on their trajectories. Some argue that states are as strong as ever (perhaps even stronger given recent efforts to strengthen domestic security in the wake of international terrorism), some argue that they are undergoing fundamental change, and others argue that they are losing power and significance (see, for example, Ohmae, 2005). The expanding effects of globalization are seen as evidence of the latter, as are criticisms of the mixed record of states in responding to transboundary problems such as terrorism, illegal immigration, the spread of disease, transboundary pollution, and climate change.

The declining power of states is also reflected in the rise of international cooperation, exemplified by the growth in the numbers and the reach of international organizations and in the signature of international treaties. Inspired at first by a desire to avoid the kind of tensions that led to two world wars, and then encouraged by the need to respond collectively to shared problems, international cooperation has grown substantially since 1945. Environmental cooperation was something of a latecomer to the agenda; while international conferences were held and treaties agreed within years of the end of World War II, it was not until 1973 that agreement was reached for the creation of a specialized environmental programme of the United Nations.

It has since been abundantly clear that many of the most pressing environmental problems inconveniently fail to respect national borders, and demand cooperative or coordinated responses, or – at the very least – the sharing of data and experiences. But while opinion is divided on the record of states in responding to environmental problems within their borders, the jury is also out on the effects of international cooperation. Betsill (2006) notes that while realists dismiss claims about the significance of transnational actors, scholars of international environmental politics have long recognized their importance, and credit them with having a stronger presence in environmental matters than in almost every other area of international cooperation, including security and trade. But while there have been advances in efforts to address cross-border acid pollution and to end man-made threats to the ozone layer, many problems persist and worsen, raising questions about the efficacy both of state responses and of international cooperation.

While there is much to be gained from the agreement of international treaties on the environment, and the development of related regimes, the environment is a relative newcomer to the world of international law, and it is hard not to conclude that most such law has been based on putting out fires rather than on taking a strategic approach based on an agreed set of guiding principles. Sustainable development probably comes closest to being a universal principle, even if there are still some doubts about exactly what it means (either in theory or in practice) and about the extent to which it has been followed in different states. The polluter pays principle and the precautionary principle (see Chapter 2) have also recurred in different treaties and sets of international declarations, moving states towards a more structured set of environmental goals. Hunter (2014) lists several other principles of international environmental law, including state sovereignty, concern for global common resources (such as Antarctica, the seabed, and the ozone layer), and a duty by states not to cause environmental harm in other states, but he also notes that they have not yet always been accepted as custom or as general principles of law.

Intergovernmental organizations

The ties that bind states are reflected in the work of **international organizations**, which are bodies set up to promote cooperation between or among states, based on the principles of voluntary cooperation, communal management, and shared interests. By one estimate, there were about 1,000 in existence in 1951, and still only about 4,000 as late as 1972. By 1989 the number had risen to nearly 25,000, and today there may be as many as 68,000 (although only about 38,000 are active) (Union of International Associations, 2016). International organizations come in two main forms:

- Intergovernmental organizations (IGOs), whose members are states or national government bodies and whose goal is to promote cooperation between or among states (covered in this section).
- International non-governmental organizations (INGOs), whose members are individuals or national interest groups, and which work outside formal government structures (discussed later in the chapter).

IGOs lack autonomy in decision-making, lack the power to impose taxes or enforce their rulings, and have few assets. Instead, they mainly act as facilitators or as venues through which states can negotiate or cooperate with one another, using a range of methods that vary from gathering information to carrying out research and hosting conferences (see Table 5.1), all designed to help shape the international policy agenda. The grandparent of them all is the UN, which was founded in 1945 and backed up by specialized UN agencies such as the World Bank, the International Monetary Fund, and the Food and Agriculture Organization (FAO). While UN agencies are open to the 193 members of the UN, the European Environment Agency has 33 European member states, and the International Joint Commission has just two: founded in 1905, it brings Canada

Table 5.1 Intergovernmental organizations with environmental interests

Institution	Headquarters	Environmental interests
United Nations Environment Programme	Nairobi, Kenya	UN programme. Coordinates environmental work of UN, generates information, and oversees treaties.
Food and Agriculture Organization	Rome, Italy	UN agency. Natural resource management, climate change and food production, bioenergy, land tenure, water management.
World Meteorological Organization	Geneva, Switzerland	UN agency. Climate change, water supply, human health.
World Bank	Washington DC	UN agency. Sustainable development.
International Maritime Organization	London, UK	UN agency. Prevention of sea pollution by ships.
International Tropical Timber Organization	Yokohama, Japan	Sustainable management of tropical forests.
Global Environment Facility	Washington DC	Funding of sustainable development projects.
International Commission for the Protection of the Danube	Vienna, Austria	Management of the Danube River basin.
European Environment Agency	Copenhagen, Denmark	Specialized agency of the European Union. Information clearing house.

and the United States together to cooperate on the management of the Great Lakes.

Another international organization, which is an unusual blend of governmental and non-governmental members, is the Swiss-based International Union for Conservation of Nature (IUCN). Founded in 1948, IUCN has more than 1,300 members, including government agencies and NGOs, as well as having observer status at the UN. It began life as the International Union for the Protection of Nature, but changed its name in 1958 to reflect its broader interest in the sustainable use of natural resources. It works to influence governments through the collection and analysis of information, supports field research and education, and has played a key role in developing several international treaties, as well as maintaining the Red List of Threatened Species (see Chapter 10).

The primary IGO with an environmental interest is the UN Environment Programme (UNEP), which was created in 1973 as a result of the Stockholm conference. Headquartered in Nairobi, Kenya, UNEP's formal mission is to 'provide leadership and encourage partnership in caring for the environment by inspiring, informing, and enabling nations and peoples to improve their quality of life without compromising that of future generations' (UNEP website, 2017). It does this primarily through monitoring environmental trends, developing and sometimes managing international treaties, and promoting education and public information (as part of which 5 June was established in 1974 as World Environment Day). It has a particular interest in climate change, environmental disasters, ecosystem management, and improving environmental governance. On climate change, for example, UNEP is co-sponsor – with the World Meteorological Organization – of the Intergovernmental Panel on Climate Change, created in 1988 to generate assessments of the state of understanding of climate change science. UNEP also facilitated the writing of the UN Framework Convention on Climate Change, which was signed at the 1992 Rio Summit, which was in turn planned and organized by UNEP.

The major problems faced by UNEP include some of those typical of IGOs, and some related more specifically to its mission. Like most other IGOs, it has no powers of enforcement, having to rely instead on voluntary agreements on the part of UN member states, or the signatories of UNEP-supported treaties, and having to sometimes base its actions on short-term opportunities rather than always working to a long-term plan. It also faces concerns about efficiency and organization similar to those experienced by many large international organizations. More particularly, UNEP is a programme of the UN rather than a specialized agency; as such, it is subsidiary to the UN General Assembly, lacks the status or independence of older and larger UN agencies such as the World Bank and FAO, and finds its mission hampered by the need to coordinate the work of other UN agencies (which sometimes resent its demands), at the same time suffering the standard IGO problem of inadequate funding, made worse by having to rely on voluntary rather than mandatory contributions from UN member states.

Writing in 2010, Ivanova concluded that there was no consensus on UNEP's performance over its first four decades, with views ranging from praise for its having achieved a great deal with few resources to criticism for its having been weak and ineffective. She reviewed its work in two major areas, drawing mixed conclusions:

- In regard to monitoring, assessment, and early warning, UNEP set up a Global Environment Monitoring System (GEMS), an International Register of Potentially Toxic Chemicals, the INFOTERRA network for global environmental information, and has published its *Global Environmental Outlook,* widely cited as a useful source on emerging environmental problems. However, UNEP does not undertake monitoring and surveillance of its own, and is instead a clearing house for information generated from other sources. Also, its information tends to be issue-driven, offering little in the way of comparative assessments from one state to another. The creation of other information systems, such as those managed by the Swiss-based Group on Earth Observations (founded 2005), seems to point to an erosion of faith in UNEP's abilities.

- As to developing international norms, standards, and policies, UNEP was expected to be a proactive advocacy organization, 'setting the global environmental agenda and prodding governments, international organizations, NGOs, and business into action' (Ivanova, 2010). But while its work has led to the development of multiple new international treaties, it has not provided as much leadership as was expected (notably on the issue of climate change), and has not been the secretariat for many of those treaties. Mee (2005) points out that while UNEP has been successful at catalysing international treaties, while working with a budget that has not increased much for more than 30 years, its capacity has been spread thinly. With many of the secretariats of those treaties becoming independent of UNEP, the result has been a loosely and sometimes poorly coordinated network. UNEP does, however, help maintain Ecolex, a database on environmental law.

Ivanova finds UNEP's main problems in three areas: its design as a programme rather than a specialized UN agency, its leadership (its structure means that its reach depends heavily on the negotiating abilities of its director general), and its location (UNEP is the only major UN body based outside Europe or North America, and Nairobi is distant from the major UN agencies and from those parts of the world where the most important economic decisions are made). UNEP's difficulties have sparked suggestions (see Biermann, 2000; Biermann and Bauer, 2005) that it should be transformed into a specialized agency of the UN: a World Environment Organization with more autonomy, an international legal personality, a stronger voice in UN environmental affairs, and a budget based on mandatory contributions from its members rather than voluntary contributions. Ivanova (2012) is not convinced of this logic, arguing that UNEP's shortcomings are not related to its institutional form so much as to the barriers to UNEP fulfilling its mission. Rather than wholesale structural change, she concludes, it would be 'bolder and more effective, and also more feasible, to focus instead on empowering UNEP to properly fulfil its original, visionary mandate'.

Box 5.1   The unusual case of the European Union

A unique intergovernmental organization that has had a substantial impact on the environmental policies of its member states is the European Union. Created in 1958 as the European Economic Community, the EU was at first an effort to build a single market among its members, with free movement of people, money, goods, and services. But in order to build such a market, a number of unexpected barriers had to be removed, one of them being different environmental standards that could interfere with free trade. Common environmental policies have since been developed, and an expanding range of laws adopted on waste, air and water quality, chemicals, biodiversity, pesticides, noise pollution, and genetically modified organisms. Such was the strength of the logic behind developing shared approaches that domestic environmental policy in the member states of the EU is now driven more by requirements set jointly at the EU level than individually at the level of member states (for more details, see Jordan and Adele, 2013).

The administrative tools of the EU include regulations that are applicable in all member states and that typically set a technical standard or objective with a target date for implementation. While the EU does not have a common environmental policy, the regulations and action plans that it has jointly agreed have come to be the main source of environmental action in the EU, particularly in poorer and newer Eastern European member states, many of which lacked much in the way of a body of environmental law or policy before joining the EU. The primary bureaucracy of the EU – the European Commission – includes four commissioners (equivalent to government ministers at the state level) responsible for climate action, energy, the environment, and transport, as well as related directorates-general (equivalent to national government departments).

The EU also has an expanding body of decentralized agencies with varied functions: the European Environment Agency is an information clearing house that reports on the state of the EU environment, while the European Chemicals Agency is responsible for overseeing the EU's scheme for the registration of new chemicals, which is the most stringent such scheme in the world, imposing obligations on EU member states and on states wanting to trade with the EU. As the world's wealthiest marketplace, with a population of just over half a billion people, the requirements of EU policy have a significant impact on its trading partners.

Treaty secretariats

A particular species of IGO is the treaty secretariat, or a body set up to oversee and monitor compliance with an international treaty. Secretariats are usually set up by governments and have the same general form and sets of responsibilities, but they differ in terms of their size, reputation, levels of influence, and the roles they play. The factors that drive those differences include the number of signatory states, the size and visibility of the problem addressed by a treaty, the amount of progress achieved in implementing the goals of a treaty, the extent of the obligations under a treaty, the amount of independence secretariats are given, and the level of credibility they establish with their government members and with NGOs. For example, the climate change secretariat (based in Bonn, Germany) has limited influence because its main job is seen to be to translate political agreements reached by its signatories into functioning procedures, while the biological diversity convention secretariat (Montreal, Canada) is seen as more of a facilitator, and thus has more influence over how decisions are reached (Siebenhüner, 2015).

Secretariats may work within pre-existing IGOs such as UNEP (which acts as secretariat for the conventions on international trade in endangered species, the ozone layer, and transboundary movements of hazardous waste), but they may also be separate bodies, making them a particular kind of IGO. Either way, they have four main tasks:

- To monitor compliance (or lack of compliance) with the treaty, and to prepare periodic reports on progress (or lack of progress). These tasks have an important role in determining the efficacy and the outcomes of treaties, but secretariats have no powers of enforcement; the best they can usually do is to report and to allow governments to decide what action to take.
- To liaise between the parties to a treaty, as well as non-parties that may have an interest in the treaty, relevant national agencies, and NGOs.
- To gather information that can be used to measure progress and to provide advice to signatories on future directions.
- To organize meetings of the signatories, usually known as Conferences of Parties. An efficient secretariat can play a key role in creating a positive environment for negotiations.

Questions have long been asked about the efficiency of treaty secretariats, many of the problems deriving from budgetary limitations, the suspicion traditionally directed at international bureaucracies, and the need for secretariats to avoid becoming involved in the politics of the exchanges over treaties. Sandford (1994) asked whether secretariats could be considered actors or stagehands, while one collection of studies of international bureaucracies (Biermann and Siebenhüner, 2009) describes the ozone secretariat as a 'good shepherd', the climate secretariat as 'making a living in a straitjacket', the biodiversity secretariat as 'a lean shark in troubled waters', and the desertification secretariat as 'a castle made of sand'.

Table **5.2** **Examples of environmental treaty secretariats**

Treaty	Office location
Convention on Biological Diversity	Montreal, Canada
UN Framework Convention on Climate Change	Bonn, Germany
Convention for the Protection of the Ozone Layer	UNEP, Nairobi, Kenya
Convention on International Trade in Endangered Species	UNEP, Geneva, Switzerland
Convention on the Control of Transboundary Movements of Hazardous Wastes	Châtelaine, Switzerland
Convention on the Prevention of Marine Pollution by Dumping of Wastes and Other Matter	International Maritime Organization, London

In her assessment of the influence and effectiveness of environmental treaty secretariats, Jinnah (2014) concludes that they have the most impact when the states involved do not have strong preferences on the issue at hand, or when there are no organizations that can better manage a particular treaty. In the case of the Convention on Biological Diversity (CBD), for example, she argues that state preferences were weak to begin with, that no other organization could better manage the treaty than the CBD secretariat, and hence the secretariat enjoys a high degree of independence. By contrast, agreements dealing with fisheries have come up against states with strong preferences about how commercially important fish stocks should be managed, while the secretariat for the Convention on International Trade in Endangered Species (CITES) has faced strong organizational competition from the UN Food and Agriculture Organization.

Treaties are often the result of – and are further developed at – international summits on the environment. **Summitry** is a particular approach to international negotiations, involving high-level person-to-person meetings – sometimes bilateral, sometimes multilateral – and focusing on strategic issues rather than on the details of policy, and designed to set the tone and character of intergovernmental relations. It typically uses a combination of brainstorming, intensive discussions, and bargaining, resulting in a general set of conclusions, a declaration of intentions, or the signature of an agreement whose details have often been worked out in advance. As we saw in Chapter 3, the 1972 Stockholm conference and the 1992 Rio Earth Summit were widely considered to be landmark events in the evolution of national and international responses to environmental problems, but opinions differ about the impact of the so-called mega-conferences. In assessing the Earth Summit, for example, Doran (1993) wrote of 'ecology as spectacle', and suggested that the achievements of the conference were modest at best. The British magazine *The Ecologist* (1992: 122) had earlier concluded that 'the spectacle of the great and the good at [Rio] casting about for "solutions" that will keep their power and standards of living intact has confirmed the scepticism of those whose fate and livelihoods were being determined'.

For his part, Death (2011) argues that summits that neither produce new agreements nor strengthen environmental regimes – such as the Rio+10 meeting in Johannesburg in 2002 – are commonly regarded as failures, and yet 'they can also be viewed as moments of political theatre, performative enactments of legitimacy and authority, and sites for the communication of particular examples of responsible conduct.' Looking at the June 2012 UN Conference on Sustainable Development held in Rio (Rio+20), Van Alstine et al. (2013) note there were a large number of delegates, but that few major world leaders attended, and no new international treaties were signed or binding pledges made. And yet the general sentiment among participants was that much was achieved, most of it in the estimated 500 official side events and 3,000 unofficial events. 'Some of the world's leading thinkers within the global sustainable development constituency attended side events but had no intention of engaging with the intergovernmental process', they noted. This is a view with which many conference attendees in general can identify; the official meetings and panels are often less interesting and productive than informal conversations in hallways or at local restaurants. The problem, of course, is that it is hard to measure the value of the agreements thus reached.

International non-governmental organizations

We saw in Chapter 4 that environmental NGOs play a critical role in influencing and shaping policy at the national level, developing sometimes symbiotic relationships with national government. A similar dynamic can be found at the international level: where intergovernmental organizations have states as members, and treaty secretariats oversee the agreements reached between or among states, international non-governmental organizations (INGOs) are bodies whose members are individuals or national associations, and which address environmental policy issues at the international level from outside the hallways of government. They relate to national governments and IGOs in much the same way as domestic NGOs relate to national governments, the goal being to bring about policy change. They come in many different forms, ranging from local grassroots organizations to national interest groups with strong international connections, groups with distinct and limited interests, groups with a broad array of interests, those working out of modest offices with limited means, and those working out of plush offices in capital cities and whose staff are often seen working alongside governments at major integrational gatherings.

The growth in the number and reach of INGOs has followed in the wake of expanded international cooperation, reflecting the emergence of a **global civil society,** or an international version of the array of groups that exist outside government at the national level and within which citizens can work to bring change. Such has been their impact that Mathews (1997) wrote some time ago of a power shift in global politics; in the wake of the rise of 'non-traditional' threats such as environmental decline, and the advent of new concerns about human security rather than national security, she concluded that national governments were 'not simply losing autonomy in a globalizing economy … [but were] sharing powers – including political, social and security roles at the core of sovereignty – with businesses, with international organizations, and with a multitude of … non-governmental organizations'. Where once NGOs were relegated to the hallways at conferences, she argued, they had come to sit at the negotiating table, their experience at the 1992 Rio Summit being illustrative:

> With the broader independent base of public support that environmental groups command, NGOs set the original goal of negotiating an agreement to control greenhouse gases long before governments were ready to do so, proposed most of its structure and content, and lobbied and mobilized public pressure to force through a pact that virtually no one else thought possible when the talks began.

The conventional view is that NGOs are created as a result of societal responses to needs and problems, and to a large extent this is true. But Reimann (2006) argues that there has been a 'top-down' dynamic at work as well: the expansion of international political opportunities in the form of funding and political access has provided a structural environment conducive to the formation and growth of NGOs, while donor states and IGOs have actively promoted the spread of NGOs to non-Western countries. The European Union and UN agencies, in particular, have subcontracted some of the responsibility for their projects to NGOs, have provided funding to NGOs, and have created networking agencies designed to encourage NGOs to work with one another. UNEP, for example, has close ties with the Environment Liaison Centre International, an 800-member NGO network based in Nairobi. NGOs are also part of the decision-making structure of the Global Environment Facility (GEF), a body set up in 1991 to channel billions of dollars of grants into environmental projects; NGOs

Box 5.2 *The role of multinational corporations*

While corporations are not usually discussed and assessed in the same manner as international non-governmental organizations, they can be seen as a form of INGO. Unlike standard INGOs, they seek to make a profit, exert control over often considerable resources, and play a key role in the economic health of states, but they are not formally part of government and they have roles in shaping policy that overlap with those of INGOs, even if their size, reach, and wealth can give them a louder voice in the hallways of government. Just as corporations (particularly the bigger ones, or the ones involved in critical sectors of the economy) play a central role in shaping policy at the state level, so **multinational corporations** (MNCs) – private enterprises that control the production of goods and services, and have facilities and other assets, in more than one country – play a central role at the international level.

Much of what we hear about the environmental role of MNCs is controversial at best, and negative at worst. They are charged with placing profits above environmental concerns, and with exploiting differences in national environmental standards by closing down operations in countries with higher standards and moving them to those with lower standards, as well as lower wage scales. They are also implicated in efforts by poorer countries to exploit natural resources at almost any cost, bringing to mind tales of multinational oil companies and their environmentally harmful extraction of oil in countries such as Nigeria.

On the other hand, there is evidence that MNCs have not been unaffected by the pressures to adopt corporate social responsibility (discussed in Chapter 2), and that many have self-regulated by adopting environmental policies and performance standards that exceed local government levels (Christmann, 2004). Few would find this line of thought very compelling, though, and could point to numerous examples of MNCs being linked to visible and substantial environmental degradation, whether in the form of pollution or the over-use of resources. To what extent, however, do the managers of MNCs seek to despoil the environment, and to what extent are they trapped in a system driven by the need to maximize profits, keep their shareholders happy, outwit the competition, and offer products and services as cheaply as possible to their customers?

Hoffman and Bansal (2012) identify three waves during which **corporate environmentalism** (the process by which businesses integrate environmental factors into their corporate decision-making) has evolved: in the 1960s and 1970s there was a new realization in the wake of the publication of Rachel Carson's *Silent Spring* that corporate activities needed regulation, in the 1980s and 1990s the focus was on strategic changes in the wake of headline-making environmental accidents, and in the twenty-first century the focus has been on a restructuring of global economies in the wake of the new debate about sustainability. The long-term effect has been to raise troubling questions about the relevance of old ways of doing business in the wake of globalization, demographic change, economic inequalities, and shifting social norms.

are part of a system of regional 'focal point' representatives, and have ten seats on the GEF Council. Finally, there are personnel exchanges between IGOs and NGOs, exemplified when Achim Steiner moved in 2006 from his position as director general of IUCN to being director general of UNEP.

Exactly how many environmental INGOs are in existence is hard to say because of the lack of comprehensive data and an agreed definition of what constitutes an INGO, but the numbers run into the thousands; some examples are listed in Table 5.3. A distinction must be made between groups with offices in multiple countries that focus on issues in those countries, and groups that are truly international; the latter include coordinating bodies made up of delegations from participating national and local NGOs, and bodies that are global in their interests and their memberships. There are also federations, or umbrella bodies that bring together different national organizations, and which might act as conduits for contacts between NGOs and an IGO. The Environment Liaison Centre International is an example.

Table **5.3 Examples of international environmental NGOs**

Name	Founded	Headquarters	Interests
Birdlife International	1922	UK	Protection of birds and their natural habitats. National 'partner' organizations in nearly 120 countries or territories.
World Wide Fund for Nature	1961	Switzerland	Protection of endangered species and habitats. International office coordinates work of national offices in nearly 70 countries.
Friends of the Earth	1969	Amsterdam	Focus on climate change, economic justice, 'food sovereignty', forests, and diversity. International office and 75 national groups.
Greenpeace	1971	Amsterdam	Direct action to stop environmental degradation. International office and 30 national/regional groups.
World Resources Institute	1982	Washington DC	Climate, energy, food, forests, water, and cities and transport. Think tank with offices in Brazil, China, European Union, India, Indonesia, United States.
Green Cross International	1993	Switzerland	Poverty, security, and the environment. Founded by former Soviet leader Mikhail Gorbachev. International office and 27 national offices.
African Biodiversity Network	1996	Thika, Kenya	Seeking African solutions to Africa's environmental problems. Has 36 partners in 12 countries.
Save China's Tigers	2000	Hong Kong	Public education and fundraising. Founded by Chinese fashion executive Li Quan.

Source: Information compiled from websites of the respective organizations, accessed May 2017.

This is no homogeneous world community of groups united by similar interests: INGOs have different methods, means, priorities, philosophies, and scopes, and a particular distinction must be made between groups based in the North and those based in the South. The former tend to focus on the environmental consequences of industrial development, and to argue in favour of adjustments in the goals of the free market, including greater regulation of industry, changes in the nature of consumerism, and investment in pollution control. Meanwhile, the latter tend to see many environmental problems in terms of the consequences of poverty, and of inequalities in the global economic system.

The work of INGOs has been less deeply studied and noticed than that of IGOs, but there have been two roles in which they have been particularly effective: as information brokers and as whistle-blowers. For example, reports to the Stockholm conference, the Rio Earth Summit, and intergovernmental discussions leading up to many international environmental treaties have been heavily influenced by research generated by INGOs, and by INGO influence over media coverage of these events. INGOs have also exerted influence by taking part in negotiations on treaties. Since only national governments can actually take decisions, INGOs usually have only observer status at meetings. But, with care, they can alter the direction of the negotiations through the information and perspectives they provide, which can alter both the negotiating process and the results (Corell and Betsill, 2008: ch. 2). One study – of the influence of indigenous peoples and local community delegates on negotiations at the 10th Conference of Parties of the Convention on Biological Diversity in 2010 – concluded that non-state delegates achieved 'moments of influence' by 'sounding an alarm for, shaming, and aligning with state actors' (Witter et al., 2015). As whistle-blowers, INGOs have used their media contacts and membership lists to draw attention to failures on the part of states to live up to their obligations, and to help treaty secretariats keep track of implementation.

Discussion questions

- Which approach to understanding international environmental governance do you find most convincing, and why?
- Are states becoming stronger, becoming weaker, or simply changing form in the face of changing demands?
- Is there a case, as has been suggested, for converting UNEP into a World Environment Organization with more autonomy and a stronger voice in UN environmental affairs?
- Are multinational corporations a force for positive environmental change or negative environmental pressures, or a combination of the two?

Key concepts

- Corporate environmentalism
- Epistemic community
- Global civil society
- Globalism
- Institution
- Intergovernmental organization
- International non-governmental organization
- International organization
- Liberalism
- Multinational corporation
- Non-regime
- Realism
- Regime
- Summitry
- Transgovernmental network
- Treaty secretariat

Further reading

Biermann, Frank, and Philipp H. Pattberg (eds) (2012) *Global Environmental Governance Reconsidered* (MIT Press). An edited collection that looks at recent developments in organizations active on environmental matters at the global level, the mechanisms they use, and the links among them.

Biermann, Frank, and Bernd Siebenhüner (eds) (2009) *Managers of Global Change: The Influence of International Environmental Bureaucracies* (MIT Press). An edited collection with studies of the work of treaty secretariats and international organizations with an environmental interest.

Bodansky, Daniel (2010) *The Art and Craft of International Environmental Law* (Harvard University Press). An accessible and real-world assessment of international environmental law, with sections on the international legal process, standard-setting, and implementation.

Harris, Paul G. (ed) (2014) *Routledge Handbook of Global Environmental Politics* (Routledge). An edited collection of chapters on the study of global environmental politics, and the key institutions, actors, ideas, and themes.

Morin, Jean-Frédéric, and Amandine Orsini (eds) (2015) *Essential Concepts of Global Environmental Governance* (Routledge). An encyclopaedia of key concepts in international environment governance, including treaties, institutions, and principles.

6 Air Pollution: Few Sources, Many Effects

Key arguments

- While the air contains gases and particles produced by natural processes, the pollution of air has grown since the Industrial Revolution, owing mainly to the burning of fossil fuels.
- The problem has been eased in older industrial states thanks to tightened regulation, but continues to worsen in newly industrializing countries.
- There are eight major pollutants, which have been the target of most air pollution law and policy.
- The threats posed by indoor pollution are often overlooked, in spite of the more immediate problems they pose to most people.
- Successful efforts to cut pollution from lead and to remove threats to the ozone layer stand as examples of what can be achieved with the right confluence of political, industrial, scientific, and public support.
- Acid pollution has been successfully addressed in Europe and North America, but continues to be a growing problem in several newly industrializing countries.

Chapter overview

Air is one of the most fundamental commodities necessary for life on earth. A combination mainly of nitrogen, oxygen, argon, and carbon dioxide, it serves one core purpose: allowing respiration, or the conversion by living organisms of oxygen into energy. While the supply of air presents no challenges (unlike the supply of water – see next chapter), the diminished quality of air has long been one of the core environmental problems: air has been increasingly polluted since the Industrial Revolution by emissions of noxious gases and particles. Because we use it every moment of our lives, it is the most immediate and intimate of the environmental problems created by human activity.

At the heart of the problem is our heavy reliance on fossil fuels, particularly the coal used in many power stations and the petroleum used in road vehicles. As the human population has increased, so has the demand for energy, the number of vehicles on our roads, and the size of towns and cities. The result has been a reduction in air quality, the threats posed to living organisms being both direct, through breathing in harmful pollutants, and indirect, through the effect of pollutants on natural processes such as the growth of plants, crops, and forests. The impacts were felt first in the original European and North American centres of industry, and spread in the wake of industrialization to Asia, South America, and parts of Africa. While levels of air pollution are down in most of Europe and North America, they are up substantially in most major Asian and South American cities, as well as in towns and rural areas downwind from those cities.

Air pollution was at first a local problem, but later developed regional and global dimensions. Acid pollution became a cross-border problem in North America and Western Europe, with emissions from the burning of fossil fuels mixing with water vapour to create acid precipitation that threatened ecosystems, materials, and human health. While agreement was reached in the 1980s to take remedial action in these regions, acid pollution remains a problem in newer industrialized countries such as India and China. At the global level, meanwhile, threats posed to the ozone layer from synthetic chemicals became a hot-button issue in the 1980s, and while remedial action was agreed, it will take decades for the ozone layer to recover.

Undoubtedly the greatest environmental problem ever faced by humanity is that of climate change. Concentrations of greenhouse gases such as carbon dioxide and methane have grown as a result of the burning of fossil fuels and changes in land-use patterns (including intensive farming and deforestation). The result has been an enhanced greenhouse effect, warming global temperatures, and the creation of an array of harmful effects ranging from changes in weather patterns to changes in ecosystems and natural landscapes. But while climate change begins with air pollution, the effects take us into a broader and more serious realm of threats, so the topic is covered separately in Chapter 12.

While air pollution has few sources, its scale varies from the local to the global, it results in a wide range of effects, and it poses different challenges to different people. This chapter begins with a review of the problem, looking at the decline in air quality, the major sources and effects of pollution and the major pollutants, and the action so far taken (or not) at the local, national, and international levels to address air pollution. It then looks at two relatively successful cases – the efforts made to remove lead from petrol and to stop production of the chemicals that created a thinning of the earth's ozone layer – before looking at the mixed policy record on acid pollution.

Defining the problem

A 2014 report by the World Health Organization (WHO) estimated that about 7 million people died worldwide in 2012 as a result of exposure to air pollution (WHO, 2014). This was more than double any previous estimate, and elevated air pollution to the unwelcome status of being the deadliest single environmental health risk. The WHO total combined all deaths from indoor and outdoor pollution, and was based on a better understanding of the health problems caused by air pollution, as well as improved measurement techniques. Worst affected were Southeast Asia and the western Pacific, regions that include China, India, Indonesia, and the Philippines, where urban and industrial growth has been fastest and regulations have often been weakest. Relatively less seriously affected were the older industrial areas of Europe and North America, which have the oldest and most comprehensive policy regimes in place to counter the problem.

Air pollution occurs when substances are introduced into the air that harm living organisms and ecosystems. Some are produced by nature and often serve a useful role: thus moderate amounts of carbon dioxide maintain the greenhouse effect that makes life on earth possible, and sulphur dioxide makes precipitation slightly acidic and helps with the breakdown of nutrients in the soil. But the air quality problem we face today stems from human activity, and the introduction of greater volumes of polluting gases and particles into the air. This has created an imbalance in phenomena such as the greenhouse effect, as well as posing a heightened threat to ecosystems and to the health of humans, animals, plants, and to the condition of materials as diverse as metals, plastics, and stone. The health risks include breathing difficulties, neurological effects, cancer, and problems with cardiovascular and reproductive systems (Vallero, 2014: ch. 7).

While air pollution is generated by a wide variety of industrial processes (including the metals industries, smelting, and the tanning of leather), and by the use of chemicals in household and commercial products, the chief source of the problem can be summarized in two words: **fossil fuels**. Formed from the decay of organic matter over millions of years, their large-scale use began with the coal used to fuel the steam engines that were at the heart of the Industrial Revolution in Britain in the eighteenth century. In the late nineteenth century, natural gas began to be used increasingly as an additional source of mainly domestic energy, and then the invention of the automobile brought petroleum into the equation. When they are burned, these fuels produce pollutants such as carbon dioxide, sulphur dioxide, and nitrogen oxides.

As this combination of technological change, industrialization, urbanization, mass transportation, and reliance on fossil fuels evolved, so air pollution worsened. It first became a problem in the eighteenth and nineteenth centuries in Europe, then in North America in the late nineteenth and early twentieth centuries, then in the Soviet Union and Japan, and more recently in Asia and Latin America. At first it was mainly a local problem, but as emissions grew it became an international problem: weather patterns carried emissions from the United States across the border to Canada, for example, from Britain and Germany north to Scandinavia, and from China to Japan. The use of synthetic chemical compounds in aerosols, refrigeration, and cooling systems made itself felt with damage to the ozone layer, and the growth in emissions of greenhouse gases eventually created the quintessential global problem of climate change.

While the older industrial states of the North have seen concerted efforts to clean their air since the 1980s, achieving new levels of green growth, the biggest problems are now being experienced in the new industrial centres of Asia and Latin America (Shin, 2016). London was once so notorious for its pollution that it became the birthplace of the term *smog*. Los Angeles later developed a similar reputation: the problem there was – and remains to a large extent – ozone created by the reaction in sunlight of pollutants created by its heavy traffic density. But they and their peer cities now rank far behind those of India and China in their levels of pollution. Figure 6.1 lists selected urban areas by levels of particulate matter (PM) pollution: Indian cities account for 13 of the 20 most polluted cities

Figure 6.1 The world's most polluted cities

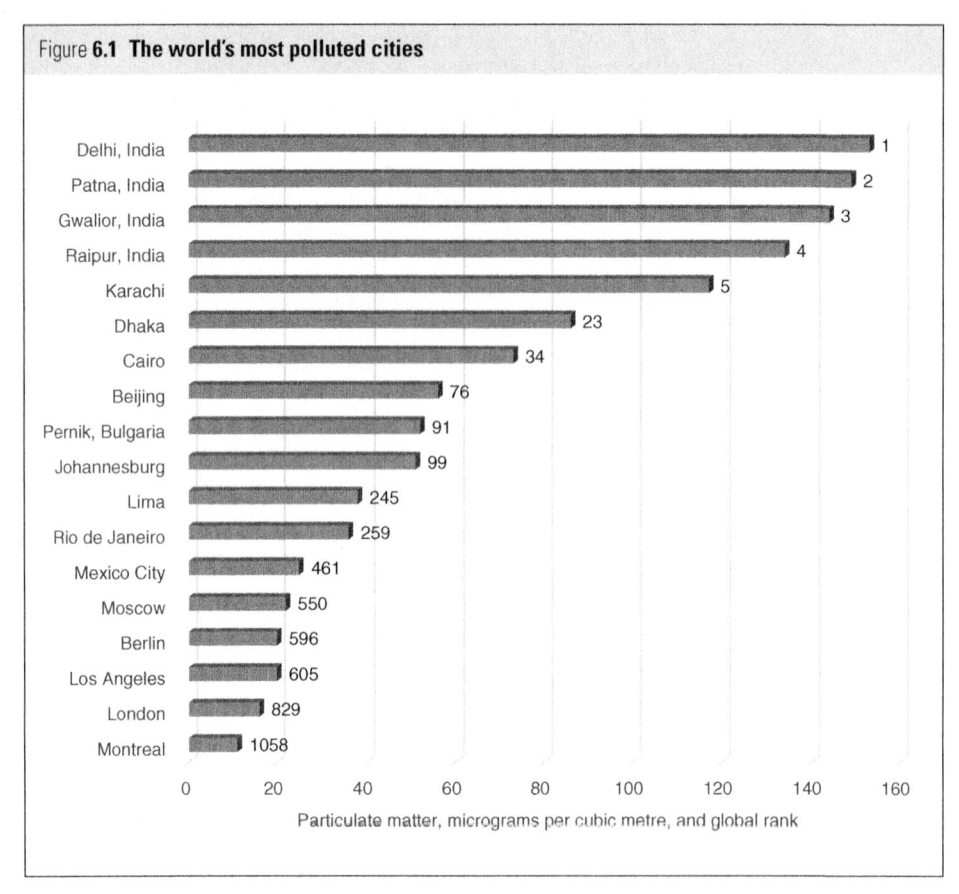

City	Particulate matter (μg/m³)	Global rank
Delhi, India		1
Patna, India		2
Gwalior, India		3
Raipur, India		4
Karachi		5
Dhaka		23
Cairo		34
Beijing		76
Pernik, Bulgaria		91
Johannesburg		99
Lima		245
Rio de Janeiro		259
Mexico City		461
Moscow		550
Berlin		596
Los Angeles		605
London		829
Montreal		1058

Particulate matter, micrograms per cubic metre, and global rank

Source: World Health Organization database, 2014, at http://www.who.int/phe/health_topics/outdoorair/databases/cities/en. Most values are for 2011 and 2012. Numbers at end of columns indicate ranking.

in the world; Asian cities account for 40 of the 50 most polluted; the most polluted European city (Pernik in Bulgaria) ranks 91st with PM concentrations that are barely one-third of those of Delhi; and all the once most polluted European and North American cities (including London, Berlin, New York, and Los Angeles) now rank far behind. Delhi's ranking at the head of the league is a result of a combination of road dust, exhaust fumes, industrial emissions, and the open fires burned by the city's poorer residents to cook and keep warm (Safi, 2016).

If fossil fuels could somehow be replaced overnight, most of our air pollution problems would quickly disappear (although the damage would take some time to be repaired). But of course they will not be replaced any time soon, because our economic systems are so heavily invested in their use: we rely on them to generate electricity, and to power our industries and our transport systems. A switch from fossil fuels would involve the restructuring of our entire economic base, at enormous cost. To be sure, there has been

Air Pollution: Few Sources, Many Effects | 117

Figure **6.2** **Electricity generation in the European Union**

[Line chart showing Terawatt hours from 1990 to 2013 for Renewables, Nuclear, Solid fuels, Gas, and Oil]

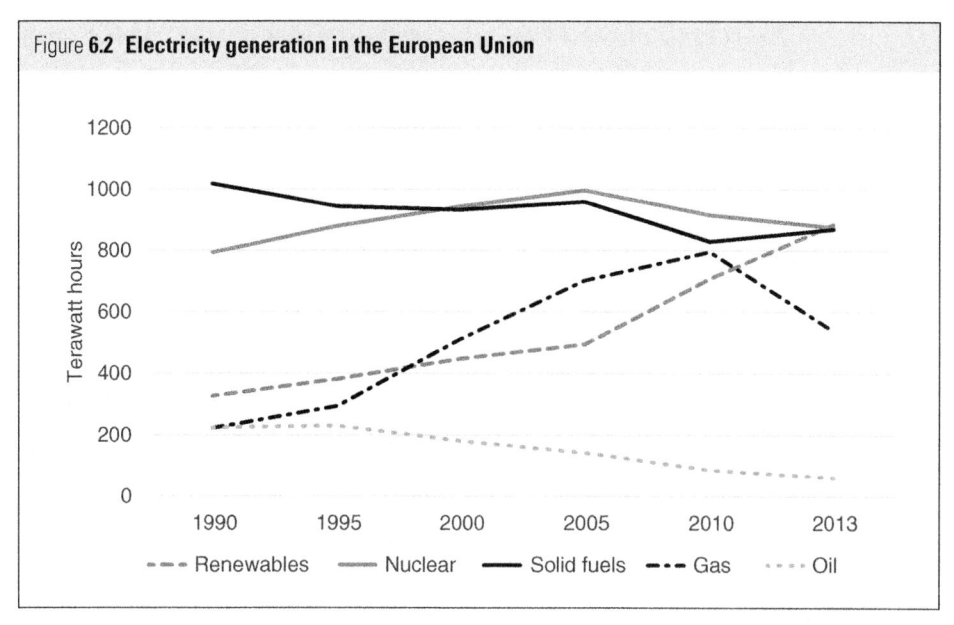

Source: Eurostat at http://ec.europa.eu/eurostat (accessed May 2016). Total gigawatt hours: 2.59 million in 1990, 3.26 million in 2013.

progress in switching away from a reliance on coal to generate electricity: Figure 6.2 shows that while electricity production in the European Union grew by 25 per cent between 1990 and 2013, the proportion generated using solid fuels such as coal fell from 39 per cent to 26 per cent, while the proportion generated by renewables

Figure **6.3** **Electricity generation in India**

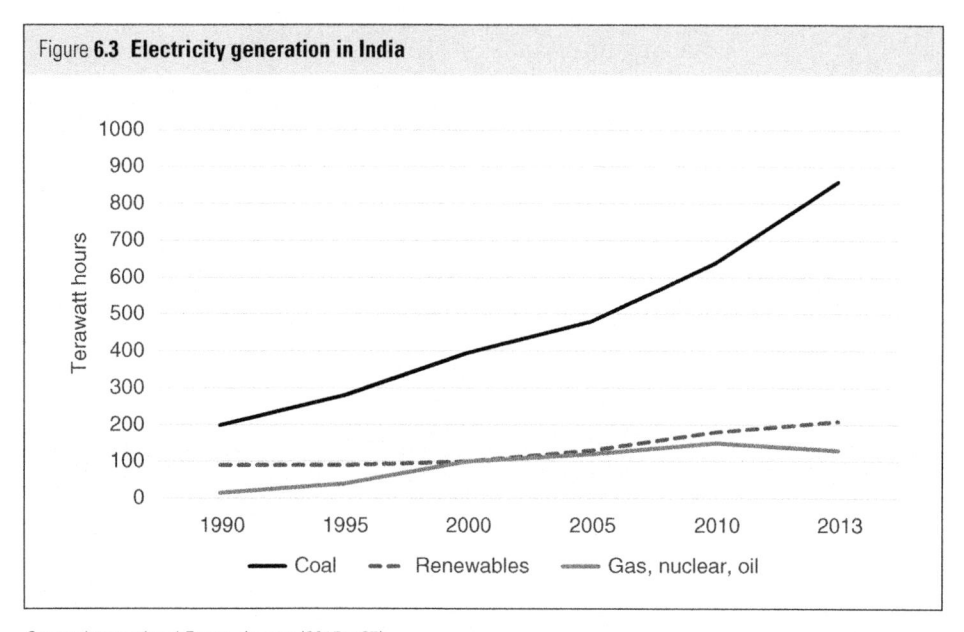

[Line chart showing Terawatt hours from 1990 to 2013 for Coal, Renewables, and Gas, nuclear, oil]

Source: International Energy Agency (2015a: 27).

grew from 12 per cent to 27 per cent. (The EU also relies heavily on nuclear power to generate electricity, which raises a separate set of concerns – see Chapter 11.) There have also been air quality gains from the switch to unleaded fuel and the production of more fuel-efficient vehicles, as well as hybrid and electric vehicles.

However, much remains to be done, and many of these gains have been offset by trends in the South, where a combination of burgeoning urban populations, investments in new coal-fired power stations, growing vehicle use density, and the use of often badly maintained vehicles have severely degraded the quality of the air. Figure 6.3 shows the heavy reliance in India on coal for generating electricity. Both India and China have made investments in hydropower, but neither has so far made significant investments in renewables. This is projected to change, though, with estimates that renewables will overtake coal as the biggest source of electricity by the early 2030s, accounting for 30 per cent of Chinese electricity by 2040 and 25 per cent of Indian electricity (International Energy Agency, 2015a).

Apart from the challenge of shifting away from fossil fuels, several other problems face policymakers in dealing with air pollution. First, there is the question of what we mean by 'clean air'. Human activity has changed the composition of air in microscopic ways, such that there is now almost no part of the earth that is not impacted, even at large distances from the centres of industry. But what should be the goal of policy: a return to pre-industrial levels, the creation of conditions that cause the least harm to the most users of air, a focus on bringing down average levels of pollution, or a focus on the most polluted areas, such as major cities?

Second, there is the problem of determining the exact dangers posed to human health and the environment by air pollution. Much of the research is carried out in laboratory conditions, with tests involving individual pollutants. But real-world damage is caused by multiple pollutants acting in concert, and different people are affected differently by different levels and combinations of pollutants; for example, airborne lead is more of a threat to children than to adults, and smog is more troubling to people with breathing problems than to those without. As a result, there is no one-size-fits-all policy response to air pollution.

Third, reducing emissions is often an expensive proposition because of the need to change production processes and to fit pollution controls, and success depends upon the cooperation of often politically powerful industries that are understandably opposed to taking on the burden of the costs involved; in spite of the polluter pays principle, they will work to pass the costs on to consumers, making their products and services more expensive. The coal, oil, and vehicle production industries have been particularly resistant, and their sheer size and economic reach have ensured that they have been able to employ political influence to slow down efforts to reduce emissions. Raising questions about the science has been a popular approach, another being the emotive charge that pollution controls costs jobs because of the added expenses, and yet another being that there are limits to the available technological solutions. On the latter point, however, regulations have often played a useful role in **technology forcing**, or setting standards that encourage the development of new solutions (see Nentjes et al., 2007).

Finally, one way by which industry in Europe and North America has been able to avoid the additional costs of pollution control has been either to outsource manufacturing to countries with weaker regulations, or to buy more from those countries. Part of the reason why Chinese emissions have been growing lies in the growth of demand for cheaper Chinese products from the West. Hence while the West argues that it is cutting greenhouse gas emissions, some of that 'reduction' is a result of polluting industries moving elsewhere. In short, some of the pollution being generated in these countries derives from the production of goods destined for the European and North American markets (Goldenberg, 2014). Ironically, a new transboundary air pollution problem has emerged in recent years with new evidence that emissions from China are finding their way across the Pacific to the west coast of the United States and Canada (Wong, 2014).

The major air pollutants

Several hundred substances have been identified as air pollutants, but eight are particularly common and widespread, and have been the target of most air pollution law and policy.

1. *Sulphur dioxide* (SO_2). A toxic gas with a pungent smell, SO_2 is created when the sulphur present in fossil fuels is released and reacts with oxygen. It is a primary component in acid pollution and smog, and causes respiratory problems in humans. Globally, about half the SO_2 in the air comes from natural sources – mainly volcanic activity – while the balance comes from human activity. The prime source of the latter is the burning of fossil fuels at power stations, with other industrial processes (such as smelting) accounting for most of the balance. Oil contains about 3 per cent sulphur while high-sulphur coal contains about 10 per cent.

    There are many options available for reducing sulphur emissions, including the use of low-sulphur coal, washing or desulphurizing coal before it is burned, removing sulphur from

Table 6.1 **Major air pollutants**

Pollutant	Main sources	Effects
Sulphur dioxide (SO_2)	Natural (mainly volcanic activity) and burning of fossil fuels.	Primary ingredient in acid pollution and smog.
Nitrogen oxides (NO_x)	Natural and road vehicles and power stations.	Primary ingredient in acid pollution; threat to ozone layer.
Carbon dioxide (CO_2)	Natural (mainly volcanic activity) and burning of fossil fuels.	Natural levels maintain greenhouse effect. Increased levels have led to climate change.
Carbon monoxide (CO)	Natural (mainly volcanic activity and forest fires) and burning of fossil fuels.	Toxic and even fatal to humans; key indoor pollutant.
Volatile organic compounds (VOCs)	Natural and found in household products and building materials.	Toxic with long-term exposure; key indoor pollutant.
Particulate matter (PM)	Natural (volcanic activity, dust storms, forest fires) and burning of fossil fuels, smoke.	Threats to human health rather than nature.
Heavy metals	Industrial activity.	Toxic or even fatal with extended exposure.
Ozone (O_3)	Reactions of other pollutants with sunlight.	Respiratory problems.

coal during the burning process, filtering sulphur out of smoke by fitting scrubbers to smokestacks, or switching away from coal for electricity generation. Emissions of SO_2 have fallen substantially in Europe and North America thanks to efforts to control acid pollution, but they are a growing problem in major Asian and Latin American cities.

2. *Nitrogen oxides* (NO_x). A collective term for nitric oxide and nitrogen dioxide, NO_x forms when combustion oxidizes the nitrogen in fuel and some of the nitrogen naturally present in the air. It is another of the primary components in acid pollution, combining with water vapour to create dilute nitric acid, and is also a factor in the depletion of the ozone layer. NO_x can cause lung irritation as well as lowering resistance to pneumonia, bronchitis, and other respiratory problems. There are several natural sources, including lightning, forest fires, and volcanic activity, but human activity has significantly increased concentrations: road vehicles account for about half of human-made NO_x, and coal-fired power stations for the balance.

The main control option has been the use of **catalytic converters**; these are devices fitted to the exhausts of combustion engines that reduce emissions of NO_x, carbon monoxide, and hydrocarbons. Emissions have fallen since the early 1990s in Europe and North America thanks to controls focused on power stations and road vehicles, but they are a problem in the larger cities of newly industrialized countries thanks to the density of traffic and the often poor maintenance of road vehicles.

3. *Carbon dioxide (CO_2)*. A colourless and odourless gas, CO_2 is produced naturally by plant and animal respiration, and by volcanoes and other geological activity. This generates only trace amounts (less than 1 per cent of the total volume of air), but plays a critical role in helping create the greenhouse effect that sustains life as we know it. The burning of fossil fuels is once again the major man-made source, carbon being a prime ingredient of such fuels. Their use has led to a 40 per cent increase in concentrations compared to pre-industrial times, the result being an enhanced greenhouse effect, which has led to climate change.

   Emissions can be reduced by cutbacks in the use of fossil fuels, or improvements in fuel efficiency. Concentrations can also be reduced by efforts to protect carbon sinks such as oceans, soils, and forests, where carbon is naturally removed from the atmosphere in a process known as carbon sequestration. Emissions of CO_2 have fallen in Europe and North America thanks mainly to moves away from coal to cleaner sources of energy, but they have grown dramatically in China, and more steadily in other major newly industrialized countries, where relatively few efforts have been made to impose controls (see Chapter 12).

4. *Carbon monoxide (CO)*. A colourless and odourless gas, CO is mainly produced by volcanic activity, forest fires, and photochemical reactions in the atmosphere, but in urban areas the major source is vehicle exhaust and the incomplete burning of fossil fuels. CO has little impact on the natural environment, but can be toxic and even fatal to humans in high concentrations, particularly indoors (see Box 6.1). The best means of control is the fitting of catalytic converters to road vehicles. Emissions have fallen substantially in Europe and North America thanks to improved controls and switches from solid fuels to gas and electricity.

5. *Volatile organic compounds (VOCs)*. This is another collective term, covering a wide range of organic compounds with a low boiling point (such as acetone, benzene, and formaldehyde), which makes them more likely to evaporate than less volatile chemicals. Some are produced naturally by chemical processes such as fires and the decay of organic matter, but VOCs are mainly a problem indoors; sources include solvents, paints, cleaning products, dry-cleaning processes,

122 | Environmental Politics and Policy

> **BOX 6.1** *Indoor pollution*
>
> Most air pollutants are a problem outdoors, but often overlooked is the more immediate and sometimes more dangerous threat posed by **indoor pollution**. Since most people (in the North particularly) spend most of their time indoors, whether at home or in the workplace, they are more immediately and persistently exposed to indoor pollutants. These include radon (from building materials, water, and soil), formaldehyde (from insulation and particle board), asbestos, the lead in old paint, mercury, synthetic fibres, chemicals in household products, microorganisms in biological activity, and tobacco smoke.
>
> As a group, VOCs pose the most serious threats; since many are found in ordinary household products, concentrations tend to be higher indoors than outdoors. Their effects range from minor eye and throat irritation to nausea and fatigue, with longer-term and more sustained exposure being linked to certain cancers. Carbon monoxide is also a dangerous indoor pollutant, created by the malfunctioning of appliances that burn fuel, such as furnaces, ovens, and water heaters (hence programmes to encourage home-owners to install CO detectors). In the South, indoor air pollution is exacerbated by the use of solid fuels such as wood, charcoal, and dung on open fires or traditional stoves (see Saksena and Smith, 2003). In spite of the immediacy and the potential depth of the problem of indoor pollution, relatively little is known about the concentrations or periods of exposure necessary to produce harmful effects, and indoor pollutants have been subject to less public concern and fewer structured policy responses than outdoor pollutants.

photocopiers and computer printers, and glues, all of which release VOCs while they are being used, and sometimes even while they are being stored. The extraction and distribution of fossil fuels is another source, although – at least in this one case – the burning of fossil fuels plays a relatively small role in the problem.

Indoors, the effects of VOCs can be limited by avoiding chemical products, following the precautions listed on product labels, and improving ventilation. Outdoors, VOCs play a key role in the production of ground-level ozone. Emissions have fallen in Europe and North America thanks in part to steps taken since the signature of the 1999 Gothenburg protocol to the Convention on Long-range Transboundary Air Pollution (see the section 'Acid pollution: A mix of success and concern' below), designed to reduce acidification, eutrophication, and ground-level ozone by cutting emissions of VOCs as well as SO_2 and NO_x.

6. *Particulate matter (PM)*. This is a collective term for solid and liquid particles suspended in the air, including ash, smoke, dust, sea salt, and pollen. They are measured in micrometres,

with particulates of 10 micrometres or less (PM10) being most likely to be breathed in by humans, and finer particulates ranging as low as PM0.1. Much PM is natural, produced by forest fires and volcanoes, but human activity has again been behind increased concentrations: in urban areas, the main problem is smoke produced by the use of solid fuel such as coal, and levels in rural areas have been exacerbated by forest fires, some sparked by drought but others set as part of efforts to clear forests.

The primary threat posed by PM is to human health rather than to natural processes, smaller particles being more dangerous than larger particles because they are easier to breathe in, and thus more likely to enter the lungs. The most effective controls include coal-washing, a switch to smokeless fuel and natural gas for domestic heating, the installation of particle-removal equipment at power stations, energy conservation, and efforts to prevent forest fires. Emissions have fallen in Europe and North America thanks mainly to a switch from solid fuels to gas and electricity in homes. But, once again, Asian and Latin American cities continue to suffer thanks to the use of solid fuels.

7. *Heavy metals.* These include arsenic, cadmium, chromium, copper, lead, mercury, nickel, and zinc. Most are introduced into both air and water as by-products of industrial activity, including smelting, waste incineration, metals production, and mining. Some – such as arsenic, cadmium, and nickel – are also by-products of the burning of fossil fuels. The metals are emitted in the form either of dust or of vapour, the more volatile among them (such as mercury) being mainly vapour. Almost all pose a threat to human health, the effects varying from one metal to another: most cause breathing problems, while arsenic is a poison, cadmium can lead to kidney disease, lead can cause brain damage, and most heavy metals are carcinogens.

The production of heavy metals can be controlled by changes in industrial processes, the more efficient (or reduced) burning of fossil fuels, and changes in road vehicle technology. Emissions of lead have decreased dramatically all over the world in the wake of the introduction of lead-free petrol, and emissions of other heavy metals have fallen thanks to changes in the use of fossil fuels, but emissions of some (such as cadmium and mercury) are increasing.

8. *Ozone (O_3).* This is the only major pollutant that is not a primary pollutant, being a by-product of interactions in sunlight involving 'precursor' pollutants such as nitrogen oxides, carbon monoxide, and VOCs, the problem being worst

in cities with heavy traffic, particularly on days with more sunlight and higher temperatures. This 'bad' ozone is found in the troposphere – from ground-level to an altitude of 10–15 km (6–10 miles) – and is different from the 'good' ozone found in the stratosphere – about 15–50 km (9–30 miles) above the surface of the earth. High levels of tropospheric ozone can cause respiratory problems in humans – particularly infants and the elderly – which usually pass once levels decline. Long-term exposure leads to more serious effects, particularly for people who already have breathing problems. Ozone can also harm sensitive vegetation and ecosystems, and crops during the growing season.

Ozone formation can be reduced with cleaner fuel burning regulations, controls on NO_x formation, and improved maintenance of road vehicles. Ozone has become less of a problem in European and North American cities thanks to the efforts to reduce precursor pollutants, although hot summer days can still lead to urban ozone warnings. The problem is greater in large tropical cities with weaker controls on precursor pollutants.

Two encouraging stories: Leaded fuel and the ozone layer

While it can sometimes seem as though humans have created more environmental problems than they have solved, two examples of responses to air pollution show that – under the right circumstances – ameliorative action can be identified, agreed, taken, and made to work. The first concerns the dangers posed to human health by the lead used in petrol, and the second concerns the relatively swift response to threats posed to the earth's protective ozone layer by a family of synthetic chemicals known as chlorofluorocarbons (CFCs), used in a variety of applications, including aerosol propellants, refrigerants, coolants, sterilisers, and solvents.

The problem with lead dates back to the early 1920s, when researchers at the US vehicle manufacturer General Motors discovered that the addition of tetraethyl lead (TEL) to petrol could prevent 'knocking' (mistiming of combustion) in vehicle engines (see Box 6.2). Lead swiftly became a standard fuel additive, with the result that vehicle engines ran more smoothly, but levels of airborne lead also grew throughout the industrialized world. Lead had long been used in plumbing (a word deriving from the Latin name for lead, *plumbum*), and was used in paint to help make whites whiter and other colours brighter. Its dangers were not unknown, and encouraged several European states to

> **Box 6.2** *Thomas Midgley: The one-man wrecking crew*
>
> The efforts to remove lead from petrol and to protect the ozone layer are not only two examples of policy that has worked, but both were responses to problems created in large part by the inventions of a single person: an American mechanical engineer named Thomas Midgley (1889–1944). He was part of the team that discovered the anti-knock qualities of lead in petrol, and while his research gave him a bad dose of lead-poisoning, the discovery went on to be described as a 'gift of God' by the vehicle industry (Markowitz and Rosner, 2013: xv). Midgley then went on to be part of the team that created CFCs, whose qualities at first seemed to offer a safer alternative to the toxic and/or flammable compounds then commonly used as refrigerants.
>
> Lead and CFCs became the standard of their respective industries, but they also came to pose health threats to hundreds of millions of people around the world: lead through its direct impact on humans, and CFCs through the damage they inflicted on the ozone layer, thereby increasing the health threats posed by ultraviolet solar radiation. Midgley was once described as causing 'more damage to Earth's atmosphere than any other single organism that has ever lived' (Walker, 2007), and *Time* magazine in 2010 listed leaded fuel and CFCs as among the 50 worst inventions of all time (*Time*, 27 May 2010). Midgley won numerous patents and several awards for his work, but ironically became his own worst enemy when – after contracting polio in 1940 – he invented a pulley system to help polio sufferers get out of bed, and was strangled to death on his own invention.

ban its use in interior paint in 1909, and prompted the League of Nations to ban lead-based paint in 1922. In spite of concerns about the effects on human health, lead was introduced into petrol in the United States in 1923 (European Environment Agency, 2013: 50), and was used in almost all the petrol being sold in the United States by 1936.

There was little general concern until the publication in the early 1970s of research confirming that even low levels of lead exposure could cause permanent learning and behavioural problems in children exposed before birth and in infancy. A phase-out of lead-based interior paint was begun in 1971 in the United States, and vehicle manufacturers were ordered to begin building engines to run on unleaded fuel by 1975. Several European states launched similar efforts, beginning with West Germany and Britain in the 1970s. In 1986, Japan became the first country in the world fully to stop the production and use of leaded fuel. Canada followed in 1990, and the United States in 1996, a move described by Carol Browner, then administrator of the US Environmental Protection Agency, as 'one of the great environmental achievements of all time' (EPA, 1996); studies had already shown a significant decrease since 1978 in blood-lead levels in the United

States. In 2000 the European Union banned sales of leaded fuel, and in 2002 the UN Environment Programme set up the Partnership for Cleaner Fuels and Vehicles with the goal of eliminating leaded fuel worldwide by 2008. While leaded fuel is today all but impossible to find, lead can still be found in cheap toys, jewellery, cosmetics, and some PVC products.

How did the story of the ban on leaded fuel evolve? The initial use of lead in fuel can be ascribed mainly to the power of large industries in the United States to have their way on policy. TEL was produced first by the Du Pont Corporation, which bought a 35 per cent stake in General Motors, which in turn agreed with Standard Oil to create the Ethyl Corporation, which became the major manufacturer of TEL. The sheer size of this combination of chemical, vehicle, and oil companies helped make sure that subsequent efforts to stop the use of lead were delayed. When it came to the eventual ban, evidence of the impact of lead on human health was overwhelming, allowing governments and interest groups to make a strong case. But the immediate spark to begin phasing out lead in petrol was a technical problem: in order to meet the requirements of the 1970 Clean Air Act, US automobile manufacturers had to begin fitting catalytic converters to their vehicles, but found that lead was poisonous to the platinum in the converters (European Environment Agency, 2013: 60).

As pressures grew for a ban in the 1980s, oil companies claimed that it would take time to develop alternatives to lead, but the value of ethanol as an alternative anti-knock agent had been known even as lead was first being introduced to fuel; it was ignored for commercial reasons. Leaded fuel was clearly a health threat to everyone who lived with and around road vehicles, and yet financial considerations meant that the phasing in of unleaded fuel had to occur in conjunction with the phasing out of older road vehicles, meaning that leaded and unleaded fuel were sold in conjunction for many years. The age of vehicles on the road was also a reason why many poorer Asian and African countries took longer to phase out unleaded fuel.

The threats posed to the ozone layer by synthetic chemicals also date back to the 1920s, and the science of the problem was understood as early as the 1930s (Gillespie, 2006: 4). Stratospheric ozone forms when oxygen molecules are split by ultraviolet (UV-B) radiation from the sun and bond with other oxygen molecules to form a thin and fragile layer of ozone that helps screen out UV-B radiation. Elevated levels of the latter can cause increased incidence of skin cancer, sunburn, eye disorders, infectious skin disease, skin ageing, and depression of the immune system. They can also kill micro-organisms and cells in animals and plants, decrease photosynthesis, damage seed quality, reduce crop yields, and limit the production of phytoplankton in aquatic ecosystems, affecting the early development stages of fish, shrimp, and other marine species (see Cockell and Blaustein, 2001).

The ozone layer problem began when Thomas Midgley and a team of researchers at General Motors was working on a safer form of refrigerant for use in air conditioning and refrigeration. They eventually created the first in a series of synthetic **chlorofluorocarbons** (CFCs) that were non-toxic and non-flammable, and were quickly and widely adopted as refrigerants and aerosol accelerants. All seemed to be well until the American and Mexican scientists F. Sherwood Rowland and Mario Molina (who, along with Paul Crutzen, won the 1995 Nobel Prize for Chemistry for their work) began to theorize that CFCs were decomposing in sunlight, releasing chlorine and chlorine monoxide that were destroying ozone. Other ozone-depleting substances (ODSs) were also identified, including halons (used in fire-fighting), carbon tetrachloride (used in medicines and agricultural chemicals), and methyl bromide (used as a fumigant). The threats were found to be greatest over the polar ice caps, where ozone levels were estimated to have fallen by as much as 40 per cent. At the same time, the amount of UV-B reaching the earth's surface was growing.

In the face of opposition from industry, the United States began taking action to limit the release of CFCs in 1977, and adopted a ban on their use in most non-essential aerosols in 1978. It also exerted pressure on the European Community (EC) – by then the biggest producer and exporter of CFCs, accounting for 38 per cent of global production – to follow suit. The Europeans agreed only to some rather modest gestures designed to demonstrate their willingness to take action on the issue, freezing production capacity rather than production. Nonetheless, these steps constituted the emergence of a distinct ozone regime.

March 1985 saw the signature of the framework Vienna Convention for the Protection of the Ozone Layer, but given the lack of a scientific consensus on the problem, it involved no obligations beyond monitoring and research (Gillespie, 2006: 162). Political and public pressure for control measures grew following the publication in June 1985 of research by a British Antarctic Survey team concluding that the ozone layer over the Antarctic had been substantially depleted. Media headlines spoke dramatically of a 'hole' in the ozone layer, when in truth it was a thinning of ozone concentrations. Discussions began on a protocol to the Vienna Convention, pitting a US/Canadian-led coalition of countries (the Toronto Group, which supported a global ban on the use of CFCs as aerosol propellants, but no limit on other uses of CFCs) against an EC-led coalition which argued that banning aerosol use would not address the problem of non-aerosol use, and that the only effective response was a blanket production capacity limit.

Majority public opinion in the United States was in favour of action, but neither government nor industry was willing to adopt a unilateral phase-out for fear that this would provide European CFC producers such as ICI and Hoechst with a larger market share than they already enjoyed. However, the positions of European industry were changing, as revealed by the support given in 1988 by the European Chemical Industry Council (CEFIC) and by ICI to a CFC phase-out. By mid-1987, the weight of scientific opinion had helped move the EC from agreement on a freeze, to agreement on a 20 per cent reduction, to agreement on a 50 per cent reduction (Morrisette, 1989). For Parson (2003: 7-9), the breakthroughs in science were critical, because they produced conclusions that were credible, authoritative, and legitimate, and encouraged several opponents of action to change their positions, thereby establishing a broad international consensus.

The Montreal protocol to the Vienna Convention was signed in September 1987, and came into force on 1 January 1989. It required that industrialized countries freeze and then reduce production of five kinds of CFC by 50 per cent by 1999, calculated from a 1986 baseline. It was immediately criticized by several countries and by environmental groups for not going far enough, and a meeting of signatories to the convention in Helsinki in May 1989 saw the 12 EC member states joining a large group of countries pushing for a complete CFC phase-out by 2000. New evidence had by then begun to emerge about the depletion of the ozone layer in the northern hemisphere (closer to home – for most industrialized countries – than the distant southern pole), and a meeting of parties to the Vienna Convention in London in 1990 led to further amendments, speeding up the timetable for the reduction and consumption of CFCs and halons, and adding more chemical compounds to the list of controlled substances, including carbon tetrachloride, hydrofluorocarbons (HFCs), and hydrochlorofluorocarbons (HCFCs). The parties met again in 1992 and agreed to bring forward the dates for the end of production and consumption of CFCs and other ODSs.

By 1998, the international ozone regime had resulted in reductions of global annual production of ozone-depleting substances of as much as 80–90 per cent. But while production has all but ceased, the problem has not gone away, and the problem has not yet been entirely solved: the stability of CFCs and halons means that they will remain intact for decades,

Table 6.2 The ozone layer and climate change: Political responses compared

Ozone layer	Climate change
Science relatively clear.	Science disputed by some.
One group of synthetic chemicals dominated the problem, with limited sources.	CO_2 is natural, and greenhouse effect essential for life on earth; many sources of greenhouse gases.
Mainly a problem created in North America and Europe.	Almost every country involved, and industrializing countries resist because of costs to economic development.
One relatively small industry involved.	The entire fossil-fuel industry involved, along with all other industries reliant on fossil fuels.
Concerted consumer response.	Consumer response, but mainly in the North.
Alternatives to ODSs found relatively easily.	Alternatives to fossil fuels exist, but the switch involves restructuring industry and transportation.

continuing to break down ozone long after they first infiltrated the stratosphere. The ozone layer is not expected to fully recover until at least 2035, and perhaps as late as 2070 (Douglass et al., 2014). Hence ultra-violet radiation levels are continuing to grow, as are their associated effects on human health. The thinning of the Antarctic ozone layer has also contributed to climate change in the southern hemisphere, the ozone layer continues to be threatened by nitrous oxide (a key greenhouse gas), and there are concerns about the impact of HFCs on climate change more widely (WMO, 2014).

The ozone layer convention – and, more importantly, the Montreal protocol – are often described as the most successful international agreements yet reached on an environmental issue, and the case of the ozone layer is sometimes wistfully pointed out as both a contrast to, and a lesson for, discussions on climate change. The success of one and the slowness of responding to the other are easier to understand when their causes and the participating political/industrial constituencies are compared (see Table 6.2). Most importantly, depletion of the ozone layer is associated with one relatively restricted group of synthetic chemicals made in a few countries and for which alternatives have been found. Climate change, by contrast, goes to the heart of our reliance on fossil fuels, involves many more actors, and demands fundamental change to the structure of economies. Little surprise, then, that political agreement on climate change has been so much harder to reach (see Chapter 12).

Acid pollution: A mix of success and concern

Acid pollution is an example of the kind of issue-attention cycle discussed in Chapter 3; it was one of the hot-button environmental issues of the 1970s and 1980s, but we hear little about it any longer because it has ceased to be a major concern in North America and Western Europe, thanks to successful efforts to reduce the emissions involved. The problem has not gone away, however, and is an increasingly worrying issue for newly industrializing countries such as India and China, which are facing the same kinds of threats as were once experienced by older industrialized states.

The problem occurs when fossil fuels are burned, releasing sulphur dioxide (SO_2) and nitrogen oxides (NO_x), which react with atmospheric water vapour to increase the acidity of precipitation (rain, snow, and fog). All precipitation is naturally acidic because of the SO_2 and NO_x produced by volcanic activity and other natural phenomena, and this acidity is helpful in – for example – breaking down the nutrients in soils. But higher levels of acidity have a string of damaging effects on the environment and human health, causing dieback in forests by making trees more vulnerable to disease, releasing heavy metals in soils, undermining the ecosystems of rivers and lakes, eroding buildings and monuments, and harming the health of people with respiratory and heart conditions (see Visgilio and Whitelaw, 2007, part I).

Acid pollution was at first mainly a local problem, but when smokestacks were built in an effort to disperse the emissions, the problem became bigger and wider. When research in the 1960s established that emissions of sulphur dioxide could travel hundreds and even thousands of kilometres, the effects of **long-range transboundary air pollution** became clear for the first time (Lidskog and Sundqvist, 2011b). The question then arose about which international institution was best placed to host negotiations on a response, and the choice fell on the UN Economic Commission for Europe, set up in 1947 to encourage regional cooperation in Europe. In spite of its name, its members usefully included the United States and Canada, as well as 37 Western and Eastern European states. Negotiations led to the signature in 1979 of the Convention on Long-Range Transboundary Air Pollution (or the ECE Convention). This committed signatories to the general goals of working to limit and reduce air pollution using the 'best available technology' that was 'economically feasible'.

In spite of the signature of the treaty, the most significant early responses to acid pollution were domestic: in Europe, West Germany was a critical actor because of its economic and political reach, and began to change policy in 1982 in the wake of research revealing substantial forest dieback, and new support for the Green party. This speeded up signature of the ECE Convention, and a large combustion plant regulation became law in West Germany in 1983, setting emissions limits for seven major pollutants, including SO_2, NO_x, and carbon monoxide. While the programme was generally considered a success, and forest dieback had ceased to be a major public issue by 1985, the view that domestic policy was not enough to deal with the problem encouraged the West German government to exert pressure for change among its European Community partners.

A draft EC directive on emissions from large industrial plants was published in April 1983, but opinion was divided on its merits: the Germans, the Dutch, and the Danish were in support; the French and the Belgians were largely indifferent because of their heavy reliance on nuclear power; and the British, the Italians, the Greeks, and the Irish were opposed. Britain was not only governed at the time by the anti-regulation Thatcher government, but, as the biggest producer of SO_2 in Western Europe, faced the greatest potential costs in making the necessary reductions, and – since most of its emissions were blown offshore – the fewest potential benefits. Britain also doubted the science, and was suspicious about the clear link with German domestic initiatives. But the growing weight of scientific evidence was confirming the extent of domestic damage from acid pollution, Britain's intransigence was harming its relations with Norway, Sweden, and its EC partners, and it ultimately conceded to the compelling weight of scientific proof.

A 1985 protocol to the ECE Convention committed signatories to cut SO_2 emissions by 30 per cent, and in 1988, after nearly five years of negotiation, agreement was reached on an EC directive on large combustion plants. The directive required a gradual reduction of emissions from existing plants and a limit on emissions from new plants, with the overall goal of cutting SO_2 emissions across the EC as a whole by 57 per cent by 2003 (from a 1980 baseline), and NO_x emissions by 30 per cent by 1998 (for details, see McCormick, 2001: ch. 8). Subsequent protocols to the ECE Convention addressed nitrogen oxides (1988), VOCs (1991), heavy metals (1998), and persistent organic pollutants (1998).

For Europe, the results of this combination of regional and international agreements have been remarkable (European Environment Agency, 2014). In 1990, today's 28 members of the European Union were producing 25.6 million tonnes of sulphur oxides among them. By 2011, emissions were down to 4.5 million tonnes, a 74 per cent reduction that took the numbers back to a level not seen since the end of the nineteenth century (see Figure 6.4). The changes were achieved by a combination of switches away from high-sulphur solid and liquid fuels to low-sulphur natural gas, the

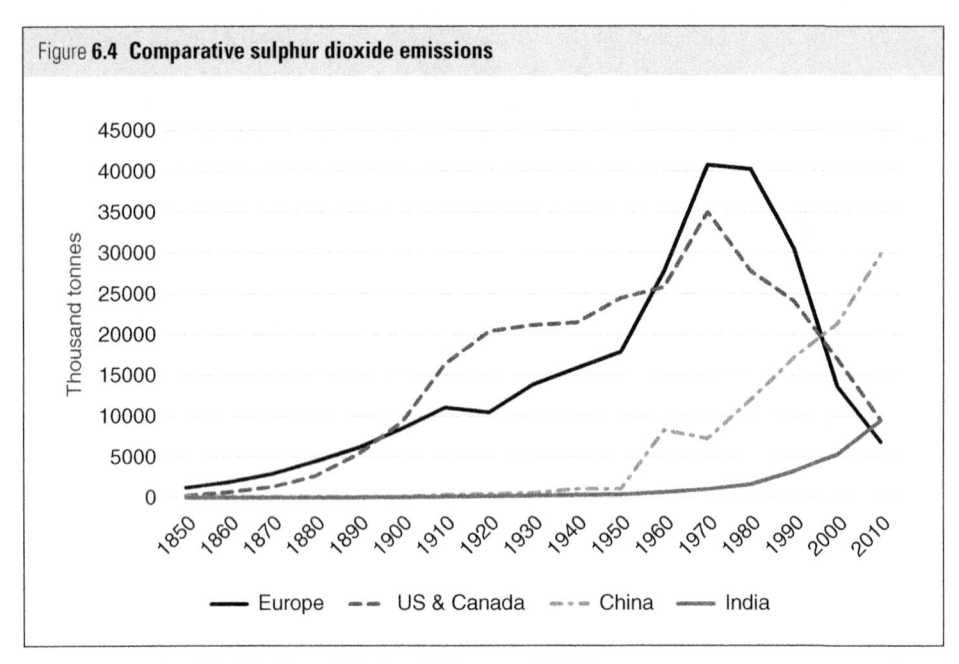

Figure 6.4 Comparative sulphur dioxide emissions

Source: Based on data in S. J. Smith et al. (2011) and Z. Klimont et al. (2013).

fitting of emissions scrubbers to industrial plants, and EU laws on the sulphur content of liquid fuels. Meanwhile, emissions of NO_x fell over the same period from 17.3 million tonnes to 8.8 million tonnes, a more modest (but still impressive) reduction of 44 per cent. These numbers were achieved through the fitting of catalytic converters to road vehicles, and changes in technology in the energy industry, including the use of low-NO_x burners, switching from coal to gas, and fitting scrubbers to industrial plants.

In North America, meanwhile, the political pressures and the emissions reductions followed a similar path. There was little effort to control emissions until changes to US clean air legislation in 1990, which capped years of growing complaints from Canada regarding emissions generated south of the border. More important, though, were changes in the balance of power in the US Congress, and in the occupancy of the White House. Numerous scientific warnings were issued during the 1980s about the effects of acid pollution on forests, lakes, soils, and buildings, but they were mainly sidestepped by the Reagan administration. Meanwhile, much of the pollution produced in the Midwestern and north-eastern United States was being carried by prevailing winds into Canada, which made great efforts to reduce its own emissions in the hope that this would encourage the United States. But American policymakers were influenced by the resistance of industrial states to take action because of fears regarding the effects on the coal and automobile industries, and by a refusal on the part of the Reagan administration to acknowledge the extent of the problem.

Even before he took office in January 1989, President George H. W. Bush had indicated his willingness to take action, helped by support from sympathetic members of Congress and continued gentle nudging from the Canadians. The 1990 amendments to the Clean Air Act introduced a cap-and-trade approach to emission reductions, setting targets for coal-fired power stations in Midwestern and eastern states, allowing them to trade emission allowances, and also allowing power companies to decide how to meet their targets (Davidson and Norbeck, 2012). There was an almost immediate reduction in SO_2 emissions: within ten years of the passage of the Clean Air Act they had fallen by 30 per cent, and by 2010 they were down nearly 60 per cent.

While acid pollution is no longer the problem that it once was in Europe and North America, history is repeating itself in newly industrialized countries. Post-war industrial growth in China, for example, resulted in the country's SO_2 emissions multiplying by nearly 3,000 per cent between 1950 and 2005, such that it is now the world's biggest producer (but has not yet overtaken the USA on a per capita basis). Studies have revealed a growing acid pollution problem near major Chinese cities (see McKibben, 2008), and while the increased use of flue gas desulphurization equipment at power stations has helped bring emissions down from a peak in 2005 of just over 32 million tonnes (Xu, 2011), little has been done to control NO_x emissions from China's road traffic. India has also fast been catching up, such that by 2010 it was producing as much SO_2 as the United States (although only about a quarter of the US total when calculated per capita). Little research has so far been undertaken into acid pollution effects in India, but the data on emissions point to the likelihood of a growing problem.

Discussion questions

- Does the blame for air pollution lie with polluting industries, with the consumers who continue to buy polluting products, or both?
- How far can industrial society reasonably be expected to go in its search for cleaner air?
- What do the cases of leaded fuel and the ozone layer tell us about the most viable answers to other air pollution problems?
- To what extent can the European and North American experience with addressing acid pollution be translated into policy initiatives in the South?

Key concepts

- Acid pollution
- Carbon dioxide
- Catalytic converter
- Chlorofluorocarbons
- Fossil fuels
- Indoor pollution
- Long-range transboundary air pollution
- Nitrogen oxides
- Ozone
- Ozone layer
- Sulphur dioxide
- Technology forcing

Further reading

Lidskog, Rolf, and Göran Sundqvist (eds) (2011) *Governing the Air: The Dynamics of Science, Policy, and Citizen Interaction* (MIT Press). A study of the international politics of air pollution, with a focus on experiences in Europe.

Markowitz, Gerald, and David Rosner (2013) *Lead Wars: The Politics of Science and the Fate of America's Children* (University of California Press). The story of how lead was allowed to become a major public health problem. For a shorter alternative, see William Kovarik (2005) 'Ethyl-leaded Gasoline: How a classic occupational disease became an international public health disaster' in *International Journal of Occupational Environmental Health* 11:4, pp. 384–97.

McGranahan, Gordon, and Frank Murray (eds) (2003) *Air Pollution and Health in Rapidly Developing Countries* (Earthscan). A survey of air pollution problems in Asian, African, and Latin American countries, contrasting the causes and responses with those in Europe and North America.

Parson, Edward A. (2003) *Protecting the Ozone Layer: Science and Strategy* (Oxford University Press). An assessment of the story behind efforts to protect the ozone layer, and some of the lessons that can be drawn.

Vallero, Daniel (2014) *Fundamentals of Air Pollution*, 5th edn (Elsevier). A comprehensive outline of the sources, effects, risks, chemistry, and control of air pollution.

7 Water: Quantity vs. Quality

Key arguments

- Unlike air, water is multidimensional in terms of the forms in which it is found, the uses to which it is put, the distribution of supplies, and the threats it faces.
- There have been improvements in access to improved water supplies and sanitation facilities, but the variable quality of water means that human health still suffers in many parts of the world.
- Water policy is still approached mainly from a local perspective, and water is still mainly seen as a private rather than a public good.
- Efforts to approach water quantity and quality from a global perspective are limited, and there is almost nothing in the way of an international water regime.
- Whether in terms of quantity or quality, water is approached mainly from the perspective of its value to humans, and less so with its ecological value in mind.
- The plight of wetlands illustrates the way in which the significance of freshwater habitats has long been overlooked.

Chapter overview

Along with air, water is one of the most essential, most fundamental, and most widely used of all natural resources. Without it, life as we know it would not be possible, and it is no surprise that almost all the world's great cities and population centres have been built on or near a ready source of surface water. Unlike air, however, which has only one use and comes in only one form, water presents a multifaceted management challenge. It comes in several different forms, it serves multiple purposes, water policy must address matters both of quantity and of quality, and while pollution is the only man-made threat to air quality, water is threatened both by pollution and by overexploitation. Too much water in the wrong place can be as much of a problem as too little water, and the environmental dimensions of water management must be seen alongside its economic, social, and even occasionally cultural dimensions.

In spite of its value, water is the subject of undeveloped and often contradictory public policy. On matters of quantity, decisions are driven less by the public interest than by commercial considerations and the interests of private owners, with political and security factors thrown in for good measure: the world has more than enough freshwater to meet the needs of humans, animals, and plants, but it is unequally distributed, creating political tensions between those parts of the world with a surfeit of water and those with a shortage. Water is also more often seen as a private good than a public good, in spite of the decision by the United Nations (UN) in 2010 to recognize the right to safe and clean drinking water and sanitation as a basic human right.

Meanwhile, quality is driven more by concerns for human health than by ecological concerns. Understandably, the provision of clean water must be a dominating planning concern, but it does not reflect well on civilized society that rivers and lakes are only minimally protected from agricultural and urban run-off, and the disposal of industrial waste and untreated sewage into surface waters remains a widespread problem. Nine per cent of the world's population still does not have access to improved sources of water – whether piped water, public taps or protected wells – and almost 850,000 preventable deaths are caused each year by dirty water or inadequate sanitation. Even in wealthy states there are still problems with incidents of pollutants entering the public water supply. And notably little effort has been made to protect freshwater supplies as habitat, whether from a domestic or an international perspective.

This chapter begins with a review of the different forms in which water is found and the many uses to which it is put, and discusses the challenges of achieving water security. It also looks at the different options available for addressing problems with supply (including the troubling effects of building dams), noting that failures to resolve water shortages can spill over into problems with security. The chapter goes on to look at the multiple threats to water quality, and at the record in achieving improved sources of drinking water and improved sanitation facilities. It then looks at the shaping of water policy, emphasizing the manner in which that policy has been mainly restricted to local and national arenas, and explaining the reasons behind the modest international response. It ends with a study of the relationship between water and ecology, illustrating the extent to which it has been overlooked by examining the case of wetlands.

Managing water supply

Freshwater constitutes only about 3 per cent of the total volume of water on earth. Most is locked up in ice caps and glaciers, and much of the balance comes in the form of groundwater, leaving less than 0.01 per cent of the total freely available to humans, animals, and plants. This is more than enough to sustain life, however, and this small fraction is constantly recycled and renewed. The problem, then, is not one of quantity but of distribution and quality: water must be available in the right place, at the right time, in the right form, and in the right quality and quantity for the many different uses to which it is put (see Table 7.1). This is a connected set of requirements that is hard to achieve: most water needs to be treated in order to make it potable (drinkable), but differences in the capacity and effort needed to provide clean water mean that much of it is contaminated, as a result of which many people die each year of water-borne diseases. And unlike

Table **7.1 A dozen different uses for water**

Domestic	Household uses, including drinking, cooking, bathing, laundry, watering grass and plants.
Commercial	Used in offices, restaurants, hotels.
Medicine	Used in multiple medical and dental procedures.
Habitat	Natural home for animal and plant species.
Navigation	Used for shipping and transportation.
Recreation	Swimming, water sports, and application to parks and sports facilities.
Industry	Used in numerous industrial processes, including mining.
Waste	A medium for the disposal of wastes and pollutants.
Nutrition	Helps keep soils naturally fertile, breaking down minerals and salts.
Energy	Used to generate hydropower.
Fisheries	A home for freshwater and marine fisheries.
Agriculture	Used for livestock, irrigation.

air, which is equally available to everyone at all times (even if its cleanliness is not always assured), and which can be neither owned nor controlled, water is unequally distributed and can be both owned and controlled.

Water security is defined by the UN as 'the capacity of a population to safeguard sustainable access to adequate quantities of acceptable quality water for sustaining livelihoods, human well-being, and socio-economic development, for ensuring protection against water-borne pollution and water-related disasters, and for preserving ecosystems in a climate of peace and political stability' (UN University, 2013). The challenges of ensuring such security begin with the five different forms in which non-saltwater is found:

- Surface water is found in rivers, lakes, and wetlands.
- **Groundwater** penetrates the soil and fills the spaces between soil particles and fractured rock.
- **Aquifers** are water-bearing rock formations that are accessed via wells and springs. While many parts of the world sit on top of large aquifers, extracting the water can be costly, and – unlike rivers and lakes, which are replenished by precipitation – aquifers are a finite resource.
- Precipitation comes in the form mainly of rain and snow.
- Frozen water is locked up in glaciers and polar ice caps.

Each of these forms present different challenges in terms of the laws and policies that pertain to ownership and distribution, the technical means for extraction and storage, and the threats posed to water quality. Some parts of the world have a water surfeit while others have a water shortage, leaving the latter with the challenge of meeting needs when nature is uncooperative, or politics intervenes. On a per capita basis, the world's two biggest states by population – China and India – both face shortfalls, as does much of the Middle East, Central Asia, Mexico and the southwest United States, most of Africa, and several European countries, including the United Kingdom, Germany, Spain, and Poland (UN World Water Assessment Programme, 2015: 12). Meanwhile, most of the rest of Europe and Latin America, along with Canada and the eastern United States, is relatively well supplied.

But the problems with distribution do not end there, because while several countries are well supplied overall, they face internal imbalances, sometimes in regions undergoing significant population growth. In the United States, for example, the Midwest and the east have few problems, but there is a deficiency in most states west of the Mississippi, made worse in the desert southwest by the rapid growth of cities such as Los Angeles, Las Vegas, and Phoenix. In South Africa, meanwhile, the constitution goes so far as to include access to sufficient water within its bill of rights, but a combination of low and unpredictable supplies, high demand, and poor use of existing resources has created water inequality (Hedden and Cilliers, 2014). The wealthy urban middle class of South Africa has enough water to keep its lawns green and its swimming pools full, while the urban poor often cannot afford to pay even for drinking water, and water shortages are increasingly common.

Piper (2015) warns of 'the coming chaos' that promises to arise from global water inequality, much of which is caused by policies that allow corporations, cities, and local governments to own the rights to water supplies. Critics argue that water is a global resource that cannot and should not be owned, but while this a simple case to make in regard to air, water is a substance that is contained, and for which investments must be made to extract it, convey it to users, divide it up among competing users, and ensure good quality. The legal and commercial logic of private water ownership is hard to oppose and deny.

Water must be managed not only to ensure needed supplies, but so as to contain its role in flooding, soil erosion, mudslides, storm surges, and siltation. All these phenomena happen naturally and have been at the heart of the formation of landscapes over the millennia, but while it is impossible to have too much air, too much water in the wrong place can lead not only to natural disasters, but to man-made disasters sparked by the building of human settlements in flood plains, the construction of faulty flood controls, the diversion of rivers, and the worsening of soil erosion as a result of deforestation.

In terms of managing supply, there are three key options:

1. Reallocating available water to meet new demands. This is not easy, because of questions relating to ownership of the water, how best to distribute it, and how to resolve disputes over competing uses. Since the ownership of groundwater is tied to the ownership of land, water shortages in some countries have been met by cities buying land far away in order to control expanded groundwater rights.
2. Using water more efficiently by conservation and recycling. About 70 per cent of freshwater is used for irrigation, the area of irrigated land worldwide having tripled since 1950, and irrigation now producing about one-third of the world's food. However, flood irrigation is inefficient because only about one-third of the water drawn off is typically used to grow crops, the rest being lost to spillage, overwatering, and evaporation. Badly managed irrigation can also turn good land into bad if soil is allowed to become waterlogged or if salt is allowed to build up in the soil.
3. Increasing the available supply of water by drilling wells and building dams. If wells are not managed and regulated, however, and if there are too many, we run the risk of reducing

the volume of groundwater. As for building dams, they have their own often serious cluster of side-effects (see Box 7.1).

The unequal supply of water – whether because of physical limits or ownership limits – is also a security issue. In 1995, then vice-president of the World Bank Ismail Serageldin warned that 'many of the wars in this century were about oil, [but] the wars of

Box 7.1 The problem of dams

Dams have been built for centuries for multiple uses: to control rivers and protect against flooding, to create inland fisheries and provide recreation, to provide reservoirs for consumers, and – more recently – to generate hydroelectricity. There are about 17,000 dams in the United States alone, generating about 7 per cent of that country's electricity supply, but China has become the leading exponent of dams, seeking to supply the water and energy needed to feed its growing population and industry; it now has approximately 25,000 large dams (Tilt, 2015). Among its biggest projects: the biggest river diversion in history, designed to move water from southern rivers to major cities 3200 km (2000 miles) to the north in three vast canal and tunnel systems, and the Three Gorges Dam, the world's largest power station by installed capacity. Built between 1994 and 2012, the dam is big enough to help China reduce its greenhouse gas emissions, but more than 1.3 million people were displaced by its construction, the dam sits on a seismic fault line, and it has disrupted ecology both upstream and downstream.

While dams can be a valuable means of managing water supply and generating electricity, they often come with multiple environmental strings attached:

- Blockage of fish migration.
- Trapping of sediments that are important for habitats and physical processes downstream.
- Interference with deltas, floodplains, and wetlands.
- Flooding or destruction of forests.
- Transformation of upstream and downstream habitats.
- Accumulation of organic matter that rots and produces greenhouse gases.
- Playing host to invasive species.
- Lowering of groundwater levels.
- The resettlement of people living in the area of the new reservoir.
- Denial of water supplies to communities living downstream.

Dams are also expensive to build and maintain, and their impact is effectively irreversible. Given the scale of the changes they introduce, Scudder (2005) asks whether governments and those who build and manage dams 'have the institutional capacity to deal with the complexity associated with such large infrastructure projects'. But he also notes their critical role in providing the growing populations of the South with electricity and with water for drinking and for irrigation. While dams can generate large amounts of hydropower, it can also be generated through the use of small water turbines that are much less expense, easier to maintain, and less environmentally disruptive.

the next century will be about water' (Crossette, 1995). He could not have anticipated that international terrorism would be about to leap to the head of the security agenda, but his warning has not been forgotten; it is reflected in the observation by Engelke and Sticklor (2015) that 'as much as oil shaped the global geopolitics of the twentieth century, water has the power to reorder international relations in the current century'. They quote the example of the drought in Syria in 2006–10 that created internal displacement that fed in to the country's civil war, and the adoption by ISIS of water access and control as primary strategic objectives. They also point to the effect of water shortages on political instability in Afghanistan, Iraq, Pakistan, and Yemen. Such problems are likely to worsen thanks to a combination of climate change, pollution, and urban expansion (Harris, 2014). Norman et al. (2015) express the problem bluntly when they argue that 'those who control water, hold power'.

Managing water quality

There are few places in the world where untreated water is uncontaminated, even if only by natural organic matter. But the problem has worsened since the Industrial Revolution owing to pollution: human activity that results in the introduction of harmful substances into a body of water at a rate exceeding the ability of the water to cleanse itself. There are multiple channels by which pollutants enter water (see Table 7.2), with implications for

Table **7.2 Sources of water pollution**

Source	Details
Industry	Chemical pollution from steel plants, the pulp and paper industry, metal foundries, and oil refineries; accidental oil and chemical spills and leaks; thermal pollution; toxic and hazardous waste disposal.
Water supply	Bacteria and other micro-organisms; heavy metals such as lead from ageing or badly maintained water supply systems; naturally occurring pollutants such as mercury.
Urban run-off	Precipitation washes oil, other petroleum products, waste, and heavy metals such as lead and cadmium off road surfaces and into rivers and streams, or leaches them down into groundwater.
Agriculture	Run-off from farmland that is treated with chemical fertilisers, pesticides, and herbicides; genetically modified crops; polluted irrigation water; animal waste.
Air pollution	Airborne pollutants entering rivers and lakes, harming or killing wildlife, undermining ecosystems, and polluting drinking water.
Sewage	Mainly (but not wholly) resolved in the North, but many in the South still suffer the effects of unimproved water supply and sanitation systems.

human health, the welfare of ecosystems and biodiversity, and the well-being of freshwater fisheries.

There are two broad sources of water pollution, each of which demands different policy responses. The first consists of **point sources**, or individual and usually identifiable sources such as factories, sewage outlets, leaks from underground storage tanks, waste dumps, or the accidental release of pollutants through oil and chemical spills. Some of these sources also generate **thermal pollution**: the release of warm water into rivers or lakes, which changes freshwater biology by encouraging the growth of non-native species of fish and plants. Because they are relatively easy to identify, point sources are also potentially containable, but this demands regulation; rivers and lakes are a handy outlet for waste, and protecting them means setting agreed limits and monitoring compliance, almost always easier said than done.

Greater challenges are created by **non-point sources**: the diffuse result of general human activity, including farming, mining, energy production, forestry, the growth of cities, and construction. They are affected by a multitude of variables such as rainfall, land use, climate, the topology of land, and local vegetation, and are mainly carried into surface waters and groundwater as a result of rainfall. We can see them and we can monitor their effects, but they are difficult to control precisely because they are so diffuse. The major non-point source of water pollution is urban run-off, which occurs when precipitation falls on city streets and buildings. Little of that precipitation is absorbed back into the soil and into groundwater, and most instead runs off into drains, and usually ends up in nearby rivers and lakes, taking with it a variety of pollutants, including oil from road vehicles, chemicals used for de-icing, animal and human waste, garbage, and the chemicals leached out of the air by rain and snow. As cities have grown and traffic flows have increased, the volume of urban run-off has grown.

Agriculture is another non-point source, posing particular problems in the North, where farming has intensified, the use of chemicals has expanded, and the volume of animal waste has grown. Run-off from farmland treated with chemicals carries potassium and nitrogen compounds into groundwater and into neighbouring rivers and lakes, and the water used for irrigation can become contaminated with salts, wastes, and chemicals. The threat posed to groundwater is particularly worrying because the pollution moves so slowly through soil that efforts to address the problem can take years to make themselves felt.

There are two major effects of water pollution. The lesser of the two is **eutrophication**: the depletion of oxygen in water as a result of excess nutrients. Naturally occurring nutrients such as nitrates and phosphates help plants grow in rivers and lakes, but their volume can be increased by discharges from sewage treatment plants and agricultural run-off, encouraging the growth of algae. This depletes the amount of oxygen in water, reduces light penetration, kills off aquatic plants, increases the acidity of the water, and creates dead zones that lack enough oxygen to support aquatic life. Water can become hypoxic (oxygen poor), or, in the worst cases, anoxic (little or no oxygen remaining). The problem is found most often in freshwater lakes and in marine coastal areas near nutrient-rich rivers. As well as degrading water quality, eutrophication can change the ecosystems found in rivers and lakes, undermine fisheries, and allow for the build-up of bacteria, making water harmful for consumption by humans, domestic animals, and wildlife.

The second and much bigger effect of pollution, and the most immediately worrying as far as human health is concerned, is the contamination of drinking water. Safe, clean water is not just one of the fundamental requirements for life on earth, but was recognized in a 2010 UN General Assembly resolution as 'essential for the full enjoyment of the right to life' (Sultana and Loftus, 2012). There are few better benchmarks for the state of the human environment than the quality of drinking water, and most people in the North take it for granted that when they turn on a tap they will be given clean water that smells and tastes good. Unfortunately, it is not always possible to rely on that one simple assumption; even less so for the urban and rural poor of the South. Contaminants have three main effects:

- Physical changes by which the appearance of water changes as a result of sediment and organic matter.
- Chemical changes brought on by naturally occurring and human-made heavy metals and chemicals, such as lead, arsenic, selenium, and uranium. More of these have found their way into water supplies in the North because so many supply pipes are old and decaying; it was normal once to use lead pipes to supply water (the word *plumber* derives from *plumbum*, the Latin for lead), and lead contamination remains a worrying problem.
- Biological changes brought on by microbial or bacterial contamination, notably faecal matter that can introduce cryptosporidium, E. coli, or legionella, and that can lead to outbreaks of cholera, typhoid, and dysentery.

The availability of clean water has improved, such that 90 per cent of the world's population now has access to 'improved' sources of drinking water, defined by the World Health Organization (WHO) as sources whose construction protects water from

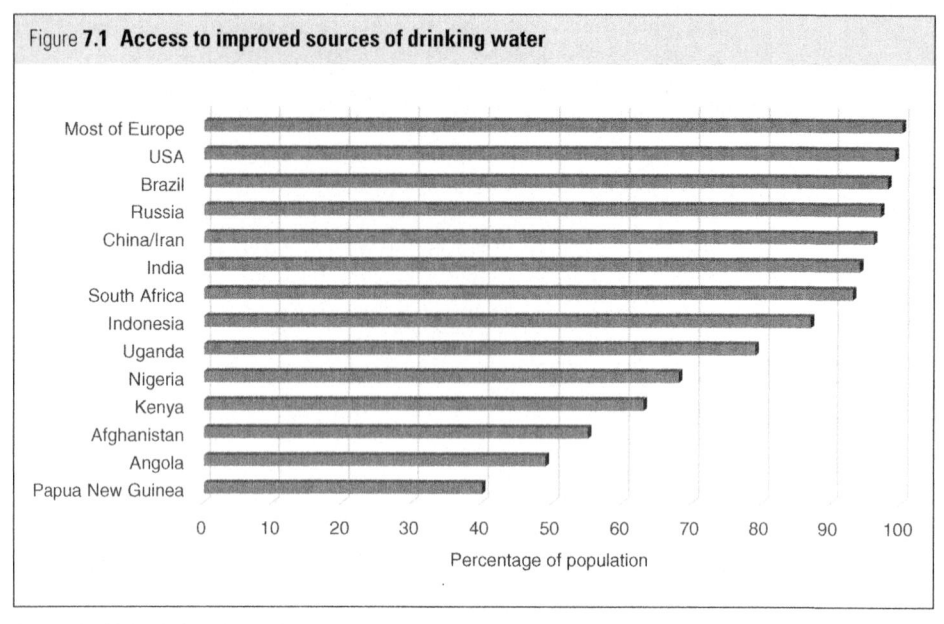

Figure 7.1 **Access to improved sources of drinking water**

Country	
Most of Europe	~100
USA	~100
Brazil	~98
Russia	~97
China/Iran	~95
India	~94
South Africa	~93
Indonesia	~87
Uganda	~79
Nigeria	~69
Kenya	~63
Afghanistan	~55
Angola	~49
Papua New Guinea	~40

Percentage of population

Source: World Health Organization database at http://gamapserver.who.int/gho/interactive_charts (accessed February 2017). Data are for 2015.

contamination, particularly from faecal matter. Although this is a marked improvement since 1990, when only 76 per cent of people had access, the rates vary by country, from 100 per cent in most of Europe to 50–75 per cent in Africa (see Figure 7.1). Out of a global population of about 7.3 billion people, WHO data suggests that 4.2 billion have access to piped water, 2.4 billion have access to other improved sources such as public taps and protected wells, but 660 million (about 9 per cent of the total) have no improved sources, including 160 million dependent on surface water (World Health Organization, 2016).

The provision of improved sources does not mean that the water they provide is perfectly clean, given the multiple channels through which contaminants can enter water supplies. Drinking water has been found to contain several hundred organic or synthetic chemicals, many of which have either never been tested for toxicity and/or remain unregulated. Of particular concern is the effect of pollution on groundwater, which accounts for a large proportion of the public water supply in many countries. Guide levels for nitrates are thought to be exceeded in groundwater beneath more than 85 per cent of agricultural land in Europe, maximum concentration limits are exceeded beneath about 20 per cent of agricultural land, and the evidence from different kinds of aquifers in different parts of Europe suggests that pollutant concentrations are growing (see later in chapter). Two recent examples from the United States offer a hint of the nature of the problem:

- One (Hu et al., 2016) found that drinking water supplies for 6 million people contained levels of polyfluoroalkyl and perfluoroalkyl substances (PFASs) above those set by the federal government. Used for decades in many applications, including food wrappers, clothing, and cooking utensils, PFASs have been linked to cancer, hormone disruption, and obesity. The report noted that while their use has been discontinued by many manufacturers, the chemicals tend to persist, and could be a more widespread problem given that data was unavailable for drinking water supplies for about one-third of the US population, or more than 100 million people.
- Another study (Andrews and Walker, 2016) found that water supplies reaching about two-thirds of the American population were contaminated by hexavalent chromium, a carcinogen whose high levels in the water supply of a town in California were the target of campaigning in the early 1990s by local resident Erin Brockovich, whose story was made into a film starring Julia Roberts.

Ironically, multiple chemicals are added to drinking water in the interests of making the water 'cleaner' and better tasting. They include purifiers such as liquefied chlorine and aluminium sulphate, the by-products of disinfectants such as bromates, and the addition of fluoride to public water supplies in many countries – beginning in the United States in the 1940s – as a mass medication programme designed to reduce tooth decay. Opinion on fluoridation is divided, with some research suggesting health threats, or – at best – no advantages, while the US Centers for Disease Control considers community water fluoridation to have been one of the 'ten great public health achievements of the 20th century' (CDC, 1999). It continues to be used in the United States, Britain, Canada, Australia, and a small group of other countries, but is no longer used in Germany, Sweden, the Netherlands, and Japan (Fawell et al., 2006).

One kind of pollution that is almost universal, and poses major health problems in poorer countries, is untreated sewage. Overall, nearly two-thirds of humans live without access to basic sanitation in the form of flush toilets and sewage treatment (Baum et al., 2013). Looking at the regional picture, the problem has been largely resolved in wealthier states with more sophisticated sewage treatment systems: in North America and Europe, and in several states in the South (such as Saudi Arabia and Singapore), there is near-universal access to improved sanitation facilities (those that separate faecal matter from human contact). In China and

Figure 7.2 **Access to improved sanitation facilities**

US/Canada
Japan/S Korea
Saudi Arabia
Germany/UK/France
Poland
Egypt
Iran/Ireland
Mexico
Brazil
Romania
China
Russia
South Africa
Indonesia
India
Kenya/Nigeria
Uganda
South Sudan

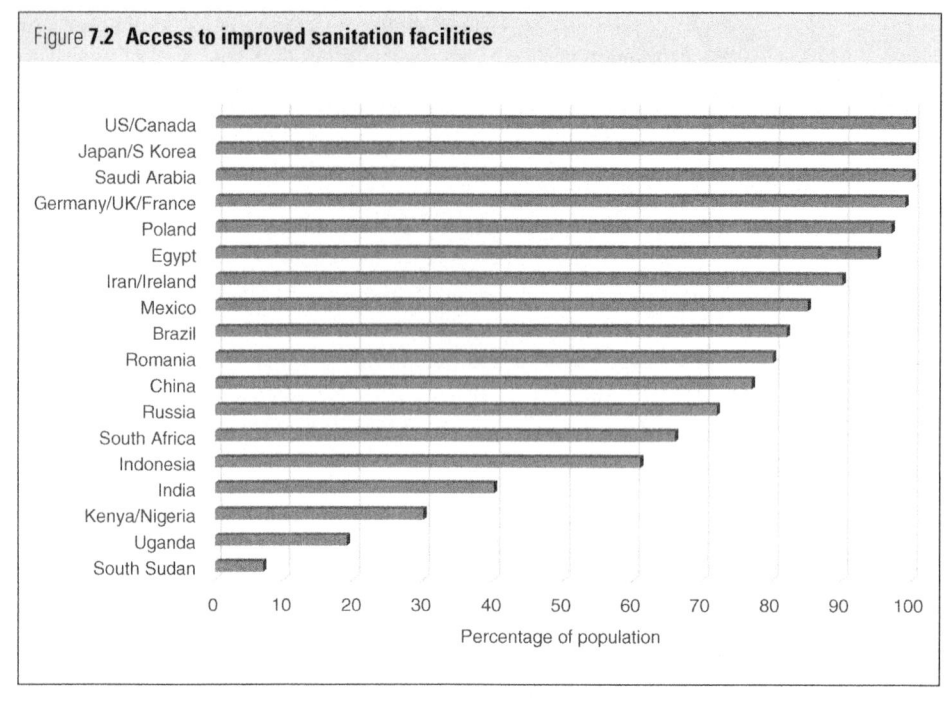

Percentage of population

Source: World Health Organization database at http://gamapserver.who.int/gho/interactive_charts (accessed February 2017). Data are for 2015.

Russia, meanwhile, there is about 75 per cent access. But only 40 per cent of Indians are protected by improved sewage treatment, the numbers falling to 25–30 per cent in more developed African states, and as low as 10–15 per cent in their less developed neighbours (see Figure 7.2).

In most cases in the South, the numbers are lower for the urban poor and for people living in rural areas. Even where people have working water-based toilets, untreated sewage may end up being discharged into drains, rivers, or coastal seas, and waste can seep out of pit latrines into local groundwater. The contamination produces a range of health effects, from dysentery to typhoid, cholera, schistosomiasis, hepatitis A, and intestinal infections. WHO estimates that almost 850,000 preventable deaths are caused each year by diarrhoea resulting from dirty water or inadequate sanitation, with young children being the most seriously impacted (World Health Organization, 2016).

Pollution and changes to freshwater ecosystems also pose a threat to biodiversity and freshwater fisheries, although the data are fragmented and we understand little about the details of the problem. Few of the world's rivers and lakes are unaffected, posing problems for species and ecosystems alike; despite making up only 0.01 per cent of the volume of the world's water, freshwater is estimated to contain about 6 percent of the described species of animals and plants (Dudgeon et al., 2006), and scientists worry that the rates of decline of species in freshwaters have overtaken those on land (Vaughn, 2010). As well as the threats described in Chapter 10 (habitat destruction, invasive species, pollution, population growth, and overexploitation), river ecology is also

---

Box 7.2 *The dubious benefits of bottled water*

Many consumers address their concerns about the quality of drinking water by turning to bottled water. This can make good sense in those parts of the world where the quality of the water supply cannot be trusted, or where water is not easily available, but bottled water makes less sense where water supply systems are improved and reliable. This is particularly so given that the standards for bottled water and for reliable tap water are approximately the same. The International Bottled Water Association (2015: 13) boasts that 'conscientious consumers' are attracted by the lack of calories and artificial ingredients in bottled water, and notes its 'healthfulness, convenience, safety, and value', the versatility that 'makes it suitable for consumption at any time of day and in just about any setting or situation', and its relatively low price compared to other 'ready-to-drink commercial beverages'. However, bottled water can cost many times more – per unit – than tap water, and the International Bottled Water Association overlooks the fact that it demands the production and safe disposal of plastic containers, as well as the transport, energy, and infrastructure costs of shipment to retail outlets. In short, bottled water increases the volume of plastic waste and the amount of energy we consume. Ironically, many of the biggest bottled water consumption figures are found in those parts of the world with the best supplies of clean drinking water (see Figure 7.3).

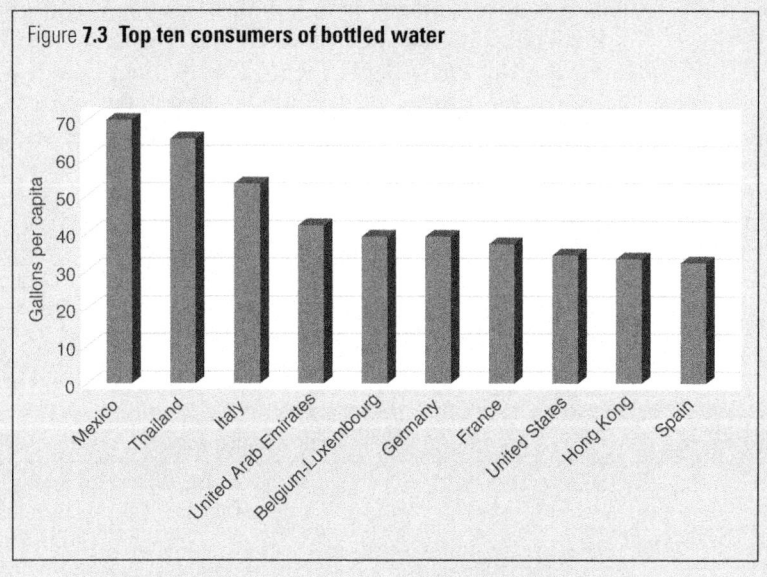

Figure **7.3 Top ten consumers of bottled water**

Source: International Bottled Water Association (2015). Figures are for 2014.

impacted by the alteration of the natural flow of rivers by the building of dams and canals. The problems become more serious further downstream as rivers approach human settlements and are more actively exploited. The result is a decline not just in common species but also entire food webs as a result of knock-on effects beyond the impacted species.

Shaping water policy

Unlike air pollution, which began as a local problem and then became international as emissions grew, smokestacks became taller, and pollutants were blown across borders, water quality is still mainly defined and approached as a local matter. While air is a global resource that cannot be owned, and to which access cannot be controlled or limited, most of the water we consume comes from local sources, is owned by corporations or governments, is subject to domestic quality laws (where they exist), and is sold as a commodity to mainly domestic end-users. Water policy can often clearly be an international matter, to be sure, as when two or more countries share a river, a lake, or an aquifer, or when pollution or silt is washed down rivers that flow through two or more countries, or into lakes or aquifers that are shared by two or more countries. Even so, the relatively contained nature of bodies of freshwater means that there is almost nothing in the way of an international water regime, and the emphasis with water policy is on domestic rather than international law and policy. (The exception, of course, is marine pollution, discussed in Chapter 8.)

It is revealing that water is rarely the named responsibility of national government departments, and in those cases where it is (such as China, India, Jordan, Kenya, Nepal, Pakistan, Tanzania, and Uganda), it is usually defined as a public good and is more

Table **7.3 Comparing air and water policy**

	Air	Water
Uses	Respiration	Drinking, farming, industry, fisheries, recreation, energy generation, habitat, transport.
Forms	Gas	Surface, groundwater, precipitation, salt water, ice.
Management	Cannot be owned	Can be (and often is) owned or controlled by governments or corporations.
Threats	Pollution, mainly from use of fossil fuels	Pollution, distribution of supply, management, security, climate change.
Pollutants	300+	Countless.
Information	Hard data on trends	Little hard data on trends or supplies.

often tied to agriculture, energy, or irrigation than to the environment. (In Australia it is tied to sport, recreation, and forestry). In short, it is considered a private commercial good where the emphasis is placed on the quality of water for direct human consumption rather than on the welfare of freshwater ecosystems.

Efforts to discuss water quality from a global perspective date back to 1977 and the convening of the World Water Conference in Mar del Plata, Argentina, which launched the water supply and sanitation decade (1981–90). The benchmark for drinking water quality is the set of guidelines provided by the World Health Organization (2011), first drawn up in 1993 and revised periodically since then. This lists the major microbial and chemical contaminants of drinking water, and discusses the best means for ensuring clean water, but does not set standards, arguing that they vary from place to place, and that there is no universally applicable approach. 'It is essential in the development and implementation of standards' argue the guidelines 'that the current or planned legislation relating to water, health and local government is taken into account and that the capacity of regulators in the country is assessed. Approaches that may work in one country or region will not necessarily transfer to other countries or regions.' The guidelines note the importance of accounting for 'local or national environmental, social, economic and cultural conditions'.

A number of gestures have been made in the direction of drawing international attention to water quality, but they have mainly been symbolic rather than substantive. In September 2000, the Millennium Summit – convened in New York to discuss the role of the UN at the turn of the millennium – resulted in the adoption of a set of Millennium Development Goals aimed at eradicating poverty and hunger, achieving universal primary education, reducing child mortality, combatting disease, and promoting gender equality, all by 2015. One of the specific targets was to halve the proportion of the global population without sustainable access to safe drinking water and basic sanitation (a target that was met five years ahead of schedule). Shortly after the summit, in 2002, the Johannesburg World Summit for Sustainable Development produced a declaration in which water quality and availability featured prominently, and the UN General Assembly then declared 2005–15 to be the international 'Water for Life Decade'. Finally, in 2010, the General Assembly adopted a resolution recognizing 'the right to safe and clean drinking water and sanitation as a human right that is essential for the full enjoyment of life and all human rights', and calling on states 'to provide financial resources, capacity-building and technology transfer … in particular to developing countries, in order to scale up efforts to provide safe, clean, accessible and affordable drinking water and sanitation for all'.

Because water pollution comes from multiple sources, and policy is driven by national rather than international interests, there is little in the way of global, international, or even regional approaches to water matters. Responses must be tailored to the particular circumstances of different states, the key distinctions being found in the contrasting needs of wealthy, industrializing, and poorer states. Institutionally, water is on the agenda of UN bodies such as the UN Environment Programme, the World Bank, the WHO, and the Food and Agriculture Organization, but for different reasons. And private control of water has been a key theme throughout. The World Bank, for example, has usually insisted on the privatization of water as a condition for its lending, emphasizing the idea of water as an economic good rather than a public good (Newig and Challies, 2014).

The World Water Council was created in 1996, but it is not what it might at first seem: it claims to be interested in promoting awareness and building political commitment on water issues, including the sustainable use of water for the benefit of all, but it charges a substantial membership fee, and has a large corporate presence. It organizes a triennial World Water Forum for its members (the eighth is scheduled for 2018), the purpose of which is to share knowledge on water issues and to encourage collaboration among its 'stakeholders', consisting of a combination of government departments, international organizations, water professionals, and private companies.

Piper (2015) is deeply critical of both the Council and the Forum, noting the visibly dominant role played in both by major corporations with a vested financial interest in controlling water supplies; they include Suez and Veolia of France, Agbar of Spain, and Thames Water of the UK. Few of these are household names, but among them they control 73 per cent of the world's privatized water supplies, and – as demand for water in China grows – they are being joined by Chinese companies such as Beijing Water Enterprises. She comments disparagingly on the 2012 meeting of the World Water Forum in Morocco at which 'predominantly white men in blue suits drink champagne and eat caviar while deciding the future of ... imaginary slum dwellers' represented by a replica slum built outside the conference hall, while access by grassroots activists was carefully controlled. In few places is the corporate role in water policy more clearly show than at the Global Water Summit held annually since 2006, and bringing together government ministers and water company CEOs. The website for the 2017 summit (held in Madrid) announced that the summit had 'always been about connections: water meets money, public meets private, business meets opportunity'.

Other institutions with an interest in water include the International Water Resources Association, an NGO founded in 1971 with the goal of promoting sustainable use of water, and the Global Water Partnership, founded in 1996 by the World Bank, the UN Development Programme, and the Swedish International Development Agency, with the goal of promoting the Dublin principles. The latter came out of the International Conference on Water and the Environment, held in Dublin in 1992 in preparation for the Rio Earth Summit. They recognized that water was finite and vulnerable, that water management should involve the participation of users and planners at all levels, that women played a special role in the provision and safeguarding of water, and that water should be recognized as an economic good. (Tellingly, there was no mention in the principles of the ecological value of water.)

On the legal front, there are numerous national laws dealing with water supply and water quality, but they are rarely as developed as laws dealing with air quality. In the United States, for example, there is a significant set of air quality standards, and there has been considerable progress in reducing airborne concentrations of key pollutants such as sulphur dioxide, nitrogen oxides, and lead. But while federal water law dates back to 1948, it has often set unrealistic targets, has generated little information about water quality, has failed to produce a reliable system for monitoring trends, and – in the view of Rosenbaum (2017) – has often been more inspirational than achievable.

In the European Union, water pollution is the target of one of the oldest and most completely developed sectors of regional environmental policy, resulting in regime-like qualities. Its development began in the 1970s, when the focus was on human health rather than environmental protection, and the focus was on setting water quality objectives which defined the minimum quality requirements needed to limit the cumulative effect of pollution, and to ensure there was no damage to human health (and later to the aquatic environment). A second phase of legislation in the 1990s included directives on urban waste water treatment and the control of nitrates used in agriculture. A third phase began in 1996 with a fundamental rethink of policy, agreement on the need for a more global approach to water quality management, and the adoption in 2000 of a framework water directive designed to offer a more strategic approach (Delreux and Happaerts, 2016: 170–72). The results have been mixed: overall, water quality in the EU has improved, with a steady application of standards across the older member states, and improvements in newer and mainly Eastern European states with less advanced water treatment systems. Pollution from agriculture continues to pose a problem, though, the main sources being fertilizers and manure (European Environment Agency, 2016).

The emphasis on local and state approaches to water policy has left little in the way of international policy beyond the management of shared lakes and river basins. There are nearly 300 shared rivers in the world, about a third of which are the subject of more than 500 international agreements (some dating back to the 1800s), and more than half of which are the subject of an international basin organization (Dombrowsky, 2008; Schmeier, 2013). The interests of these agreements and organizations run the gamut from water quality and quantity to hydropower, flood control, navigation and irrigation. Examples include the International Commission for the Protection of the Rhine (a river that runs through nine countries), the Mekong River Commission, and the Niger Basin Authority. Many of these bodies are members of regional or continental basin organizations, which have their own coordinating body in the form the Paris-based International Network of Basin Organizations. Not all these basin organizations have lived up to expectations, however, as a result of which many rivers remain overexploited (Schmeier, 2014).

Watercourses are also the subject of the only two international (actually, regional) framework agreements on freshwater: the 1992 Convention on the Protection and Use of Transboundary Watercourses and International Lakes (which, like the Convention on Long-range Transboundary Air Pollution discussed in Chapter 6, is maintained by the UN Economic Commission for Europe), and the 1997 UN Convention on the Law of the Non-Navigational Uses of International Watercourses (otherwise known as the UN Watercourses Convention). The former has been ratified by the EU and 40 European states, and aims to encourage cooperation on water quality and quantity among states that mainly have a strong record of cooperation in numerous policy areas. Meanwhile, the UN Watercourse Convention traces its roots back to the first discussions about watercourses in the UN in the 1950s, and more specifically to a 1970 UN resolution hinting at the need for an international agreement. But the treaty was not adopted until 1997, and while more than 100 UN member states voted in favour of adoption, only 36 had ratified by the time it came into force in 2014. The main problem has been a tension between upriver and downriver states over the goal built into the treaty of reasonable use, overlapping with concerns about loss of sovereignty (Salman, 2007).

Pahl-Wostl et al. (2008) argue the importance of taking a more global approach to water governance, based on four principles: the hydrological system is a global system; the driving forces behind water-related problems often lie outside the reach of local or state government; many of the local environmental phenomena that surround water (such as erosion, loss of biodiversity, and urbanization) imply worrying global trends; and many of the direct and indirect impacts of the loss of water quality and quantity are likely to have global implications on food production, the spread of disease, and migratory species, for example. These are all sound arguments, but progress on international water agreements remains limited.

Water and ecology: The case of wetlands

Much of the political debate about water has centred on its quality and supply, with a clear emphasis on its importance to humans; but even then, as we have seen, progress on water policy has been halting. Much less of the debate has focused on the ecological dimension of clean and unpolluted water, and yet the welfare of water as a resource and as a habitat go hand in hand. One aspect of water as habitat concerns **wetlands**, or the kind of water-saturated land that we usually refer to as swamps, bogs, and marshes. They are found on every continent except Antarctica, and play a critical role in feeding rivers, trapping floodwaters, recharging supplies of groundwater, regulating water levels in watersheds, purifying water, sustaining fisheries, supporting biodiversity, functioning as important stopovers for migratory species of animals and birds, and mitigating climate change through their role as carbon sinks. Famous examples include the Camargue of France, the Okavango Delta of Botswana, the Sundarbans of Bangladesh, the Everglades of the United States, and the Pantanal of Brazil, Bolivia, and Paraguay.

Regrettably, wetlands have long been seen as wastelands and as barriers to development, the emphasis being placed on their 'reclamation' in the interests of making room for expanded agriculture and urban settlement. As a result, they face more serious threats than any other type of ecosystem. Smardon (2009) describes them as 'the world's most important environmental resources', but also worries that they 'remain among the world's least understood and most seriously abused assets'. It is hard to say how much wetland has been lost, because so much had already been converted before records began to be kept, but estimates suggest that about half the original area of specific kinds of wetland in North America, Europe, and Australasia was lost during the twentieth century alone (Smardon, 2009).

In policy terms, wetlands face similar challenges to water resources more generally: they have been approached mainly as a local or national resource (even though they often have regional and global ecological significance), many are privately owned, and wetland protection has been the subject of only modest international cooperation. The major international agreement is the Convention on Wetlands of International Importance, usually known as the Ramsar Convention for the Iranian city where it was agreed in 1971. Signatories undertake to include wetlands conservation in their national development plans, to each designate at least one wetland within their borders as having international significance, and to include wetlands among their protected areas. Just over 160 countries have signed the convention, and more than 2,200 sites have been added to the list of wetlands, covering 2.1 million square kilometres (an area equivalent to that of Greenland) (Ramsar Convention website, 2017). Wetlands have also been given special designation as World Biosphere Reserves under the UNESCO Man and the Biosphere Programme, and under the Convention on the Conservation of Migratory Species (see Chapter 10).

The numbers, however, often tell a better story than the realities of protection: designations and fine rhetoric do not necessarily translate into meaningful action. This is illustrated by the story of the Everglades of Florida, among the most internationally famous of wetlands. They have suffered as a result of economic development dating back to the late 1800s (Grunwald, 2006), including the construction of levees and canals designed to divert water to the growing cities of Miami and Fort Lauderdale, and conversion of land to sugarcane farms. As a result, about half the original area of the Everglades was lost during the twentieth century, in spite of the declaration of the Everglades National Park in 1947 (which only covered the southern half of the wetlands). A Comprehensive Everglades Restoration Plan was agreed by the US Congress in 2000, but little progress has since been made in pursuing the plan thanks to political resistance. The debate about the Everglades has recently expanded to focus on the value of the region as a carbon sink, but this argument continues to come up against the scepticism of those who deny the link between climate change and human action (see Chapter 12).

The much lesser known Pantanal – found mostly in Brazil but spilling over into Bolivia and Paraguay – benefits from being far away from major population centres, but suffers the effects of being mainly privately owned. It covers an area about the size of nearby Uruguay, making it the world's largest freshwater wetland, and has the highest concentration of wildlife in South America. But only a small part of the area is protected by the Pantanal National Park, and despite the region's designation (like that of the Everglades) as a World Biosphere Reserve and a World Heritage Site, there have been plans to dredge rivers in the area, and to build hydropower projects.

The wetlands dilemma is ultimately one of attitude. When most people think of marshes and swamps, positive images rarely come to mind. They have often been portrayed in popular culture as dark and threatening, and the prevailing economic view is that they are wasted space. This is slowly changing as more people understand their ecological significance, and as they become a draw for tourists seeking wilderness experiences. But the political and policy responses to wetlands have lagged far behind the notion of their intrinsic ecological value, and will continue to do so until the practical arguments to protecting wetlands are more widely understood and accepted.

Discussion questions

- If access to safe and clean drinking water is a human right, how have we failed to effectively protect that right, and what changes are needed to improve the record?
- With states thinking of water as a national resource, how can we encourage them to work together on water policy?
- Are the lessons of our record with air quality transferrable to the approaches we take to water quality?
- Is the development of a global water regime possible, or even desirable?

Key concepts

Aquifer	Point source
Eutrophication	Thermal pollution
Groundwater	Water security
Non-point sources	Wetlands

Further reading

Conca, Ken (2006) *Governing Water: Contentious Transnational Politics and Global Institution Building* (MIT Press). Assess the complex political struggles behind the development of a system of global governance for water, arguing the case of alternative institutions in the wake of the weaknesses of traditional interstate regimes.

Feldman, David L. (2017) *Water Politics: Governing Our Most Precious Resource* (Polity Press). An assessment of the politics of water supply and quality, drawing on examples from multiple countries and underling the urgency of improved cooperation.

Piper, Karen (2015) *The Price of Thirst: Global Inequality and the Coming Chaos* (University of Minnesota Press). A study that is critical of the role of business in water supply, charging that financial considerations play more of a role than human need in shaping water distribution.

Salzman, James (2013) *Drinking Water: A History* (Overlook Duckworth). A study of the politics and economics behind the provision of a glass of safe drinking water.

Smardon, Richard C. (2009) *Sustaining the World's Wetlands: Setting Policy and Resolving Conflicts* (Springer). A study of wetlands policy, comparing cases from different parts of the world.

8 Natural Resources: Forests, Oceans, and Fisheries

Key arguments

- Approaches to natural resources vary according to whether they are renewable or non-renewable, finite or infinite, global or local, and private, public, or common pool goods.
- Developing policy on natural resources pits economic considerations against environmental considerations.
- Forests are seen as a domestic resource, and efforts to build a global forestry regime – or even to encourage states to take common approaches – have failed.
- The regional approach to managing forests, oceans, and fisheries has so far resulted in more progress than the global approach.
- Oceans face threats on four fronts – overfishing, pollution, climate change, and habitat destruction – and we know remarkably little about their condition.
- The political response to managing fisheries has lagged far behind the demand for fish and improvements in the efficiency of fishing.

Chapter overview

Environmental policy is not just concerned with qualitative matters such as clean air and water, but also with quantitative matters, prime among them being the management of **natural resources**. These are materials or commodities found naturally on earth that have value to humans, and include land, water, plants, animals, soil, minerals, fossil fuels, forests, fisheries, and the open ocean. They can be consumed directly, as in the case of food and drinking water, or indirectly, as in the case of forests that provide timber and fuelwood. Their value and necessity demands that they be managed to ensure continued availability, but how they are managed depends upon their type, of which there are four:

- Some are finite in supply, and once used will not naturally regenerate. Examples include fossil fuels (oil, natural gas, and coal) and groundwater in certain aquifers.
- A few – such as solar and wind energy – are infinite in supply, no matter how much we use them.
- Others – such as fisheries and forests – are also infinite in supply, but only if managed so as to ensure constant replenishment.
- Some are infinite in supply because they can be reused or recycled. Examples include water and minerals.

Cross-cutting these types, resources can be classified as either ubiquitous or localized. As examples of the former, solar energy and air are found everywhere on earth and are accessible to everyone, free of the limitations that arise from ownership or territorial boundaries. Most resources, however, are localized, meaning that they are geographically restricted, with different parts of the earth being relatively well or badly endowed. Some parts of the world have extensive forests, for example, while others have none, and some parts of the world have large stocks of freshwater while others are deserts. Thus distribution becomes a problem, giving some states advantages and others disadvantages, prompting different perspectives on how they should be used.

Further cross-cutting these types (and as we saw in Chapter 2), resources can be classified as public, private, common, and toll. All land, freshwater, soil, minerals, fossil fuels, and forests are owned in some fashion, whether privately, by corporations, by local governments, or by states, so their management is determined by the policies of their owners, and by laws governing their extraction and use. In economic terms, such resources are both rivalrous (consumption by one user precludes consumption by others) and excludable (those who do not own them cannot use them). But many resources – notably air, most fisheries, and the open oceans – are common pool goods that are also rivalrous, but non-excludable, meaning that others cannot be prevented from using them.

> This chapter begins with a review of natural resources and their qualities, focusing particularly on the economics of the relationship between humans and natural resources, and the tension between exploitation and preservation. It then takes an example of a private resource (forests) and two common pool resources (the oceans and fisheries), and compares and contrasts the policy record in managing them. National and international responses have had mixed results, for sometimes different reasons, while regional responses have often been more successful.

Defining the problem

Whether directly or indirectly, we all need access to food, air, water, land, energy, and minerals. These are all examples of natural resources, which need careful use and efficient management in order to guarantee supplies in the right form, in the right place, at the right time, at the right price, and of the right quality. As we saw with the case of water, achieving this goal has not always been easy, thanks to a combination of imbalances in supply and demand, questionable priorities, competing political and economic interests, poor management decisions, and a failure always to keep up with changing needs. Since the beginning of the Industrial Revolution and the accompanying explosion in human population, the demand for natural resources has grown. This has not – in itself – been a problem, but we have often undermined supply through unsustainable exploitation and inefficient use, and exploitation has often come with environmental costs, such as pollution. In short, it has been a story less of management than of mismanagement.

At the heart of the dilemma lie the contrasting challenges of managing resources that are renewable and non-renewable. In the latter case, a combination of history, technology, and geography started us out on a path that resulted in a deep economic and political reliance on sources of energy that are finite: we rely for more than 80 per cent of our energy needs on coal, oil, and natural gas, all of which will eventually run out. True, this will not happen any time soon, but our continued reliance only postpones the day when change must come, and we are meanwhile failing fully to address the environmental harm created by their extraction, transport, and consumption. We are also holding ourselves hostage to the problems created by an imbalance in their supply; about half of known global oil reserves are found in the Middle East, giving the region a level of global influence that is out of all proportion to the size of its population (3 per cent of the world total) or to the reach of its non-oil economic activities.

In the case of renewable resources, we must further sub-divide them into those that are infinite in supply, those that are infinite only if managed sustainably, and those that are reusable or recyclable (see Table 8.1). Each demands different policy responses, the general rule so far having been that we have invested relatively little in the few truly renewable resources (such as solar and wind power), have a mixed record on the sustainable management of fisheries and forests, and are not investing enough in recycling or reuse. We have also tended to approach many of these resources from a national rather than a global perspective, and have failed to develop the kinds of universal responses to their management that would better ensure their continued supply.

To begin with domestic resources, our stocks of fossil fuels, forests, arable land, fresh water, and inland or coastal fisheries vary, and being well-endowed in a resource is not necessarily the advantage it might seem; it poses challenges to the making of domestic policy because of competing ideas about how those resources are best used and shared. As we saw in Chapter 4, some countries suffer from a resource curse: abundant supplies of oil or minerals, for example, which come to dominate politics and economics. Others – including Colombia, Côte d'Ivoire, the Democratic Republic of the Congo, Liberia, Rwanda, and Sudan – have found themselves emerging from civil conflict only to face the challenge of ensuring peace through the careful management of resources; such management, argue Bruch et al. (2016), is 'crucial to rebuilding governance and the rule of law, combatting corruption,

Table 8.1 **Types of natural resources**

Type	Examples	Qualities
Non-renewable, finite in supply	Fossil fuels (oil, coal, natural gas) and groundwater in certain aquifers	Cannot be remade, regrown, or regenerated Gone once used, giving them the least long-term value.
Renewable, infinite in supply	Solar, wind, and geothermal energy	Universally available, and will never run out no matter how much we use them, giving them the greatest long-term value.
Renewable, potentially infinite in supply	Fisheries, forests, animals, plants, soil	Will only remain available if managed sustainably. Otherwise subject to shortages and depletion.
Reusable	Water	Indefinitely reusable, but unequal allocation, and depletable.
Recyclable	Minerals, paper, glass	Either finite but indefinitely reusable (minerals) or recyclable and replenishable (paper and glass).

improving transparency and accountability, engaging disenfranchised populations, and building confidence after conflict'.

Others find themselves with large resources for which competing demands remain unresolved. Take, for example, forests in the United States. The country is well-endowed in temperate forest, which was the natural vegetation of large swathes of the region before the advent of European settlement, and which still covers about a third of the land area of the United States. The main federal government agency responsible for forest management is the US Forest Service, which must operate – according to the 1960 Multiple Use and Sustained Yield Act – on the basis of ensuring that forests be 'administered for outdoor recreation, range, timber, watershed, and wildlife and fish purposes. But these are often conflicting demands, and efforts to achieve compromises have resulted in gridlock as lobbies have developed to promote each of the five uses, resulting in a zero-sum game dominated by the view on the part of each lobby that it must restrict the others in order to protect its own interests (Cawley and Freemuth, 1997).

At the international level, the difficulties are multiplied. Since states are sovereign, the default position is that they have freedom to exploit their domestic resource however they wish so long as problems are not caused for other states; for example, deforestation in one state should not be allowed to cause soil erosion that leads to river siltation downstream in a neighbouring state. But access to natural resources can become a security problem, as we saw in Chapter 1; those parts of the world best endowed in resources will be under pressure from those that are less well-endowed.

Meanwhile, resources that lie outside the boundaries of states – such as the air, the oceans, and fisheries – suffer the standard problem associated with common pool resources: over-use by some at the expense of others, and little or nothing in the way of a legal or institutional structure that can ensure more equal and sustainable use. Political initiatives may or may not be able to produce a solution, but economics also enters the equation, to the extent that **natural resource economics** has emerged as a distinct field within the discipline (see Tietenberg and Lewis, 2016). It works to understand the economic impact of supply, demand, and allocation in natural resources, looking at the connections and interactions between economies and natural systems. It is interested not just in economic efficiency, but also in the development of sustainable means for managing resources, studying the dynamics of extraction, depletion, and management.

Developing policy on natural resources pits economic considerations against environmental considerations. From the economic perspective, resources are defined by their value to humans, and they are there to be exploited as a source of wealth, profit, and power. Exploitation is best done as quickly and as inexpensively as possible, and nature is something to be reshaped for our convenience. From the environmental perspective, nature either has its own intrinsic value, whether ecological or ethical, and should be left undisturbed as far as possible, or else – sitting somewhere between exploitation and preservation – we should try to build green economies by exploiting resources in a sustainable manner that produces economic benefits while recognizing ecological value and the importance of management in the interests of ensuring continued supply. Sustainable exploitation is the compromise, but as the three cases that follow show, we have made only limited progress in developing workable natural resource regimes.

Forests: Domestic or global resources?

Forests not only serve essential ecological functions as natural habitats, carbon sinks, producers of oxygen, managers of water supply, and generators of clouds and rain, but they are a renewable source of timber for construction and fuelwood (see Sands et al., 2013; Peh et al., 2015). As a land-based natural resource, they sit within state boundaries, where they are subject either to public, commercial, or private control. It could reasonably be argued – particularly given their role in shaping weather and offsetting climate change – that they are a global resource, but states still see them as a domestic resource, and efforts to build a global forestry regime have failed, while efforts to move states in similar directions on domestic forestry policy have had only mixed results.

The area of natural forest has been greatly reduced over the centuries with the spread of agriculture and human settlement, but enough remains in most parts of the world to ensure that forests continue to fulfil their biological and economic roles, and there are signs of a reversal of fortune as rates of **deforestation** (the transformation of forests into cleared land) start to slow. The proportion of the world's land surface that is covered by forest has fallen from about 45 per cent in the pre-industrial era to just over 30 per cent today, leaving us with about 4 billion hectares (10 billion acres). Forests are cut down for a variety of reasons: to make way for farmland and urban settlement, to allow access to minerals in the ground beneath the forests, and to provide fuelwood. They are also damaged by fire, natural disasters, and air pollution. While the economic and financial incentives to fell trees are usually clear, the problem arises when they are removed at a rate that exceeds their replacement. The results include soil erosion, flooding, the siltation of rivers and dams, the extinction of animal and plant species, and the spread of desert conditions.

FAO data suggest that the pace of forest loss was fastest in the 1990s, when it was being removed at a rate of about 16 million hectares per year. It then slowed to just over five million hectares per year between 2000 and 2010, but gains in Europe and parts of Asia have been offset by continuing losses in Africa and South America (see Figure 8.1). The sharpest falls have come in some of the poorest and/or most politically unstable countries, such as Benin, Myanmar, North Korea, Timor-Leste, Uganda, and Zimbabwe; the latter saw its forest cover fall from 57 per cent to 36 per cent between 1990 and 2015. Meanwhile, the sharpest rises have come mainly in high income countries (the EU saw its forest cover increase from 35 per cent to 38 per cent between 1990 and 2015, with Spain alone seeing a 33 per cent increase), but China and India have also seen recent increases in cover.

The contrasting record with forests in Europe and Africa offer useful insights. Europe's forests cover about a third of the land area of the region, a proportion that has been growing in recent decades even while the amount harvested has also grown. Much less European forest is primary than is the case anywhere else in the world, because centuries of agricultural change have left little virgin forest behind (Kirby and Watkins, 2015). Most existing forest has been planted, and much of it carefully harvested and managed to ensure ongoing supplies; about 80 per cent of the EU's wood is used for construction or for paper and pulp, the balance being used for fuelwood. Building on domestic policy, the EU

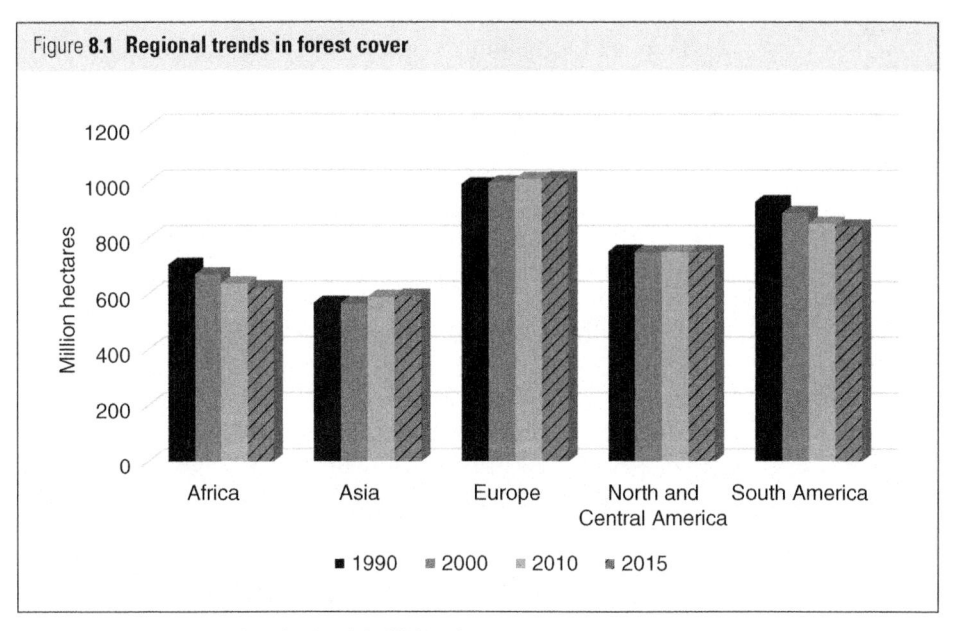

Figure **8.1** **Regional trends in forest cover**

Source: Food and Agriculture Organization of the UN (2015).

adopted a Forestry Strategy in 1998 which leaves responsibility for forest policy with the member states but encourages them to work together on shared principles of sustainable management. An updated Forestry Strategy was published in 2012 with the goal of guiding policy until 2030.

Meanwhile, sub-Saharan African forests face very different conditions: they cover a smaller area (about a quarter of the land area of the region), few African countries have developed sustainable management policies, and forests face the quadruple threats of growing population, the unregulated removal of trees for fuel, logging to meet growing demand from China, and new demands for access from mining, oil and gas companies. Policy is marked by a reliance on decentralization (Germain et al., 2010), but while this can theoretically help build policies based on local interests, and strengthen local institutions, it also provides more opportunities for corruption and mismanagement as local elites exploit opportunities for their own short-term benefits (Tacconi, 2007).

There is little in the way of a global forestry regime, the body of international forestry law having been described by Humphreys (2005) as, at best, 'fragmented and opaque'. The absence of binding international laws has long been cited as one of the explanations for the ongoing threats faced by forests (Davenport, 2005), including illegal logging. Most forest policy is made at the domestic level, and the community of international organizations with an interest in forestry is modest, while international treaties only address forests indirectly. Institutionally, the major IGO is the Food and Agriculture Organization of the UN (FAO), whose primary interest is in food security, for which the sustainable use of natural resources is a supporting goal, and forests are only one of several items on its agenda. The World Bank has addressed forestry in its development goals, and has seen its policy priorities change from a focus on timber as a resource, to forest preservation in the 1990s, to sustainable development and poverty alleviation more recently (Hajjar and Innes, 2009).

The 1992 Rio Earth Summit resulted in agreement on a set of non-binding Forest Principles, which emphasized the right of states to exploit their own forests while also making a plea for the application of sustainable use and improved international cooperation. One of the results was the creation in 2000 of the UN Forum on Forests, charged with encouraging political commitments to the sustainable use of forests. It has helped develop a global strategic plan for forests, and has set the goal of increasing the area of global forests by 2030 by 3 per cent, or 120 million hectares (300 million acres). A noble goal, to be sure, but it has been left to individual states to achieve it, and they are motivated more by market utility than by environmental concerns. It is revealing that while the negotiations leading to the 1992 Convention on Biological Diversity saw countries being represented mainly by negotiators from national environmental departments, the Forum on Forests saw countries being represented mainly by negotiators from national agricultural and economic departments (Giessen et al., 2014).

> **Box 8.1** *The plight of tropical rainforests*
>
> While the trends with temperate forests in Europe and North America may be positive, the story is different with **tropical rainforests**. So called because they are found in the tropical regions of South America (particularly Brazil), Africa (particularly the Democratic Republic of the Congo), and Southeast Asia (particularly Indonesia), and attract heavy rainfall (making them dense and luxuriant), they cover only about 6 per cent of the earth's land area but contain about 80 per cent of the its vegetation. They may receive as much as 10 metres (30 feet) of rain per year, and trees may grow as high as 60–90 metres (200–300 feet).
>
> They have traditionally been viewed by developers and farmers as wasted and as a ready source of valuable timber (including ebony and mahogany), as well as a barrier to accessing minerals such as iron ore and gold, and hence have been cleared aggressively. Gathering data on forest trends has not been easy, but the increased use of satellite imagery suggests that about 5 per cent of the world's tropical rainforest cover was lost between 2000 and 2012. This was equivalent to an area the size of Switzerland, with the biggest percentage loss (11.5 per cent) occurring in south and Southeast Asia (Martin, 2015: 44). Brazil lost 6 per cent of its forest cover between 1990 and 2015 (building on already substantial pre-1990 losses), Guatemala 11 per cent, Paraguay 14 per cent, Indonesia 15 per cent, and Honduras 32 per cent (Food and Agriculture Organization of the UN, 2015). These developments raise two key problems. First, since tropical rainforests took centuries to evolve, once cleared it would take decades – and possibly centuries – to restore them to anything like their original state. Second, even though they are luxuriant and teeming with life, most of their nutrients are stored in the vegetation, and the soil beneath them is relatively poor, making it good only for ranching, and not for raising crops.
>
> In Brazil, the political story has been one involving the conflicting views of loggers and ranchers on the one hand, and environmentalists and indigenous peoples on the other. Political initiatives have resulted in an expansion of the area of protected forests and a steady decline in the rate of deforestation, the latter coming in part from a decline in population growth, improved satellite monitoring that allows the government to more quickly identify problem areas and those responsible for violations, and Brazil's strengthened democracy; tropical rainforests are generally less safe in authoritarian states, where opposition politicians, environmental groups, and the media have less freedom to press for policy change (*The Economist*, 2014a).

On the legal front, there is no binding international agreement on forests, nor even a set of more focused agreements. Efforts to draft a global convention in time for the Rio Earth Summit ended when it became obvious that governments were far from reaching a consensus on its potential content and goals, with a clear North–South split (Bass and Guéneau, 2005). While most Northern states wanted forests to be considered a global resource, and thus subject to the protection of a convention, the United States led the opposition, prompted by the influence of its domestic timber industry, which saw a treaty as involving too much intervention and regulation. Meanwhile, most Southern countries – notably big forest states such as Brazil, India, and Malaysia – argued that forests were a national resource and were concerned about the potential effect of an agreement on their sovereignty (Humphreys, 2005). As a result, plans for a convention failed, and forests today are only addressed tangentially in international agreements focused on other topics:

- Protocols to the 1992 Convention on Climate Change have acknowledged the role that forests play in absorbing carbon dioxide. Much of the discussion about climate change has focused on reducing emissions from deforestation in developing countries, or REDD. There are estimates that anything between 12 and 30 per cent of greenhouse gas emissions are the result of changes in land use, including deforestation, and hence better forest management could help reduce net emissions.
- The 1992 Convention on Biological Diversity recognizes the importance of forests as habitat.
- The 1994 Convention to Combat Desertification recognizes their importance in mitigating the effects of drought and preventing the spread of deserts.

One of the key trends in international environmental law in recent decades has been its regionalization, based on groups of countries with shared interests developing coordinated policies and signing regional agreements. In the face of the drift and obstructionism that is so often found at the global level, regions seem to be more pragmatic in scale, and more conducive to policy diffusion (Conca, 2012). Forestry is an example, with more having been achieved at the regional than the international level. Building on the cooperation that was achieved in addressing acid pollution, the Helsinki Process was launched in Europe in 1993 and the Montreal Process in North America in 1994. They inspired the Tarapoto Process in the Amazon, and the creation in 1996 of the African Timber Organization. All are designed to bring together focused groups of countries with shared interests in the sustainable use of forests, and there are suggestions that these sectoral approaches might have a better chance of encouraging the adoption of common approaches in multiple countries than the work of standard international organizations. In other words, international norms can emerge from well-organized domestic interests (Gale and Cadman, 2014).

NGOs have been on the margin of making forest policy, having mainly been discouraged by the lack of political will, and also marginalized by governments more interested in utility than in the environment (Bass and Guéneau, 2005). Even so, several NGOs are active at the international level on forest science and management, including the following:

- The International Union of Forest Research Organizations (based in Vienna) was founded in 1892 and networks scientists from several hundred member organizations.
- The Global Forest Coalition (headquartered in Asunción, Paraguay) brings together interest groups and indigenous peoples organizations working on behalf of people dependent on forests.
- The Forest Stewardship Council (based in Bonn, Germany) runs a certification and labelling scheme for forest products.
- The Rainforest Action Network (based in San Francisco) focuses on changing the policies of corporations and consumers through direct action, including consumer boycotts.

While there is no broad global forestry regime, there is something of a mini-regime – although not a very successful one – focused on tropical timber. In 1985, FAO coordinated the development of a Tropical Forestry Action Plan (later Programme) that identified the major threats to tropical forests, encouraged the development of national sustainable forestry plans, and recommended $8 billion of spending over five years to address such threats. But the plan was criticized for failing to even slow the rate of deforestation, to build an international consensus, to place deforestation within its wider economic context, and to take into account the needs, rights or advice of local forest dwellers (Humphreys, 1996: 43–45). The programme was reorganized in the 1990s, but by then had lost momentum.

Also in 1985, the International Tropical Timber Agreement was signed, and was to be overseen by the International Tropical Timber Organization (ITTO), established in 1986 under the auspices of the UN and headquartered in Yokohama, Japan. The goal of both is to monitor trade in tropical timber and to make sure that exports come from sustainable sources. Only states that are either producers or consumers of tropical timber are allowed to be members of the ITTO, whose work has been undermined by the conflict between maximizing trade and profits and imposing environmental safeguards that might restrict trade. Questions were early being raised about the effects of the conflict (Colchester, 1990), and subsequent analyses of the work of the ITTO have been mainly negative; Nagtzaam (2014), for example, concludes that the international tropical forestry regime has been a failure, mainly because the economic interests of both producer and consumer timber states 'are best served by allowing the harvesting of tropical timbers to continue virtually unabated at the expense of good environmental outcomes'.

Shearman et al. (2012) suggest that the production of tropical timber is following the **Hubbert curve** that was proposed in the 1950s by an American geologist named M. King Hubbert to predict the future of the oil industry. He argued that production would rise rapidly to a peak in the 1970s before falling off, a model that has since been applied to other resources. Shearman et al. point to three problems afflicting tropical forests, and pushing them along the trajectory of this curve: a standard cutting cycle of 30–40 years that is too brief to allow forests to regrow, the deforestation caused by logging, and the fact that most logging is undertaken by multinational corporations that place short-term profits over long-term sustainability.

Oceans: A classic common pool resource problem

While forests are a national resource, and their management is approached from a stubbornly national perspective, oceans are a global resource, and as such pose a different set of challenges. They cover about 71 per cent of the surface area of the earth, and play five key environmental roles:

- Home to enormous biological wealth, including reefs and mangrove forests, and numerous species of animals and plants, many of which have not been deeply studied.
- Home to plants that produce about half the planet's oxygen.
- A critical sink for carbon dioxide, absorbing about a quarter of the emissions we produce.
- Regulate weather patterns and climate, their currents distributing heat globally.
- Home to fisheries with high nutritional and economic value.

In spite of their clear value, we know remarkably little about the oceans as a habitat, or about their overall condition, but we know that they face human-made problems on four fronts: overfishing, pollution, climate change, and habitat destruction. We have a sound body of data on all four problems, and we have a good list of potential solutions, but we have so far failed to develop the political will to act in a coordinated and effective manner. Fisheries continue to be used unsustainably, there is a growing but patchy body of international law on marine pollution, climate change continues to contribute to rising sea levels, and habitats continue to suffer; less than 3 per cent of the oceans are protected, and most marine parks and reserves are protected in name only.

Oceans present a classic common pool resource problem. As long ago as 1609, the Dutch jurist Hugo Grotius argued that the seas had to be free, if only because they could not be occupied (quoted by Treves, 2015). This idea of the freedom of the seas was defended by the major maritime powers, and continues to explain the manner in which oceans are exploited, and the failure to build an effective international maritime regime. Until 1994, everything outside a coastal band that was three nautical miles (5.6 km) wide was considered international waters, and thus outside the jurisdiction of states and regulated only by narrow agreements on pollution and marine species. Changes under international law have created a more complex set of designations for maritime zones, including **Exclusive Economic Zones** (EEZs) stretching as far as 200 nautical miles from the coast (see Table 8.2). Beyond

Table **8.2 Maritime zones under international law**

Type	Location	State rights
Archipelagic waters	Within clusters of islands such as those found in Indonesia and the Philippines	State has sovereignty, including right to limit 'innocent passage' by foreign boats and ships (passage that does not threaten peace or security of the state).
Territorial waters	Up to 12 nautical miles (22 km) from coast	State has sovereignty and jurisdiction over waters (and over airspace above and seabed below), but cannot restrict innocent passage.
Contiguous zone	Up to 24 nautical miles (44 km) from coast	State allowed to prevent or punish 'infringement' of its 'customs, fiscal, immigration or sanitary laws and regulations' within territorial waters.
Exclusive Economic Zone	Up to 200 nautical miles (370 km) from coast	State controls economic resources within its EEZ, including fisheries, mining, and oil or gas exploration.
Continental shelf	Up to 200 nautical miles (370 km) from coast	Once claimed, states have sovereign rights over resources on the shelf.
High seas	Outside territorial waters	None.
International sea bed	Outside territorial waters	None. Resources must be treated as global common heritage, and used only for peaceful purposes.

territorial waters, and regardless of the rights given in contiguous zones, EEZs, and even the nearby continental shelf, the oceans are considered international waters, which means that they belong to no one, are a common pool resource, and are subject only to the limitations agreed under international law.

This arrangement comes as a result of the UN Convention on the Law of the Sea (UNCLOS), which was signed in 1982 after lengthy debate. It superseded four treaties drawn up as a result of negotiations that began in 1949, and were signed in 1958 at the first UN Conference on the Law of the Sea. A second conference met in 1960 and soon failed, and a third met between 1973 and 1982, combining and expanding earlier agreements into a new convention, which did not come into effect until 1994, more than 40 years after negotiations had first begun. The main institution associated with UNCLOS is the Jamaica-based International Seabed Authority, which was set up under the terms of the treaty, and given the task of coordinating the activities of states in managing the international seabed.

A small but growing sub-regime focuses on efforts to control pollution at sea, and is centred on the work of the London-based International Maritime Organization (IMO), a specialized agency of the UN set up 1958. IMO's work was originally focused on safety at sea, but expanded to the prevention and control of pollution following the 1967 *Torrey Canyon* disaster. Legal efforts to address the latter date back to the 1954 International Convention for the Prevention of Pollution of the Sea by Oil (OILPOL), which prohibited the discharge of oil from tankers within 80 km (50 miles) of the coast (or up to 240 km/150 miles in some parts of the world). It was superseded in 1973 by the International Convention for the Prevention of Pollution from Ships (MARPOL), adopted in the wake of a spate of tanker accidents. It began with a focus on oil, and was expanded by annexes to require double hulls for oil tankers, and to cover chemicals, sewage, garbage, and air pollution from ship exhausts.

Campe (2009) argues that while the IMO has been influential in providing technical expertise on ship design and construction, it has been less influential on environmental policy. It helps encourage negotiations among its member states, but is torn between demands for efficient and low-cost shipping (from ship owners, traders, and oil companies) and for clean seas (from environmental, tourism, and fishing interests). To date, shipping interests have had the bigger political and economic interest, and have dominated the IMO agenda.

As in the case of forestry, much of the movement on marine environmental policy can be found at the regional level. At the heart of these efforts has been the UNEP Regional Seas

Table **8.3** International treaties on marine pollution

Signature	Focus
1954	Prevention of pollution of the sea by oil.
1969	Civil liability for oil pollution damage.
1969	Intervention on the high seas in cases of oil pollution casualties.
1971	International fund for compensation for oil pollution damage.
1972	Prevention of marine pollution by dumping of wastes and other matter.
1973	Prevention of pollution from ships.
1990	Oil pollution preparedness, response and cooperation.
2000	Liability and compensation for damage in connection with carriage of hazardous and noxious substances by sea.
2001	Control of harmful anti-fouling systems on ships.
2004	Control and management of ships' ballast water and sediments.
2009	Safe and environmentally sound recycling of ships.

Programme (RSP), which was begun in 1974 and works to pull together neighbouring states with a shared interest in a regional sea. UNEP acts as a coordinator, encouraging the countries involved in each regional programme to draw up an action plan based on a combination of local environmental needs and the political and economic situation of the participating states. This might involve new research into trends with pollution and biodiversity, agreement on a set of priorities, the creation of regional trust funds to pay the costs of action, and agreement of a regional convention.

The model for regional marine agreements was provided by developments in the Mediterranean, where an action plan was agreed in 1976, the same year as agreement of the Barcelona Convention for the Protection of the Mediterranean Sea Against Pollution. Since then, a total of 18 regional programmes have been developed, including those for the Caribbean, East Asia, the northwest Pacific, and the Caspian (all run by UNEP), and those for the Black Sea, the Red Sea, South Asia, and parts of the Pacific (all run outside UNEP). All but four are based on legally binding treaties, and several of the treaties have expanded to protocols dealing with protected areas and land-based pollution.

The RSP has the advantage of including countries with a clearly shared stake in the welfare of their contiguous marine environment, and UNEP has overcome its institutional limitations to play the role of facilitator. The programme has even brought together clusters of wealthy and poor states, and democracies and authoritarian states, as in the case of the Mediterranean Action Plan. But

Box 8.2 *Saving the whales*

One focused and emotive example of the overexploitation of marine resources is found in the problem of **whaling**. There are eight families of whales, containing multiple species, among which is the blue whale, the largest animal ever known to have existed. Subsistence whaling among coastal communities has a long history, but with the introduction of organized industrial whaling in the 1600s, and then of factory ships capable of catching whales, and processing and freezing the catch, whaling became increasingly unsustainable. In 1946, the International Whaling Commission (IWC) was created under the terms of the Convention for the Regulation of Whaling, an agreement whose main goal was to ensure the sustainable use of whale stocks. A worldwide moratorium on whaling went into force in 1985, while the Indian Ocean Whale Sanctuary was created in 1979 and the Southern Ocean Whale Sanctuary in 1994, providing areas within which all commercial whaling is prohibited (see Dorsey, 2013).

The number of whales killed has fallen dramatically since the agreement of the moratorium, from a peak of 30,000–35,000 annually in the early 1960s to a total of about 1,500–2,000 annually since the year 2000. In spite of their protection under law, Japan continues to whale, purportedly for scientific reasons, while Norway has objected to the moratorium and thus is not bound by it, and Iceland has resisted IWC pressure, resuming commercial whaling in 2006. In order to help it maintain its policies, Japan has recruited several non-whaling and non-coastal states to the IWC, seeking their votes in return for official development aid. The International Court of Justice ruled in 2014 that Japan's whaling programme was unscientific and thus illegal, but Japan has disputed the jurisdiction of the court over whaling matters. It argues that eating whale meat is an important historical tradition, and that trying to stop it from whaling is a threat to its national culture. In fact, few Japanese eat whale meat, leaving critics of Japanese policy struggling to understand its motivation. One theory holds that the problem is political: whaling in Japan is run by a government department whose employees would see shame in having their numbers and their budget cut, while legislators from a small number of whaling constituencies feel the need to keep promising a return of commercial whaling (Wingfield-Hayes, 2016).

the problems faced by the marine environment have changed; when the programme was first set up, the focus was on pollution from land-based sources and shipping. These are still risks, but the problems have expanded to include deeper and more complex threats to biodiversity and habitats, threats to the high seas, and climate change. The RSP has responded with a host of new agreements and protocols to original agreements, but it faces the standard problem of implementation at the national level (Oral, 2015). While the regional approach has many advantages, there is also the danger of contradictory approaches among regions, and a case to be made for developing a global agreement on oceans that would overlap with regional agreements (Rochette et al., 2014).

While managing regional seas has seen progress, the deep sea (200 metres and deeper) and the open ocean (beyond the limit of EEZs) present greater challenges because of their depth and/or size. Little effort has been made to think about how they might best be governed, a problem that achieves new significance as changes in technology make it easier to go further and deeper in the search for fish and new sources of energy. Environmentally, the deep sea is poorly understood, UNCLOS is more concerned with territorial matters than environmental matters, and the only body with jurisdiction over the seabed – the International Seabed Authority – is interested primarily in minerals, paying little attention to ecosystems and having only limited contacts with environmental interest groups (Moore and Squires, 2016).

Fisheries: Free-for-all on the high seas

Marine fisheries are another example of a common pool resource, and of the political challenges involved in managing such resources. Within EEZs, management is the responsibility of coastal states, and there are benefits to the regional approach, but matters are different in the open oceans, where the record has been weak:

- There is no clear global regime, and there has been little significant political progress in building one.
- Too many boats are chasing declining numbers of fish.
- Too many fish are being caught when they are too young or are being discarded as waste.
- The sheer size of the oceans makes it difficult to track fishing boats.
- There is no global authority that can oversee the development and implementation of such rules on fishing as have been agreed.

The annual global fish catch grew between 1950 and 2014 from 20 million tonnes to 167 million tonnes, catching up and overtaking the rate of human population growth (see Figure 8.2). Per capita consumption doubled from about 10 kg per year in the 1960s to 20 kg per year today (Food and Agriculture Organization of the UN, 2016). As a result, FAO warns that the number of fish stocks exploited sustainably has fallen from 90 per cent in 1970 to just over 70 per cent in 2011, by when 61 per cent were fully fished and 30 per cent were being overfished. It points out that many of the most popular fish (such as tuna) are being caught unsustainably, and that matters will only worsen with

Figure **8.2 Global fish catch**

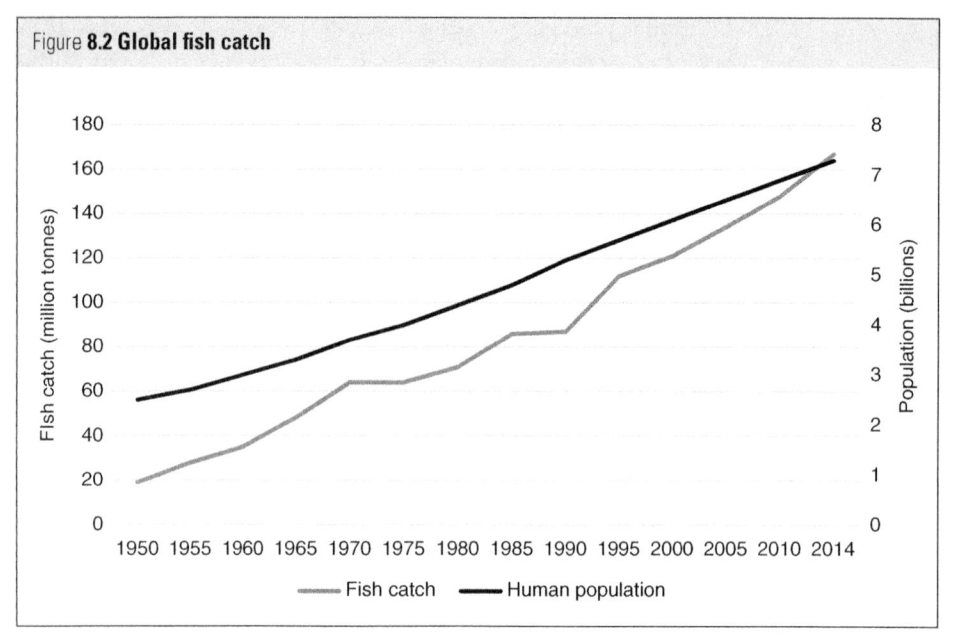

Source: Fish catch data from Food and Agriculture Organization of the UN (2016). Population data from UN Population Division (retrieved May 2016), *The World at Six Billion*.

projections that fish production will increase by 17 per cent between 2016 and 2025 (Food and Agriculture Organization of the UN, 2016).

Improved technology has allowed more fish to be caught further from home ports, while government subsidies – driven by fishing as an economic opportunity, and as a cultural symbol in many coastal communities – continue to flow even in the face of questionable economic logic (Barkin and DeSombre, 2013). The fish that could once be caught using small boats or rods close to shore are almost all gone, and we have come close to exhausting stocks of pelagic fish (those found in the open ocean, neither close to the shore nor to the ocean bottom) such as herring and tuna. Fishing fleets have ranged further away from home and have cast their nets deeper, paying little heed to waste: when young fish are caught and thrown away, they do not become big fish. There is also the problem of **bycatch**: fishing can involve the unintentional catching of marine species such as sea turtles, porpoises, albatross, crabs, and starfish.

The potential impact of unrestricted fishing is illustrated by the case of the collapse of the Peruvian anchovy industry in 1972. Resource management is based in part on the idea of **maximum sustained yield** (MSY), a figure for the amount of fish (or timber, or other renewable resource) that can be harvested while leaving enough for the resource to replace itself. It had been calculated that the MSY for the Peruvian anchovy industry was 9.5 million tonnes per year, but catches were routinely exceeding that number, meaning that fish were being taken faster than new fish were being hatched. The annual take began falling, and the fishery eventually collapsed in 1972. By the late 1970s, the annual take was down to about 1.5 million tonnes.

Institutionally, fisheries have been addressed mainly by the FAO as part of its interest in food security. A group of 17 **regional fisheries management organizations** (RFMOs) have also been set up among clusters of countries that have a shared interest in managing and conserving commercially valuable fish stocks in a particular part of the world; five of them focus on tuna and other large species such as swordfish and marlin (they include the International Commission for the Conservation of Atlantic Tunas), while others have a broader interest; these include bodies responsible for the south Pacific, the Mediterranean, and three of the four quadrants of the Atlantic. While their work is helpful, they are only marginally interested in the broader marine environment, they have not yet developed effective systems for recording and monitoring the activities of fishing boats, large areas of the open ocean do not come under their jurisdiction, and – as a result – they have failed to prevent overfishing.

In her assessment of RFMOs, Rayfuse (2015) points out that they are subject to all the same weaknesses as standard international organizations, including the desire by states to protect their sovereignty. In addition, there is no obligation on states to join RFMOs, the agreements on which they are based allow for opt-outs by states that wish to join but do not want to be held to all the obligations of membership (this has led, for example, to a dispute between Australia and Japan on access to southern Bluefin tuna), ships from member states of RFMOs have been known to be reflagged to non-state members and thus to skirt the obligations, and there is a tradition in law of the sea matters to allow only 'flag states' to have jurisdiction over their vessels. The overall effect has been to provide almost no limits on what is called 'illegal, unreported and unregulated' (IUU) fishing.

One example of a regional agreement that has failed is the Common Fisheries Policy of the European Union, launched in 1983 with the goal of bringing sustainable management to the world's third biggest fishing industry (after those of China and Japan). The plan was to conserve fish stocks by imposing national quotas, setting rules on fishing gear and mesh sizes for fishing nets, requiring accurate reporting of catches and landings, and limiting the size of EU fishing fleets. In spite of these goals, there was a failure of enforcement, and a clear difference of opinion between major fishing states such as Spain, Britain, and France (on the one hand) and countries with smaller fishing industries, such as Germany and most of Eastern Europe (on the other). Fishing also played an important economic role in poorer parts of the EU, whose governments opposed caps and continued to subsidize fishing. North Atlantic fisheries continued to be overexploited, and the EU fishing fleet was clearly too large, so a major overhaul of policy was undertaken in 2013. This included the establishment of MSY numbers for fish stocks, more emphasis on reducing the impact of fishing on marine ecosystems, and a breaking down of the regional approach into sub-regions (Penas Lado, 2016).

There are no global treaties on fisheries, and until the passage of UNCLOS it was mainly a free-for-all on the open sea. The writing and signing of the convention was motivated by events such as the 'cod wars' between Britain and Iceland in the 1950s and 1970s. Before the era of EEZs, fishing trawlers would range far and wide in their search for fish, among them British trawlers that sailed into fish-rich waters off Iceland. This led to a conflict between the two countries, escalating to the point where Britain despatched naval cruisers to protect its trawlers.

UNCLOS defused these kinds of problems with the creation of EEZs, and went further in 1995 with the signature of the UN Fish Stocks Agreement. This was designed to manage fish that straddle or migrate through EEZs, encouraging coastal states to take a precautionary approach and recognize that changes to ecosystems in one zone can have an impact on neighbouring zones. It also allows states to monitor and inspect fishing vessels of other states in order to ensure compliance with the rules. There are also a few more focused treaties, such as the 1966 Convention on the Conservation of Atlantic Tuna, and the 1980 Convention on the Conservation of Antarctic Marine Living Resources. The latter is managed by a commission of the same name based in Hobart, Australia, which has 24 member states that are either located in the southern hemisphere or have scientific interests in the Antarctic. The Commission has been working since 2005 to set up two marine protected areas in the Antarctic, a goal that has persistently been blocked by Russia, joined occasionally by China, both of which operate fishing fleets in the area. Progress was made in 2016 with the declaration of the world's largest marine park (and the first in international waters) in the Ross Sea, south of New Zealand.

There is no shortage of potential answers to the global fishing problem, including the creation of marine protected areas, a reduction in the capacity of global fishing fleets, changes to fishing methods, the elimination of harmful fishing subsides, and improved monitoring and surveillance. The problem is that states have failed to achieve much in the way of agreement on how to respond to what is clearly a rapidly worsening problem. For Barkin and DeSombre (2013), the answer lies in the reform of regional fisheries management organizations so that they can set and monitor realistic catch limits, in addition to which an international fisheries organization needs to be created that could oversee efforts to encourage sustainability at the global level.

Discussion questions

- How can the economic and environmental considerations involved in managing natural resources be reconciled?
- Which is the most realistic approach to forests: seeing them as a global resource and developing policy accordingly, or treating them as domestic resources and encouraging states to follow common policies?
- Is the regional approach the only realistic way of effectively managing the world's oceans?
- To what extent are fisheries an example of the tragedy of the commons, and to what extent is it possible to develop solutions to the tragedy?

Key concepts

Bycatch

Deforestation

Exclusive Economic Zone

Hubbert curve

Maximum sustained yield

Natural resources

Natural resource economics

Regional fisheries management organizations

Tropical rainforests

Whaling

Further reading

Balliett, James Fargo (2010) *Oceans* and *Forests* (Routledge). Two brief survey books by the same author in a five-part series on separate environments, each providing scientific background, offering cases from around the world, and discussing human impact.

Chiras, Daniel D., and John P. Reganold (2009) *Natural Resource Conservation: Management for a Sustainable Future*, 10th edn (Pearson). A textbook offering a survey of natural resource challenges, and discussing sustainable solutions.

Harris, Jonathan M., and Brian Roach (2015) *Environmental and Natural Resource Economics*, 3rd edn (Routledge), and Tom Tietenberg and Lynne Lewis (2016) *Environmental and Natural Resource Economics*, 10th edn (Routledge). Two examples of the many texts offering surveys of natural resource economics, including case studies of energy, water, forests, fisheries, and other resources.

Hilborn, Ray, and Ulrike Hilborn (2012) *Overfishing: What Everyone Needs to Know* (Oxford University Press). A survey of the causes of overfishing, the options available addressing the problem, and the difficulties of adopting those options.

Sands, Roger (ed) (2013) *Forestry in a Global Context*, 2d edn (CAB International). A survey forestry, with chapters on how forests are used, their environmental value, sustainable use, and global policy.

9 Waste: A Failure of Consumer Society

Key arguments

- The problem of waste exemplifies much that is wrong with modern consumer society, and with our collective approach to the management of resources.
- Nothing is wasted in nature, begging the question of how best to define waste, which comes in multiple forms and can be addressed in multiple ways.
- We are producing more waste as the human population grows and as wasteful habits spread from the North to the South.
- There are many options to dealing with waste – including prevention, recovery, and disposal – but the political and economic pressures shaping these options vary significantly by country.
- Increased production of toxic, hazardous, and radioactive waste has added troubling new dimensions to the question of how best to deal with waste.
- An international dimension has been added to the debate over waste by efforts either to ship it elsewhere or to dump it into the ocean.

Chapter overview

The problem of waste exemplifies much that is wrong with modern consumer society, and with our collective approach to the management of resources. Waste was all but unknown until the beginning of the twentieth century, the low levels of consumption combining with the scarcity of goods and money to encourage producers and consumers to reuse almost everything. But as consumers became wealthier, as they demanded and were given more choice, and as they increasingly saw belongings as temporary and disposable, so they created more waste: the consumer society became the disposable society.

The global middle class today buys and consumes more than it needs, expects its purchases to be attractively presented in disposable packaging, wastes almost as much food as it eats, and approaches waste disposal as little more than tossing something into a bag and placing it on the street for municipal services to take away. Consumers routinely replace their belongings not because they have ceased to function but because of a desire to replace them with newer versions. Thus, says Campbell (2015), the 'curse of the new' has come to drive hyper-consumption. Waste production figures have risen as a result.

And these are only the wastes that individuals generate; far more waste (about 90 per cent of the total in industrialized countries) is generated by agriculture and industry as it produces the food and goods that consumers demand, using often inefficient processes and methods. Much of that waste is either toxic or hazardous, posing a heightened level of threat to the environment, and ultimately to consumers. Meanwhile, the growth of the middle class in the South promises more consumption and more waste unless the lessons of the North are learned and applied.

Waste takes five major forms: human, municipal, agricultural, industrial, and toxic or hazardous. Each has different qualities, each is subject to different economic and financial pressures, and each demands different sets of policy responses. Overall, though, we have three main options: prevention, recovery, and disposal. The first means reducing the amount of waste produced, the second involves recycling or reusing waste materials, and the third (assuming waste cannot be reused or there is no plan for reuse) involves either burial or destruction, via incineration, for example. In the case of hazardous and radioactive waste, we must develop policies for safe long-term storage. All three options have their advantages and disadvantages, no approach has yet proved ideal, the mix of policies changes by time and place, and the result is that most communities have adopted a multifaceted approach.

This chapter begins with a review of the problem of waste, first offering a definition of the meaning of the term, then reviewing the different forms that waste takes, and assessing trends in production, particularly of municipal waste. It then goes on to look at the shaping of waste policy,

> reviewing the varied record with – in turn – prevention, recovery, and disposal. Waste production is down in most Northern states, but policies vary in terms of their efficacy, and rates of production are growing in the South. The chapter then looks at the particular challenges posed by dealing with toxic, hazardous, and radioactive waste, problems mainly for industrialized countries. It ends with a review of the dynamics of the international export and dumping of waste, and the mixed record of the international waste regime. Trends on waste transfer are hard to measure, and data are available only for legal transfers. Meanwhile, efforts to stop exports have suffered from difficulties of definition and enforcement, as well as anomalies in international law.

Defining the problem

The production of waste symbolizes the failure of modern society to use materials and energy efficiently. As industrial and consumer demand have grown, and as industrial and agricultural production have increased, so the production of waste has increased. Where once almost all by-products of consumption could and would be reused, they have increasingly been cast aside as having no value. Much is discarded without much underlying motivation beyond either laziness or efforts to avoid spending money; the result is trash lying on our city streets, more trash washing up on beaches or floating in the open oceans, and toxic wastes dumped illegally into rivers and lakes. But most wastes are now disposed of via increasingly structured (but also expensive) means: the organized weekly collection of municipal waste, complex sewage transport and treatment systems, and waste storage sites and incinerators. Meanwhile, the toxicity of wastes has grown as more chemicals have been used in industry and agriculture, while the growth of plastics has generated a new form of perpetual inorganic waste.

There is the potential for waste at every stage of the production process, from the extraction of raw materials to their conversion into manufactured commodities and their final consumption. But what exactly is waste, and is there even such a thing as true waste? Strictly speaking, material can only be defined as waste if it has no further value. But if we examine the natural world we find – in line with Commoner's second law of ecology (see Chapter 1) – that it wastes nothing: biological processes ensure that all the by-products of consumption by animals, plants, and other organisms are reformed and reused. Only humans have decided that the by-products of their consumption should either be discarded or placed in indefinite storage with no view to further use. This waste is not simply material that is undesirable or that has no immediate further use – whether it is human waste, rotting food, used packaging, or a broken television set – but includes material that is either defined as being excess to needs or that has been replaced by something newer and more desirable: hence we often throw away unfashionable clothes, dated household appliances, and empty containers. In short, **waste** has come to be defined as any solid or liquid commodity or material that is no longer of use or of value to the producer or the owner, and that is either discarded or intended to be discarded (Gillespie, 2015: 8–9).

As the volume and variety of waste has grown, and as humans have adopted the idea that discarding something is easier and cheaper than reusing or recycling, so the legal and policy response has become broader, deeper, and more sophisticated. Waste has also moved beyond being a local problem to being both national and in some cases international. Landfill has become more expensive to establish and maintain, the variety and chemical composition of wastes has expanded, the toxicity of much of the waste has deepened, and – with the introduction of plastics since the 1950s – we have introduced a new form of waste that does not break down naturally and is all but permanent. Where once it was assumed that producers would take care of their own waste, the responsibility for managing and disposing of waste has been passed on to others, whether legally or illegally.

Human waste is the most immediate form of waste, since it is produced by everyone. Its safe disposal is taken for granted by the residents of the North and the middle classes of the South, and yet – as we saw in Chapter 7 – nearly two-thirds of humans live without access to improved sanitation in the form of flush toilets and sewage treatment, and a combination of dirty water and inadequate sanitation causes nearly 850,000 preventable deaths each year. The amount of waste produced per person does not change, but human population is growing, and while it might be assumed that the greatest challenges to sewage management are faced by the fastest growing cities in the South, the greatest health problems are faced in many of the least urbanized states, with Angola, the Democratic Republic of the Congo, Sierra Leone, and Somalia topping the list of mortality rates in 2012.

For the average middle-class consumer, waste mainly takes the form of **municipal waste**: the garbage that is thrown away every day by homes and workplaces in cities and towns, and that consists mainly of packaging, food, clothing, containers, plastics, glass, tins and drink cans, paper, yard and garden waste, and street sweepings. (It is also sometimes known as solid waste.) But there is almost none of this that could not be reused or recycled, meaning that the problem of waste is not so much one of the creation of 'waste' materials as one of our failure to develop habits, policies, or incentives that place these materials back into the stream of production and consumption. Unfortunately, as noted later in this chapter, the economic benefits of reuse and recycling are not always as clear as they might be, and it is sometimes cheaper and more 'efficient' simply to dispose of municipal waste.

Box 9.1 *Waste and the consumer society*

It is often said that there is nothing certain in life but death and taxes, but waste could be added to the list. Humans have always created waste, its volume and content expanding first with the Agricultural Revolution, then with the Industrial Revolution, and finally with the arrival of the era of mass consumerism. The **consumer society** – one in which social and economic status is driven and defined by the acquisition of material goods – has been with us since the late nineteenth century. Prior to that, the ownership of commodities was based mainly on practical considerations, although most people were too poor to own much beyond essential clothes and household goods. Consumerism has meant the replacement of needs with wants, the advent of mass production, and a combination of social and economic pressure (fed by rapid technological change) to own the newest and most advanced car, television, cell phone, or computer, or the latest fashions, or the most recent fad games and toys, all driven by notions such as conspicuous consumption, instant gratification, convenience, and ownership as a status symbol.

Consumerism has also meant increased disposability and waste, reflected in the comparative World Bank data for municipal waste production in the North and the South shown in Figure 9.1. Globally, the numbers continue to increase:

- In 2002, nearly 3 billion urban residents were producing about 0.64 kg of waste per person per day, for a total of 0.68 billion tonnes per year.
- By 2012, 3 billion people were producing nearly twice as much: 1.2 kg of waste per person per day, or 1.3 billion tonnes per year.
- By 2025, it is projected that 4.3 billion people will be producing 1.42 kg per person per day, or 2.2 billion tonnes per year.

The wealthiest OECD countries produce the most, while Latin America is catching up, and Africa and South Asia (including India) lag behind. The World Bank data suggest that the OECD countries produce almost half the world's municipal waste, that urban residents produce almost twice as much as rural residents, that the most waste is produced in the most economically developed countries, and that the greatest growth is expected in East and South Asia, thanks mainly to China and India. The story does not end with quantity; the content of the waste produced by the consumer society can tell us much about the nature and the priorities of that society. 'You get a real sense of life's rich variety and mystery' by examining trash, says the narrator of a novella titled *The Dump*. 'In fact you probably end up knowing more about life [in the real world] than [its inhabitants] do themselves' (Sharp, 1998: 57).

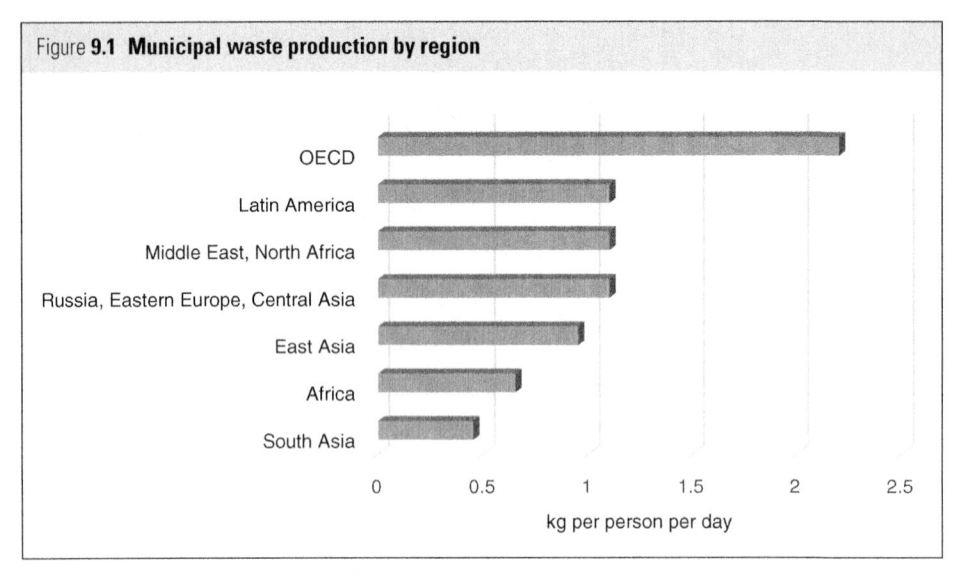

Figure 9.1 Municipal waste production by region

Region	kg per person per day
OECD	~2.2
Latin America	~1.1
Middle East, North Africa	~1.1
Russia, Eastern Europe, Central Asia	~1.1
East Asia	~1.0
Africa	~0.8
South Asia	~0.5

Source: World Bank (2012).

The problem is greatest in the 35 member states of the OECD, the data (see Figure 9.2) showing that in spite of efforts to cut back on waste production, and to promote recycling, municipal waste production among its members grew by 12 per cent between 1995 and 2013, while its population grew over the same period by 13 per cent. Although several OECD countries – notably Germany and Sweden – have found effective means of collecting municipal waste and using it to generate energy, overall waste production has remained level at best (although population growth means that per capita production is down). For the European Union, per capita waste production has fallen only slightly, from 554 kg (1220 lbs) per person in 2000 to 511 kg (1130 lbs) per person in 2013. In the United States, overall production has not changed much so far this century in spite of a growing population, but on a per capita basis Americans still create more waste than most of their OECD peers (see Figure 9.3).

Municipal waste is something that most of us see and produce every day, and for which we must arrange for disposal from our homes and offices. But it is only a small part of overall waste production, 90 per cent of which (in industrialized countries, at least) comes from agriculture and industry:

- Agricultural waste is mainly but not exclusively organic, and includes manure, harvest waste, refuse, salt and silt drained from fields, sludge from water treatment plants, used oil from machinery, and chemical run-off from pesticides and fertilizers used in farming.

Waste: A Failure of Consumer Society | **185**

Figure 9.2 Municipal waste production in the OECD

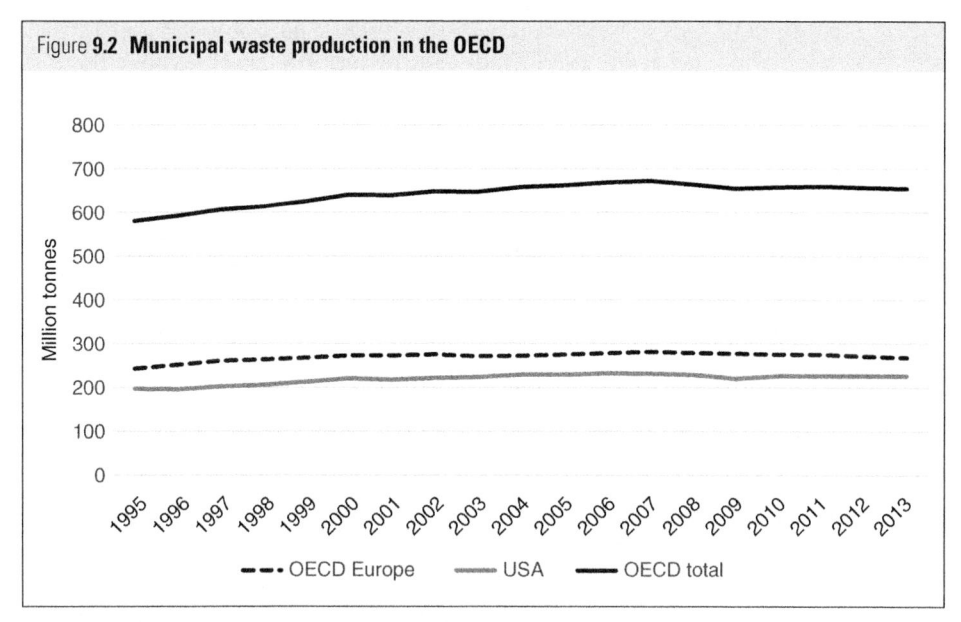

Source: OECD statistics at https://stats.oecd.org/Index.aspx?DataSetCode=MUNW (retrieved March 2017). OECD member states include most of Europe, as well as Australia, Japan, South Korea, and the USA.

Figure 9.3 Comparative municipal waste production

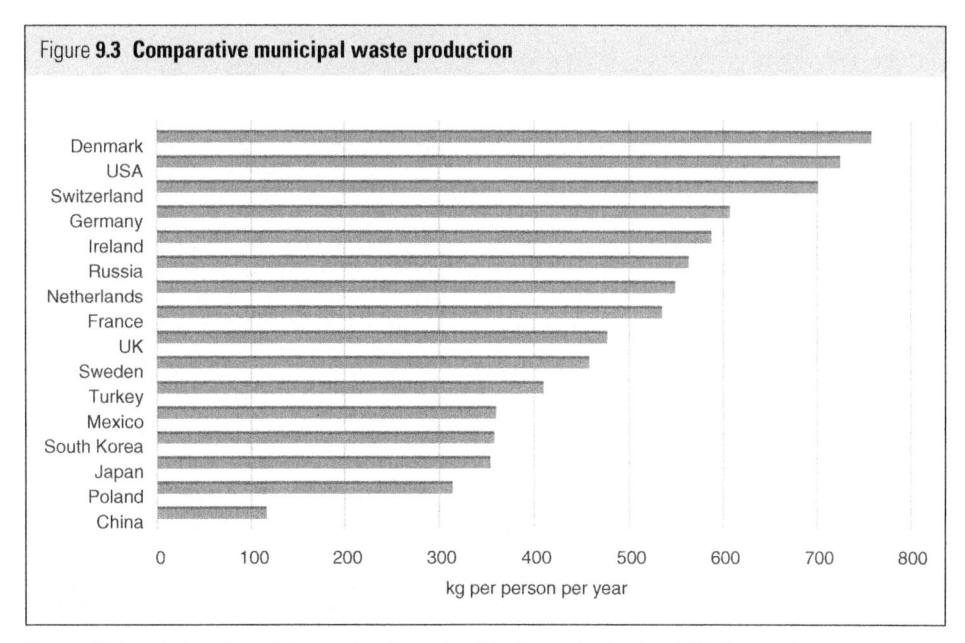

Source: OECD statistics at https://data.oecd.org/waste/municipal-waste.htm (retrieved March 2017). Data are for 2012, except China (2009) and Japan (2010).

- Industrial waste is mainly but not exclusively solid and inorganic, and includes any material that is a by-product of manufacturing, such as solvents, waste water, heavy metals, empty containers, packaging, the chemicals used in petroleum refining, waste materials from construction, tailings and rubble left behind after mining operations, and depleted or abandoned mines and quarries.

Since much of this is regarded as pollution rather than waste (although there is often no clear line between the two), it is addressed by the kinds of policies on pollution control and management discussed in Chapters 6 and 7. One exception is the challenge of safely disposing of toxic and hazardous waste, which demands particular care because of the dangers it poses to humans and other living organisms, either because of its physical properties or through its pollutive effects (see the section 'Toxic and hazardous wastes' below).

Shaping waste policy

The shaping of effective waste policy faces several challenges. First, we are producing more waste as human population grows and as the wasteful habits of the North spread to middle-class consumers in the South. Second, waste comes in multiple forms that need different responses. Disposing effectively of human waste, for example, demands the construction of sophisticated sewage transport and processing plants (which are more viable in urban than in rural areas), while the disposal of radioactive waste poses challenges of a higher order. Third, the debate over waste prompts numerous troubling questions. If we cannot (or choose not to) recycle or reuse, what options are available for the disposal of waste, should 'disposal' be defined as destruction or safe storage, and how can we guarantee safe storage? If waste is burned to generate energy, for example, does that constitute 'recovery' or 'disposal'? When should we consider waste to be hazardous, and what is the difference between 'hazardous' and 'toxic'? Should states be self-sufficient in disposal or is waste a 'good' that can be traded? If it *can* be traded, what should be the terms of the trade, and how can we avoid creating pollution havens? These are all questions that have muddied the waters as policy on waste has evolved, and the pressure for answers is only growing as industrializing countries produce more waste.

Policies to date have focused on three different points in the waste stream: the prevention of waste production, the recovery of waste, and the safe disposal of waste that either cannot be reused or where there is no plan for reuse (see Table 9.1).

Table 9.1 **Waste policy options**

Stages	Options	Features
Prevention	Zero waste	Changing procedures and habits so as to eliminate the production of waste.
	Product stewardship	Designing products and services so as to minimize their environmental impact.
	Low-waste consumption	Avoiding products and services based on wasteful production processes.
	Extended producer responsibility	Make producers responsible for managing their products at the end of their useful life.
Recovery	Recycling	Using waste material to make a new version of the same product.
	Reuse	Using waste material for different purposes.
Disposal	Burying in landfill	Oldest and most common form of waste management.
	Incineration	May or may not be used to generate energy.
	Exporting	Increasingly restricted.
	Dumping	Typically illegal.
	Storage	Obligatory for radioactive wastes.

Prevention. In terms of reducing production, the baseline goal is to change the habits of consumers, agriculture, and industry so as to achieve a **zero waste** society: one in which all waste is at least recovered and reused, but ideally in which production and consumption systems are restructured so as to minimize the generation of waste to begin with (see Lehmann and Crocker, 2012). More an ideal than a hard goal, the concept of zero waste was born in California in the 1970s, but has only been adopted in practice since the early 2000s by a few local governments. While it may be feasible in regard to municipal waste, and has spawned numerous self-help guides to creating a zero waste home (by, for example, eliminating the use of paper), it is a harder goal to reach in agriculture and industry. This leaves – in practical terms – three main preventative options:

- **Product stewardship** involves efforts to minimize the environmental impact of a product or service throughout its life cycle, for example by reducing the amount of packaging, redesigning products to use fewer harmful ingredients, or giving consumers a financial incentive not to produce waste. One example is the use of container deposits, by which a fee is charged to the consumer for a container, and the fee is returned if the empty container is returned. Another example is making efforts to reduce the amount of packaging used in consumer products. The European Union has been active in adopting laws on packaging waste, and most European supermarkets charge customers for plastic shopping bags in an effort to encourage them to use reusable cloth bags instead.

- Low-waste consumption. Consumers can steer away from products whose manufacture and sale involves wasteful methods. Unfortunately, convenience usually tops environmental concerns in consumer choice, which explains – for example – the attraction of disposable over reusable diapers, or the ongoing attractions of bottled water (see Chapter 7).
- **Extended producer responsibility** (EPR) makes manufacturers responsible for what happens to products at the end of their useful life. First used in Sweden in the 1990s, EPR overlaps with product stewardship and usually involves a commitment by a manufacturer to reuse, buy back, or recycle their used products. A modest case in point is the arrangement made in some US states and several European countries to buy back empty bottles. In the Netherlands, a recycling fee is charged to the buyers of new road vehicles, and when those vehicles reach the end of their useful life, their parts are recycled by a company named Auto Recycling Nederland. A particular effort has been made in Europe to control the production of **e-waste**: used cell phone, televisions, computers and printers that contain plastics as well as toxic substances such as lead, mercury, and cadmium. The production of e-waste, and the failure to develop safe disposal practices, is becoming a growing problem in the South as well (Johri, 2008).

Recovery. The second approach to dealing with waste is to recover and reuse useful commodities, such as paper, glass, and metals. A distinction must be made between **recycling** (which involves using waste material to make a new version of the same product, such as recycled paper or glass) and reuse (which involves using waste material for different purposes, as in turning scrap metal to new uses, or using old tyres as a component of bitumen for roads or safety surfaces in playgrounds). Recycling is pursued most actively in wealthier societies and has come to be hailed as an option where mainly middle-class consumers can play a collective part in addressing an environmental problem, allowing them to feel virtuous and engaged along the way. It also reduces the need to make new products from scratch, and keeps valuable materials in the production and consumption cycle, instead of burying them in landfill.

Unfortunately, the benefits of recycling are not clear (Tierney, 2015). It can be more expensive to recycle materials than to dispose of them in landfill, particularly if it moves beyond paper and metals, and includes different kinds of glass and plastics. There are also often few incentives for consumers: recycling is usually a voluntary undertaking, and the volume of municipal waste that is recycled depends largely on the creation of recycling schemes by entrepreneurs or local government. Consider also the following limitations to recycling:

- Metal and glass can be remelted and reused indefinitely, but both are heavy and thus expensive to transport, and not all glass is equal: there is more market demand for clear glass than for green or brown glass, as a result of which many used wine and beer bottles find their way into concrete aggregate.
- Paper cannot be recycled indefinitely, because its quality deteriorates with each round of recycling.
- Plastics come in different forms and are being used more often, creating a growing problem for which solutions are harder to find. The economics of plastics recycling also depends on the global price of oil; when it is low, it is cheaper for companies to make new plastic than to recycle.
- Some products are 'down-cycled' in the sense that they are made into different and sometimes less valuable products. For example soda bottles are made into the fibres in clothing and carpeting.
- Some materials (such as glass) are more energy-intensive to recycle than others (such as aluminium).
- Transporting products for recycling is more expensive in some parts of a country than others.

The result is that recycling rates vary from one country to another: among OECD member states (see Figure 9.4), Germany, Switzerland, Japan, and Sweden have the best records, using landfill for almost none of their municipal waste, which they either recycle, compost, or incinerate. So successful have Germany and Sweden been, that both are obliged to import waste from other countries to feed their waste-to-energy incineration plants (see later in this section). At the other end of the scale, New Zealand places all its waste in landfill, having made only modest and recent efforts to encourage recycling or to introduce zero waste policies. Its relative slowness to change is explained by a combination of its geographical isolation, the non-interventionist style of its national government, a lack of leadership from the national Ministry of the Environment, and the dominating role of private companies in making waste policy (Davies, 2008: ch. 6).

Mexico and Turkey also rely heavily on landfill (a reflection of the extent to which developing countries have not yet caught up with policies on recycling and reuse), while three other big

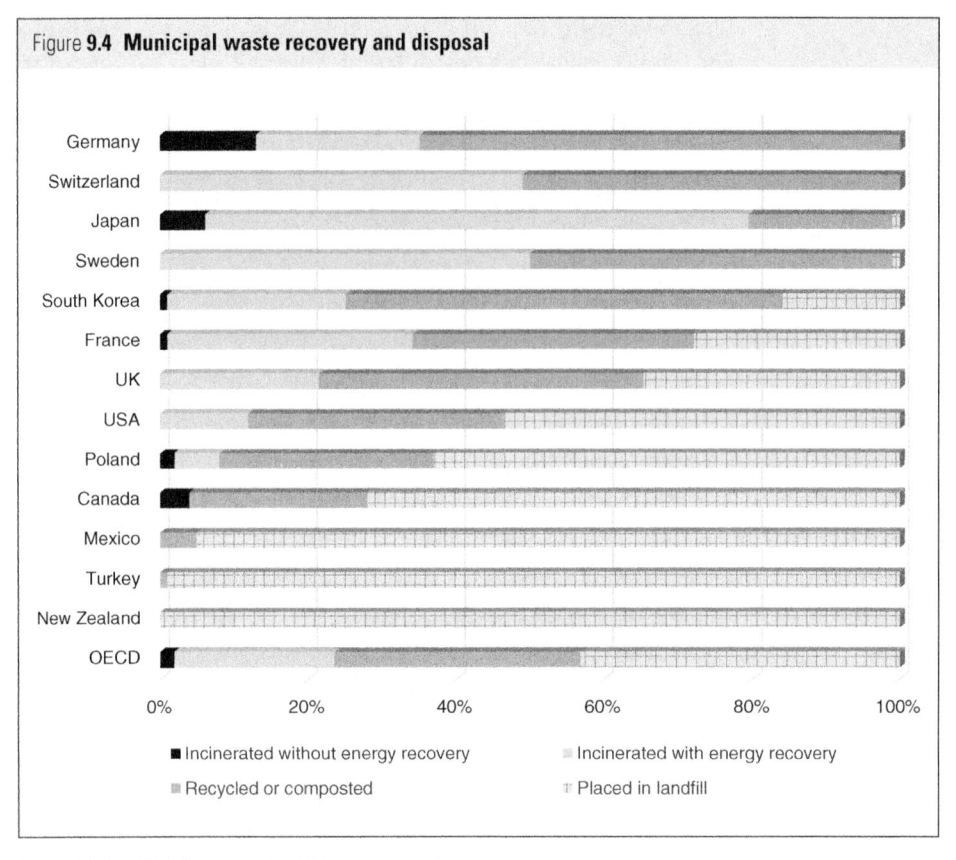

Figure 9.4 Municipal waste recovery and disposal

- Incinerated without energy recovery
- Incinerated with energy recovery
- Recycled or composted
- Placed in landfill

Source: OECD (2015). Figures are for 2013 or most recent.

producers of waste – the United States, the United Kingdom, and France – have mixed records, recycling or composting only 35–43 per cent of their waste. For the OECD as a whole, only about one-third of municipal waste is recycled or composted. Industry has successfully resisted efforts to change policy, which – in the case of the United States – has created 'the illusion of progress while allowing industry to maintain the status quo and place responsibility on consumers and local government' MacBride (2012).

The economic pressures involved in recovery and reuse are quite different in poorer countries. As was the case in pre-twentieth-century Europe and North America, much less waste is produced to begin with, so the amount that is available for recycling is smaller, as are the pressures to develop policies on recycling; China, for example, produces one-sixth as much municipal waste per person as the United States, and one-third as much as Japan. (Ironically, the poorest rural societies are closer to achieving the goal of California-style zero waste than wealthy societies whose residents worry so much more about waste; for the poor, waste is simply not an option.)

At the same time, population growth means that waste production is growing rapidly in many poorer countries, while efforts to recover and reuse are rarely managed by local government; in many cases, recycling only happens because poor people sift through dumps in their search for materials to sell for reuse. In other words, recovery happens, but less as a result of policy than as a result of the poor seeking income and making a virtue out of a necessity. In India, local people known as 'ragpickers' (many of whom are children) make an income from searching through the dumps for recoverable materials. But they face new dangers from the increasingly hazardous quality of waste (particularly e-waste), and their work cannot be expected to keep up with the accelerating production of waste in India. It does not help that few Indians are willing to segregate their waste in order to help with recycling efforts; only about one-third, according to a recent survey in six major cities (Energy and Resources Institute, 2013).

Disposal. Assuming that there is either limited capacity or desire to reduce the production of waste, or to recover and reuse, then policymakers must consider the best means of disposing of it. In some cases, such as radioactive waste, safe storage is the only viable option, although it raises a multitude of problems that have not yet been resolved. Otherwise, waste can be buried in landfill or burned in incinerators, or – raising legal and troubling ethical questions – it can be shipped somewhere else or dumped illegally.

The default option is to bury waste in **landfill**: a site that is created, designed, and ideally managed for the burial of waste. This is the oldest form of waste management, and remains the preferred option in many parts of the world. Landfill has the financial advantage of being relatively cheap and convenient, and it can be arranged at almost any scale where space is available. It has even been used to extend land into coastal waters (including around New York City), and old landfill can also be used to grow forests, and has been used in Australia, Hong Kong, Israel, Singapore, and the United States to build new parks and playgrounds. But landfill also creates several problems:

- Unless carefully managed, waste in landfill can produce gases such as methane and carbon dioxide (both implicated in climate change), can lead to chemicals and heavy metals being leached into water and soil, and can attract pests.
- Landfill sites can be expensive and difficult to buy and maintain, particularly where land is at a premium, such as in or near large and growing cities. It can be transported or shipped further afield, but this generates additional costs.

- The development of landfill sites is often opposed by local residents, sparked by the **NIMBY syndrome** ('not in my back yard') and encouraging them to launch organized opposition (McAvoy, 1999).
- Burying waste means taking resources out of the production and consumption cycle. The value of those resources is illustrated by the way in which landfill has occasionally been mined in an effort to recover valuable materials.

Among OECD countries (see Figure 9.4), 44 per cent of municipal waste ends up in landfill, the highest proportions being in New Zealand (100 per cent), Chile and Turkey (99 per cent), and Mexico (95 per cent). The United States places 54 per cent of its waste in landfill, and Britain about a third of its waste. But several countries – including Belgium, Denmark, Germany, Japan, the Netherlands, Sweden, and Switzerland – have been able to almost entirely do away with landfill, sending all their municipal waste for recycling, composting, or incinerating. Switzerland has long had a policy of shunning landfill, which was expanded in 2000 with a ban on the placing of combustible waste in landfill, and in 2001 with the introduction of a landfill tax. It was also able to send more than half its waste to recycling between 2001 and 2013 despite a 16 per cent increase in the amount of municipal waste generated. The balance was burned in a network of 30 waste-to-energy incinerators (Herczeg, 2013).

Landfill is the most popular option for waste disposal in the South, but often less as a result of deliberate policy than out of habit. Dump sites are usually on the surface, are only minimally maintained, and typically ignore local ordinances on being kept at a distance from inhabited areas. A review in the *Hindustan Times* (Banerjee, 2016) makes several key points about waste in India: the country as a whole produces relatively little garbage (just 3 per cent of the global total, in spite of being home to 17 per cent of the world's population), but most of the waste from its biggest cities (such as Mumbai, Delhi, and Chennai) is placed in a few large dumps that are filled beyond capacity, little of the waste is treated, and local statutes on the distance to be maintained between dumps and local residential areas are mainly ignored. Mumbai's biggest dump has been in operation since the 1920s, covers 132 hectares, stands 15 metres high in some places, and is surrounded by densely populated suburbs (*Indian Express*, 2016).

For its part, the burning of waste is a method that has been used for centuries, and remains common in developing countries. In the North, municipal legislation on air pollution has placed restrictions on burning, which is now an option associated mainly with commercial incineration. First used in the 1890s, this is today a $17 billion global industry with advanced capacity in Europe and

North America, and work is under way in China to build several hundred new plants, including one in the city of Shenzhen that is projected to become the biggest in the world. Incineration has the advantage of permanently removing waste, but incinerators can also be used to generate energy, thereby addressing two environmental challenges at once. Oil-poor Japan disposes of more than 70 per cent of its municipal waste by burning it to generate energy, while the four Scandinavian countries dispose of between 40 and 60 per cent of their waste by the same means. There are almost 500 waste-to-energy plants in Europe, with 99 in Germany (using 25 million tonnes of waste) and 126 in France (using nearly 15 million tonnes of waste) (Confederation of European Waste-to-Energy Plants, 2016). There are 71 plants in the United States, but while they account for 12 per cent of the country's waste, they generate only 0.4 per cent of the country's electricity needs, a proportion that has been static since the mid-1990s (US Energy Information Administration, 2016a).

In spite of their advantages, incinerators pose their own raft of problems (see Table 9.2), not least of which is – once again – the NIMBY syndrome. In spite of technological achievements that have allowed plants to filter out almost all harmful pollutants, there is still public resistance to having incinerators sited near residential areas. Cynics argue that public disquiet about incinerators, landfill, or almost any kind of industrial installation deserves the more uncompromising acronym BANANA: Build Absolutely Nothing Anywhere Near Anything.

Table 9.2 **Incinerators: Benefits and costs**

Benefits	Costs
Reduce the need to dispose of waste in landfill.	Produce ash, much of which is toxic, and all of which must be disposed of safely.
Waste is in constant supply, and landfills can be mined for more.	Their use reduces incentives to reduce waste production.
Incineration is a form of recycling, with recyclable materials being removed before or after incineration.	Destroy materials that could be usefully recycled.
Generating energy from incinerators reduces the need to burn fossil fuels.	Generate air pollutants; much of the cost of construction goes into building pollution controls.
The costs of building incinerators can be offset by generating and selling energy.	Incinerators are more expensive to build and run than coal or nuclear power stations, although costs are coming down.
Constitute a form of domestic energy supply.	Are often built in poorer areas where local opposition will not mobilize so effectively.

Toxic and hazardous wastes

The most troubling aspect of the waste dilemma is how to deal with the toxic and hazardous by-products of industry and energy generation, which must be either carefully reformulated, destroyed, or placed into safe storage. A toxic substance is one that is poisonous or damaging to the health of living organisms, while a hazardous substance is dangerous because of its physical properties: it may be corrosive, ignitable, or reactive (see Table 9.3). Given their advanced levels of industrial development, North America and Western Europe have faced the greatest problems with these kinds of wastes.

In the United States, political attention was first drawn to the problem of the unmanaged disposal of toxic waste by events in Love Canal in upper New York state. In the 1940s, the Hooker Chemical Company began dumping wastes into the abandoned Love Canal in upper New York State. By the time it was covered over in 1953, it contained more than 21,000 tonnes of waste. The land was then sold to a local school board, the contract of sale absolving Hooker of responsibility for any damage or injury that might result, and by 1955 a school and several hundred homes had been built on the site. It was not until 1970 that a story broke in the local press about the dangers posed by the dump, prompting local residents to mobilize and to testify before the US Congress. Ten years later, $15 million was set aside to buy the land and the homes, and almost all residents left the area (for details, see Newman, 2016).

Inspired by such incidents, three pieces of legislation were adopted that have since formed the basis of the US response to the problem of toxic and hazardous substances:

- The Toxic Substances Control Act of 1976 regulates the manufacture and distribution of chemicals, requiring

Table 9.3 **Toxic and hazardous substances**

	Features	*Examples*
Toxic	Poisonous to humans, animals, or plants.	Pesticides, weed killers, household cleaners.
Corrosive	Chemically capable of eating away other substances.	Acid.
Ignitable	Can be set on fire.	Oil, petrol, paint, furniture polish.
Reactive	Can explode and/or release poisonous gas when mixed with other substances.	Chlorine bleach + ammonia = toxic chloramines. Bleach + vinegar = chlorine gas.

manufacturers to inform the US Environmental Protection Agency (EPA) when new chemicals are released onto the market. They are then supposed to be screened and tested, so that the most dangerous can be identified. But the EPA is understaffed and responsible for multiple environmental regulations, there is no obligation on the chemical industry to take the initiative or to test new chemicals, and thousands of such chemicals are pending review. There will, however, be an occasional success story, as with the case of polychlorinated biphenyls (PCBs), which were long used in paint, insulators, and electrical circuits before their dangers were discovered, and production was almost entirely phased out.

- The Resource Conservation and Recovery Act of 1976 regulates solid waste management. It requires the EPA to develop minimum standards for municipal waste landfills, which must then be monitored to ensure that no problems develop. But there were more than 20,000 sites on the EPA list in 2016, making monitoring difficult. The EPA is also required to track hazardous waste from the point of production to the point of disposal ('cradle to grave'), and to work to develop new ways to commercialize waste recovery.

- Finally, the Comprehensive Response, Compensation and Liability Act of 1980 (otherwise known as Superfund), requires the EPA to identify all existing toxic waste sites in the country, and to maintain a National Priority List of abandoned waste sites (including accidental spills and illegal dumps). It must also work towards cleaning them up, ideally by placing responsibility in the hands of those who created the problem (assuming they can be found), but otherwise paying with taxpayer funds. In spite of enormous spending, more than 1,300 sites remained on the priority list in 2016, while 400 others had been cleaned up and removed from the list. Recouping the costs has involved legal proceedings that have in some cases been going on for multiple decades and have generated substantial legal fees.

The European Union has gone further than the United States in terms of controlling new chemicals coming onto the market. In 2007 it launched the REACH programme (Registration, Evaluation, Authorization, and Restriction of Chemicals), which applies to all chemicals made or marketed in the EU. REACH places the burden of proof on the chemical companies, which must identify and manage the risks created by their chemicals, or face government restrictions. It is estimated that there are about 100,000 chemicals in regular use in the EU, of which about one-third are minimally exposed to people, and about 20,000 pose only minimal health risks, leaving about 40,000 that might pose stronger risks.

Box 9.2 The problem of radioactive waste

A unique problem is that created by radioactive waste, which is any material containing dangerous levels of radionuclides (unstable atoms containing excess nuclear energy). There are several different kinds of waste: that created during the mining or processing of uranium, that produced during the operation or decommissioning of nuclear reactors (including spent filters), that produced as a by-product of the construction of nuclear weapons, and that resulting from nuclear weapons testing or accidents at nuclear installations, such as the one in Chernobyl, Ukraine, in 1986, and the one in Fukushima, Japan, in 2011. Wastes are classified and handled differently according to their half-life and levels of radioactivity: very short-lived waste needs storing for only a few years, while high-level waste remains deadly to living organisms for thousands of years, and demands sophisticated and expensive storage (Lee et al., 2013: ch. 1).

The amounts involved are small: about 400,000 tonnes per year, or about 0.1 per cent of the total amount of hazardous waste produced annually (Nuclear Energy Agency, 2016). The problem also immediately affects only the 30 countries that generate electricity from nuclear power, several of which also possess nuclear weapons. But while the idea of nuclear energy has widespread support (except in countries such as Australia, Denmark, Germany, Italy, New Zealand, and Norway), the storage and disposal of radioactive waste is a highly emotive issue (see Blowers, 2016). Nuclear waste has only been with us since the beginning of the nuclear age (dated from the first nuclear explosion in July 1945), but the early years of processing waste were marked by limited understanding and poor design of storage facilities. There is general agreement that high-level waste is best stored underground, where it can be allowed centuries to cool down while ideally posing no threat to life, but efforts to build long-term underground storage sites have so consistently come up against local opposition that no country has yet been able to build an operational underground storage facility. (Most waste is currently stored at or near nuclear facilities.) Technical questions also pose a challenge, including confidence about the geological stability of storage facilities, and the challenge of keeping them dry and intact for thousands of years.

The story of Yucca Mountain in the US state of Nevada is a case in point. First identified in 1977 as a prospective storage facility, it was carefully studied between 1987 and 2002, and building of the facility began. But local opposition was vocal and enthusiastic, particularly given that are no nuclear power stations in Nevada (but overlooking the fact that the Nevada Test Site – which contains Yucca Mountain – was used for almost 1,000 nuclear tests between 1951 and 1992). Doubts were also raised about the geological safety of the site. In 2009, the Obama administration determined that it was not a suitable storage site, construction ended, and the site was fenced off and abandoned, having consumed $15 billion in spending, and leaving the United States without a long-term nuclear waste storage facility.

Less than 1 per cent had been tested as of 2007, creating a culture of 'toxic ignorance' in which little was known about the effects of chemicals in general use or in the waste stream (see Vaughan, 2015). The REACH programme has since changed the direction of EU chemicals policy, and has also had a global impact: all non-EU chemicals manufacturers wishing to do business in the EU must meet EU chemicals standards, which – in turn – places pressure on their home governments to change domestic policy, which means that closer attention will be paid to the chemical content of waste.

Exporting and dumping waste

While landfill and incineration are primarily domestic options for dealing with waste disposal, an international dimension has been added by efforts either to ship waste elsewhere or to dump it into the ocean. As an option, shipping assumes that producers can find other countries willing to take the waste, even for a fee, but it raises legal and ethical questions. China needs materials to feed its growing industry, and has been willing to take metal wastes for recycling, but it is relatively rare in this regard. A different set of challenges is posed by exports of hazardous waste: the increased use of chemicals in industrial processes has led to massive growth since World War II in the production of hazardous waste, from an estimated 5 million tonnes in 1945 to 400 million tonnes in 2000 (Hunter et al., 2010), most of it in the North. This poses a major waste management challenge, particularly in the key producing countries, the four biggest of which are Russia, the United States, Germany, and China.

Exactly how much is moved across borders is unknown, because the data include only legal transfers. But the rising volume of waste produced, combined with the rising costs of processing or storing it properly, and the vocal opposition in the North to the creation of hazardous waste processing or storage facilities, make the prospect of sending it to developing countries attractive. For their part, some in developing countries have seen this as a handy source of income. These factors have combined to create the problem of **toxic colonialism**, meaning the export from the North to the South of materials (including waste) that are illegal or undesirable in their source countries. In some cases the plan was to dispose of the wastes in the target countries, but claims were also sometimes made that the wastes would be processed for reuse, which rang hollow given the lack of processing facilities in many of the target countries.

The first efforts to control movements of hazardous waste were made in the United States during the Carter administration (1976–80), and the conditions placed on such exports became the model for OECD policies adopted in the mid-1980s, which were sparked in part by two headline-making incidents.

- The first happened when several thousand tonnes of ash from waste incinerators in the United States was loaded aboard a ship named the *Khian Sea* in August 1986 and sent to the Bahamas for disposal. The Bahamian government denied it entry and the ship spent the next 16 months sailing to multiple countries as far away as Sri Lanka and Singapore, twice changing its name in an effort to hide its identity. Some of the ash was dumped in Haiti and the rest was thrown overboard in the Atlantic and the Indian Oceans.
- Soon after, producers of radioactive waste in Italy made an arrangement with a Nigerian farmer willing to take 18,000 barrels of waste into storage for $100 per month. But when the Nigerian government found out, they insisted that Italy take the waste back. It was loaded on board a German ship named the *Karin B*, which was denied entry into European ports for two months, and was eventually obliged to return the waste to Italy.

Determined to prevent a recurrence of these kinds of incidents, governments opened negotiations under the auspices of the UN Environment Programme, resulting in the signature of the 1989 Basel Convention on the Control of Transboundary Movements of Hazardous Wastes and their Disposal. The agreement is based on the **proximity principle** (waste should be disposed of as close as possible to its source), encourages parties to minimize the production of waste, and restricts transboundary movements to those instances where 'it is the best environmental solution' and disposal is performed 'in an environmentally sound manner'. A global system for notification and prior consent was arranged, but the focus was on controlling the movement of wastes rather than imposing an outright ban on their export (except to non-party states, one of which – ironically – is the United States). As a result, and in spite of ongoing negotiations, and the signing of a 1999 protocol to the Basel Convention on liability and compensation for damage arising from waste shipments, there is still no agreement on prohibiting the shipment of hazardous wastes for final disposal to any part of the world except Antarctica, where it is prohibited (Gillespie, 2015: 21–31).

African states were sufficiently disappointed in these developments to draw up the regional Bamako Convention on the Ban of the Import into Africa and the Control of Transboundary Movement and Management of Hazardous Wastes within Africa, which went into force in 1998. Unfortunately, the limited political and technical ability of most African states to implement the terms of the convention has meant that it has had little real effect. A case in point is the phenomenon of all the e-waste from Europe that ends up in dumps in locations such as the Agbogbloshie area of Accra, the capital of Ghana (Biello, 2014), in spite of the terms either of the Basel or the Bamako conventions.

Pratt (2011) lists several problems with the Basel Convention:

- It has been unable to stop fraudulent shipments of wastes (which can be hidden, misrepresented, or described as materials destined for recycling).
- Many countries lack the means to prevent or punish illegal activities.
- The convention does not define hazardous waste sufficiently tightly, does not allow for differences among countries in the way they define hazardous waste, and does not take account of new substances being defined as hazardous.
- A total ban would be difficult because it would undermine bona fide recycling and reclamation efforts.
- The meaning of the term *developing country* is changing as several Asian and Latin American countries undergo rapid economic growth (and improve their abilities to process and store waste).

Another problem with hazardous waste (and hazardous materials more generally) is that they can be moved across borders because of anomalies in the law; they may not be hazardous when they are moved, but they become hazardous as a result of what is done with them in the target country. For example, used batteries turned in for recycling by American consumers are often sent to Mexico, where the lead is extracted using methods that are illegal in the United States (Partlow and Warrick, 2016). Similarly, diesel containing sulphur at levels far higher than is allowed in the European Union is exported quite legally to Africa, where standards are lower. The EU limit is ten parts of sulphur per million, but many African states use colonial-era standards that have only recently been revised: several West African countries allow 2,000 parts per million, while Egypt, Somalia and Tunisia allow 5,000 parts per million (BBC News, 2016). Several have recently tightened their standards and have worked to block imports of high-sulphur European diesel.

The shipping of waste from the point of production to the point of disposal is only one part of the challenge of building a workable international waste regime. Unscrupulous producers have long dumped waste into handy local rivers or lakes, but as laws tightened on tracking and disposal, and companies faced substantial fines, so dumping moved out into the open oceans.

There was little control or interest until the early 1970s, but even though the 1972 Convention on the Prevention of Marine Pollution by Dumping of Wastes and Other Matter (the London Convention) prohibits the dumping of waste from ships and aircraft, there was no prohibition from land-based sources until the passage of a 1996 protocol to the convention. This bars almost all kinds of waste from ocean dumping; listed exceptions include dredged material, industrial fish processing waste, offshore platforms and other human-made structures, and organic material of natural origin. However, there are still fewer than 90 parties to the convention, with few south/southeast Asian, Middle Eastern, or African countries having signed. While the treaty is based on the precautionary and the polluter pays principles, it is hard to enforce.

If managing the transboundary movement and dumping of toxic or hazardous wastes is hard enough, even more difficult is the challenge of controlling the accumulation in the ocean of more mundane garbage, much of it plastic and coming from discarded fishing gear and land-based sources. The precise quantities are unknown, current data being based on a combination of beach surveys, computer modelling, and estimates of the amount of garbage entering the oceans (Parker, 2015). Little is also known about the long-term ecological effects, although the evidence based on the damage caused to wildlife does not paint an encouraging picture. The trash tends to congregate on the basis of ocean currents, which have helped create the Great Pacific Garbage 'Patch': a concentration of garbage floating (mainly beneath the surface, and invisible even to satellite images) over large swathes of the north Pacific. Since such waste has come from multiple sources over an extended period of time, stopping further accumulation and cleaning up the existing waste is an international challenge of almost unimaginable proportions.

Discussion questions

- Is there such a thing as true waste?
- Which is the best approach to waste policy: prevention, recovery, disposal, or some combination of these three options?
- Is the zero waste option practical or viable, at least for individual consumers?
- Does the export of waste provide a valuable financial opportunity for target countries, or is it simply a lazy option for producer countries?

Key concepts

- Consumer society
- E-waste
- Extended producer responsibility
- Landfill
- Municipal waste
- NIMBY syndrome
- Product stewardship
- Proximity principle
- Radioactive waste
- Recycling
- Toxic colonialism
- Waste
- Zero waste

Further reading

Brunnengräber, Achim, Maria Rosaria Di Nucci, Ana Maria Isidoro Losada, Lutz Mez, and Miranda A. Schreurs (eds) (2015) *Nuclear Waste Governance: An International Comparison* (Springer). A comparative study of the problem of nuclear waste, looking at how the problem has been addressed in 11 European countries and the United States.

Gillespie, Alexander (2015) *Waste Policy: International Regulation, Comparative and Contextual Perspectives* (Edward Elgar). A broad-ranging overview of the problem of waste, with chapters on its production and disposal, and on the different forms that it takes.

Pratt, Laura A. (2011) 'Decreasing Dirty Dumping? A Reevaluation of Toxic Waste Colonialism and the Global Management of Transboundary Hazardous Waste' in *William & Mary Environmental Law and Policy Review* 35:2, pp. 581–623. A short and clear discussion of international law and policy on the problem of transboundary movements of hazardous waste.

Shinkuma, Takayoshi, and Shunsuke Managi (2011) *Waste and Recycling: Theory and Empirics* (Routledge). Mainly a study of the economics of recycling, but includes several useful chapters on the dynamics of the international trade in waste.

Stokes, Raymond G., Roman Köster, and Stephen C. Sambrook (2013) *The Business of Waste: Great Britain and Germany, 1945 to the Present* (Cambridge University Press). A comparison of how waste policy has evolved in Britain and Germany, two similar countries that have followed different policy paths.

10 Biodiversity: Species, Genes, and Ecology

Key arguments

- The threats posed by human activity to biological diversity go to the heart of our environmental dilemma, and yet we know little about the true breadth or depth of the problem.
- The extinction of species is part of the evolutionary cycle of life, but the current cycle of extinctions is mainly human-made.
- Threats to biodiversity come mainly from habitat destruction, invasive species, pollution, population growth, and overexploitation.
- Habitat destruction poses particular threats to tropical forests, migratory species, and coral reefs.
- Climate change has become the latest and most troubling threat to biodiversity, posing systemic problems that can be resolved only through coordinated international action.
- There are numerous international conventions and programmes with biodiversity as their focus, but whether this amounts to an identifiable biodiversity regime is debatable.

Chapter overview

This chapter focuses on what human actions have meant for other living things, a notion encapsulated in the term *biodiversity*. Related to the more general term *wildlife*, and coined in 1986 for a conference on the topic (Harper and Hawksworth, 1994), it is both a synonym for and a contraction of the term *biological diversity*, and is concerned with the variety and the population of species, and their place in the natural system. Hall (2010a) defines biodiversity as 'the total sum of biotic variation, ranging from the genetic level, through the species level and on to the ecosystem level', while biological diversity is defined in the 1992 Convention on Biological Diversity as 'the variability among living organisms from all sources including ... terrestrial, marine and other aquatic ecosystems and the ecological complexes of which they are part; this includes diversity within species, between species and of ecosystems.'

The concept has three different dimensions:

- Species diversity refers to the variety of species.
- Genetic diversity describes the variety of genes within a species.
- Ecological diversity refers to the variety of ecosystems, natural communities, and habitats.

There is no longer any part of the earth's **biosphere** (those parts of the earth – including land, oceans, and the atmosphere – within which living organisms exist) that has not felt the impact of human action, such that we may now be living in the new geological epoch of the Anthropocene. There also may be no more fundamental measure of the impact of humans on the natural environment than the implications for biodiversity. In spite of this, the threats to biodiversity continue to build, the successful efforts to protect and manage outnumbering the failures. Individual species – particularly the largest and most eye-catching – tend to attract the most attention, but it is the smaller, more numerous and often overlooked species that have the most biological and ecological significance.

The chapter begins with a discussion of the core problem we face in our efforts to measure human impact on biodiversity: we do not know how many species there are on earth, nor do we know the exact populations of most, and thus we cannot be entirely clear about population trends. Estimates of the number of species range from a few million to a trillion or more, a range that means that the authoritative source on endangered species – the Red Data List – is not much more than a study in informed speculation.

The chapter then goes on to review the five major threats to biodiversity: habitat loss, the spread of invasive species, the pressures from human population, the dangers of pollution, and the effects of overexploitation, including the particular problem of trade in endangered species. In each case it looks at the policy response, reviewing the difficulties of making policy, and assessing achievements and failures. The chapter ends with a discussion of the directions so far taken in addressing the threats to biodiversity, including the

> ethical, ecological, and practical arguments involved, and the unbalanced interest in so-called charismatic megafauna. It also looks at the development of protected areas, weighing up their advantages and disadvantages.

Defining the problem

The effectiveness of a policy is determined at least in part by how fully we understand the dimensions of the problem we are addressing. Understanding those dimensions, in turn, is only as good as the available data and the care with which we interpret that data. In the case of biodiversity, we have the peculiar dilemma of having a fairly good grasp of the causes and effects of the pressures it faces, but gaps in the science mean that we can make only educated guesses regarding the numbers and scales involved: we have no complete and agreed system for classifying **species** (defined as actually or potentially interbreeding natural populations), we do not know how many species have existed in the past or exist today, and even in the cases of those species we have identified and studied, we have only variable knowledge regarding their population numbers and trends. We know for certain that many species have become extinct, we are fairly sure that many others are extinct in the wild, and we have strong data suggesting that the numbers of yet others have declined, but the overall picture resembles a jigsaw puzzle from which most of the pieces – as well as the picture of the puzzle we are working on – are missing.

Consider three recent estimates:

- The biologist E.O. Wilson (2007) refers to 'the dark matter of the biological world of bacteria', and suggests that the number of species of bacteria alone could run into the tens of billions.
- In research supported by UNEP, Mora et al. (2011) used the number of species so far catalogued to calculate that the earth supports a total of 8.7 million, within a range of 1.3 million either way (see Table 10.1). However, they also pointed out that only 1.2 million had been described, and that 86 per cent of the species on land and 91 per cent of the species in the oceans awaited description.
- In more recent work, based on combining government datasets on microbes, plants, and animals, Locey and Lennon (2016) concluded that there could be as many as 1 trillion species of microbes alone, with 99.999 per cent of them still unidentified.

On land, the greatest concentration of known species is in tropical regions, with about half of all such species living in the 6 per cent of the earth's land area that is covered by tropical rainforests.

Table **10.1** **Number of species identified**

Class	Features	Number catalogued	Number catalogued as percentage of total predicted
Animals	Species that are motile (capable of motion), including mammals, birds, amphibians, reptiles, insects, fish, sponges.	1,124,000	11
Plants	Trees, flowers, ferns, and mosses.	224,600	21
Fungi	Include yeasts and moulds.	44,000	72
Chromists	Include algae and mildews.	17,900	50
Protozoa	Single-cell organisms with animal-like behaviour.	16,200	50
Bacteria	Micro-organisms; first form of life to appear on earth.	11,050	100

Source: Calculated from Mora et al. (2011). Numbers rounded out.

Table **10.2** **The megadiverse countries**

Australia	India*	Peru*
Brazil*	Indonesia*	Philippines*
China*	Madagascar*	South Africa*
Democratic Republic of Congo*	Malaysia*	United States
Colombia*	Mexico*	Venezuela*
Ecuador*	Papua New Guinea	

* Together with Bolivia, Costa Rica, and Kenya, these countries are members of the Group of Like-Minded Diverse Countries.

Seventeen countries (see Table 10.2) have been classified as 'megadiverse' because of the number and variety of species to which they are home. In 2002, 12 of these countries signed the Cancun Declaration, forming the Group of Like-Minded Diverse Countries in an effort to encourage mutual cooperation. But while this effort draws attention to species density on land, we know much less about the number and variety of species in the oceans, which cover 71 per cent of the area of the planet. The problem is illustrated again by E.O. Wilson (2007), who gives the example of a class of marine phytoplankton known as *Prochlorococcus*: they are responsible for much of the photosynthetic production of oxygen in the oceans, and may be the most abundant organisms on earth, with numbers ranging perhaps into the octillions (10 to the power 27); and yet they were not discovered until 1988.

Extinction of species is part of the evolutionary cycle of life, but science has identified five major 'extinction events' during which there have been particularly large numbers of losses. Some argue that we might now be going through a sixth such event – the **Holocene extinction** (otherwise known as the Anthropocene extinction) dating from 10,000 BCE (Kolbert, 2014) – with human activity as the major cause. Indicating once again how little we actually know, Martens et al. (2003) estimate the current rate of extinction to be anywhere between 100 and 1,000 times the natural rate, while the World Wildlife Fund (2016) suggests that it may be between 1,000 and 10,000 times the natural rate. There have been multiple catalogued examples of extinctions during the Holocene, including the following:

- Perhaps the most famous extinction was that of the dodo, a flightless bird native to the Indian Ocean island of Mauritius that was hunted by Dutch sailors and by introduced invasive species. The last generally accepted sighting of a dodo was in 1662.
- The quagga, a species of southern African zebra that looked like a cross between a zebra and a donkey, was hunted because it competed for forage with livestock. The last one died in Amsterdam Zoo in August 1883.
- The passenger pigeon of North America, once so numerous that passing flocks could block out the sun, was hunted for sport and food. The last one – a female named Martha – died in Cincinnati Zoo in 1914.

While these three species are known to be extinct, there are many others that we can only suppose are extinct, others that we speculate are extinct in the wild, and yet others that were thought to be extinct before being rediscovered. (An example of the latter is the coelacanth, a fish that was thought to have gone extinct about 65 million years ago at the end of the Cretaceous period, but was rediscovered off the coast of South Africa in 1935.) In short, we know remarkably little about the number of species in existence or the number of endangered species. The authoritative catalogue of the latter is the **Red List**, which has been maintained since 1964 by the International Union for Conservation of Nature (IUCN). Its 2015 list contained evaluations of just over 77,000 species, of which just over 23,000 were classified as either critically endangered, endangered, or vulnerable. These included just over 10,500 flowering plants, 2,000 amphibians, 1,375 birds, 1,200 mammals, 1,000 insects, and 730 corals (IUCN, 2015). Several individual examples illustrate the extent of the problem:

- The number of tigers in the wild in their 14 home countries has fallen to about 5,000–7,000.
- African elephant numbers have been halved to 500,000 since the 1980s.

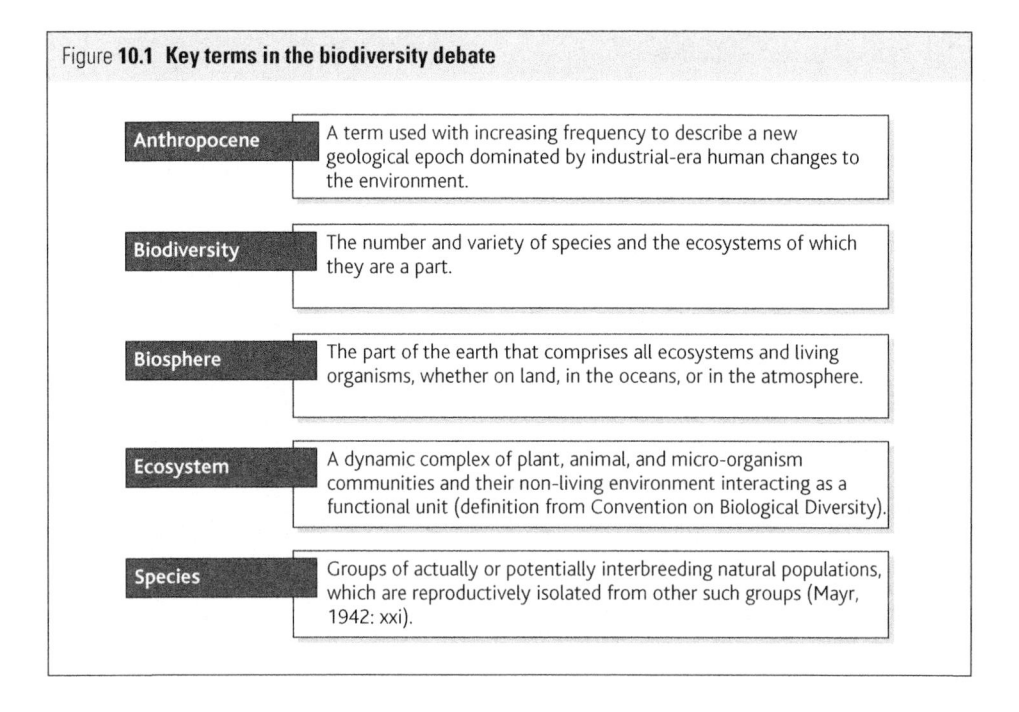

Figure 10.1 Key terms in the biodiversity debate

Anthropocene — A term used with increasing frequency to describe a new geological epoch dominated by industrial-era human changes to the environment.

Biodiversity — The number and variety of species and the ecosystems of which they are a part.

Biosphere — The part of the earth that comprises all ecosystems and living organisms, whether on land, in the oceans, or in the atmosphere.

Ecosystem — A dynamic complex of plant, animal, and micro-organism communities and their non-living environment interacting as a functional unit (definition from Convention on Biological Diversity).

Species — Groups of actually or potentially interbreeding natural populations, which are reproductively isolated from other such groups (Mayr, 1942: xxi).

- The number of black rhinos was cut by 97 per cent during the second half of the last century.
- Blue whales were hunted almost to extinction before being protected in 1966, and there are estimated to be about 5,000–12,000 remaining.

The major threats to biodiversity

While we have only an approximate idea of the scale of the diversity of species, and of the numbers currently threatened, we have a much better idea regarding the threats they face. These fall into five main categories, handily grouped by E.O. Wilson using the acronym HIPPO: habitat destruction, invasive species, pollution, population growth, and overexploitation (see Figure 10.2).

Habitat destruction. This is the most serious threat to biodiversity, occurring when a natural habitat is altered so deeply that it no longer supports the species it originally sustained, with plant and animal populations destroyed or displaced, leading to a loss of biodiversity (Laurance, 2010). The problem comes from multiple sources, prime among them being the clearance of forests and other natural vegetation for agriculture and urban development. The bulk of the clearance has already happened in Europe and North America, where there is now little habitat left in its natural state, and considerable public and political pressure

Figure **10.2** **Threats to biodiversity**

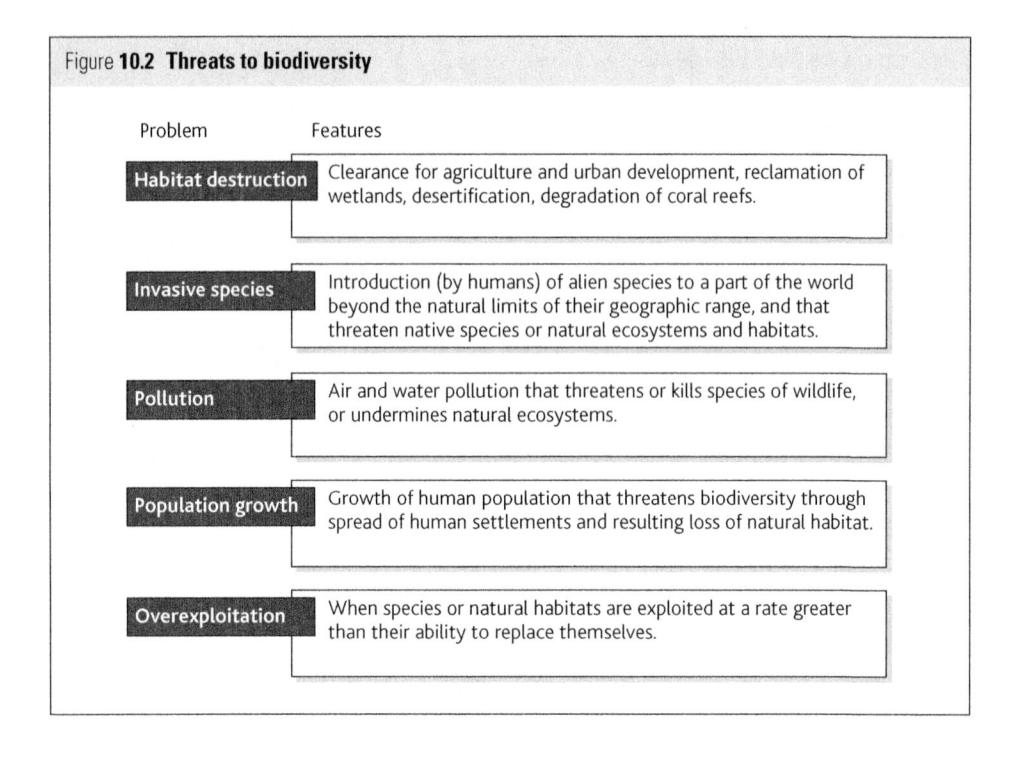

Problem	Features
Habitat destruction	Clearance for agriculture and urban development, reclamation of wetlands, desertification, degradation of coral reefs.
Invasive species	Introduction (by humans) of alien species to a part of the world beyond the natural limits of their geographic range, and that threaten native species or natural ecosystems and habitats.
Pollution	Air and water pollution that threatens or kills species of wildlife, or undermines natural ecosystems.
Population growth	Growth of human population that threatens biodiversity through spread of human settlements and resulting loss of natural habitat.
Overexploitation	When species or natural habitats are exploited at a rate greater than their ability to replace themselves.

to protect what remains. As we saw in Chapter 7, wetlands such as swamps and marshes were long seen as wasted space and were often 'reclaimed' for agriculture or urban development, but it is now understood that they play several critical ecological roles. As a result, they have been mainly better protected and managed.

The most pressing threats to habitats are instead found in South America, Africa, and in south and Southeast Asia, which are witnessing rapid change as populations grow, human settlements spread, farmers seek to produce more off a shrinking land base, and timber and grazing companies exploit resources more aggressively. We saw in Chapter 8 that tropical rainforests face particular threats, because – like wetlands – they are often seen as wasted space, as well as being a valuable source of timber. They are renowned for the diversity of the species they contain and support; they cover only 6 per cent of the earth's land area but contain about half of all known species. They are home to an unknown number of species of animals and plants, are home to many important food plants (including coffee, cocoa, potatoes, and bananas), and play a key role in global weather and climate: as well as attracting rain, which they store and gradually release into rivers, they also recycle carbon dioxide and produce oxygen, helping regulate the global climate and earning themselves the title 'lungs of the earth'. Their role in climate is so critical that the debate over their status and value has recently shifted away from biodiversity to climate change (Martin, 2015: 39).

Migratory species are particularly prone to the problems caused by habitat destruction because their mobile nature means that they are potentially exposed to an array of threats facing different ecosystems, and will have greater trouble adapting to changes. The Convention on the Conservation of Migratory Species of Wild Animals (otherwise known as the Bonn Convention) was signed in 1979 and came into force in 1983, and while it provided recognition of the needs of migratory animals, it focuses on their movements across borders rather than from one biological zone to another. It was also drawn up well before we understood the full implications of climate change; with migratory animals moving in order to seek out the most productive seasonal habitats, and adjusting their behaviour in line with annual changes in the weather, the combination of habitat change and climate change has already resulted in unfortunate examples of mis-timed migration (Robinson et al., 2009).

One response to habitat loss lies in encouraging better understanding and exploitation of the economic value of **wild genetic resources**, the heritable characteristics of wild plants and animals. All domesticated crop plants – such as wheat, corn, rice, and beans – were once wild, but domestication has led over the centuries to reduced genetic diversity (a problem known as the domestication bottleneck), making crops more prone to the effects of disease or climate change. Reaching back through the bottleneck to the wild relatives of these crops has the potential to help address the problem (Dempewolf and Guarino, 2015), as well as opening up human diets to a greater selection of fruits, vegetables, cereals, and pulses than the three dozen or so that currently account for the majority of most people's consumption.

Tropical forests have also been the source of major medicinal drugs that we take for granted, and could be the source of many more; those with tropical forest origins include curare (used as a muscle relaxant for surgery), quinine (an ingredient in anti-malarial medication), diosgenin (derived from the wild yam, and used for birth control and to lower cholesterol), and reserpine (used as a sedative). If tropical forests were to be seen less in terms of their value as a source of timber and land, and more for their plant and animal genetic content, there might be more motivation to ensure their better management. However, there has been a problem with **biopiracy**, meaning the exploitation of indigenous knowledge for profit, without permission or compensation. In an effort to provide more focus on genetic resources, a protocol to the Convention on Biological Diversity was signed in 2010 at Nagoya in Japan, coming into force in 2014. Its goal is to stop biopiracy, and to promote the fair and equitable sharing of benefits arising out of the use of genetic resources, thereby promoting the sustainable use of biodiversity. There were almost immediately concerns that the protocol would slow down access to valuable genetic resources because of the bureaucratic procedures involved (Cressey, 2014).

Moving from the land to the oceans, marine habitats face their own set of challenges, the greatest problems being faced by coastal regions. Coral reefs are the underwater equivalents of tropical rainforests in terms of their biodiversity, being home to about one-third of known marine species. They face threats from pollution, from the warming of ocean temperatures in the wake of climate change (which kills the algae that live in an endosymbiotic relationship with coral polyps, and give corals their colour, leaving them bleached), from the absorption of greater quantities of carbon dioxide and the resulting acidification of seawater, and from deep-sea trawling that scrapes entire ecosystems off underwater mountain ranges. Meanwhile, coastal mangrove forests are cleared for shrimp production or to build new resorts and marinas for tourists. These forests are the ecological backbone of many tropical coastlines, being an important natural habitat, playing a key role in maintaining water quality, and protecting coasts from erosion and the damage wrought by storms.

Tourism plays a critical role in the damage inflicted on habitats, which is ironic given how much it relies upon the attractions of nature. Few tourists set out deliberately to cause harm to nature, but many are unaware of the effects of their actions, whether direct or indirect, and the arrival of growing numbers of visitors usually means the provision of infrastructure to meet their needs (including roads, airports, hotels, restaurants, marinas, shopping malls, and golf courses), and tourism has also had a history of encouraging the introduction of alien species. The cumulative effects include the disruption of ecologically sensitive areas, migration networks, and food chains. Tourism is one of the biggest industries in the world, a major employer and source of foreign exchange and investment, and it continues to expand: the number of international tourist arrivals grew from 25 million in 1950 to 530 million in 1995, and 1.3 trillion in 2014 (World Tourism Organization, 2016; World Bank, 2016).

While the value of tourism to many communities could be turned into a compelling economic argument for better environmental management, there has been a general failure to balance its demands on natural capital, or to achieve what Hall (2010b) describes as 'steady-state tourism'. While he defines sustainable tourism as the kind that involves 'development without growth in throughput of matter and energy beyond regenerative and absorptive capacities', he considers steady-state tourism to be different in that it 'encourages qualitative development but not aggregate quantitative growth to the detriment of natural capital'. A reaction to the problems of tourism has emerged with **ecotourism**, giving visitors opportunities to visit natural environments while also encouraging

Box 10.1 *The special place of wilderness*

Routinely forgotten or overlooked in environmental policy – whether at the national or at the international level – is **wilderness**, defined by Watson et al. (2016) as 'biologically and ecologically largely intact landscapes that are mostly free of human disturbance'. It might be argued that true wilderness is more accurately defined by deleting the words *largely* and *mostly* from this sentence, but it is an indication of just how far the effects of human activity have been felt that we must use these adverbs. In other words, the reach of human-made change has been such that no true wilderness remains. The term *wilderness* now implies simply the absence of permanent human development or settlement in the form of roads, buildings, or energy supply, for example. This is reflected in its definition in the 1964 Wilderness Act in the United States, which was the first attempt at the national level to systematically define and protect wilderness. The definition, which reportedly took more than 15 years and more than 60 drafts to win approval (Harvey, 2005), defines wilderness as an area of undeveloped land 'retaining its primeval character and influence without permanent improvements or human habitation, which is protected and managed so as to preserve its natural conditions'.

Wilderness has long been regarded as dangerous, threatening, undesirable, as a handicap to progress, and as something to be conquered rather than to be preserved and appreciated. More recently, though, its value has been better understood, partly in symbolic terms and partly in ecological terms. In regard to the former, wilderness is often seen to represent the pure and the unchanged, and as an opportunity for visitors to reflect and contemplate. In regard to the latter, wilderness plays multiple critical roles as a stronghold for biodiversity, as a carbon sink, as a buffer and regulator of local climates, and as a home for some the world's most marginalized human communities.

In spite of changes in the way it is perceived, the challenges faced by wilderness have been relatively little studied (for a rare and recent review of wilderness policy in Europe, see Bastmeijer, 2016), and the protection of wilderness is barely addressed in international environmental treaties, and continues to be threatened by human action. With almost a quarter of the earth's land area consisting of wilderness (mostly in North America, northern South America, North Asia, North Africa, and Australia), it may seem as though there is little cause for concern, but Watson et al. found that nearly 10 per cent had been lost in the period 1990–2015 alone.

---

in them a greater appreciation of biodiversity. Its educational qualities are reflected in the definition of ecotourism offered by the International Ecotourism Society (2016): 'responsible travel to natural areas that conserves the environment, sustains the well-being of the local people, and involves interpretation and education'.

Invasive species. The second source of threats to biodiversity comes from bioinvasion, or the introduction of alien or **invasive species**. These are non-native species that are introduced by humans to a part of the world that lies beyond the natural limits of their geographic range, and that can threaten native species or natural ecosystems and habitats. The spread of species into new ecological niches is nothing new, but the phenomenon has expanded on the back of international trade and mass tourism. One estimate (Pimentel et al., 2005) suggests that as many as half a million species have been accidentally or deliberately introduced to areas outside their natural range. Whether accidental or deliberate, the results have often been disruptive or devastating for species native to a region. The effects are made worse by climate change and its impact on weather patterns, and bioinvasion has become so widespread that it has spawned its own sub-field of ecology, known as invasive biology (Stoett, 2010). Three examples illustrate the problem:

- The classic example of deliberate introduction was the release of a few rabbits in Australia in 1859 for hunting and sport. From a single farm, they quickly multiplied and spread, threatening many of the species of fauna and flora that are unique to Australia. Numerous efforts have since been made to contain them, including the building of rabbit-proof fences, the introduction of myxomatosis (a disease that is lethal to rabbits), and organized efforts to shoot rabbits, but the effects have been limited. Along with soil erosion, rabbits are the single most significant threat to biodiversity in Australia.
- Kudzu is a perennial vine that is native to Asia and was introduced into the United States as an ornamental bush and shade plant at the Philadelphia Continental Exposition in 1876. Farmers were encouraged to use it to control soil erosion in the 1930s and 1940s, and it is now common along roadsides, where it climbs over trees and shrubs, creating unnatural shading that can kill native species.
- The water hyacinth is native to western Brazil, but is now found in about 50 countries, where it often blocks waterways and changes the natural ecology of rivers and lakes by preventing sunlight and oxygen from reaching submerged native plants.
- Diseases have been spread by humans that have taken their toll on plants and animals. One example is Dutch elm disease, a fungus spread by elm bark beetles, and so-named because it was identified in the 1920s in the Netherlands. Originating in Asia, it was accidentally introduced into Europe and the Americas, where it has killed native populations of elms, once common in many northern forests.

The accidental introduction of invasive species comes through many different channels: they are spread through shipments of biological materials such as food and soil, through the pet trade (part of the reason why so many Burmese pythons are now found in the Everglades National Park of Florida), through the carrying of diseases by humans, through the escape of ornamental plants into the wild, and through the introduction of insects in wood. International shipping has long been a source of the problem, unintentionally introducing rats all over the world, and creating problems when marine organisms contained in ballast water are set free and colonize non-native environments. (The International Convention for the Control and Management of Ships' Ballast Water and Sediments was adopted in 2004, but has not yet come into force because it has not won enough ratifications.) Once released, invasive species can cause damage by preying on or competing with native species, introducing and spreading disease, and altering ecosystems.

Pollution and climate change. Pollution is another threat to biodiversity, with multiple sources involved: agricultural and urban run-off pollute rivers and lakes, sewage contributes to the problem of eutrophication discussed in Chapter 7, oil drilling and transportation threaten sensitive ecosystems, and shipping generates a variety of problems for habitats, including oil spills, ship groundings, anchor damage, and the dumping of waste and ballast water. We are all too familiar with disturbing images of seabirds covered in oil after a major spill, or washed up dead from suffocation on beaches. This is usually just the tip of the iceberg, however, with spills often causing medium- to long-term environmental, economic and social disruption, as well as generating large clean-up bills.

Although large events win the most attention – such as the blowout of the Ixtoc I oil well in the Gulf of Mexico in 1979–80, the Gulf war oil spills of 1991, and the *Deepwater Horizon* explosion in the Gulf of Mexico in 2010 – many of the problems stem from more routine events such as accidental spills during the loading and unloading of oil. With growing international demand for oil over the last few generations, the threat of oil spills has grown, even if the number of spills has fallen as better safety procedures are used. The International Tanker Owners Pollution Federation, created in the wake of the *Torrey Canyon* disaster of 1967, has collected data on about 10,000 spills since 1970, and notes that the number of spills has fallen from an annual average of 24.5 in the 1970s to 1.8 in 2010–15, with more than 80 per cent being spills of less than 7,000 tonnes (International Tanker Owners Pollution Federation, 2017). The league of the biggest tanker disasters is headed by incidents such as *Atlantic Empress* (off Tobago, 1979), *Amoco Cadiz* (off France, 1978), and *Exxon Valdez* (off Alaska, 1989), and it is reassuring that they mainly happened many years ago.

While it is more than pollution, because of its multiple environmental effects, climate change has become the latest and most troubling threat to biodiversity. Hunting, overexploitation, and encroachment on natural habitat have all played their role in reducing the numbers and the range of species, but they have all been relatively isolated (and isolatable) events. Climate change, but contrast, is a systemic problem that can be resolved only through focused and coordinated international action. The threats it poses to biodiversity are discussed in more depth in Chapter 12.

Population. The growth of human population is clearly a threat to biodiversity because of the spread of human settlements and the resulting loss of natural habitat, but it is perhaps the most ambiguous of the five major threats. It took until 1960 for the human population to cross the 3 billion mark, but only another 51 years for it to cross the 7 billion mark, and while growth has begun to even out – the 10 billion mark is not projected to be crossed for another 70 years (UN Population Fund, 2016) – the pressures of population growth are felt most keenly in many of the tropical regions that are home to the greatest biodiversity.

Urban growth is the key problem: in 1960, just over one-third of the human population lived in cities, a proportion that had risen to 54 per cent in 2014. This period has seen the rise of megacities (those with a population greater than 10 million), including Tokyo, Shanghai, Jakarta, Beijing, Karachi, Mexico City, and Sao Paulo. Tokyo today tops the list with a population of nearly 40 million people; by way of comparison, the world's biggest city in 1950 was New York, with a population of 13 million. The problem is not just urban spread as cities reach further into neighbouring rural areas, but the growing demand for resources such as water and food crops from growing urban populations, the construction of supporting infrastructure such as roads and dams, and more pollution deriving from urban sources.

Overexploitation. The final threat posed to biodiversity takes the form of overexploitation, which occurs when species or natural habitats are exploited at a rate greater than their ability to replace themselves. We saw in Chapter 8 the problems faced by forests and fisheries as natural resources, but those same problems also have implications for biodiversity; the loss of forests means also the loss of the animal and plant species that live within those forests, while overfishing undermines biodiversity through the loss of fish stocks, the unintentional taking of other marine species, and damage to marine ecosystems.

A particular form of overexploitation is created by the international trade in endangered species, whose rarity makes them valuable to collectors. Rhino horn offers an example: valued in several Asian markets for its (mythical) medicinal properties, and becoming harder to find as a result of declining numbers of rhinos, it has been rumoured to be fetching prices on the black market that would make it more valuable by weight than gold, diamonds, or cocaine. The international trade in ivory has had similar dynamics and caused similar problems for the remaining populations of African elephants.

The legal response centres on the Convention on International Trade in Endangered Species of Wild Fauna and Flora (CITES), which was opened for signature in 1973 and came into force in 1975. Supported by a trust fund made up of contributions from its signatories, the convention maintains a list of the most endangered species (including gorillas, tigers, and rhinos) and a separate list of species that could be threatened in the event that trade is not controlled. Meetings of the parties are held every three years, but opinion differs on the efficacy of the convention. It is criticized for the failure of its parties to expand the list of endangered species, their unwillingness to take action against countries that are failing to live up to their obligations, and for its focus on individual species rather than on taking a more holistic approach to protecting the ecosystems in which they live (see Bowman, 2013; Couzens, 2013).

Shaping biodiversity policy

Most of the environmental problems we have so far reviewed have a measurable and direct effect on humans: air and water pollution, for example, threatens our health, and we can often see, smell, or taste it. It has a clear political and economic dimension, can influence the outcome of elections, and is directly related to the kind of industrial activity of which we are almost all consumers. With biodiversity, the links with human action are often less clear, and the responses are often more emotionally driven; when we hear that tropical forests or coral reefs are under threat, or we are shown images of giant pandas and tigers, we might be worried or saddened, but the political connection is usually softer and more tenuous. And biodiversity policy is complex, because there are at least three different perspectives to consider:

- The ethical argument holds that all species should be respected in their own right.
- The ecological argument holds that all species have a place and a purpose, and that the loss of species degrades ecological stability.
- The practical argument focuses on the utility value of species: how much they are worth for food, medicines, drugs, or tourism.

There are numerous international conventions and programmes with biodiversity as their focus, including many at the regional level, and some focused on particular ecosystems and even

Box 10.2 *The dominance of charismatic megafauna*

Biodiversity policy is shaped in part by human emotion: we do not think of all species as being equal, with the result that the policy agenda is driven less by the relative ecological importance of species than by the appeal of different species to humans. In terms of generating public awareness and political support for changes in policy, it tends to be the big mammals that draw the most attention, because they elicit the most sympathy and excitement, and have come to play the role of flagship species, or rallying points around which to attract public attention and support for conservation. Their dominance is exemplified by the phenomenon of **charismatic megafauna** such as elephants, lions, tigers, leopards, pandas, bald eagles, and polar bears. Visitors are drawn to them at zoos, they attract the most research grants, and they are the subject of the most TV documentaries, but they are rarely the most ecologically important members of their respective ecosystems.

In ecological terms, we should be most concerned about the smaller, the less charismatic, and the less visible species. Prime among these are insects, which we mainly regard with something ranging between fear, disgust, irritation, mild interest, and indifference, and yet upon which we rely in more ways than we realize. As E.O. Wilson (2007) puts it, 'If we were to wipe out insects alone … on this planet – which we are trying hard to do – the rest of life and humanity with it would mostly disappear from the land. And within a few months.' There was cause for concern, for example, about Colony Collapse Disorder impacting bees on both sides of the Atlantic in the 1990s. Bees have a critical ecological roll in their work as pollinators, most importantly (for humans, at least) in regard to crop plants. Climate change, disease, parasites, and the use of chemicals in agriculture were all blamed, although there was no certainty about which factors had the most impact. By 2015 it seemed that the numbers were recovering, but again the explanation was unclear (Ingraham, 2015).

When it comes to generating public concern about the condition of biodiversity, no single species plays as visible a role as the giant panda of China. Brought to international attention when it was chosen in 1961 as the symbol of the World Wildlife Fund, efforts to breed giant pandas in captivity repeatedly attract news headlines, and they have even become actors in international diplomacy with agreements between the government of China and zoos around the world to borrow pandas. At the domestic level, other charismatic megafauna have come to symbolize efforts to protect biodiversity, as in the case of polar bears in the Arctic, bald eagles in the United States, tigers in India, and rhinos and elephants in eastern and southern Africa.

Even if the human bias towards charismatic megafauna can be distracting, it can be leveraged for the benefit of other species and entire ecosystems: charismatic species are flagships that can be used as symbols or rallying points to stimulate public awareness (Heywood, 1996). Protecting such species in their natural environment can have an **umbrella effect** of protecting all other species in the same habitat or ecosystem, and their marketing value can be exploited to use them as surrogates to raise funds for the protection of all species living in that ecosystem (Di Minin and Moilanen, 2014), or to draw attention to the wider threats to biodiversity. But the umbrella effect also has drawbacks: the plight of an umbrella species may not be indicative of broader problems in its natural habitat, and to a large extent it is a matter of faith rather than scientific certainty.

particular species (see Table 10.3 for examples). But whether this amounts to an identifiable biodiversity regime, given its piecemeal nature and the lack of much convergence of policy, is debatable. UNESCO was the sponsor of the launch in 1971 of the Man and the Biosphere Programme, designed to encourage scientific research on the relationship between humans and their environment. The programme is behind the designation of World Biosphere Reserves, of which there are now almost 700 in 120 countries. This designation gives these reserves a status of global significance, and encourages protection and research. Related designations are given under the 1972 World Heritage Treaty, which identifies sites of global cultural and natural significance, including the Galapagos Islands, Yellowstone National Park in the United States, Serengeti National Park in Tanzania, and the Great Barrier Reef off Australia. A philosophical basis for biodiversity policy was provided in 1982 when the UN adopted the World Charter for Nature, which argued that nature should be respected, the population levels of all forms of life should be at least sufficient for their survival, that special protection should be given to unique areas and representative

Table **10.3 International treaties on biodiversity**

Signature	Focus
1951	Plant protection.
1971	Wetlands of international importance especially as waterfowl habitat.
	Man and the Biosphere Programme.
1972	Protection of the world cultural and natural heritage.
1973	International trade in endangered species of wild fauna and flora.
1974	Polar bears (signed by five Arctic states).
1979	Conservation of migratory species of wild animals.
	Conservation of European wildlife and natural habitats.
1980	Antarctic marine living resources.
1992	Biological diversity.
2001	Plant genetic resources for food and agriculture.

samples of different ecosystems, that ecosystems and organisms used by humans should be managed sustainably, and that such principles should be reflected in national and international policy.

Globally, the most significant international treaty is the Convention on Biological Diversity (CBD), opened for signature in 1992 with the goal of encouraging governments to develop national biodiversity strategies. Almost all member states of the UN have ratified the convention, with the notable exception of the United States, which was also alone in failing to support the World Charter for Nature. This is particularly puzzling given that the United States was a leader in developing national and local-level law and policy on species protection, revolving around the 1973 Endangered Species Act. Blomquist (2002) explains the anomaly in terms of an internal struggle between presidents and Congress over foreign policy, a resistance among American conservatives to the strengthening of environmental law (whether at the domestic or the international level), and the influence of the US corporate sector in biotechnology. The United States has participated in all CBD conferences, supports the work of the convention, and has strong domestic law on biodiversity, while its corporate interests cannot work independently in a globalized world. Nonetheless, the absence of a major actor from a key international agreement is rarely without political implications.

In 2002, the goal was set under the CBD of significantly reducing the rate of biodiversity loss by 2010, but it proved too ambitious. The 2010 meeting of CBD signatories in Aichi, Japan, set several new targets, based on a general goal of 'mainstreaming biodiversity across government and society' by, for example, making people aware of the value of biodiversity, at least halving the rate of habitat loss, ensuring that all fish were harvested sustainably, ensuring that all agriculture was sustainable, and preventing the extinction of known threatened species: all of this was to be done by 2020. By 2014 it was clear that few of the targets would be met. The periodic report published that year by the CBD secretariat noted that there was a time lag between taking action and seeing an outcome, the responses were insufficient relative to the pressures, there was limited knowledge on which actions were having the most positive impact, and regional variation meant that progress in some parts of the world was being offset by failure in others (Convention on Biological Diversity, 2014: 10, 18–19).

The case of protected areas

The major implement in the toolbox of approaches to protecting biodiversity is the setting aside of **protected areas** such as national parks or nature preserves where development is either restricted or banned. While the idea was not new, the United States became a global leader in 1872 when it created the world's first national park at Yellowstone, presaging the creation of many more: the United States now has nearly 60 national parks, as well as a network of national forests, wilderness areas, wildlife refuges, rangelands, monuments, and state parks, giving protection to about 14 per cent of its land area. Almost every country today has some protected land, although the proportion varies significantly, from a high of 54 per cent in Venezuela and Slovenia to a low of 0.2 per cent in Turkey (see Figure 10.3). (It is interesting to note that several members of the Group of Like-Minded Diverse Countries lag well behind in terms of the declaration of protected land; they include South Africa, India, and Madagascar.) The world's biggest terrestrial protected area is the Northeast Greenland National Park, which was established in 1974 and covers

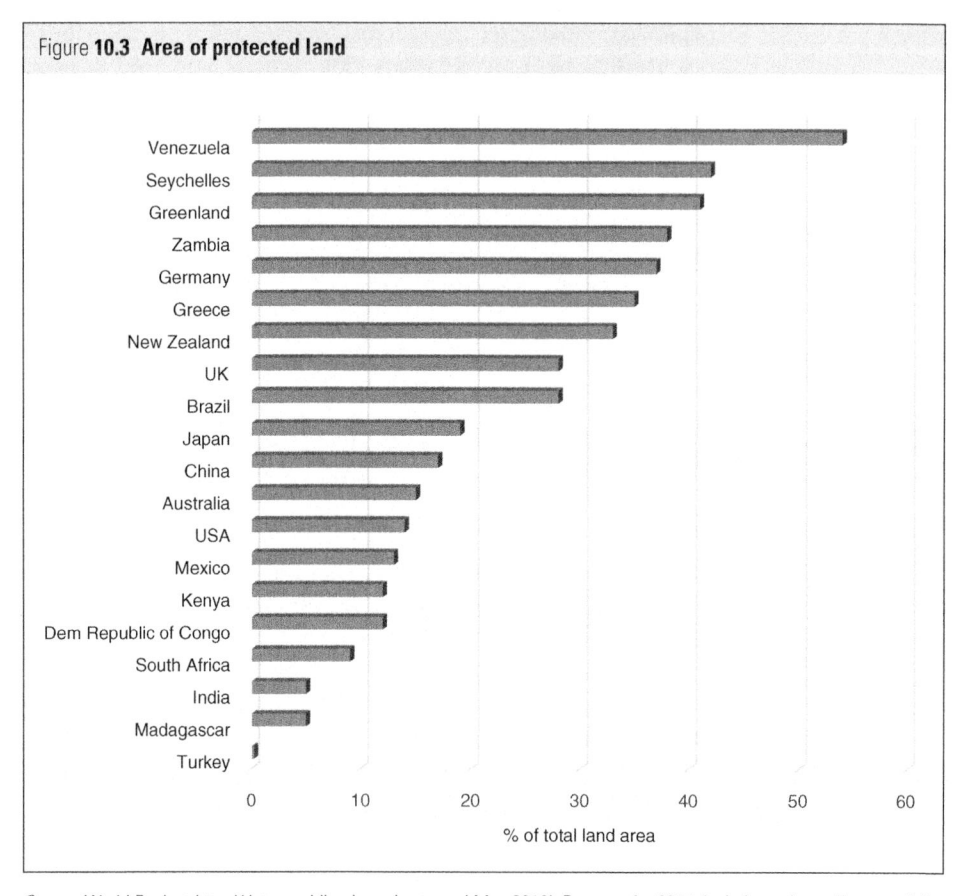

Figure **10.3** Area of protected land

Source: World Bank at http://data.worldbank.org (accessed May 2016). Data are for 2014. Includes only totally or partially protected areas of at least 1,000 hectares that are designated by national authorities as scientific reserves with limited public access.

972,000 square kilometres, or an area bigger than that of France and Italy combined.

Quantity is less important than quality in terms of the efficacy of protected areas, there being no guarantee that designation will lead to protection. They have sometimes been criticized as islands of nature in a sea of humanity, and in some cases have become a victim of their own success: national parks in the North have often attracted so many visitors that roads, buildings, hotels, and restaurants have often followed in their wake, and the parks are being loved to death. Elsewhere, protected areas have caused resentment among local populations either because they deny access to other users, such as mining and timber companies, or because – particularly in poorer countries – they might be seen as being of more interest to wealthy tourists than to land-starved local residents. This can sometimes make them irresistible magnets for **poaching**: the illegal capture, removal, or killing of wild animals and plants.

Trade in endangered species has overlapped with security in the sense that many biodiversity-rich African states suffer from internal instability, making it difficult to protect hunted species and to control poaching, which sometimes overlaps with the activities of organized crime, and with corruption in authoritarian (and even democratic) states. This means, in turn, that the more peaceful means for guarding protect areas and for addressing the root causes of poaching may no longer always work. There has been a debate over the use of the military to hunt down poachers, but as well as the legality of such methods, Duffy (2014) is critical of the failure of militarized responses to address the bigger picture: such approaches fail, she argues, because 'they do not resolve the underlying reasons why people poach in the first place; and they do not tackle either the role of global trading networks or the continued demand in end-user markets. Ultimately, they result in coercive, unjust and counterproductive approaches to wildlife conservation'.

There has been a particular growth in the creation of protected areas since the 1960s, a new boost being given after 1992 with the passage of the Convention on Biological Diversity, which includes a commitment by signatories to establish 'a system of protected areas or areas where special measures need to be taken to conserve biological diversity'. The term *protected area* takes many different forms with different regulations: some areas are so ecologically sensitive that public access is strictly controlled, others welcome visitors but restrict construction other than roads and visitor centres, and yet others – particularly in Europe – were created long after all land was settled or changed, so they contain roads, towns, and farms, but further development is restricted and

Table **10.4 Protected areas: Benefits and costs**

Benefits	Costs
Protection for species, habitats, and ecosystems, and places to study ecology with limited human disruption.	Many species and ecosystems remain mainly or wholly outside the boundaries of protected areas.
Source of employment and income for often remote and isolated regions.	Can be a source of frustration for poorer and/or more rural local populations who have few independent opportunities outside those provided by the protected areas. Some may have been forcibly moved in order to make way for a protected area.
Protection for local economies and cultures linked to natural environment.	Protection usually prevents any other use for the designated area.
Protected status can turn wildlife into a valuable commodity, providing an economic incentive for conservation.	The value of animals and plants as commodities can encourage poaching.
Protection confirms the commitment of states to respect the value of biodiversity.	Many protected areas exist only in name, lacking adequate funding or a supportive legal framework.
Protection helps emphasize the value of species and natural landscapes as symbols of a country or a locality.	Nature is separated from humans, discouraging people from thinking of themselves within their natural environment.

Source: For more detailed discussion, see Hayes and Ostrom (2005) and Brockington et al. (2008): ch. 4.

monitored. In most cases the areas are owned and maintained by local or national government, and as such are subject to legal regulation, but in others the land is privately owned and managed on a different basis.

In an effort to provide some consistency for an otherwise ambiguous term, IUCN has defined a protected area as 'a clearly defined geographical space, recognised, dedicated and managed, through legal or other effective means, to achieve the long term conservation of nature with associated ecosystem services and cultural values' (Dudley, 2008: 8). Using this definition, IUCN (2016) calculates that about 10 per cent of the earth's land surface – an area about the size of South America – is protected in some way. While this might seem impressive, it falls far short of the target set by the Convention on Biological Diversity: the protection of 17 per cent of the earth's land surface by 2020.

Efforts have also been made to protect marine biodiversity through the creation of marine reserves or underwater national parks, and the designation of protected 'no-take' areas designed to allow the most sensitive marine environments to recover from human stresses. However, while the oceans contain the two largest protected areas on earth (the Natural Park of the Coral Sea around the French overseas territory of New Caledonia, and the Pacific Remote Islands Marine National Monument administered by the US government), only 3.4 per cent of the total area of oceans has protected status. And, even more than is the case on land, much of the protection is in name only, with few meaningful safeguards actively implemented. Indeed, protection of marine areas emphasizes the many advantages and disadvantages of protection in general, on whose merits the jury is still out (see Table 10.4).

Discussion questions

- Does it matter how little precision we have in our understanding of the extent of the threats posed to species?
- What kinds of arguments in favour of biodiversity protection are likely to have the most appeal to people in different countries?
- In making the case for biodiversity protection, are charismatic megafauna an opportunity or a diversion?
- Critically assess the IUC definition of a protected area. Does it need further development and more precision?

Key concepts

Biodiversity

Biopiracy

Biosphere

Charismatic megafauna

Ecosystem

Ecotourism

Holocene extinction

Invasive species

Poaching

Protected areas

Red List

Species

Umbrella effect

Wild genetic resources

Wilderness

Further reading

Brockington, Dan, Rosaleen Duffy, and Jim Igoe (2008) *Nature Unbound: Conservation, Capitalism and the Future of Protected Areas* (Earthscan). A study of therise of protected areas, their social impact, and their current social and economic position.

Kolbert, Elizabeth (2014) *The Sixth Extinction: An Unnatural History* (Henry Holt). An assessment of the sixth mass extinction in recorded history – the one caused by humans – told through the stories of species that are already gone and others that are in danger.

Lovejoy, Thomas E., and Lee Hannah (2005) *Climate Change and Biodiversity* (Yale University Press). An edited collection with cases studies on the effects of climate change on biodiversity.

Schneider, Jacqueline L. (2012) *Sold into Extinction: The Global Trade in Endangered Species* (Praeger). A review of the problem, with chapters on the structure of trade in endangered species, examples of the problem, and suggestions for solutions.

Wilson, Edward O. (2010) *The Diversity of Life* (Harvard University Press). A review (first published in 1992) of the scale of earth's biodiversity by the Pulitzer Prize-winning American biologist.

11 Energy: The Slow Road to Renewables

Key arguments

- The world still relies heavily on fossil fuels, sources of energy that are still mainly cheap and plentiful, but that are also finite in supply, and highly pollutive.
- The contribution of coal and natural gas to energy supply has grown in recent decades, while that of oil has fallen, and nuclear power goes through ups and downs.
- The contribution of renewable sources has grown little in recent decades, thanks mainly to the hold of fossil fuels on economies and governments, and the need for upfront investments in the development of renewables.
- Debates over energy policy have long been driven by concerns over the security of supplies, but are increasingly driven by concerns about air pollution and climate change.
- Few states have an energy policy that goes much beyond a concern with security of supplies, although acid pollution – and, more recently, climate change – has pushed the environment further up the agenda in Europe and North America.
- New scientific understanding, public opinion, technological change, and international peer pressure promise to continue changing the directions taken with energy policy.

Chapter overview

The source of many of our environmental problems can be found in our reliance on fossil fuels: coal, oil, and natural gas that were created over millions of years by the decomposition and compression of organic matter. The seeds of that reliance were sown during the Industrial Revolution when new inventions in Britain brought structural change in production methods: the steam engine, the flying shuttle, the spinning jenny, the water frame, and new methods for smelting iron all transformed their respective enterprises. They also needed cheap and ready sources of energy, and since Britain had plenty of coal, it became the foundation of the Industrial Revolution and started us on the road to our current reliance on fossil fuels. Coal was later joined by petroleum (the major source of energy for transport) and – after World War II – by natural gas (used for heating, electricity generation, and transport). Coal was also increasingly used to generate electricity for lighting, heating, and powering appliances.

While the industrial world thereby became reliant on sources of energy that were cheap and plentiful, they are also finite in supply, and are highly pollutive: the extraction and transport of fossil fuels has numerous environmental effects, and their combustion produces harmful air pollutants, including sulphur dioxide, nitrogen oxides, and carbon dioxide. It is interesting to speculate what might have happened had inventors and leaders of industry instead investigated and developed renewable sources of energy, such as wind power, water power, and solar power. To be sure, windmills and watermills had long been used on a localized basis, but they were never developed to the same extent as coal-fired power stations or petrol-powered road vehicles. Industry, transport, and domestic consumers instead came to rely on sources of energy whose long-term costs were not fully understood, or were – at least – ignored in the interests of short-term needs and profits.

The realization that fossil fuels are dirty and that they will eventually run out has pushed us slowly towards other sources of energy. The first major step in that direction was taken in the 1950s with the development of nuclear power. But while it had much promise, it was also tied uncomfortably closely to the development of nuclear weapons, it generated radioactive waste that has proved difficult to manage, and a series of accidents and near-misses at nuclear power stations raised concerns about safety and security. More recently, there has been more interest and investment in biofuels, solar power, wind power, and water power, all of which have the advantage of being renewable, but which also raise a variety of technological problems and in some cases pose their own sets of environmental threats.

> This chapter begins with a review of our major sources of energy, and looks at the trends taking place in each sector, and the environmental problems they generate. It goes on to look at the changing prospects for renewable energy, which currently meet only 14 per cent of our global energy needs, but will inevitably continue to play an ever bigger role in the supply of commercial energy as technology changes and market forces push us away from fossil fuels. The chapter ends with an assessment of energy policy, the main feature of which is its underdevelopment. Few states have a clear set of policy goals (beyond the security of supply), there is little in the way of an international energy regime, and it has mainly been left to the private sector to take the lead on change.

Defining the problem

At a minimum, we need energy to cook our food and to keep us warm (or cool in hot climates). But we also need it to power our industries and transport systems, and to supply the electricity that runs the appliances that most of us in the North and the urban South take for granted in homes and offices: lights, computers, phones, photocopiers, printers, televisions, radios, fridges, and stoves. As human population and needs grow, so does demand for energy, the annual consumption of which has more than doubled since 1973 to nearly 13.7 million tonnes of oil equivalent (Mtoe). The North still accounts for the lion's share of demand and consumption, but the South is catching up: its growing demand for fossil fuels has led to more pressures on declining global supplies, and has produced more pollution because regulation is weaker. China has been the key actor; its share of global energy consumption grew from 7 per cent in 1973 to 22 per cent in 2014.

Prior to the Industrial Revolution, wood was the major source of energy for most people, being converted in some societies to charcoal: a lightweight residue created by heating wood and other organic materials without oxygen, and that is still used widely as a source of energy in Brazil, India, China, Thailand, Haiti, and many African states. **Fuelwood** more broadly provides less than 10 per cent of global energy supply, but is still the major source for the poorer and mainly rural residents of the South, and its use is often overlooked in Europe, where it is the biggest source of renewable energy: it accounts for as much as 80 per cent of non-fossil fuel consumption in Finland and Poland, for example, and 40 per cent in Germany (*The Economist*, 2013). If forests are managed properly, and efficient wood-burning technology is used, wood can be a carbon-neutral energy source because the emissions created in its burning can be offset by the role of forests as carbon sinks (see Chapter 12 for more details). Carbon dioxide production can also be offset by converting power stations to run on a mix of coal and wood, or even – potentially – entirely on wood.

There are many different ways of slicing the energy pie (see Figure 11.1), as a result of which it is not always easy to see the big picture without complex flow diagrams that account for production (the amount of energy extracted from different sources), supply (a figure derived from combining production, imports and exports), consumption, and the variety of end users. Also, different energy sources are used in different proportions from one activity to another and from one region or another, and the challenges faced by industrialized countries are different from those faced by countries that are still industrializing or still mainly agricultural. We must also make a distinction between three contrasting technical pairings:

- **Primary energy** consists of sources of energy in their original state, such as coal and oil, while secondary energy is derived from primary sources, and includes electricity from coal or petroleum from oil.
- The finite qualities of coal and oil (which took so long to naturally form that once used, they are effectively gone forever) stand in contrast with the infinite qualities of **renewable energy** such as solar and wind power (which, if managed well, are effectively infinite sources of energy).

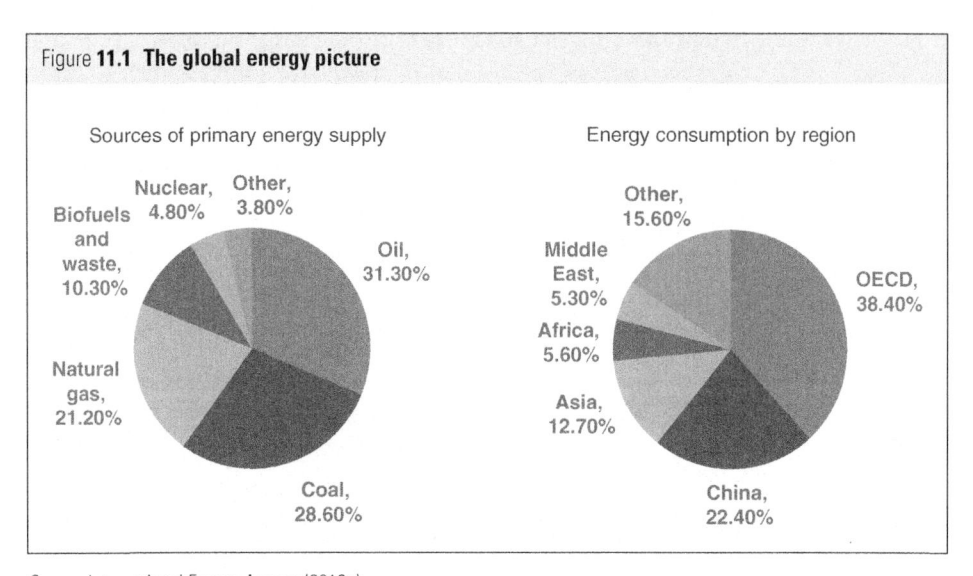

Figure **11.1 The global energy picture**

Sources of primary energy supply:
- Biofuels and waste, 10.30%
- Nuclear, 4.80%
- Other, 3.80%
- Oil, 31.30%
- Natural gas, 21.20%
- Coal, 28.60%

Energy consumption by region:
- Other, 15.60%
- Middle East, 5.30%
- Africa, 5.60%
- Asia, 12.70%
- China, 22.40%
- OECD, 38.40%

Source: International Energy Agency (2016a).

- Potential energy describes stored energy, such as the energy we extract from oil and coal, while kinetic energy refers to the kind we can extract from movement, as in wind and water power.

Today's global energy system has two key characteristics: we rely for the vast majority of our energy needs on pollutive and limited supplies of fossil fuels, and we use energy in a remarkably inefficient fashion. The average road vehicle has such poor aero dynamism, such low energy conversion ratios, and so much heat loss from the engine that only about 40 per cent of the petroleum pumped into the tank is converted into useful energy. Most homes are also energy-inefficient, with heat often escaping through roofs and windows, and electricity being wasted because of the poor energy-efficiency of appliances.

Most of our energy needs today come from five major sources (see Table 11.1), each of which has its own set of possibilities and limitations.

Coal is the oldest source of primary energy in the industrial era, today accounting for about 29 per cent of global energy supply, slightly up from its 25 per cent share in 1973. It is used mainly to fuel industry and to generate electricity (about 40 per cent of the world's electricity is generated by coal-fired power stations), with the five biggest producers being China, the United States, India, Australia, and Indonesia. Production has more than doubled since 1973, and while the OECD share has fallen from 56 per cent to just under 25 per cent, the Chinese share has more than tripled to nearly 46 per cent.

Environmentally, the challenge posed by coal is summed up neatly by *The Economist* (2014b): it is an abundant fuel that is found in politically stable parts of the world, is not 'beset by state interference and cartels', and is 'cheap and simple to extract, ship and burn', leaving it with just one major problem: it is 'devastatingly dirty'. Most of the world's coal is still mined underground, a task that not only threatens the health of miners, but is also dangerous, and can lead to land subsidence, changes in the water table, the production of often toxic waste earth and rock, the contamination of water, the production of methane (a greenhouse gas), and the setting of fires that can smoulder for years or even decades, releasing pollutants into the air. Coal is also extracted through surface mining (otherwise known as open cast, open pit, or mountain-top mining), but while this is less laborious and expensive than underground mining, it creates its own set of problems: the clearance of forests, disruption to ecosystems and habitat, permanent change to landscape, and local air and water pollution.

When coal is burned, it generates chemicals and heavy metals (such as arsenic, lead, and mercury), airborne particulates that pose a threat to human health (particularly in the major cities of industrializing countries such as China and India), the sulphur

Table 11.1 The major sources of energy

	% share	Trends	Environmental implications
Fossil			
Coal	29	Abundant supplies, but use falling in older industrialized countries, offset by growth in China and India.	Dirty to extract and use, unless treated.
Oil	31	Percentage share has declined with increased efficiency.	Dirty to extract, transport, and use. Potentially combustible.
Natural gas	21	Cleanest fossil fuel.	Cleaner than coal and oil, but extraction and transport can cause problems. Potentially explosive.
Non-fossil			
Nuclear	5	Optimistic start, controversial present, uncertain future.	Concerns about safety and about storage of radioactive waste.
Renewables	14	Little change in contribution to energy supplies.	Vary by source (see Table 11.2).

dioxide and nitrogen oxides implicated in acid pollution, and the major greenhouse gas: carbon dioxide (CO_2). Fortunately, there are multiple options available for reducing pollution from coal:

- Using low-sulphur coal.
- Cleaning coal using physical or chemical processes that remove some of the sulphur or nitrogen content before it is burned.
- Preventing the formation of pollutants during combustion either by injecting additives or using low-pollution combustion techniques.
- Screening pollutants from exhaust and flue gases by fitting scrubbers to flues in power stations and factories.

All these options have been available for many years and more come along as technology evolves, but there is no consensus on the most efficient alternatives, and retrofitting old installations is expensive. Also, most cleaning techniques were developed to control sulphur and nitrogen emissions with a view to reducing acid pollution, and it has only been recently that the focus has shifted to CO_2 controls. **Carbon capture** involves extracting the CO_2 from gases generated by coal-fired power stations and placing it in safe storage, or injecting the CO_2 in liquid form into disused gas or oil fields, or porous rock formations.

In spite of its problems, coal continues to play a key role in global energy supply. Even as there been a shift towards cleaner natural gas in the United States, with electricity companies even closing coal-fired generation plants or switching them to gas, demand for coal grows in leaps and bounds in China and India, and even Japan has looked more favourably on coal as public and political support for nuclear power has waned since the 2011 Fukushima accident. Coal usage may have fallen in the United States, the world's biggest producer of coal, but its exports have grown as demand has grown in Europe and Asia, emphasizing the need for continued efforts to develop clean coal technology.

Oil is our biggest source of energy globally, but its 31 per cent share represents a significant decline from its 46 per cent share in 1973, a result mainly of improved fuel economy in road vehicles. It is used mainly to produce petroleum to fuel transport, and while it has the advantage of being relatively cheap, it has critical economic and security drawbacks: changes in the global price of oil have knock-on effects throughout most economies, and the fact that most oil stocks are found in relatively few countries (Saudi Arabia, the United States, Russia, Canada, and China are the five biggest producers) causes stresses between importers and exporters and has given the major producers a sometimes inflated global political and economic role.

Oil has multiple negative primary and secondary environmental effects, ranging from the damage created by drilling and transportation to the pollution created when oil and its derivatives are burned. While most drilling and extraction once occurred on land, the depletion of terrestrial oil reserves has pushed exploration and extraction (of both oil and natural gas) out to sea, a trend that is more expensive in both financial and environmental terms. About one-third of global oil production now comes from offshore areas such as the Gulf of Mexico and the Persian Gulf, and so intense has the competition become to control new reserves that – as we saw in Chapter 2 – a dispute has been brewing in the South China Sea as China expands its maritime claims as a means of winning more control over oil reserves in the area. Alongside the more infamous drilling disasters – such as Ixtoc I in 1979–80 and *Deepwater Horizon* in 2010 (both in the Gulf of Mexico) – there are many more smaller spills that attract fewer headlines but cumulatively cause enormous environmental damage and can take months or years to clean up.

As we saw in the previous chapter, the transportation of oil adds another set of problems, with the construction of pipelines that can disrupt ecosystems or habitats and generate spills, and with the operations of the fleet of large oil tankers needed to move oil from source to market. Fortunately, improvements in the design and management of tankers and navigation systems has meant a decrease in the number of spills and the amount of oil spilled, even as the amount of oil transported by sea has grown from about 6,000 billion tonne-miles in the 1980s to about 10,000 billion tonne-miles today (International Tanker Owners Pollution Federation, 2017).

The decline in global oil consumption is in large part due to developments in the United States, long the largest consumer in the world: it burned more than 19 million barrels of oil per day in 2015, or almost 20 per cent of the global total; the EU was second at 14 per cent; and China third at nearly 13 per cent (see Figure 11.2). But US consumption has fallen even as the country's population and economic productivity have grown. As well as a reduction in the number of vehicle miles travelled in the United States, and increased use of ethanol (which now accounts for about 10 per cent of total volume of petroleum consumed by Americans), there have been improvements in road vehicle technology (Cox, 2015), including more efficient engines and the use of lighter materials. This example of technology forcing has come mainly from regulations that have set higher targets for fuel economy. As a result, vehicles on American roads run more cleanly and are more fuel efficient, even though Americans still like to drive big trucks and sport utility vehicles (known elsewhere as four-by-fours or utility vehicles). Average fuel economy

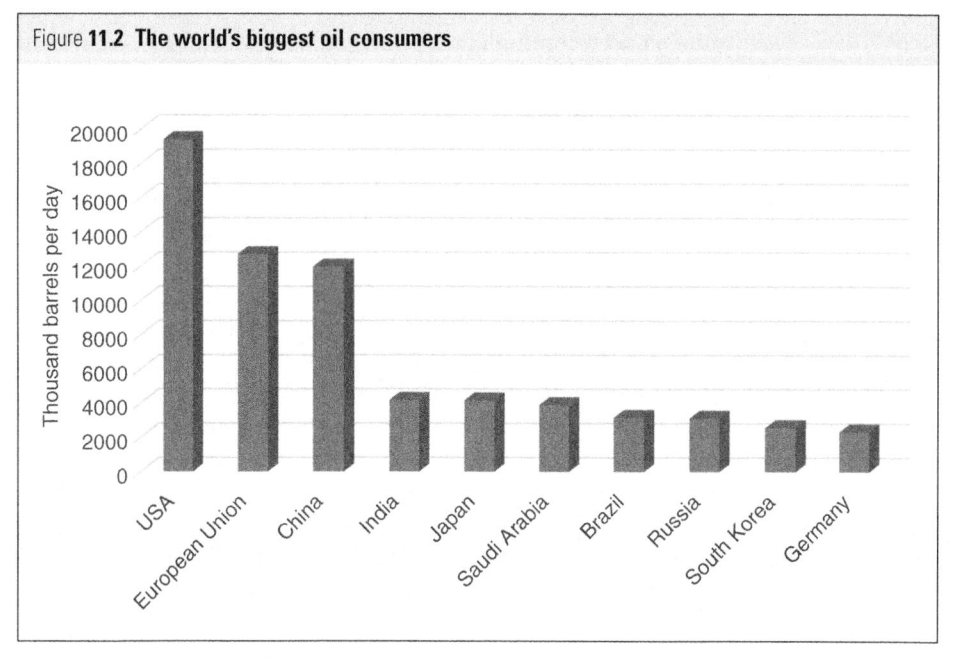

Figure **11.2 The world's biggest oil consumers**

Source: BP (2016) Statistical Review of World Energy at https://www.bp.com/content/dam/bp/pdf/energy-economics/statistical-review-2016/bp-statistical-review-of-world-energy-2016-full-report.pdf

for cars and trucks in the United States was about 12 miles per gallon (mpg) in 1975, had grown to 22 mpg ten years later before tailing off, then grew again after 2005, reaching a new high of 26 mpg (9 litres per 100 km) in 2016 (US Environmental Protection Agency, 2016).

In Europe, meanwhile, fuel consumption has fallen for other reasons. Road vehicles have long been more efficient thanks in part to their smaller size, but Europeans also pay high prices for petroleum (thanks mainly to higher taxes), face worsening congestion, have turned to bicycles in growing numbers, and have many options for efficient public transport, a growing proportion of which is powered by electricity. But public transport is only financially viable in large cities with high population density, which is partly why its plays much less of a role in the United States, with its more widely dispersed population. In many cities in the South, meanwhile, population growth has overwhelmed the capacity of national and local government to provide enough public transport.

Oil consumption is also declining in the wake of the improved design of electric and hybrid vehicles, although progress has been slow: in 2015 the number of electric vehicles on the road passed the 1 million mark for the first time (International Energy Agency, 2016b), but they made up only 0.1 per cent of the estimated 1.2 billion vehicles on the world's roads in 2014, a number that is predicted to reach 2 billion by 2035 (Voelcker, 2014), with most of the growth coming in the South. Also, most electric and hybrid vehicles are found in just a few countries (mainly the United States, Canada, Japan, China, and those in Western Europe), and their benefits are more than offset by the pollutive effects of the large number of old and badly maintained vehicles on the road, particularly in the South.

Natural gas is the third major fossil fuel, and – mainly because it is cleaner than coal and less controversial than nuclear energy – the fastest growing source of primary energy; its share of global energy supply grew from 16 per cent in 1973 to about 21 per cent today. Gas is used mainly for industrial processes and to generate electricity (nearly a quarter of global electricity generation comes from natural gas), for heating and cooking in many Northern countries, and to fuel transport (a small but growing segment). The five major producers are the United States (21 per cent of the world total), Russia, Iran, Qatar, and Canada.

Even though it is mainly methane (a greenhouse gas), natural gas produces about half as much carbon dioxide per unit burned as either coal or oil. But exploration and transport can pose problems: drilling for gas can harm natural habitats and produce

Box 11.1 *The energy–transport nexus*

The environmental effects of energy use are largely determined by the way in which the transport sector has evolved. Road vehicles are a remarkably inefficient way of moving people and goods from one point to another:

- Most of the potential energy in petroleum is wasted because of vehicle design flaws.
- Most vehicles on Northern roads contain one driver and no passengers or baggage.
- Vehicles produce large amounts of pollution, particularly in the South where they are often older and less well maintained.
- We have had to build expensive and environmentally disruptive systems of roads and highways to carry traffic.
- The bigger cities have been built around higher densities of population but have not provided enough parking spots to keep up with demand, meaning that a significant amount of the traffic on the road consists of people driving around looking for somewhere to park.
- Congestion means that drivers spend much of their time sitting in vehicles that are idling in traffic jams or waiting for traffic lights to change or accidents to be cleared.
- Investments in public transport vary in terms of the quality of their results.

The potential for improvements in road transport is illustrated by recent trends in Europe and the United States; these have included policies aimed at improving the energy efficiency of vehicles, increasing taxes on petroleum, and investing in public transport, but they have also included growing congestion that has encouraged more people to use public transport, and changes in technology that have allowed more people to work at home. More changes are in the pipeline as advances are made in self-driving and electric vehicles, mag-lev (magnetic levitation) trains that are fast and energy efficient, and even possibly urban transport pods (automated single-passenger urban carriers) and the Hyperloop being developed by Elon Musk (CEO of Tesla Motors and SpaceX) that might one day carry passengers between cities in almost airless tubes at up to 1,300 kph (800 mph). The improved efficiency of transport promises to have far-reaching implications for energy use and its environmental effects.

both air and water pollution, while laying pipelines to move gas supplies can be unsightly and environmentally disruptive, and natural gas is also potentially explosive. One particularly controversial technique aimed at gaining access to more gas and oil is **fracking**, or hydraulic fracturing. This involves injecting water, sand, and chemicals at high pressure into subterranean rocks so as to force open fissures and release oil and gas. It has been used most actively in the United States, and is still only under consideration in most other parts of the world, but is criticized for its heavy water consumption, for concerns about the release of pollutants and the contamination of groundwater, and for distracting energy companies from investing more in renewables.

Nuclear power accounts for only 5 per cent of global energy supply, although this is a more than fivefold increase since 1973. It involves harnessing nuclear reactions to generate heat, which is used to drive steam turbines to generate electricity, and its use is limited to countries with nuclear technology; the United States accounts for about a third of global nuclear electricity production, followed by France (17 per cent) and eight other countries, including Russia, Germany, Japan, and Britain. It was once considered the great new hope for energy production, the first chairman of the US Atomic Energy Commission (Lewis Strauss) once famously predicting that the cost of nuclear electricity would one day be 'to cheap to meter'. France has taken it further than any other country, building a network of 58 nuclear power reactors that generate 75 per cent of the country's electricity.

But nuclear energy has long been controversial because of concerns about its links with nuclear weapons, concerns about the safety of nuclear power stations, and the challenges of safely storing radioactive waste (see Box 9.2). Its most telling problem, however, is that nuclear power plants are expensive to build, the costs running into billions of dollars, and the nuclear energy industry must often rely heavily on government subsidies to keep nuclear electricity affordable. In spite of its problems, political and public support for nuclear energy has grown in recent decades, even against the background of the Fukushima accident. Baker and Stoker (2015) concede that the debate is 'complex and conditional', point out that the story of the nuclear industry has been 'littered with new dawns and false starts', and conclude that public opposition may be less an issue than the 'limits of governance capacity'.

The prospects for renewable energy

Our fifth source of energy is a cluster of renewable sources, including biofuels, hydro, solar, wind, and geothermal energy. Together they meet 14 per cent of our current needs, but this is only a modest increase on the 12 per cent share in 1973. (For the current state of renewable energy, see International Energy Agency, 2015c.) There are doubts that the target set by the 2015 Paris agreement on climate change (holding the global average temperature to less than 2°C above pre-industrial levels) can be met without a rapid acceleration in the adoption of improved renewable energy technologies. Unfortunately there is such an intimate relationship between fossil fuels and the technology we use, and such a vast political and economic investment in fossil fuels by governments, oil companies, and key sectors of industry, that the resistance to change is palpable. Renewables, meanwhile, each have their own advantages and disadvantages.

Biofuels and waste (otherwise known as bioenergy) are the biggest source of renewable energy, together accounting for about 10 per cent of global energy supply, most of it in the South. In contrast to fossil fuels, which are the remains of long-dead organic matter, **biofuels** are produced directly from biomass, which is organic material that includes plant matter, animal waste, and municipal waste. They come in many different forms, the simplest being traditional sources such as wood, charcoal, or crop waste (which are considered primary biofuels), while secondary and more advanced biofuels include ethanol made from sugars and starches, and biodiesel made by combining alcohol with vegetable oil or animal fat. Ethanol can be blended with petroleum or burned by itself in modified engines, but it takes a large area of corn or sugar cane to generate the quantities of ethanol needed to make a significant difference to energy supply and demand.

Firewood and other forms of vegetation are the oldest forms of energy brought under human control, and – if managed properly – are renewable, cheap, and accessible. They are usually the readiest form of fuel for the rural residents of poorer Southern countries, but they have low conversion efficiency and their unregulated use can spark several environmental problems: the removal of trees and vegetation for use as firewood can lead to soil erosion, the siltation of rivers and lakes, floods, and the spread of desert conditions, as well as threatening the natural habitat of species. As population grows and more people must travel further to cut down trees and vegetation, the problem widens and supplies become less sustainable. Opinion is also divided about the prospects for biofuels as a replacement for fossil fuels; supporters point to the greater energy security they provide, their reduced environmental impact, and their accessibility to poorer rural societies (see Demirbas, 2008). But critics charge that the large-scale development of biofuels could undermine global food supply and pose a substantial threat to biodiversity (Giampietro and Mayumi, 2009).

Hydropower meets about 2.5 per cent of global energy needs, and is normally generated by the building of dams that are used to run turbines and generate electricity. At its simplest, though, water power can be used to turn water wheels attached to mills. It is a clean form of energy, limited only by the number of generating stations that can be built, and has enormous unmet potential given the number of rivers in the world. China has emerged as a

Table 11.2 **Renewable sources of energy: Benefits and costs**

	Benefits	Costs
Biofuels	Cheap and readily available if managed properly.	Wood, charcoal and residues have low conversion efficiency, and supplies often unsustainable.
Hydro	Clean and cheap, reliable, flexible, can be generated wherever there is a river.	Ecologically disruptive, sometimes high initial investment costs, can be impacted by droughts, dams expensive to build and maintain.
Solar	Infinite in supply, available everywhere, many different applications.	Technology still evolving, weather dependent, problems with energy storage, development reliant on government subsidies.
Wind	Infinite in supply, available everywhere, mature technology.	Weather dependent, visual pollution of wind farms.
Geothermal	Multiple applications, minimal cost fluctuations, not weather dependent, minimal above-ground disruptions.	Technology still evolving, high initial investment costs, can demand high use of water, development reliant on government subsidies.
Tidal/wave	Considerable unmet potential.	Undeveloped technology.

major producer of hydropower, accounting for just over a quarter of the world total, but its production meets only about one-fifth of Chinese electricity needs. Norway meets almost all its electricity needs from hydropower, while Venezuela, Brazil, and Canada are also major producers. Hydropower presents a number of problems, as we saw in Chapter 7: dams can be expensive to build and maintain, they disrupt the ecology of rivers and estuaries, they create lakes that may cover valuable fertile land (although they can also create fisheries and new sources of recreational income), and they can be damaged by silt washed down rivers from upstream. One answer to some of these problems is to build more and smaller dams, which – while less efficient – can be less disruptive.

Solar power meets only a fraction of global energy needs, and about 1 per cent of global electricity needs, but these figures do not include the passive solar power that many people derive from the sun shining through the windows of their homes and offices, creating a mini-greenhouse effect. Photovoltaic (PV) systems use solar panels to convert the rays of the sun into electricity, and that are built in a modular form that allows them to be installed at scales ranging from the structure of buildings (with roofs made of solar panels, for example) to large solar farms built on unused land or in desert and semi-desert areas that otherwise have no practical use; solar energy has considerable potential for those Southern and tropical states that are otherwise energy-poor.

Improvements in their design means that PV cells can even generate electricity when the sun is obscured by clouds. Although the amount of electricity generated by solar power has increased dramatically in recent years – a more than 300 per cent increase in the amount of energy generated from PV cells between 2006 and 2016 (International Energy Agency, 2015b) – government subsidies remain essential to its development.

Wind power also meets only a fraction of global energy needs, but it has been harnessed for hundreds of years, windmills come in many different sizes and applications, the technology is constantly improving, and there is enormous unmet potential. Windmill farms can be built on farmland, making more use of that land and providing a source of additional income to farmers. The major technical handicap is the variability of winds, the sight of extensive wind farms is not one that meets universal acclaim, and wind farms have become more controversial as they have moved offshore. Locating them in coastal areas is the most advantageous because they are close to consumers and can exploit differences in the temperature of land and sea during the day and at night. Local opposition can result in their being moved out to sea in areas with shallow water, but the further they are from consumers, the more they will need to rely on expensive long-distance transmission grids.

Geothermal power involves harnessing the heat naturally produced by the earth to provide heating or cooling, or to generate electricity. It can mean tapping into the ground immediately beneath our feet, which has a nearly constant temperature of 10–16°C (50–60°F), or, with the hot rock method, drilling deep wells into the earth, injecting water into the wells so as to fracture the rock, and then drilling more wells to recover the heated water. Wells can also be drilled to tap naturally occurring hot water or steam, which can be used in heating systems or to drive turbines to generate electricity. The contributions of geothermal energy are currently modest except in Iceland, which sits on top of volcanoes and other geothermal activity, and generates 25 per cent of its electricity from geothermal power.

Ocean power is based on harnessing incoming and outgoing tides, tidal currents, wave power, temperature differences between the surface and the depths of oceans, and salinity differences in estuaries. This is one of the least developed forms of renewable energy, much of the technology still being under development.

In summary, renewable sources of energy have the key advantages of being both clean and infinite in supply, as well as widely available. But they often have the disadvantages of needing significant upfront investment and government subsidies. The economics of renewables will change as the technology improves and as they provide a greater share of our energy needs, but fossil fuels continue to have a strong grip on economies and the support of strong vested political and economic interests. They will eventually run out, but they promise to continue to be a key part of the global energy picture for decades to come.

Shaping energy policy

The need for cheap and reliable sources of energy lies at the heart of the capitalist paradigm, and many powerful actors have a stake in ensuring the ongoing dominance of fossil fuels in sustaining that paradigm, including the oil, coal, transport, and manufacturing industries. How we derive and use energy raises complex social, economic, and political questions, but also has important environmental implications; decisions must be made on the effects of the extraction, transportation, and use of energy, all of which have consequences for human health, the quality of air and water, and the welfare of biodiversity and ecosystems. Where debates over energy policy have long been driven by concerns over the security of supplies, they are now as often driven by concerns about problems such as urban air pollution and climate change.

Overall, energy has fallen into the trap that afflicts most public policy: a concern with short-term interests and profits at the expense of long-term planning. We are addicted to fossil fuels, we know they are running out, and we know that they are dirty; but we have been remarkably slow – as individuals, communities, and states – to change the way we live in order to account for these realities. Much of our technology is rooted in an era of cheap and plentiful sources of coal and oil, most economic actors (particularly oil companies and vehicle manufacturers) are too deeply vested in the status quo to willingly embrace change, and elected officials are mainly too focused on conceding to these economic actors to rock the boat by supporting anything more than piecemeal change.

At the national level, we can tell something of the character and status of energy policy by looking at where it sits in the institutional structure of governments (see Table 11.3). Energy is often mingled with the environment or economic affairs, several countries have no departments of energy in spite of being either energy-rich or energy-poor, some sub-divide responsibility for energy into its different sources, major oil producer states are interested mainly in petroleum, and only a few have a department or ministry of energy as such. Even in the latter case, though, all is not necessarily as it seems. In the case of the US Department of Energy, for example, it is one

Table 11.3 **The place of energy policy in national government**

Country	Main government department/s
Britain	Department of Business, Energy and Industrial Strategy.
Germany	Federal Ministry for Economic Affairs and Energy.
France	Ministry of the Environment, Energy and Marine Affairs.
Spain	Ministry of Energy, Tourism and the Digital Agenda.
Brazil	Ministry of Mines and Energy.
Australia, Denmark, Sweden	Departments or ministries of environment and energy.
Canada, China, Japan	No national departments of energy.
India	Separate departments of power; new and renewable energy; and petroleum and natural gas.
Nigeria, Norway, Saudi Arabia	Ministries (respectively) of Petroleum Resources, Petroleum and Energy, and Petroleum and Mineral Resources.
Mexico, Russia, South Africa, United States	Department or Ministry of Energy.

Source: Government websites of respective countries, accessed January 2017.

of the weaker US federal government departments, its interests have barely gone beyond nuclear security and energy research, and it has long been the target of Republican efforts to close it down on the basis that its original concern with security has been resolved.

Clearly, there is no consensus on the question of where best to place responsibility for energy policy, in large part because it is so central to all of our political and economic concerns that the work of a true national department of energy would need to overlap with that of departments responsible for industry, transport, commerce, technology, national security, land, resources, urban development, and the environment. As we saw in Chapter 4, government departments are jealous of their preserves, constantly jostling with one another for bigger shares of political influence and budgetary allocations. The result is that cross-cutting departments are unpopular, and thus often ineffective.

At the international level, and in spite of the fact that so much of our energy supply crosses borders and creates environmental problems with international dimensions, there is little in the way of an energy regime, or even of separate regimes focused on different sources of energy, or the environmental fallout of energy use. The overriding interest in energy-rich countries is with extraction and export, while the overriding interest in energy-poor countries is with achieving energy security, which usually means ensuring reliable imports, but may also involve working to improve energy efficiency and invest in renewables. To complicate matters, a meaningful global energy regime must address the same three related challenges that face national policymakers: security, efficiency, and sustainability (Lesage et al., 2010: 37). In other words, energy needs to be plentiful, cheap and clean, three qualities that do not always coincide. Coal and oil are plentiful for many countries, for example, but they are not clean, while energy security is usually seen in national and not international terms.

Institutionally, energy is part of the interests of more broad-based bodies such as the World Trade Organization and the OECD, but there is no UN agency or programme with responsibility for energy matters, except in a peripheral way: for example, the work of the UN Industrial Development Organization and the World Bank includes helping with energy development, the International Maritime Organization has an interest in preventing oil pollution at sea, and the International Atomic Energy Agency is as much interested in inhibiting the use of nuclear technology to build weapons as it is in promoting nuclear energy.

Outside the UN, the few international energy organizations have narrow interests:

- The Vienna-based Organization of Petroleum Exporting Countries (OPEC, founded 1960) is an oil producer club with a primary interest in prices and supplies.
- The Paris-based International Energy Agency was founded in 1974 in the wake of the 1973 oil crisis to coordinate the efforts of oil importers to ensure steady supplies. Its mission statement includes an interest in 'reliable, affordable and clean energy', but it was founded within the framework of the OECD and has only 29 members: all OECD members except Chile, Iceland, Israel, Latvia, Mexico, and Slovenia.
- The Riyadh-based International Energy Forum was founded in 1991 with the goal of encouraging meetings between consumer and producer countries, but it has achieved little.
- The Paris-based International Partnership on Energy Efficiency Cooperation (IPEEC) was founded in 2009 by the members of the Group of Seven (G7) biggest economies, and membership has since expanded to include almost all of the Group of 20 (G20) economies. Among them, the G20 account for 80 per cent of global energy use and greenhouse gas emissions, but they have only agreed (according to their joint declaration) to 'facilitate those actions that yield high energy efficiency gains ... on a voluntary basis'.

- The Bonn-based International Renewable Energy Agency (IRENA) was also founded in 2009, with the general goal of promoting the development and use of renewables on a global basis. Most members of the UN are also members of IRENA.

China, India, and Brazil are among the biggest energy consumers, and also face some of the most pressing energy-related environmental problems, but they cannot join the IEA (because they are not OECD members), they do not see their interests as being represented by other institutions, and as latecomers to the global energy market they feel disadvantaged relative to established players (Kuzemko et al., 2015: 81). The environmental interests of such latecomers are also different from those of older established industrial states; the latter went through their Industrial Revolution decades ago, and have reached the point where there is more political and economic support for balancing economic growth and environmental quality, while the latecomers are still at an earlier stage of their economic development, and there is a tendency – as there was in Europe and North America in the nineteenth century – to rank quantity above quality.

Meanwhile, there is little in the way of a body of international energy law, one study of the subject describing the concept as important but elusive (Talus, 2014). Where agreements have been reached they tend to be narrow in their focus; hence there are treaties on nuclear energy, for example, but they are addressed mainly at the consequence of accidents. The Vienna Convention on Civil Liability for Nuclear Damage was adopted in 1963, and the 1986 Convention on Early Notification of a Nuclear Accident was adopted immediately after the Chernobyl accident. Meanwhile, the Energy Charter Treaty was launched in 1991, but it is less than it sounds: it was aimed at integrating the energy sectors of the former Soviet Union and Eastern Europe with those of Western Europe, and now has 52 signatories bound by an interest in more open energy markets. In 2003, an Environment and Security Initiative was agreed that works to combine the efforts of major international organizations (including UNEP, NATO, and the Organization for Security and Cooperation in Europe, or OSCE) on a combination of energy, environmental, and security needs.

If there is one area of energy policy where there is clearly the potential for building a compelling international regime, it is renewable energy. But the history of IRENA does not inspire optimism. The idea for such an agency was first suggested at a UN conference on renewables in Nairobi in 1981, but it took another 27 years before a preparatory conference was held in Berlin, with IRENA being founded a year later. It has barely two dozen staff, and its state members have made few substantial commitments.

Box 11.2 Europe leads the way on energy

If there has been only modest activity on energy policy at the international level, there has been much activity and progress at the regional level in Europe, which has come closer than any other part of the world to building a transnational energy regime. There have been several motivations: the influence of progressive national energy and environmental policies, the region's sensitivity to its reliance on imported energy (including oil from the Middle East and natural gas from Russia), and efforts by the EU to address climate change. Since the EU is the third largest consumer of energy in the world after the United States and China, the results have global significance.

The most progress has been made specifically by the European Union, which – after many decades without much activity – has made what Birchfield and Duffield (2011) describe as 'unprecedented strides toward the creation of a common energy policy' in recent years (although Kuzemko et al. (2015: 91) charge that it has failed 'to fully live up to its own aspirations'). While energy security and an open EU energy market have been the dominating goals, there have been important consequences for environmental policy and the future of renewables. The following four steps have been the most telling:

- In 2009, the EU's 20–20–20 programme was launched with the goals of cutting greenhouse gas emissions by 20 per cent (on 1990 levels), meeting 20 per cent of energy needs with renewables, improving energy efficiency by 20 per cent, and meeting 10 per cent of energy demand in transport with renewables, all by 2020. The EU had already met the greenhouse gas goal by 2014, but the other goals are proving more difficult to achieve (see Chapter 12).
- In 2015 it launched efforts to build a European Energy Union aimed at pooling the negotiating power of the member states relative to other countries, opening up the energy industry, developing joint investment plans, and looking more actively into alternative energy sources, such as renewables.
- By 2030, the EU hopes to have achieved a 40 per cent cut in greenhouse gas emissions, to be meeting 27 per cent of its energy needs with renewables, and to have improved energy efficiency by 27 per cent.
- By 2050, it hopes to have reduced greenhouse gas emissions by 85–90 per cent, a goal to be achieved through investments in new low-carbon technologies, renewable energy, energy efficiency and improved grid infrastructure.

As a regional body, the EU has the benefit of being a club of countries with similar economic structures, energy sources, and environmental interests, so the extent to which the EU model can be exported is debatable. Even so, it offers valuable pointers (for more details, see Schubert et al., 2016).

At the same time, the problem of climate change – where, as we will see in Chapter 12, there is a strong global regime – has triggered a new set of institutional arrangements and legal obligations with telling effects on energy decisions. As Kuzemko et al. (2015: 82) put it, climate change is now 'overwhelmingly viewed as being rooted in existing patterns of energy production and use, warranting a fundamental decarbonisation of the global energy system'. Hence the climate change convention and its protocols can be seen, along with the work of the Intergovernmental Panel on Climate Change, as part of the global energy regime.

In contrast to many other areas of environmental policy, private companies and state-owned corporations play a key role in shaping energy decisions. In the oil industry, for example, patterns of global oil production and sales were dominated until the creation of OPEC by just seven major British and American oil companies, known as the Seven Sisters (including Anglo-Persian (now BP), Gulf Oil, and Texaco). Western oil companies such as Royal Dutch Shell, Exxon Mobil, and BP still play a dominating role, but they have been joined in recent years by state-owned oil companies from the South such as Sinopec and CNPC from China, Saudi Aramco, Petrobras from Brazil, and Petronas from Malaysia. Other energy sectors also have their key corporate players, such as Peabody Energy and Arch Coal (the biggest coal producers in the United States), China Shenhua Energy and Coal India, Gazprom (which dominates the Russian natural gas sector), and Areva and Electricité de France (the mainly state-owned companies that dominate the French nuclear energy industry). And it is not just energy companies that have a stake in policy; trends in oil consumption and the pollution created by petroleum have been driven by decisions taken by the major automobile manufacturers.

History suggests that a combination of new scientific understanding, public opinion, technological change, and international peer pressure can produce remarkable and positive changes in energy-related environmental policy. We saw in Chapter 6 that once the science of acid pollution was understood, and once agreement was reached among two sets of actors (the Americans and the Canadians on one hand, and the Western Europeans on the other), the problem was addressed remarkably quickly. Fossil fuels were burned in ever larger quantities in factories, power stations, and growing numbers of road vehicles, and yet the application of clean coal technology, emissions scrubbers, and filters on vehicle exhausts – combined with the use of a cap-and-trade system in the United States – produced impressive results, with a 74 per cent reduction in sulphur dioxide emissions in the EU and a 60 per cent reduction in emissions in the United States, along with related falls in nitrogen oxide emissions.

The challenge now is to work on similar achievements in the industrializing countries of Asia and Latin America, and to address carbon dioxide emissions as well. The fragmented nature of the global energy system, the contrasting positions of energy-rich and energy-poor countries, the extent to which economic systems are built on a reliance on fossil fuels, and the still-developing nature of renewable sources of energy – all combined with the lack of much in the way of a global energy regime – indicate that change will be hard to achieve. Sooner or later, though, we will have to wean ourselves off our reliance on fossil fuels, and better to do it sooner rather than later.

Discussion questions

- Which is the most likely route to changing energy policy: declining supplies of fossil fuels, security concerns, technological change, government regulation, or market forces?
- Is coal dying?
- Has climate change meant a change in the direction of the debate about energy?
- Given its central role in our lives, why is there no global energy regime?

Key concepts

Biofuels	Nuclear power
Carbon capture	Ocean power
Fracking	Primary energy
Fuelwood	Renewable energy
Geothermal energy	Solar power
Hydropower	Wind power

Further reading

Boyle, Godfrey (ed) (2012) *Renewable Energy: Power for a Sustainable Future*, 3rd edn (Oxford University Press). An assessment of the practical and economic potential for renewable sources to meet global energy needs.

Kuzemko, Caroline, Andreas Goldthau, and Michael F. Keating (2015) *The Global Energy Challenge: Environment, Development and Security* (Palgrave). A good general survey of the global energy picture, including details on the environmental implications.

McElroy, Michael B. (2016) *Energy and Climate: Vision for the Future* (Oxford University Press). A review of the links between energy use and climate change, assessing causes, effects, and future options, with a focus on the American and Chinese experiences.

Schubert, Samuel R., Johannes Pollak, and Maren Kreutler (2016) *Energy Policy of the European Union* (Palgrave). A survey of the energy picture in the EU, and its efforts to build common policies and a single energy market.

Talus, Kim (2014) *Research Handbook on International Energy Law* (Edward Elgar). One of the few broad studies of international energy law, which serves mainly to show how little has yet been achieved in terms of international policy development.

12 Climate Change: The Ultimate Global Test

Key arguments

- Other than the threat of nuclear holocaust, no other human-made phenomenon has ever threatened the well-being of life on earth in such a wholesale manner as climate change.
- Global average temperatures are clearly rising, and the effects of those rises are evident and well established.
- In spite of a near-consensus on the science of climate change, many continue to doubt its seriousness or its roots in human activity.
- States are divided on their levels of responsibility and their commitments to change, much of the focus being on the major industrial powers that generate the most greenhouse gas emissions.
- The most support for policy change has tended to come from states that are dependent on imported energy while the most opposition has tended to come from those states most well endowed in energy.
- The European Union has been a leader in addressing climate change, while the two major producers of greenhouse gases – China and the United States – have equivocated.

Chapter overview

Without question, the most serious environmental problem we face is human-induced climate change (otherwise known as global warming). At source, it is an air pollution problem because it stems from an enhanced greenhouse effect created by a growth in atmospheric concentrations of greenhouse gases such as carbon dioxide and methane. But the effects – which include changing weather patterns, more extreme weather events, melting ice caps and glaciers, rising sea levels, changing crop-growing patterns, and threats to biodiversity – mean that climate change is not just a pollution problem or even an environmental problem, but has become a broader political, economic, and social problem. It has moved since the 1990s from being a mainly scientific concern to being the ultimate test of our political and economic systems to respond to long-term ecological change of a kind that impacts all humans and other living organisms. Other than the threat of nuclear holocaust, no other human-made phenomenon has ever threatened the well-being of life on earth in such a wholesale manner.

The greenhouse effect is a natural phenomenon, which makes life on earth possible as we know it because water vapour, carbon dioxide, and methane trap enough solar radiation to keep global temperatures stable. The problem is that human activity has led to a rise in the volume of carbon dioxide and methane in particular, leading to warmer average global temperatures. Despite the stakes, agreement on remedial action has proved elusive, pitting states and industries with different political and economic priorities against one another. Opinion is divided on the degree of the problem, the best responses to adopt, and how best to share the burden of those responses. And while there is a near-consensus in the scientific community that climate change has been exacerbated by human action, there are still many who question the science, albeit for political or commercial reasons, rather than because of the science per se.

The political response has been shaped by the multiple sources and types of greenhouse gases, the differences of opinion between multiple blocks of countries (particularly developed and developing countries), and the slowness of the two major producers of greenhouse gases – the United States and China – to provide leadership. While a World Climate Conference was held as long ago as 1979, and the Convention on Climate Change was signed in 1992, it was not until 1997 that binding reductions in emissions of greenhouse gases were agreed at the Kyoto meeting of parties to the convention, but the Kyoto protocol did not receive enough ratifications to go into effect. A new agreement was reach in Paris in 2015, while the European Union has meanwhile taken independent action leading to big reductions in its greenhouse gas emissions by 2020. But the lack of progress in most other parts of the world has been very clear.

This chapter begins with an outline of the science of climate change, discussing the key greenhouse gases and their sources, trends in emissions, the effects of climate change, and the dynamics of public opinion. It then reviews the political response, contrasting the opposing positions of key players in the debate, and assessing the different steps in the political debate leading up to the conclusion of the Paris accord by which signatories agreed to try to hold the global average temperature to no more than 2°C above pre-industrial levels and to achieve a peaking of greenhouse gas emissions 'as soon as possible'. It ends with an analysis of the results achieved so far with climate policy, including several potential explanations for the evolution of that policy.

Defining the problem

At the core of climate change is the **greenhouse effect**, a natural phenomenon by which life on earth is made possible through the absorption of solar energy in the earth's atmosphere. Some of the heat is released back into the atmosphere as infrared radiation, where it is absorbed by **greenhouse gases** (GHGs), thereby slowing or preventing the escape of heat back into space. This process creates the conditions that make it possible for life (as we know it) to exist. Global temperatures have changed naturally over time as a result of changes in levels of solar energy reaching the earth and of natural changes in concentrations of GHGs, affected particularly by volcanic eruptions. We know of at least five ice ages, for example (the last ended about 12,000 years ago), each of which produced elemental changes in climate and natural systems. But while all earlier climate cycles were the product of natural causes, such causes do not – by themselves – explain the relatively rapid changes in climate that have taken place over the last century. It is more convincingly explained by the burning of fossil fuels, and is thus a result of human activity, not of natural change.

There are three primary GHGs:

- The most problematic – accounting for two-thirds of global GHG concentrations – is carbon dioxide (CO_2), which – as we saw in Chapter 6 – is produced naturally by plant and animal respiration, and by volcanoes and other geological activity. In its natural form it is vital to life on earth, the carbon cycle involving the circulation and transformation of carbon among living organisms. But when fossil fuels are burned, the carbon stored within them is released, and one of the effects of our reliance on fossil fuels has been a 40 per cent increase in atmospheric CO_2 concentrations since 1800, most of the growth coming since 1945. The amount of carbon in the atmosphere can be offset by its removal (or sequestration) when it is absorbed by plants, forests, or the oceans; part of the policy debate about climate change has revolved around the impact of these so-called **carbon sinks**.

- Methane (CH_4) is produced naturally by bacterial activity in bogs, swamps, rice paddies, and digestive processes in livestock, as well as by forest fires and by the release of natural gas (which is mainly methane). The volume in the atmosphere has more than doubled since 1800 as a result of human activity, particularly the intensification of agriculture. At the same time, however, methane is relatively easy to control because it has a life of just ten years in the atmosphere, and a 10–20 per cent cut in production would be enough to halt the increase in atmospheric methane concentrations. Such a cut could be achieved by improving feed and nutrition for cattle and sheep.
- Often overlooked in discussions about climate change is atmospheric water vapour, the most abundant GHG and also the one with the shortest lifetime. It is visible in the form of clouds, which play a key role in absorbing heat and reflecting solar radiation back into space. While it is not directly

Table **12.1 Greenhouse gases**

	Sources	*Trends*
Carbon dioxide (CO_2)	Natural (mainly volcanic activity) and human-made (burning of fossil fuels, deforestation).	Concentrations (parts per million) up 40 per cent since 1800, with 75 per cent of the increase coming since 1945. Forests and oceans are sinks for CO_2.
Methane (CH_4)	Natural (from natural gas) and human-made (from intensive livestock farming, rice paddies, wetland changes, landfill emissions).	Concentrations up 140 per cent since 1800. As the Arctic tundra thaws, concentrations will increase.
Water vapour (H_2O)	Natural.	Clouds play a key role in reflecting solar radiation.
Ozone (O_3)	Human-made (from burning of fossil fuels).	Unequal concentrations around world, so hard to measure trends.
Nitrous oxide (N_2O)	Human-made (from burning of fossil fuels, industrial and agricultural processes).	Concentrations up 20 per cent since 1800.

Source: Data on changes in concentrations from European Environment Agency at http://www.eea.europa.eu (accessed February 2017).

produced by human activity (unlike CO_2 and methane), the concentration of water vapour in the atmosphere is driven by temperature; as global temperatures continue to rise, so cloud formation changes, in turn contributing to climate change.

As GHG concentrations have grown, so have global temperatures, which have risen at an average rate of 0.07°C (0.13°F) per decade since 1880 and at an average rate of 0.17°C (0.31°F) per decade since 1970 (see Figure 12.1). The ten hottest years on record have all occurred this century (Figure 12.2), and unless action is taken to reduce GHG emissions, average global temperatures are projected to continue rising, with an increase of between 1.4°C and 5.8°C (2.5–10°F) by 2100, on a 2000 baseline. (The variation in the projections reflects different emissions models.) The Intergovernmental Panel on Climate Change (see Box 12.2) has argued that just to stabilize GHG concentrations would require a 60 per cent cut in CO_2 emissions and a 20 per cent cut in methane emissions. Even then there would be little short-term impact on temperatures because of the longer term effect of higher concentrations.

Just as the rise in global temperatures is indisputable, so are many of the consequences:

- Weather patterns are changing. With temperature differences between the poles and the equator driving most of the world's weather, the changes in temperature are producing changes in weather: this is particularly evident in higher latitudes, where

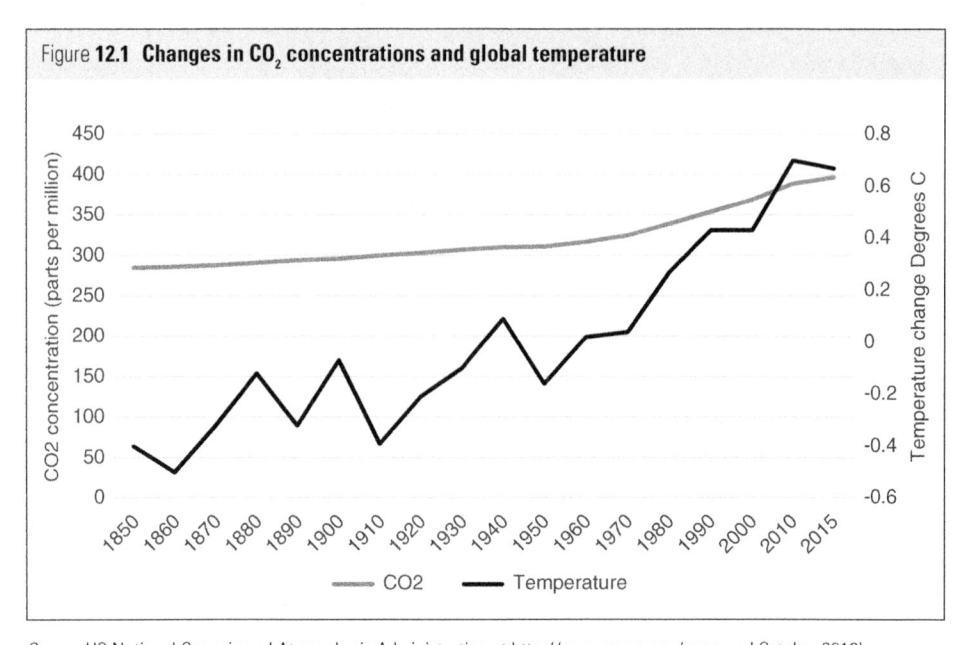

Figure **12.1 Changes in CO_2 concentrations and global temperature**

Source: US National Oceanic and Atmospheric Administration at http://www.noaa.gov (accessed October 2016).

Figure **12.2** **The ten warmest years on record**

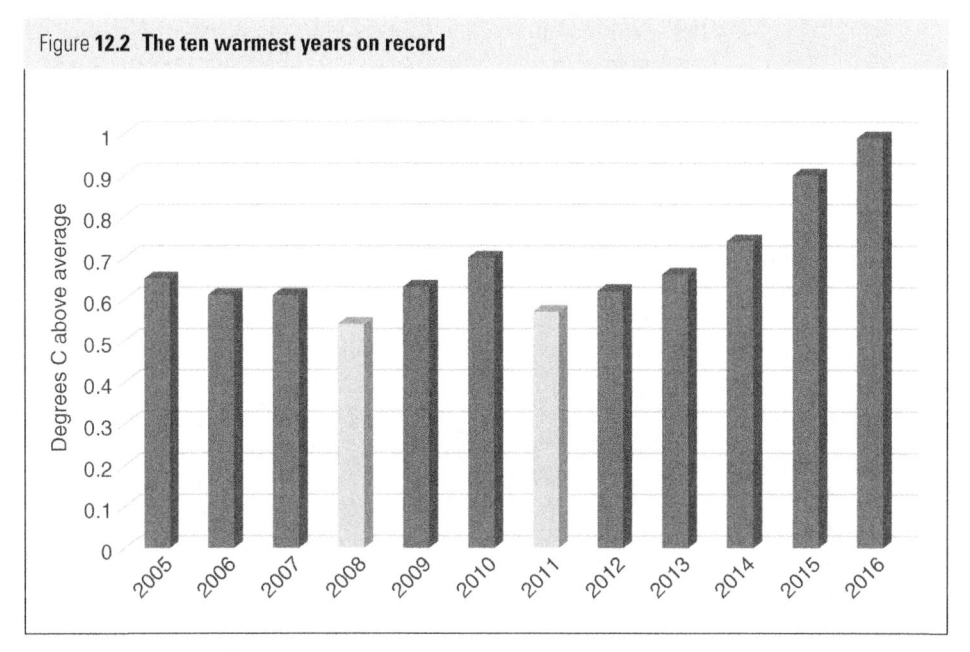

Source: US National Oceanic and Atmospheric Administration at https://www.ncdc.noaa.gov/sotc/global/201513 (accessed April 2016). NASA Press Release 17-006, 18 January 2017, 'NASA, NOAA Data Show 2016 Warmest Year on Record Globally'.

both summers and winters are becoming milder. A critical unknown factor is the influence of changes in cloud cover: the formation of clouds is unpredictable, and different kinds of clouds have different reflective capacities. For example, tropical storm clouds are so thick that they trap three times as much heat as northern temperate clouds, and also reflect more sunlight back into space, perhaps offsetting some of the dangers of climate change. But changes in cloud cover threaten to harm the ecosystems found in cloud forests and rainforests.

- There have been more extreme weather events, including tropical storms, hurricanes, tornadoes, blizzards, heat waves, droughts, floods, and forest fires. At one end of the scale, records for temperatures and precipitation totals are being routinely broken. At the other end, more and greater natural disasters – added to the greater potential for drought and water shortages – raise the likelihood of more people being displaced (often permanently), creating a climate refugee problem.
- Ice caps, glaciers, snow pack, and floating ice are melting, while the oceans are becoming warmer, causing ocean water to expand. As a result, sea levels are rising, with the effects already being seen in accelerated coastal erosion and more damage from high tides and storms. Low-lying coastal areas

face the most immediate threats, with the prospect of rising sea levels hovering over large coastal cities such as London, Amsterdam, Mumbai, Shanghai, and New York. Questions have even been raised about the continued existence of island states such as the Maldives in the Indian Ocean and Fiji in the Pacific.
- Crop-growing patterns are changing, with the potential that they could move closer to the poles. The frost-free growing season is lengthening in temperate regions, yields of crops such as wheat and maize are threatened, and the stability of fisheries is being impacted by changing ocean currents.
- Climate change poses an array of ecological threats, with landscapes changing as a result of changes in temperature and patterns of rainfall, shifts in vegetation, increased soil erosion, and altered river flows. Coastal ecosystems are under threat, particularly wetlands and mangrove forests. As the oceans absorb more carbon, they become more acidic, posing threats to the life cycle of marine organisms and the bleaching of corals. As climate changes, there is also the increased prospect of vector borne disease such as malaria (carried by mosquitoes), and waterborne diseases.

While the rise in temperatures and most of the effects of climate change are undisputed, there still remains resistance to the idea that the problem is as serious as it is often portrayed, or even that it is human-made (see Box 12.1). At source, climate change is an energy problem, linked to our heavy dependence on fossil fuels. Individually and collectively, we all have a **carbon footprint** based on our direct consumption of fossil fuels, and our indirect consumption through the products and services we buy. As we saw in Chapter 11, all sources of energy have their own particular sets of political and economic considerations that play into policy, not least being the powerful influence of oil and coal companies and vehicle manufacturers; the former want to exploit oil and coal reserves for as long as they last, while the latter are only slowly moving their products away from petrol and towards electricity. Climate change must also compete for political and public attention with many other problems that might seem more immediate, such as terrorism or economic decline. Science is rarely absolute, scientific understanding routinely changes, and opinions are typically based on a consensus view rather than firm agreement; these are all qualities that have been exploited by those opposed to action on climate change, whatever their underlying reasons.

Box 12.1 *Climate change doubters and deniers*

Environmental policy has long had to wrestle with the problem of scientific uncertainty, which has often been exploited by opponents of regulation to resist change. In few areas of policy has this been more obvious than that of climate change, where many of those opposed to action – whether for political or commercial reasons – have based their opposition on claims that the science remains unclear. Global climate is clearly changing, but doubters and deniers question assertions that humans are causing the change.

A Pew Research Centre poll in 40 countries in 2015 found that just over half of those surveyed regarded climate change as a 'very serious' problem, with rates being highest in Latin America and lowest in the Middle East (see Figure 12.3). Levels of concern had not changed much since a 2010 survey, the poll found, had fallen in Japan, South Korea, and Russia, and were lowest in China. The poll also found significant ideological differences, with those holding conservative political views being less likely to regard climate change as a problem than those holding liberal political views: in the United Kingdom, 53 per cent of those on the left and 34 per cent on the right considered it to be a problem, while in the United States the relative figures were 68 per cent and 30 per cent.

Meanwhile, significant minorities in some countries argue that climate change is not caused by human action but is part of a natural cycle, and some go so far as to argue that the problem is nothing more than an elaborate hoax. In the United States, for example, where one in three Americans do not support the view that climate change is caused by human activity, it has been suggested (Begley, 2007) that climate change denial is promoted by an organized, well-funded and well-coordinated 'denial machine'. In 2012, several years before running for the US presidency, Donald Trump tweeted that 'the concept of global warming was created by and for the Chinese in order to make US manufacturing non-competitive'. Upon becoming president in 2017, he appointed several climate change sceptics to his administration, and soon withdrew the United States from the Paris accord. This was a futile political gesture given than many cities, states, and industries in the United States support the goals of Paris, and given that the US coal industry is declining as a result of market forces.

Economic interests – notably the fossil fuels industry – have been at the heart of efforts to cast doubt on the science of climate change, and for obvious reasons: they stand to bear most of the financial and organizational costs involved in cutting carbon dioxide emissions. Climate change denial is also partly motivated by what is seen to be the growing burden of government regulation (Dunlap and McCright, 2011). One recent study suggests that the absence of clear climate change policies in the United States can be explained by the influence of an inner circle within the American corporate elite that is concerned about the effect of regulations on profits, and has been able to oppose the support for change shown by a 'public interest sector' composed mainly of corporate law and media companies and leaders of higher education (Hein and Jenkins, 2017). Evangelical religious fundamentalism has also been found to play a role in US climate change scepticism (Shao, 2017).

Figure 12.3 Public opinion on climate change

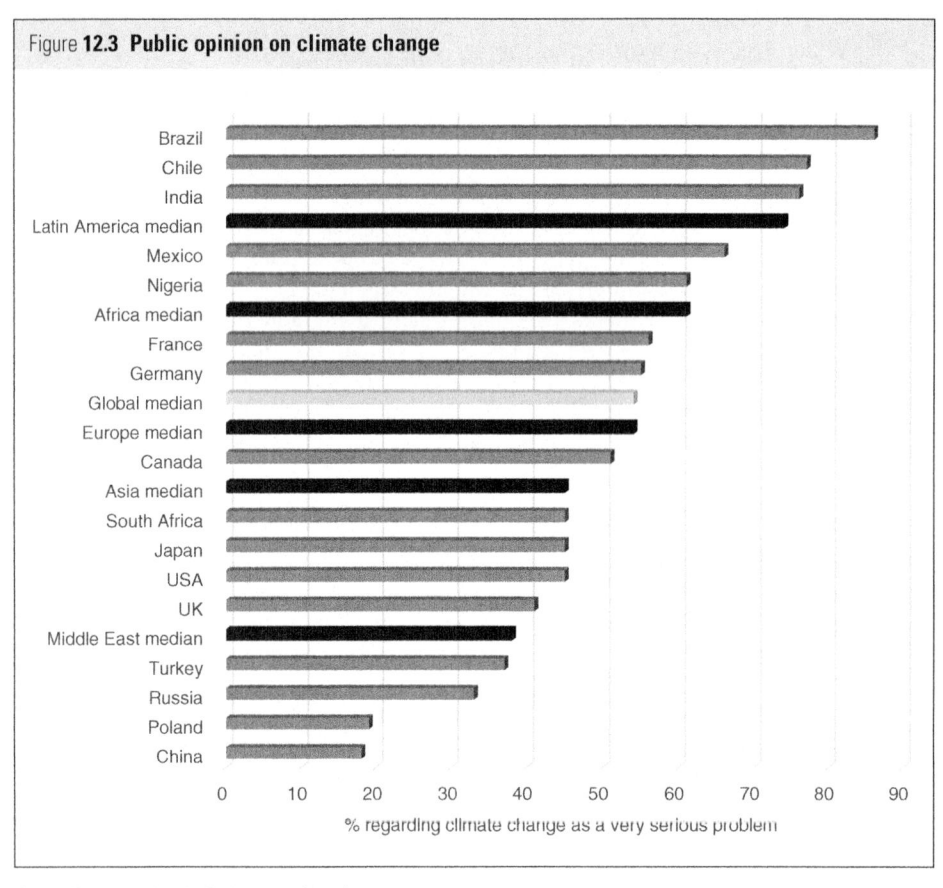

% regarding climate change as a very serious problem

Source: Based on data in Stokes et al. (2015).

Shaping climate change policy

While the political response to climate change has only a short history, theories and concerns about rising CO_2 levels and the enhanced greenhouse effect are far from new. The science of the absorption of solar radiation has been understood since the late nineteenth century, and the first scientific article making a link between rising temperatures and rising carbon dioxide concentrations was published in 1896 (Arrhenius, 1896). The phenomenon remained more theoretical than factual until data gathered at the Mauna Loa observatory in the 1950s provided the earliest evidence of an actual rise of CO_2 levels in the atmosphere. In 1969, President Richard Nixon was warned that CO_2 emissions were 'clearly' a problem, that global temperatures could rise, and that global sea levels could also rise (Moynihan, 1969). In 1988, during an unusually hot summer, James Hansen of the US National Aeronautics and Space Administration (NASA) told a US Senate hearing that it was 99 per cent certain that climate change was not a natural variation, and that it was 'time to stop waffling so much and say that the evidence is pretty strong that the greenhouse effect is here' (Shabecoff, 1988).

But just as science was providing more detail on the dynamics of climate change, and the body of data provided more certainty and understanding, so there was a reaction from scientific doubters, many supported in their work by industries that feared the potential costs of changes in policy. This was far from the first example of this phenomenon at work; the dangers posed by airborne lead and tobacco had also been questioned by powerful interests, but those interests were much smaller than those invested in the fossil fuel and transport industries, which lie at the heart of modern economies. Their fears were reflected in the manner in which climate scientists were accused of doctoring the results of their research, books and websites were published that questioned the science, and active efforts were made to undermine the arguments of scientists by what Oreskes and Conway (2010) describe as the 'merchants of doubt'.

The solutions to the problem of climate change have also long been known; they include a reduction in the use of fossil fuels, a switch to renewable sources of energy, improved energy efficiency, the planting of forests as carbon sinks, a reduction in the removal of tropical rainforests, improved land management, changes in the ingredients of the nutrition given to livestock so as to reduce methane production, and the promotion of public transport, with an emphasis on electric buses and trains. Some of these changes, such as improved energy efficiency, have undeniable consumer benefits, and should be pursued with or without the prompting of climate change. Others, however, are not cost-free, and demand a shift in economic practices that many are unwilling to make or pay for, at least unless they can be assured that the burden of change is being equally shared.

The essence of the problem, argue Bailey and Compston (2010), is that 'measures that are seen to impose high or unevenly distributed costs are likely to be strongly resisted by business groups, national parliaments, electorates, and … political parties, whilst uncertainty surrounding the international climate regime adds to concerns about losses in competitiveness – and political retribution – if governments move substantially beyond the commitments made by other countries'. Economic resistance and political resistance feed off one another, the debate over climate change having been driven by the divergent and contrasting positions of multiple negotiating groups:

- Although climate change is a global problem, the biggest shares of GHG emissions can be laid at the door of just a few countries: collectively, China, the United States, members of the European Union, India, Russia, and Japan account for about 70 per cent of carbon dioxide production. Although it might seem that concerted action in these countries would be enough to make a big dent in the problem, they have different views about their economic futures and about relative levels of responsibility.

- Members of the Organization for Economic Cooperation and Development (OECD) – the club of the world's 35 wealthiest developed countries – argue that they should not bear an excessive share of the financial burden, and have been divided by the contrasting support for action on the part of the EU and by the resistance to action of the United States, Japan, and even occasionally Canada and Australia.
- Newly industrializing states do not want to see their development plans compromised, and argue that they should be allowed to follow the same economic trajectory as the industrialized states. The so-called BASIC states (Brazil, South Africa, India and China) have played a particularly prominent role in the debate (Hochstetler and Milkoreit, 2015), committing to work together at the 2009 Copenhagen climate conference, and even to walk out as a group if their demands were not met by developed states.
- Oil-producing states such as Saudi Arabia, Nigeria, and Venezuela – with substantial global economic influence – are concerned about the loss of income that would result from a conversion to renewables.
- The Alliance of Small Island States (AOSIS) includes coastal and island states, for some of which climate change is an existential matter. But while the group includes 44 members (including the Bahamas, Cuba, Fiji, the Maldives, and Singapore), they collectively account for only 5 per cent of the world's population, giving them limited influence. The government of the Maldives – whose highest point is 2.5 metres (8 feet) above sea level – colourfully illustrated its concerns in 2009 when it held an underwater cabinet meeting with ministers wearing scuba gear.
- The Coalition for Rainforest Nations is broadly interested in promoting careful use of rainforests, but has also campaigned for developed countries to invest in the preservation of forests as carbon sinks. Members include Indonesia, Malaysia, the Democratic Republic of Congo, and Argentina, but not rainforest-rich Brazil.

Building a climate change regime has meant trying to achieve a compromise among states with different economic priorities, emissions levels, levels of vulnerability, and abilities to respond. The absolute numbers are clear (see Figure 12.4), but they can be interpreted and massaged in different ways, raising questions

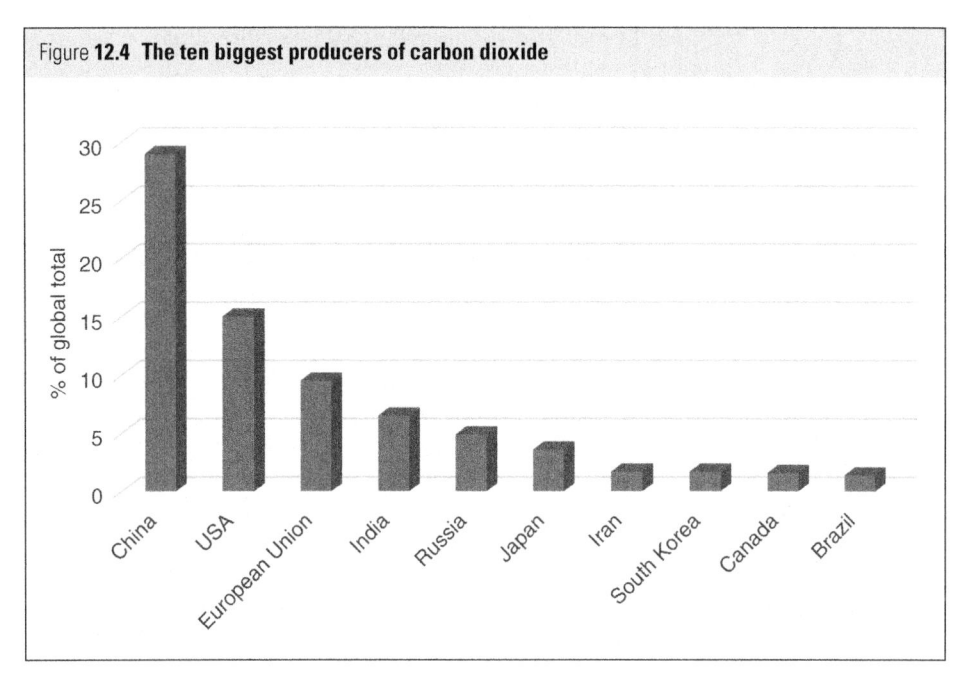

Figure **12.4** The ten biggest producers of carbon dioxide

Source: European Commission (2014), Emissions Database for Global Atmospheric Research (EDGAR) at http://edgar.jrc.ec.europa.eu (retrieved October 2016).

about the fairest and most efficient means for calculating levels of responsibility: should targets be based on the total output of individual states (or groups of states), per capita output, output per unit of GDP, current emission levels, or historic emission levels? How much credit should be given for past reductions? (At one point in the discussions, there was talk of giving credit to Russia and other former Soviet states for emission reductions they had already achieved, not as a result of policy decisions but as a result of the closure of pollutive Soviet-era factories and power plants.)

Often overlooked in the debate about climate change is the question of environmental justice (or, actually, injustice). Ciplet et al. (2015: 5) point to the 'heightened and disproportionate vulnerability to climate-related harm by disadvantaged social groups, who in general are far less responsible for the problem and are excluded from decision making about its resolution'. They note the negative impact of fossil fuel extraction and transport on those who live near mines, wells, and refineries, the vulnerability of such groups to the fallout from climate change (including famine, drought, flooding, and extreme weather events), and even the impact on such groups of changes in technology aimed at addressing climate change, such as the mining of silicon and lithium for solar panels and batteries. To this list they might also add the unbalanced role of smaller and poorer (and often more vulnerable) states in the climate debate, which has been dominated by the major industrialized and industrializing countries.

The climate change convention

The political response to climate change dates backs to a series of conferences in the 1970s, culminating in the 1979 World Climate Conference in Geneva, which was sponsored by the World Meteorological Organization (WMO) and brought together scientists interested in the emerging evidence of the problem. A 1985 conference in Austria on the role of GHGs in climate change led to more focused demands for political action, sparking a call by the UN General Assembly in 1988 for a climate change treaty, and the creation that same year of the Intergovernmental Panel on Climate Change (IPCC) (see Box 12.2). The charge of the IPCC has been to provide a common scientific basis for thinking about climate change, dating from the release of its first assessment in 1990. This warned that if states continued to pursue a policy of 'business as usual', there would be a rise in global average surface temperatures that would be unprecedented in human history. Also in 1990, the Second World Climate Conference was convened and negotiations were opened on the UN Framework Convention on Climate Change, which was signed at the Rio Earth Summit 1992 (for a brief review of climate change diplomacy, see Harris, 2011).

Negotiations on the convention saw political and economic divisions that persist to this day, even if some of the details have changed. Among the lead supporters were states that were dependent on imported energy and had learned the value of wise use (they included Sweden, Finland, and the Netherlands), while states that were well endowed in energy (notably the United States and Russia) offered the most opposition. The outcome was a general agreement under the terms of the convention to stabilize GHG concentrations by cutting emissions and enhancing carbon sinks, but without any specific targets. The convention came into force in 1994, was quickly ratified by almost every member state of the UN, and was followed in 1995 by the first in a series of Conferences of the Parties to the convention (COPs), held in Berlin.

The Berlin conference saw the introduction of the idea of 'common but differentiated responsibilities', meaning that while there was agreement on a shared responsibility

Box 12.2 *The Intergovernmental Panel on Climate Change*

More than many other environmental problems, the debate over climate change has revolved around science. Climate change doubters point to the absence of certainty about the links with human action, overlooking the fact that science is rarely certain, and the near-consensus on the science of climate change. At the heart of the evolving scientific debate has been the work of the Intergovernmental Panel on Climate Change, which was created in 1988 and is sponsored by the World Meteorological Organization and the UN Environment Programme. An example of the science and technology studies approach to understanding international relations discussed in Chapter 5, it brings together scientists and other experts from the UN member states to produce assessments of the state of understanding on climate change. The first of these was published in 1990 and the fifth in 2013. Among them they offer a road map through the changing scientific understanding of climate change, work that earned the IPCC the 2007 Nobel Peace Prize.

The conclusions outlined in its assessments are conditioned by different levels of confidence, ranging from *very low* to *very high*, and from *exceptionally unlikely* to *virtually certain*, but the Fifth Assessment (IPCC, 2013) makes several important points:

- Warming of the climate system is unequivocal, and since the 1950s, many of the observed changes are unprecedented over decades to millennia (p. 4).
- Human influence on the climate system is clear. This is evident from the increasing greenhouse gas concentrations in the atmosphere, positive radiative forcing, observed warming, and understanding of the climate system (p. 15).
- Human influence has been detected in warming of the atmosphere and the ocean, in changes in the global water cycle, in reductions in snow and ice, in global mean sea level rise, and in changes in some climate extremes ... It is *extremely likely* that human influence has been the dominant cause of the observed warming since the mid-twentieth century (p. 17).
- Continued emissions of greenhouse gases will cause further warming and changes in all components of the climate system. Limiting climate change will require substantial and sustained reductions of greenhouse gas emissions (p. 19).

to address climate change, developing countries wanted industrialized countries to take on the biggest commitments to reducing GHG emissions. The third COP – which met in Kyoto, Japan, in 1997 – promised more substance because developed states agreed to 6–8 per cent reductions in GHG emissions by 2008–12 from 1990 levels, without any commitments being imposed on developing states. But while the Clinton administration in the United States signed the Kyoto protocol, it was not ratified by the US Congress, and it was rejected in 2001 by the Bush administration, removing a key player from leadership on climate change. Other conservative administrations also proved resistant: Australia did not ratify Kyoto until the defeat in 2007 of the conservative government of John Howard, while Canada – normally a leader on environmental matters – ratified Kyoto in 2002 but then saw resistance from the conservative administration of Stephen Harper in 2006, and withdrew from Kyoto in 2011 (see Kutney, 2014).

The ambitious goal set in the climate change convention of a reduction in emissions of GHGs by developed countries to 1990 levels by 2000 had long fallen by the wayside, and so clear were the signs of climate change that participants at the eighth COP in New Delhi in 2002 were talking less about reducing GHG emissions than about how developed countries could help developing countries adapt to the effects of climate change (Harris, 2011). The Kyoto protocol finally won enough ratifications to enter into force in 2005, but efforts to achieve its goals were piecemeal, the modest record reflecting – in the words of UN secretary-general Kofi Annan – a 'frightening lack of leadership' (Gettleman, 2006). The debate revolved mainly around three points on a triangle: support by the European Union for substantial action, efforts by the Bush administration in the United States to block such action, and demands by developing countries for lower targets and more technological and financial help.

The European Union has long been the major champion of climate change policy (see Delreux and Happaerts, 2016: ch. 9), having early taken the initiative to develop its own internal goals

Table **12.2 Key events in the climate change debate**

1979	First World Climate Conference, Geneva.
1985	Conference on climate change science, Austria.
1988	Formation of Intergovernmental Panel on Climate Change.
1990	Release of first IPCC assessment.
	Second World Climate Conference, Geneva.
1992	Signature of UN Framework Convention on Climate Change at Rio Earth Summit.
1995	First Conference of Parties (COP) to the climate change convention, Berlin.
1997	Third COP, Kyoto.
2009	Third World Climate Conference, Geneva.
2013	Release of fifth IPCC assessment.
2015	Twenty-first COP, Paris.

in the hope that it would encourage other states to act. It began drafting a joint climate change policy in the 1990s, with a commitment to cut CO_2 emissions by 2000, and at Kyoto set itself a target of an eight per cent reduction in CO_2 emissions. In 2007 it adopted a 20-20-20 package designed to achieve a 20 percent reduction in GHG emissions by 2020 (from a 1990 base), a switch to renewable sources for 30 per cent of its energy needs, and a 20 per cent improvement in energy efficiency. It also agreed an emissions trading system that included sources responsible for 45 per cent of the EU's GHG emissions, and targeted 11,000 power plants and factories. It did all this without comparable obligations from either the United States or China.

The result has been not just a steady decrease in EU carbon dioxide emissions that have kept it on track to meet its 2020 target, but also the elevation of the EU to a position of global leadership on climate change. It has not been an easy path to follow, because there has been a division of opinion among member states of the EU, with some (mainly in Eastern Europe) seeing climate action as detrimental to economic growth, while others (such as Germany and the UK) have taken the opposite view (Skovgaard, 2014). The EU also went through major economic problems in the wake of the 2007-09 global financial crisis, which helped spark a debt crisis in several eurozone countries. Ironically, though, the cutbacks in production and consumption helped it more quickly meet its GHG reduction targets.

Illustrating the California effect discussed in Chapter 4, research has found that trading with the EU has encouraged developing countries to reduce their CO_2 emissions, and even their emissions of sulphur dioxide. Although the EU has not adopted binding regulations that require importing countries to reduce their greenhouse gas emissions, developing countries see the EU's commitment to emission reductions since Kyoto as a signal of its plans, and – given their export dependence on the large EU market – have taken steps to cut their CO_2 emissions (Prakash, 2017).

The approach of developing countries has often been quite different. In absolute terms, China is by far the biggest producer of CO_2, although in per capita terms its role is modest: it produces about 8 tonnes per capita per year, compared to 16 tonnes per capita in the United States. India is an even more modest contributor, accounting for about 7 per cent of global emissions but only 4 tonnes per person. Brazil, meanwhile, is a growing producer of CO_2, but contains a massive carbon sink in the form of its extensive tropical rainforests, and also has a large and growing biofuels industry. The traditional alliance among China, India, and Brazil in climate change negotiations creates a substantial voting block that has been used to good effect to demand more of developed countries and less of developing countries (Bailey and Compston, 2012.) At the same time, Held et al. (2013) argue that several of these countries may not deserve the reputations they have earned as laggards, and point to unilateral decisions they have made that are at least comparable to – and in some cases more ambitious than – the targets adopted by industrialized countries. China, for example, currently has plans in place to peak its CO_2 by 2030 (and ideally earlier) by reducing the contribution of coal to its energy needs and increasing its forest cover. Ciplet et al. (2015) also question the long-held view of a North–South divide in climate politics, pointing to the variety within the major negotiating groups.

To Paris and beyond

While there has been encouraging news on emissions reductions in Europe, there has been less encouraging news globally. International negotiations on climate change continued after Kyoto with annual meetings of signatories to the climate change convention, agreement being reached at the 15th COP in Copenhagen in 2009 for specific GHG reduction by all major economies, including China for the first time. However, no binding commitments were made. Meanwhile, the target date of 2012 established at Kyoto came and went without the planned 6–8 per cent reduction in GHG emissions by rich countries (CO_2 emissions instead remained static overall), and while an extension was agreed until 2020, only 75 countries ratified the extension. In many ways, the goal of achieving agreement among nearly 200 states on a topic tied so deeply to fundamental economic change of the kind needed to address climate change was always doomed to failure (Kutney, 2014). While it has been shown to be possible to achieve deep agreement among a small group of countries on a focused problem (as in the case of the agreement on the ozone layer), or superficial agreement among many countries on a broad problem (as in the case of biodiversity), achieving deep agreement among all the states of the world on a broad problem – even if climate change is dominated by a handful of major players – is a challenge of a different order.

The 21st COP was held in Paris in December 2015 amid high hopes of a breakthrough, given not just new evidence of the severity of the problem of climate change (2015 was the warmest year on record at the time), but also progress on cutting emissions in the EU, and the support of the Obama administration in the United States. A new agreement was reached (rather than another

Table **12.3** Key articles in the 2015 Paris climate change accord

2.1	This Agreement ... aims to strengthen the global response to the threat of climate change ... by: (a) Holding the increase in the global average temperature to well below 2°C above pre-industrial levels and pursuing efforts to limit the temperature increase to 1.5°C above pre-industrial levels ... (b) Increasing the ability to adapt to the adverse impacts of climate change and foster climate resilience and low greenhouse gas emissions development, in a manner that does not threaten food production. (c) Making finance flows consistent with a pathway towards low greenhouse gas emissions and climate-resilient development.
2.2	This Agreement will be implemented to reflect equity and the principle of common but differentiated responsibilities and respective capabilities, in the light of different national circumstances.
4.1	Parties aim to reach global peaking of greenhouse gas emissions as soon as possible, recognizing that peaking will take longer for developing country Parties, and to undertake rapid reductions thereafter in accordance with best available science, so as to achieve a balance between anthropogenic emissions by sources and removals by sinks of greenhouse gases in the second half of this century, on the basis of equity, and in the context of sustainable development and efforts to eradicate poverty.
4.3	Each Party's successive nationally determined contribution will represent a progression beyond the Party's then current nationally determined contribution and reflect its highest possible ambition, reflecting its common but differentiated responsibilities and respective capabilities, in the light of different national circumstances.
4.4	Developed country Parties should continue taking the lead by undertaking economy-wide absolute emission reduction targets. Developing country Parties should continue enhancing their mitigation efforts, and are encouraged to move over time towards economy-wide emission reduction or limitation targets in the light of different national circumstances.
4.5	Support shall be provided to developing country Parties for the implementation of this Article ... recognizing that enhanced support for developing country Parties will allow for higher ambition in their actions.

extension of Kyoto), and enough states had ratified for the agreement to come into force in November 2016. The key details of the Paris accord are reproduced in Table 12.3 as a means of illustrating the kinds of conditional clauses that often appear in international agreements.

Overall, signatories agreed to make efforts to hold the global average temperature to 'well below' 2°C above pre-industrial levels, and to achieve a global peaking of GHG emissions 'as soon as possible'. Unlike previous agreements, which were top-down in the sense of giving countries targets and timetables, Paris was bottom-up: it set a temperature ceiling but allowed signatories to develop their own plans, the emphasis being on the need to move away from fossil fuels and towards renewables. The plan also refers once again to 'common but differentiated' responsibilities and capabilities for taking action, emphasizing the continued absence of a one-size-fits-all approach, and also opening the door to the prospect of countries being able to interpret their responsibilities and contributions differently. There is also a clear emphasis in the agreement on the responsibilities of developed countries, with developing countries being asked only to 'continue enhancing their mitigation efforts' and to move 'over time' to achieving reductions in light of 'different national circumstances'.

While the Paris accord was widely hailed as a significant advance, the absence of clear targets and the use of several fudge-phrases left much room for flexibility. It had also taken a long time even to reach this point; it had been six decades since the first clear evidence of rising CO_2 concentrations came to light, and many governments continue to resist significant action on climate change even in the face of ever more certain evidence of the problem, and steadily rising global temperatures. The work of the IPCC has strengthened the foundations of the scientific debate, but the institutional aspect of the climate change regime remains modest. Busch (2009) wrote several years ago of the secretariat of the climate change convention as 'making a living in a straitjacket', meaning that while it had filled all the standard roles of a treaty secretariat (including the provision of information, support for negotiations, and the hosting of technical workshops), it had neither generated new knowledge, contributed to understanding of climate change, helped shape the public and political debate, nor played a key role in keeping the climate change debate on the agenda. It has been expected to remain neutral in its work, considering all policy options that might be of interest to the bickering signatories of the convention.

To a large extent, progress on climate change has come either out of the separate initiatives of states or groups of states (the EU being the prime example of the latter), or else as a result of market forces or developments in technology that are incidental to the specific problem. At least part of the reason why GHG emissions are down in Europe, for example, is – ironically – because of reduced energy use in the wake of milder winters brought on by climate change. Also – as we saw in Chapter 8 – Europe has seen an increase in the area of its forest cover, and thus an improvement in its carbon sink capacity. Meanwhile, part of the explanation for recent declines in emissions in the United States lies less in deliberate policy than in market forces: coal in the eastern United States tends to have a higher sulphur content and to exist further underground than coal in the western United States, making it not only dirtier to burn but also more expensive to extract. Coal is also expensive to transport, while record production of natural gas has made it cheaper (US Energy Information Administration, 2016b). For reasons that have

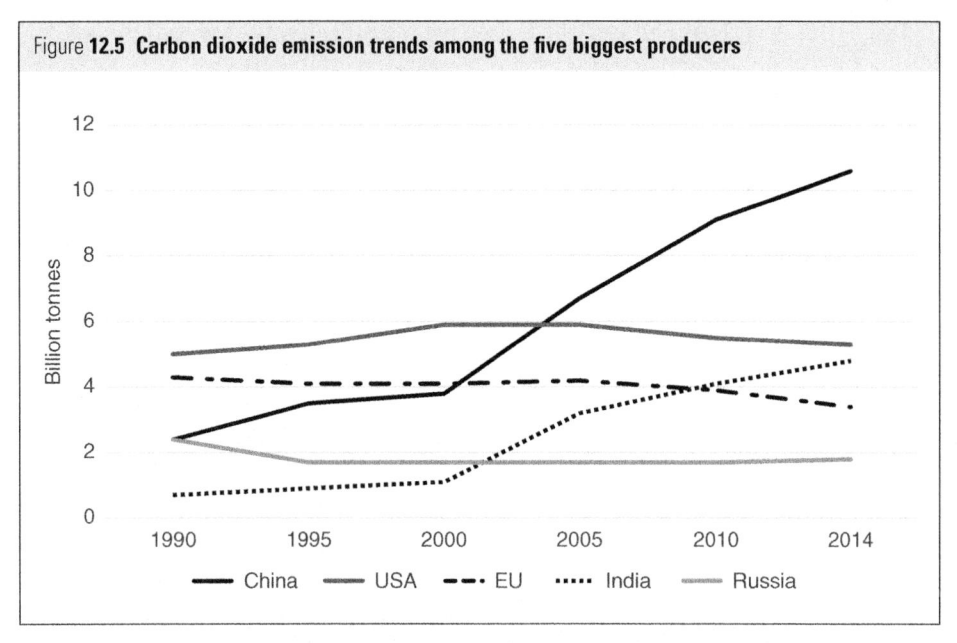

Figure 12.5 Carbon dioxide emission trends among the five biggest producers

Source: Based on data in Netherlands Environmental Assessment Agency (2015) *Trends in Global CO₂ Emissions: 2015 Report* (The Hague: Netherlands Environmental Assessment Agency).

had little to do with government policy, then, there has been a move away from coal to cleaner and cheaper natural gas.

A recent summary of the data on CO_2 emissions (Netherlands Environmental Assessment Agency, 2015) paints a mixed picture (see Figure 12.5):

- Globally, they grew by nearly 60 per cent between 1990 and 2014, from 22.5 billion tonnes to 35.7 billion tonnes. Most of the growth occurred in the opening decade of the century, and the rate of growth has tailed off since 2010.
- China more than quadrupled its emissions during this period, from 2.4 million to 10.6 billion tonnes, making it by far the biggest single producer in the world (although it remains a modest producer on a per capita basis, with numbers about the same as those for the EU). It now accounts for nearly 30 per cent of global CO_2 emissions.
- The United States saw its numbers rise slowly to a peak of 5.9 billion tonnes in 2005, after which they fell to 5.3 billion tonnes in 2014, a 10 per cent cut. It now accounts for 15 per cent of global CO_2 emissions, but remains one of the world's biggest producers on a per capita basis; it takes two Chinese to produce as much CO_2 as one American.
- The European Union collectively made the greatest reductions, with emissions falling from 4.3 billion tonnes in 1990 to 3.4

billion in 2014, a drop of 21 per cent. It now accounts for just under 10 per cent of global CO_2 emissions.
- India saw its emissions grow between 1990 and 2014 from 0.7 billion tonnes to nearly 5 billion tonnes, an almost sevenfold increase. Like China, though, it remains a modest per capita producer.

An interesting insight into the comparative records of states on climate change is offered by the Climate Change Performance Index maintained by two interest groups, the Bonn-based Germanwatch and the Brussels-based Climate Action Network Europe. Based on a set of criteria that include trends in emissions, energy efficiency, and investments in renewables, the index ranks countries as either *Very Good, Good, Moderate, Poor,* or *Very Poor*. In the 2017 index (Burck et al., 2017), no countries earned the status of Very Good, but 14 mainly European countries (including the UK) were ranked as Good, 16 (including India and Germany) were ranked as Moderate, 15 (including Brazil, China, and the United States) were ranked as Poor, and 13 (including Canada, Russia, and Japan) were ranked as Very Poor. (More than 130 countries were not ranked, reflecting the extent to which the problem of climate change is associated with the larger industrial states.) Britain was expected to fall in the rankings because it had not followed up on earlier policy changes, India was given credit for an active renewable energy programme, Germany fell because of a failure to keep up with its 2020 emission reduction targets, concerns were expressed for the future in a United States governed by Donald Trump, Canada was still impacted by the effects of the Harper government (which left office in 2016), and Japan was hurt by emphasizing nuclear energy at the cost of renewables.

There are several potential explanations for the story of climate change policy:

1. There is the realist idea that states seek above all to protect their self-interest, and do not wish to bear the costs of taking action so long as doubts exist that other states are also doing their fair share, however 'fair' is defined.
2. Much can be attributed to the role of large corporations and their profit motives within their respective economic sectors, including the energy and transport industries that are most affected by changes in national regulation.
3. Another explanation is offered by the extent to which modern economies are invested in the often inefficient use of polluting fossil fuels; it is clear what can and should be done, but the investments needed in order to ensure the more efficient use of energy, and a switch to non-pollutive and renewable sources, are substantial.

4. There is the desire of industrializing countries such as China and India to follow the path of economic development that was established by the older industrialized states of Europe and North America. They seek to expand their economic base so as to meet the needs of their expanding populations and to exploit opportunities for trade, and ask why they should handicap themselves with regulations and clean-air technology of the kind that Europeans and Americans felt no need to adopt when they were industrializing.
5. Finally, there is the problem of scientific uncertainty, although this is used as much as anything as a cover for the kinds of commercial concerns that the energy and transport industries have about the costs of change.

Harris (2011) focuses on the influence of the Westphalian international system, a term that refers back to the 1648 Peace of Westphalia that is often considered to be the landmark event in the emergence of the modern state system. He accuses states of fighting for their 'narrowly perceived interests', and placing them above those of the broader human interest. He is particularly critical of the United States and China, and of their long-pursued refusal to compromise on demands that the other must act first. He also points to the problem of the pollution arising from material consumption and other aspects of modern lifestyles that are spreading from developed to developing states as the global middle class expands. He argues that the solution to climate change lies in a combination of climate diplomacy that puts people first, a formula by which the 'common but differentiated' responsibilities of states are matched by a willingness on the part of the world's affluent classes to take on a greater burden of change, and a campaign to encourage people to define happiness and well-being through sufficiency and environmental sustainability.

Discussion questions

- Do we know enough about the science of climate change to blame its effects of human activity?
- Which is the fairest basis for assigning responsibility for emission reductions: total output, per capita output, output per unit of GDP, current emission levels, or historic emission levels?
- Whether or not climate change is human-made, should we not be cutting back on our reliance on fossil fuels anyway?
- Given recent changes in the climate positions of the United States and China, how much do the arguments made by Harris in 2012 still apply?

Key concepts

Carbon footprint   Greenhouse effect

Carbon sink   Greenhouse gases

Further reading

Bailey, Ian, and Hugh Compston (2012) (eds) *Feeling the Heat: The Politics of Climate Change in Rapidly Industrializing Countries* (Palgrave), and David Held, Charles Roger, and Eva-Maria Nag (eds) (2013) *Climate Governance in the Developing World* (Polity). Most books on climate change focus on wealthy industrialized countries; these two offer a helpful perspective on industrializing and developing countries.

Ciplet, David, J. Timmons Roberts, and Mizan R. Khan (2015) *Power in a Warming World: The New Global Politics of Climate Change and the Remaking of Environmental Inequality* (MIT Press). An assessment of the story of climate change politics, offering six potential future scenarios.

Giddens, Anthony (2011) *The Politics of Climate Change*, 2nd edn (Polity Press), and Paul G. Harris (2013) *What's Wrong with Climate Politics and How to Fix It* (Polity Press). Two of the many studies of the politics of climate change, the latter blaming the failure to make more progress largely on the self-interest of states.

Kutney, Gerald (2014) *Carbon Politics and the Failure of the Kyoto Protocol* (Routledge). An analysis of the negotiations over the Kyoto Protocol, offering insights into carbon politics and placing the blame for the failure of Kyoto at the door of inequitable targets.

Sweet, William (2016) *Climate Diplomacy from Rio to Paris: The Effort to Contain Global Warming* (Yale University Press). An assessment by a journalist of the evolution of climate change diplomacy since the signature of the climate change convention.

Glossary

Acid pollution. Pollution caused by emissions of sulphur dioxide and nitrogen oxides, which react with airborne water molecules to acidify precipitation.

Administrative fragmentation. The phenomenon by which policy responsibilities are divided up among multiple governmental institutions.

Anthropocene. A geological epoch dating from the end of the last ice age 10,000 years ago and characterized by the extent to which humans have changed global ecological systems.

Anthropocentrism. The view that human interests have priority over those of the rest of the natural world, and defines the value of nature extrinsically in terms of its value to humans. *See also* **Ecocentrism**.

Anti-environmentalism. A general term for opposition to the arguments of environmentalists.

Aquifer. Water-bearing rock.

Authority. The acknowledged right to rule and govern.

Biodiversity. A term describing the variety and the population of species, and their place in the natural system.

Biofuels. Energy generated from biomass or organic material, including plant matter, animal waste, and municipal waste.

Biopiracy. The exploitation of indigenous knowledge of plant and animal species for profit, without permission or compensation.

Biosphere. Those parts of the earth – including land, oceans, and the atmosphere – within which living organisms exist.

Bycatch. Marine species such as sea turtles, porpoises, albatross, crabs, and starfish that are unintentionally caught during fishing operations.

California effect. The phenomenon by which exporting industries in the South are obliged to meet stronger environmental standards in order to be allowed to export to Northern markets that require those standards.

Carbon capture. Extracting the carbon dioxide from the gases generated by burning coal and placing it in safe storage.

Carbon dioxide. A colourless and odourless gas produced naturally by plant and animal respiration, volcanoes, and other geological activity, and by the burning of fossil fuels. The primary element in the **greenhouse effect**.

Carbon footprint. The amount of carbon dioxide emitted by a particular person, industry, activity, community, or group.

Carbon sink. Natural elements that absorb carbon, including plants, forests, and oceans.

Carbon tax. An effort to reduce the use of fossil fuels by assessing a fee on the carbon content of such fuels, or a tax on carbon dioxide emissions from burning such fuels.

Catalytic converter. A device fitted to the exhausts of combustion engines, and designed to reduce emissions of nitrogen oxides, carbon monoxide, and hydrocarbons.

Charismatic megafauna. The large animal species that attract most human interest and efforts to both exploit and protect.

Chlorofluorocarbons. Non-toxic and non-flammable chemical compounds use as refrigerants and aerosol accelerants, that were found to degrade the earth's **ozone layer**.

Civil society. The arena within which citizens and interest groups work to promote the common interest and to influence public policy.

Collective action problem. The conflicting priorities or additional costs that discourage individuals from working together on a common goal even when they can see how they would benefit as individuals.

Command-and-control. An approach to pollution control based on setting goals, quality standards, and emissions levels, and making government responsible for enforcement.

Common pool resources (or common goods). Resources whose size or extent makes it difficult or impossible to prevent individuals from making use of them.

Conservation. The scientific exploitation and management of resources in order to ensure sustained output. *See also* **Sustainable development**.

Consumer-led solutions. An approach to addressing environmental or resource problems based on the idea that the actions of individual consumers can change the demand system from below.

Consumer society. One in which social and economic status is driven and defined by the acquisition of material goods.

Contingent valuation. An effort to place a price on a commodity that does not have a market value because it is not directly sold.

Corporate environmentalism. The process by which businesses integrate environmental factors into their corporate decision-making.

Corporate social responsibility. The idea that companies should place social and environmental issues at the core of their decision-making because it is in their financial interests so to do.

Cost-benefit analysis. A planning tool by which the costs and benefits of different courses of action are calculated with a view to designing the most economically efficient policies.

Deep ecology. An ecocentric (nature-centred) concern for the environment for its own sake (as opposed to how environmental damage will impact humans).

Deforestation. The transformation of forests into cleared land.

Dumping. The export of polluting industries or activities to poorer countries with weaker (or less stringently enforced) environmental regulations and cheaper labour.

Ecocentrism. The view that nature has intrinsic value, and that humans should not see themselves apart from nature but as part of an interconnected web of relationships. *See also* **Anthropocentrism**.

Ecofeminism. A philosophy that likens men's control and exploitation of women to their control and exploitation of nature.

Eco-labelling. The practice of awarding government- or NGO-sanctioned rights to label consumer products as environmentally friendly.

Ecological democracy. A form of democracy based on the elimination of attempts to dominate the natural world, and on efforts to reintegrate humans and nature.

Ecological modernization. The argument that environmental reform is possible within existing economic systems, and that there is no need for a radical revision of conventional economic ideas. *See also* **Reformist environmentalism**.

Ecological state. One in which the environment takes precedence over the economy.

Ecologism. A political ideology based on the idea that sustainability requires that humans make radical changes to their relationship with the natural world. *See also* **Radical environmentalism**.

Ecology. The branch of biology that studies the relationships among organisms and between organisms and their physical surroundings.

Ecosystem. A dynamic complex of plant, animal and micro-organism communities and their non-living environment interacting as a functional unit.

Ecotourism. A form of tourism aimed at giving visitors opportunities to visit natural environments while encouraging in them a greater appreciation of biodiversity.

Emissions trading. An approach to pollution control based on setting air quality standards in a given area, setting caps on emission levels, and allowing affected industries that are below the levels to trade the right to pollute with those that are above the levels.

Environment. The physical surroundings in which an entity – whether a human, animal, plant, insect, bacterium, or an inanimate object – exists.

Environmental authoritarianism. A response to environmental problems that is shaped by a government that has a greater capacity to impose change on industry and consumers than is the case in democratic systems.

Environmental citizenship. The obligation that individuals have for acting responsibly and positively towards the environment of which they are a part.

Environmental ethics. Moral questions pertaining to the relationship between humans and their environment.

Environmental justice. A paradigm concerned with ensuring the meaningful involvement and fair treatment of all parties involved in making and implementing environmental policy, regardless of race, wealth, religion, or any other political, social, or economic category.

Environmental peacekeeping. Integrating the management of natural resources into conflict prevention or mitigation, with equitable access removing the pressures that lead to environmental mismanagement as well as conflicts arising from scarcity.

Environmental policy instruments. The tools and means available to shape and implement environmental policy.

Environmental refugees. People forced to move or relocate as a result of human-made environmental disruptions such as soil erosion, desertification, and climate change.

Environmental scarcity. The declining availability of natural resources that leads to instability or conflict.

Environmental state. A state that possesses a significant set of institutions and practices dedicated to the management of the environment and societal–environmental interactions.

Environmentalism. A philosophy or ideology that promotes deeper understanding of the threats faced by the environment.

Epistemic community. A transnational network of professionals with recognized skills and knowledge in a particular area, who share a set of practices, and whose influence and power lies in their specialist knowledge of the issues being addressed.

Eutrophication. The depletion of oxygen in water as a result of the introduction of excess nutrients.

E-waste. Electronic waste, including used cell phones, televisions, computers, and printers.

Exclusive Economic Zone. A maritime zone stretching as far as 200 nautical miles (370 km) from the coast within which neighbouring states control resources such as fisheries, minerals, oil, and natural gas.

Extended producer responsibility. An arrangement that makes manufacturers responsible for what happens to their products at the end of their useful life.

Fossil fuels. Fuels formed from the decay of organic matter over millions of years, including coal, oil, and natural gas.

Fracking. Hydraulic fracturing, or injecting water, sand and chemicals at high pressure into subterranean rocks so as to force open fissures and release oil and natural gas.

Fuelwood. Wood that is burned to generate energy for heating and cooking.

Garbage-can policy model. One in which problems and needs are addressed in a manner that is partial, fluid, anarchic, incomplete, disorganized, and opportunistic.

Geothermal energy. Energy generated by tapping the natural heat of the earth.

Global civil society. An international version of **civil society**.

Globalism. The idea that institutions and ideals other than state citizenship attract the loyalty of humans.

Globalization. The process by which the links between people, corporations, and governments in different states have become integrated through trade, investment, and technology.

Governance. The process by which public decisions are made, with or without the input of formal institutions, and with or without formal mechanisms.

Government. The institutions and offices through which societies are governed.

Green economy. One that generates growth in a manner consistent with **sustainable development**, simultaneously advancing economic, social and environmental well-being.

Green growth. A process building on **sustainable development** by achieving growth based on economic, social and environmental sustainability.

Greenhouse effect. A natural phenomenon by which life on earth is made possible through the absorption of solar energy in the earth's atmosphere.

Greenhouse gases. A combination of natural and man-made gases that absorb solar energy, warming the earth's atmosphere.

Green politics. A political philosophy that seeks to build a sustainable society rooted in environmentalism, social justice, nonviolence, diversity, and grassroots democracy.

Green state. A democratic state whose regulatory ideals and democratic procedures are informed by **ecological democracy** rather than liberal democracy.

Greenwashing. A deliberate effort to give the false impression that a company's products or aims are environmentally friendly.

Groundwater. Water that penetrates the soil and fills the spaces between soil particles and fractured rock.

Holocene extinction. An 'extinction event' dating from 10,000 BCE during which notably large numbers of species became extinct, with human activity as the major cause.

Hubbert curve. A graphic that attempted to predict the future of the oil industry (production would rise rapidly to a peak before falling off), and that has been applied to other resources.

Hydropower. Energy captured from water, primarily by using water to generate electricity from turbines.

Incremental policy model. One in which a problem or a need is identified, and change is achieved by building incrementally on what has come before, responding less with a comprehensive plan than with a series of minor adjustments.

Indoor pollution. Pollutants found mainly indoors, including radon, formaldehyde, asbestos, lead, mercury, synthetic fibres, and tobacco smoke.

Institution. A set of rules, decision-making procedures, and programmes that defines practices, assigns roles to participants in these practices, and guides interaction among those in the different roles.

Intergovernmental organization. A body whose members are states or national government bodies and whose goal is to promote cooperation between or among states.

International non-governmental organization. A body whose members are individuals or national interest groups, and which works outside formal government structures.

International organization. A body set up to promote cooperation between or among states, based on the principles of voluntary cooperation, communal management, and shared interests.

Invasive species. Non-native species that are introduced by humans to a part of the world that lies beyond the natural limits of their geographic range.

Issue-attention cycle. The idea that policy issues go through cycles of attention that are driven by media interest, the costs of action, and competition by other issues.

Landfill. A site that is created, designed, and managed for the burial of waste.

Leader–laggard dynamic. The phenomenon by which leader states pull others behind them to more ambitious standards and goals, while laggard states either follow along later or force compromises that result in more modest goals.

Liberalism. A theory which argues that states believe in cooperation, and emphasizes the importance of international organizations and law. *See also* **Realism**.

Long-range transboundary air pollution. Air pollution that is carried across political borders by wind and precipitation.

Market-based incentives. An approach to addressing environmental problems by setting goals and standards while leaving it to the marketplace to deliver the results.

Maximum sustained yield. A figure for the amount of fish, timber, or other renewable resource that can be harvested while leaving enough for the resource to replace itself.

Mega-conferences. Big international conferences that involve most or all governments and that are designed to address broad global or international problems.

Multinational corporation. A private enterprise that controls the production of goods and services, and has facilities and assets in more than one country.

Municipal waste. The garbage that is thrown away every day by homes and workplaces in cities and towns, and that includes packaging, food, plastics, glass, tins, and paper.

Natural resources. Materials or commodities found naturally on earth that have value to humans, and include land, water, plants, animals, soil, minerals, fossil fuels, forests, fisheries, and the open ocean.

Natural resource economics. A field of study that works to understand the economic impact of supply, demand, and allocation in natural resources, looking at the connections between economies and natural systems.

Neoliberalism. The view that the market can resolve most social, economic, and political problems, and that the general social interest is maximized by the pursuit of self-interest.

NIMBY syndrome. Meaning 'not in my back yard', and describing the opposition of local residents to the siting nearby of landfill, power stations, incinerators, and so on.

Nitrogen oxides. A collective term for nitric oxide and nitrogen dioxide, formed when combustion oxidizes the nitrogen in fuel and some of the nitrogen naturally present in the air.

Non-point sources. Diffuse sources of water pollution, including urban and agricultural run-off.

Non-regime. An arena within which policies are pursued among countries without a formal **regime** being in place.

Nuclear power. Harnessing nuclear reactions to generate heat, which is used to drive steam turbines to generate electricity.

Ocean power. Generating energy by exploiting incoming and outgoing tides, tidal currents, and waves.

Ozone. A ground-level pollutant created as a by-product of interactions in sunlight involving pollutants such as nitrogen oxides and carbon monoxide, the problem being worst in cities with heavy traffic.

Ozone layer. The stratospheric ozone that forms when oxygen molecules are split by ultraviolet radiation from the sun to form a thin layer of ozone that helps screen out ultraviolet radiation.

Paradigm. A widely shared pattern or set of values, beliefs, and ideas that guides action.

Poaching. The illegal capture, removal, or killing of wild animals and plants.

Point source. An individual and usually identifiable source of water pollution, such as a factory, a waste dump, or an oil or chemical spill.

Policy convergence. The phenomenon by which policies become more similar across countries.

Policy diffusion. The phenomenon by which policies spread from one country to another.

Policy cycle. A means of understanding policy by seeing it in terms of a never-ending cycle of formulation, adoption, and implementation.

Political ecology. An interdisciplinary field of study interested in the relationships among politics, economics, society, culture, and the environment.

Politics. The process by which people decide collectively how to manage and share the resources of the society in which they live.

Polluter pays principle. An approach to environmental management based on addressing problems by making the polluter or the producer pay the costs of amelioration or clean-up.

Pollution haven hypothesis. The suggestion that high regulatory demands in the North will encourage corporations to move their operations to countries in the South with cheaper labour and weaker environmental regulations.

Post-environmentalism. A call for new environmental approaches and strategies that would define wealth not in gross economic terms but in terms of overall well-being.

Post-materialism. A focus on quality of life issues such as environmental protection and gender equality, as distinct from more traditional materialist interests in economic growth and security.

Power. The capacity to control in the sense of being able to bring about change or to resist pressures to change.

Precautionary principle. The idea of proceeding with caution if there are suspicions that a problem might emerge.

Preservation. Protecting nature by preventing development in **wilderness** areas.

Primary energy. Sources of energy in their original state, such as coal and oil.

Product stewardship. Efforts to minimize the environmental impact of a product or service throughout its life cycle.

Protected areas. National parks, nature preserves, and similar areas where development is either restricted or banned.

Proximity principle. The idea that waste should be disposed of as closely as possible to its source.

Public goods. Goods provided by nature, government or business that are free for general use.

Public policy. The actions taken – or deliberately avoided – by those in positions of authority in order to achieve public goals.

Radical environmentalism. Argues that we face urgent dangers that cannot be resolved within existing structures, and that we need fundamental change and new approaches to economic growth and environmental protection. *See also* **Ecologism**.

Radioactive waste. Any waste material containing dangerous levels of radionuclides (unstable atoms containing excess nuclear energy).

Rational policy model. One in which a problem or a need is identified, alternative approaches studied and weighed, goals and schedules agreed, preferred approaches implemented, and the problem is solved, or the need is met.

Realism. A theory which argues that states are autonomous, self-interested actors in a global system that is dangerous and anarchic (lacks a central authority), and that they are not inclined to trust other states or to place their faith in co-operation. *See also* **Liberalism**.

Recycling. Using waste material to make a new version of the same product, such as recycled paper or glass.

Red list. A catalogue of endangered and vulnerable species maintained since 1964 by the International Union for Conservation of Nature.

Reformist environmentalism. Supports human-centred change within existing political, economic, and social structures, and argues that economic growth and environmental protection can be compatible. *See also* **Ecological modernization**.

Regime. The principles, norms, rules, and decision-making procedures related to a structured area of international relations. See also **Non-regime**.

Regional fisheries management organizations. Bodies that bring together clusters of countries with a shared interest in managing and conserving commercially valuable fish stocks.

Regulation. A rule, standard, or restriction imposed by an executive agency operating under the authority of a legislature.

Regulatory agency. A body set up to exercise autonomous authority over a focused area of policy by implementing government regulations.

Renewable energy. Energy generated by sources that are potentially or actually infinite in supply.

Resource curse. Exists when a country is well endowed in a natural resource that is so valuable that it becomes the target of almost all political and economic attention, and is exploited at almost any cost, including harm to the environment.

Risk assessment. The methodical assessment of the degree and the nature of environmental risks posed by human action.

Solar power. Energy captured from the sun.

Species. Actually or potentially interbreeding natural populations of living organisms.

Sulphur dioxide. A toxic gas that is created when sulphur is released by natural processes such as volcanic activity, or by the burning of fossils fuels, and reacts with oxygen.

Summitry. An approach to international negotiations based on high-level person-to-person meetings and focusing on strategic issues.

Sustainable development. Development that meets the needs of the present without compromising the ability of future generations to meet their own needs. *See also* **Conservation**.

Technology forcing. Setting standards that encourage the development of new solutions to environmental problems

Technology transfer. The channels by which advanced technologies might be made available to emerging states.

Thermal pollution. The release of warm water from industrial plants into rivers or lakes, causing harm to freshwater ecosystems.

Toxic colonialism. The export from the North to the South of materials (including waste) that are illegal or undesirable in their source countries.

Tragedy of the commons. An economic theory which argues that individual self-interest encourages the over-use of **common pool resources**, personal gain prevailing over the well-being of society.

Transgovernmental network. An informal horizontal peer-to-peer web of cooperation that brings together national regulators, legislators, judges, specialized agencies, and other actors, going beyond ad hoc communication but stopping short of the creation of international organizations.

Treaty. A written agreement under international law between or among states that holds them responsible for meeting specified goals and deadlines.

Treaty secretariat. A body set up to oversee and monitor compliance with an international treaty.

Tropical rainforests. Dense and luxuriant forests that attract heavy rainfall, and that are found in the tropical regions of South America, Africa, and Southeast Asia.

Umbrella effect. The idea that protecting a specific umbrella or flagship species will extend the benefits of protection to all other species in the same habitat or **ecosystem**.

Waste. Any solid or liquid commodity or material that is no longer of use or of value to the producer or the owner, and that is either discarded or intended to be discarded.

Water security. The capacity of a population to ensure access to sustainable supplies of clean water and to guard against water-related disasters.
Wetlands. Water-saturated land of the kind usually referred to as swamps, bogs, and marshes.
Whaling. The organized catching of whales for food, 'research', and other uses.
Wild genetic resources. The heritable characteristics of wild plants and animals.
Wilderness. Landscapes that are largely intact in biological and ecological terms, and mostly free of human disturbance.
Wind power. Energy captured from the wind.
Zero waste. An arrangement by which all waste is recovered and reused.

References

Adams, W.M. (2006) 'The Future of Sustainability: Re-thinking Environment and Development in the Twenty-first Century'. Report of the IUCN Renowned Thinkers Meeting, 29–31 January 2006 (Gland, Switzerland: IUCN).

Agola, Nathaniel O., and Joseph L. Awange (2014) *Globalized Poverty and Environment* (Berlin: Springer).

Andresen, Steinar (2012) 'Do We Need More Global Sustainability Conferences?', in Peter Dauvergne (ed), *Handbook of Global Environmental Politics* (Cheltenham: Edward Elgar).

Andrews, David, and Bill Walker (2016) "Erin Brockovich' Carcinogen in Tap Water of More than 200 million Americans', at Environmental Working Group, 20 September, http://www.ewg.org/research/chromium-six-found-in-us-tap-water

Arrhenius, Svante (1896) 'On the Influence of Carbonic Acid in the Air upon the Temperature of the Ground', in *Philosophical Magazine* 41, pp. 237–76.

Auld, Graeme, Steven Bernstein, and Benjamin Cashore (2008) 'The New Corporate Social Responsibility', in *Annual Review of Environment and Resources* 33, pp. 413–35.

Bailey, Ian, and Hugh Compston (2010) 'Geography and the Politics of Climate Policy', in *Geography Compass* 4, pp. 1097–114.

Bailey, Ian, and Hugh Compston (2012) (eds) *Feeling the Heat: The Politics of Climate Change in Rapidly Industrializing Countries* (Basingstoke: Palgrave).

Baker, Keith, and Gerry Stoker (2015) *Nuclear Power and Energy Policy: The Limits to Governance* (Basingstoke: Palgrave Macmillan).

Baldwin, Robert, Martin Cave, and Martin Lodge (2013) *Understanding Regulation: Theory, Strategy, and Practice*, 2nd edn (Oxford: Oxford University Press).

Banerjee, Poulomi (2016) 'Gone to Waste: How India is Drowning in Garbage', in *Hindustan Times*, 9 February.

Barkin, J. Samuel, and Elizabeth R. DeSombre (2013) *Saving Global Fisheries: Reducing Fishing Capacity to Promote Sustainability* (Cambridge, MA: MIT Press).

Barry, John, and Robyn Eckersley (eds) (2005) *The State and the Global Ecological Crisis* (Cambridge, MA: MIT Press).

Bass, Steven, and Stéphane Guéneau (2005) 'Global Forest Governance: Effectiveness, Fairness and Legitimacy of Market-Driven Approaches', in Sophie Thoyer and Benoît Martimort-Asso (eds) *Participation for Sustainability in Trade* (Aldershot: Ashgate).

Bastmeijer, Kees (ed) (2016) *Wilderness Protection in Europe: The Role of International European and National Law* (Cambridge: Cambridge University Press).

Baum, Rachel, Jeanne Luh, and Jamie Bartram (2013) 'Sanitation: A Global Estimate of Sewerage Connections without Treatment and the Resulting Impact on MDG Progress', in *Environmental Science and Technology* 47:4, pp. 1994–2000.

BBC (2016) 'Fuel "too dirty" for Europe sold to Africa', on BBC News web site at http://www.bbc.com/news, 15 September.

Beeson, Mark (2016) 'Environmental Authoritarianism and China', in Teena Gabrielson, Cheryl Hall, John M. Meyer, and David Schlosberg (eds) *The Oxford Handbook of Environmental Political Theory* (Oxford: Oxford University Press).

Begley, Sharon (2007) 'The Truth about Denial', in *Newsweek*, 13 August, pp. 20–29.

Bell, Michelle L., Devra L. Davis, and Tony Fletcher (2004) 'A Retrospective Assessment of Mortality from the London Smog Episode of 1952: The Role of Influenza and Pollution', in *Environmental Health Perspectives* 112:1, January, pp. 6–8.

Bemelmans-Videc, Marie-Louise, Ray C. Rist and Evert Vedung (eds.) (1998) *Carrots, Sticks, and Sermons: Policy Instruments and Their Evaluation* (New Brunswick, NJ: Transaction).

Betsill, Michele M. (2006) 'Transnational Actors in International Environmental Politics', in Michele M. Betsill, Kathryn Hochstetler, and Dimitris Stevis (eds) *Palgrave Advances in International Environmental Politics* (Basingstoke: Palgrave Macmillan).

Biello, David (2014) 'E-Waste Dump among Top 10 Most Polluted Sites', in *Scientific American*, 1 January.

Biermann, Frank (2000) 'The Case for a World Environment Organization', in *Environment* 42:9, pp. 22–31.

Biermann, Frank (2006) 'Global Governance and the Environment', in Michele M. Betsill, Kathryn Hochstetler, and Dimitris Stevis (eds) *Palgrave Advances in International Environmental Politics* (Basingstoke: Palgrave Macmillan).

Biermann, Frank and Steffen Bauer (eds.) (2005) *A World Environment Organization: Solution or Threat for Effective International Environmental Governance?* (Aldershot: Ashgate).

Biermann, Frank, and Bernd Siebenhüner (2009) (eds) *Managers of Global Change: The Influence of International Environmental Bureaucracies* (Cambridge, MA: MIT Press).

Birchfield, Vicki L., and John S. Duffield (eds) (2011) *Toward a Common European Union Energy Policy: Problems, Progress, and Prospects* (Basingstoke: Palgrave Macmillan).

Blackstone, William T. (1974) 'Ethics and Ecology', in William T. Blackstone (ed) *Philosophy and Environmental Crisis* (Athens, GA: University of Georgia Press).

Blomquist, Robert F. (2002) 'Ratification Resisted: Understanding America's Response to the Convention on Biological Diversity, 1989–2002', in *Golden Gate University Law Review* 32:4, January, pp. 493–586.

Blowers, Andrew (2016) *The Legacy of Nuclear Power* (Abingdon: Routledge).

Bodansky, Daniel (2010) *The Art and Craft of International Environmental Law* (Cambridge, MA: Harvard University Press).

Bowen, Howard R. (1953) *Social Responsibilities of the Businessman* (New York: Harper and Row).

Bowman, Michael (2013) 'A Tale of Two CITES: Divergent Perspectives upon the Effectiveness of the Wildlife Trade Convention', in *Review of European Community and International Environmental Law* 22:3, pp. 228–38.

Breitmeier, Helmut, Arild Underdal, Oran R. Young, and Michael Zürn (2006) *Analyzing International Environmental Regimes: From Case Study to Database* (Cambridge, MA, MIT Press).

Brennan, Andrew, and Yeuk-Sze Lo (2015), 'Environmental Ethics', in Edward N. Zalta (ed) *The Stanford Encyclopedia of Philosophy* (Winter Edition) at http://plato.stanford.edu/archives/win2015/entries/ethics-environmental

Brockington, Dan, Rosaleen Duffy, and Jim Igoe (2008) *Nature Unbound: Conservation, Capitalism, and the Future of Protected Areas* (London: Earthscan).

Brown, Lester R., Patricia L. McGrath, and Bruce Stokes (1976) 'Twenty Two Dimensions of the Population Problem'. Worldwatch Paper 5, March (Washington: Worldwatch Institute).

Brown, Lester R. (1977) 'Redefining National Security'. Worldwatch Paper 14, October (Washington: Worldwatch Institute).

Bruch, Carl, Carroll Muffett, Sandra S. Nichols (eds) (2016) *Governance, Natural Resources, and Post-conflict Peacebuilding* (Abingdon: Earthscan).

Brundtland, Gro Harlem, et al (1987) *Our Common Future: World Commission on Environment and Development* (Oxford: Oxford University Press).

Burck, Jan, Franziska Marten, and Christoph Bals (2017) *Climate Change Performance Index: Results 2017* (Bonn: Germanwatch).

Busch, Per-Olof (2009) 'The Climate Secretariat: Making a Living in a Straitjacket', in Frank Biermann and Bernd Siebenhüner (eds) *Managers of Global Change: The Influence of International Environmental Bureaucracies* (Cambridge, MA: MIT Press).

Büscher, Bram, Wolfram Dressler, and Robert Fletcher (eds) (2014) *Nature Inc: Environmental Conservation in the Neoliberal Age* (Tucson, AZ: University of Arizona Press).

Busenburg, George J. (2013) *Oil and Wilderness in Alaska: Natural Resources, Environmental Protection, and National Policy Dynamics* (Washington DC: Georgetown University Press).

Caldwell, Lynton Keith (1970) *Environment. A Challenge for Modern Society* (Garden City, NY: Natural History Press, 1970).

Caldwell, Lynton Keith (1990) *International Environmental Policy: Emergence and Dimensions*, 2nd edn (Durham: Duke University Press).

Campbell, Colin (2015) 'The Curse of the New: How the Accelerating Pursuit of the New is Driving Hyper-Consumption', in Karin E. Ekström (ed) *Waste Management and Sustainable Consumption: Reflections on Consumer Waste* (Abingdon: Routledge).

Campbell, Kurt M, and Christine Parthemore (2008) 'National Security and Climate Change in Perspective', in Kurt M. Campbell (ed), *Climatic Cataclysm: The Foreign Policy and National Security Aspects of Climate Change* (Washington DC: Brookings Institution).

Campe, Sabine (2009) 'The Secretariat of the International Maritime Organization: A Tanker for Tankers', in Frank Biermann and Bernd Siebenhüner (eds) *Managers of Global Change: The Influence of International Environmental Bureaucracies* (Cambridge, MA: MIT Press).

Cannon, Tom (2012) *Corporate Responsibility: Governance, Compliance and Ethics in a Sustainable Environment*, 2nd edn (Harlow: Pearson).

Carson, Richard T. (2011) *Contingent Valuation: A Comprehensive Bibliography and History* (Cheltenham: Edward Elgar).

Carter, Neil (2007) *The Politics of the Environment: Ideas, Activism, Policy*, 2nd edn (Cambridge: Cambridge University Press).

Cawley, R. McGreggor, and John Freemuth (1997) 'A Critique of the Multiple Use Framework in Public Lands Decision-Making', in Charles Davis (ed) *Western Public Lands and Environmental Politics* (Boulder, CO: Westview Press).

Centers for Disease Control (1999) 'Ten Great Public Health Achievements – United States, 1900–1999' at https://www.cdc.gov/mmwr/preview/mmwrhtml/mm4850bx.htm. European Environment Agency (2016).

Christmann, Petra (2004) 'Multinational Companies and the Natural Environment: Determinants of Global Environmental Policy Standardization', in *The Academy of Management Journal* 47:5, October, pp. 747–60.

Christoff, Peter (2005) 'Out of Chaos, a Shining Star? Towards a Typology of Green States', in John Barry and Robyn Eckersley (eds) *The State and the Global Ecological Crisis* (Cambridge, MA: MIT Press).

Christoff, Peter, and Robyn Eckersley (2013) *Globalization and the Environment* (Lanham, MD: Rowman & Littlefield).

Ciplet, David, J. Timmons Roberts, and Mizan R. Khan (2015) *Power in a Warming World: The New Global Politics of Climate Change and the Remaking of Environmental Inequality* (Cambridge, MA: MIT Press).

Cockell, Charles S., and Andrew R. Blaustein (eds) (2001) *Ecosystems, Evolution and Ultraviolet Radiation* (New York: Springer Science).

Cohen, Michael D., James G. March, and Johan P. Olsen (1972) 'A Garbage Can Model of Organizational Choice', in *Administrative Science Quarterly* 17:1, March, pp. 1–25.

Cohen, Steven (2014) *Understanding Environmental Policy* (New York: Columbia University Press).

Colchester, Marcus (1990) 'The International Tropical Timber Organization: Kill or Cure for the Rainforests?' in *The Ecologist* 20:5, September/October, pp. 166–73.

Commoner, Barry (1971) *The Closing Circle: Nature, Man and Technology* (New York: Knopf).

Conca, Ken (2012) 'The Rise of the Region in Global Environmental Politics', in *Global Environmental Politics* 12:3, August, pp. 127–33.

Confederation of European Waste-to-Energy Plants. Home page at http://www.cewep.eu/information/data/studies/index.html (retrieved December 2016).

Convention on Biological Diversity (2014) *Global Biodiversity Outlook 4* (Montréal: Secretariat of the Convention on Biological Diversity).

Corell, Elisabeth, and Michele M. Betsill (2008) 'Analytical Framework: Assessing the Influence of NGO Diplomats' in Michele M. Betsill and Elisabeth Corell (eds) *NGO Diplomacy: The Influence of Nongovernmental Organizations in International Environmental Negotiations* (Cambridge, MA: MT Press).

Couzens, Ed (2013) 'CITES at Forty: Never Too Late to Make Lifestyle Changes', in *Review of European Community and International Environmental Law* 22:3, pp. 311–23. 228–38.

Cox, Lydia (2015) 'The Surprising Decline in US Petroleum Consumption' on World Economic Forum web site at https://www.weforum.org/agenda/2015/07/the-surprising-decline-in-us-petroleum-consumption

Crane, Andrew, Dirk Matten, Abagail McWilliams, Jeremy Moon, and Donald Siegel (eds) (2009) *The Oxford Handbook of Corporate Social Responsibility* (Oxford: Oxford University Press).

Cressey, Daniel (2014) 'Biopiracy Ban Stirs Red-Tape Fears', in *Nature* 514, 20 September, pp. 14–15.

Cross, Mai'a K. Davis (2013) 'Rethinking Epistemic Communities Twenty Years Later', in *Review of International Studies* 39:1, January, pp. 137–60.

Crossette, Barbara (1995) 'Severe Water Crisis Ahead for Poorest Nations in Next Two Decades', in *New York Times*, 10 August.

Crutzen, Paul J. (2002) 'Geology of Mankind', in *Nature* 415;6867, 3 January, p. 23.

Curwin, Daniel (2015) 'How Resource Wealth Fuels War', in *The National Interest*, 6 February.

Dahlman, Carl J. (2012) *The World Under Pressure: How China and India are Influencing the Global Economy and Environment* (Stanford: Stanford University Press).

Dasgupta, Partha, and Veerabhadran Ramanathan (2014) 'Pursuit of the Common Good', in *Science* 345:6203, 19 September, pp. 1457–58.

Dauvergne, Peter (2009) *Historical Dictionary of Environmentalism* (Lanham, MD: Scarecrow Press).

Davenport, Deborah S. (2005) 'An alternative Explanation for the Failure of the UNCED Forest Negotiations', in *Global Environmental Politics* 5:1, pp. 105–30.

Davidson, Jonathan, and Joseph M. Norbeck (2012) *An Interactive History of the Clean Air Act* (London: Elsevier).

Davies, Anna R. (2008) *The Geographies of Garbage Governance: Interventions, Interactions and Outcomes* (Aldershot: Ashgate).

Death, Carl (2011) 'Summit Theatre: Exemplary Governmentality and Environmental Diplomacy in Johannesburg and Copenhagen', in *Environmental Politics* 20:1, February, pp. 1–19.

Delreux, Tom, and Sander Happaerts (2016) *Environmental Policy and Politics in the European Union* (London: Palgrave).

Demirbas, Ayhan (2008) *Biofuels: Securing the Planet's Future Energy Needs* (London: Springer).

Democracy Index maintained by Economist Intelligence Unit at http://www.eiu.com (retrieved April 2017).

Dempewolf, H., and L. Guarino (2015) 'Reaching back through the domestication bottleneck: Tapping wild plant biodiversity for crop improvement', in *Acta Horticulturae* 1101, pp. 165–68.

Di Minin, Enrico, and Atte Moilanen (2014) 'Improving the Surrogacy Effectiveness of Charismatic Megafauna with Well-Surveyed Taxonomic Groups and Habitat Types', in *Journal of Applied Ecology* 51: 2, January, pp. 281–88.

Dimitrov, Radoslav S., Detlef Sprinz, Gerald Di Giusto, and Alexander Kelle (2007) 'International Nonregimes: A Research Agenda', in *International Studies Review* 9:2, Summer, pp. 230–58.

Dinar, Shlomi (ed) (2011) *Beyond Resource Wars: Scarcity, Environmental Degradation, and International Cooperation* (Cambridge, MA: MIT Press).

Dobson, Andrew (2007a) *Green Political Thought*, 4th edn (Abingdon: Routledge).

Dobson, Andrew (2007b) 'Environmental Citizenship: Towards Sustainable Development', in *Sustainable Development* 15:5, September/October, pp. 276–85.

Dobson, Andrew, and Derek Bell (eds) (2005) *Environmental Citizenship* (Cambridge, MA: MIT Press).

Dombrowsky, Ines (2008) 'Integration in the Management of International Waters: Economic Perspectives on a Global Policy Discourse', in *Global Governance* 14:4, October–December, pp. 451–77.

Doran, Peter (1993) '"The Earth Summit" (UNCED) Ecology as Spectacle', in *Paradigms: Kent Journal of International Relations* 7:1, Summer, pp. 55–65.

Dorsey, Kurkpatrick (2013) *Whales and Nations: Environmental Diplomacy on the High Seas* (Seattle: University of Washington Press).

Douglass, Anne R., Paul A. Newman, and Susan Soloman (2014) 'The Antarctic Ozone Hole: An Update', in *Physics Today* July, p, 42.

Downs, Anthony (1972) 'Up and Down with Ecology – The "Issue Attention Cycle"', in *The Public Interest* 28.

Doyle, Timothy, Doug McEachern, and Sherilyn MacGregor (2016) *Environment and Politics*, 4th edn (Abingdon: Routledge).

Dryzek, John S. (2013) *The Politics of the Earth: Environmental Discourses*, 3rd edn (Oxford: Oxford University Press).

Dudgeon, David, Angela H. Arthington, Mark O. Gessner, Zen-Ichiro Kawabata, Duncan J. Knowler, Christian Lévêque, Robert J. Naiman, Anne-Hélène Prieur-Richard, Doris Soto, Melanie L. J. Stiassny, and Caroline A. Sullivan (2006) 'Freshwater Biodiversity: Importance, Threats, Status and Conservation Challenges', in *Biological Reviews* 81:2, May, pp. 163–82.

Dudley Nigel (2008) *Guidelines for Applying Protected Area Management Categories* (Gland, Switzerland: IUCN.

Duffy, Rosaleen (2014) 'Waging a War to Save Biodiversity: The Rise of Militarized Conservation', in *International Affairs* 90: 4, July, pp. 819–34.

Dunlap, Riley E., and Aaron McCright (2011) 'Organized Climate Change Denial', in John S. Dryzek, Richard B. Norgaard, and David Schlosberg (eds) *The Oxford Handbook of Climate Change and Society* (Oxford: Oxford University Press).

Duit, Andreas (ed) (2014) *State and Environment: The Comparative Study of Environmental Governance* (Cambridge, MA: MIT Press).

Duit, Andreas (2016) 'The Four Faces of the Environmental State: Environmental Governance Regimes in 28 Countries', in *Environmental Politics* 25:1, pp. 69–91.

Duit, Andreas, Peter H. Feindt, and James Meadowcroft (2016) 'Greening Leviathan: The Rise of the Environmental State?', in *Environmental Politics* 25:1, pp. 1–23.

Durant, Robert F., Daniel J. Fiorino, and Rosemary O'Leary (eds) (2004) *Environmental Governance Reconsidered. Challenges, Choices, and Opportunities* (Cambridge, MA: MIT Press).

Eckersley, Robyn (1992) *Environmentalism and Political Theory: Toward an Ecocentric Approach* (Albany, NY: State University of New York Press).

Eckersley, Robyn (2004) *The Green State: Rethinking Democracy and Sovereignty* (Cambridge, MA: MIT Press).

The Ecologist (1992) 'Editorial', 22:4, July/August.

The Economist (2013), 'Wood: The Fuel of the Future', 6 April.

The Economist (2104a) 'A Clearing in the Trees: New Ideas on What Speeds Up Deforestation and What Slows it Down', 23 August.

The Economist (2014b) 'The Fuel of the Future, Unfortunately', 19 April.

Ehrlich, Paul (1968) *The Population Bomb* (New York: Ballantine Books).

Energy and Resources Institute (2013) *TERI Environmental Survey 2013* (New Delhi: The Energy and Resources Institute).

Engelke, Peter, and Russell Sticklor (2015) 'Water Wars: The Next Great Driver of Global Conflict?', in *The National Interest*, 15 September.

Epstein, Charlotte, and Kate Barclay (2013) 'Shaming to "Green": Australia-Japan Relations and Whales and Tuna Compared', in *International Relations of the Asia-Pacific* 13:1, pp. 95–123.

European Environment Agency (2013) *Late Lessons from Early Warnings: Science, Precaution, Innovation* (Luxembourg: Publications Office of the European Union).

European Environment Agency (2014) Data on Sulphur Dioxide Emissions at http://www.eea.europa.eu/data-and-maps (retrieved May 2016).

European Environment Agency (2016) 'European Water Policies and Human Health'. EEA Report No. 32 (Luxembourg: Publications Office of the European Union).

Evelyn, John, Fumifugium: or the Inconvenience of the Aer and Smoake of London Dissipated, reproduced in James P. Lodge (1969), *The Smoake of London: Two Prophecies* (New York: Maxwell Reprint Company).

Falkner, Robert (2008) *Business Power and Conflict in International Environmental Politics* (Basingstoke: Palgrave Macmillan).

Faure, Michael, and Marjan Peeters (eds) (2008) *Climate Change and European Emissions Trading: Lessons for Theory and Practice* (Cheltenham: Edward Elgar).

Fawell, J., K. Bailey, J. Chilton, E. Dahi, L. Fewtrell and Y. Magara (2006) *Fluoride in Drinking-water* (Geneva: World Health Organization).

Food and Agriculture Organization of the UN (2015) *Global Forest Resources Assessment 2015* (Rome: FAO).

Food and Agriculture Organization of the UN (2016) *The State of World Fisheries and Aquaculture 2016* (Rome, FAO).

Foss, Jeffery E. (2009) *Beyond Environmentalism: A Philosophy of Nature* (Hoboken, NJ: John Wiley).

Foster, Kenneth R., Paolo Vecchia, and Michael H. Repacholi (2000) 'Science and the Precautionary Principle', in *Science* 288:5468, 12 May, pp. 979–81.

Fotopoulos, Takis (2001) 'Inclusive Democracy', in R. J. Barry Jones (ed) *Routledge Encyclopedia of International Political Economy, Vol. 2: Entries G-O* (London: Routledge).

Gale, Fred, and Timothy Cadman (2014) 'Whose Norms Prevail? Policy Networks, International Organizations, and "Sustainable forest Management"', in *Society and Natural Resources* 27:2, pp. 170–84.

Galtung, Johan (1973) 'The "Limits to Growth" and Class Politics', in *Journal of Peace Research* 10:1/2, pp. 101–14.

Germain, Laura A., Alain Karsenty, and Anne-Marie Tiani (eds) (2010) *Governing Africa's Forests in a Globalized World* (London: Earthscan).

Gettleman, Jeffrey (2006) 'Annan Faults 'Frightening Lack of Leadership' for Global Warming', in *New York Times*, 16 November.

Giampietro, Mario, and Kozo Mayumi (2009) *The Biofuel Delusion: The Fallacy of Large-scale Agro-biofuel Production* (London: Earthscan).

Giessen, Lukas, Max Krott, and Torsten Möllmann (2014) 'Increasing Representation of States by Utilitarian as Compared to Environmental Bureaucracies in International Forest and Forest–Environmental Policy Negotiations', in *Forest Policy and Economics* 38, January, pp. 97–104.

Gilardi, Fabrizio (2012) 'Transnational Diffusion: Norms, Ideas, and Policies' in Walter Carlsnaes, Thomas Risse and Beth Simmons (eds) *Handbook of International Relations* (Thousand Oaks, CA: Sage).

Gillespie, Alexander (2006) *Climate Change, Ozone Depletion and Air Pollution* (Leiden: Martinus Nijhoff).

Gillespie, Alexander (2015) *Waste Policy: International Regulation, Comparative and Contextual Perspectives* (Cheltenham: Edward Elgar).

Goklany, Indur M. (2007) *The Improving State of the World: Why We're Living Longer, Healthier, More Comfortable Lives on a Cleaner Planet* (Washington DC: Cato Institute).

Goldenberg, Suzanne (2014) 'CO_2 Emissions are Being "Outsourced" by Rich Countries to Rising Economies', in *The Guardian* 19 January.

Goodin, Robert E., et al (2006) 'The Public and its Policies', in Moran, Michael, Martin Rein, and Robert E. Goodin (eds) *The Oxford Handbook of Public Policy* (Oxford: Oxford University Press).

Grunwald, Michal (2006) *The Swamp: The Everglades, Florida, and the Politics of Paradise* (New York: Simon and Schuster).

Guha, Ramachandra (2013) 'Mahatma Gandhi and the Environmental Movement in India', in Arne Kalland and Gerard Persoon (eds) *Environmental Movements in Asia* (Abingdon: Routledge).

Gupta, Arti (2015) 'Precautionary Principle' in Jean-Frédéric Morin and Amandine Orsini (eds) (2015) *Essential Concepts of Global Environmental Governance* (Abingdon: Routledge).

Haas, Peter (1992), 'Introduction: Epistemic Communities and International Policy Coordination', in *International Organization*, 46:1, Winter, pp. 1–35.

Haas, Peter M. (2002), 'Constructing Environmental Conflicts from Resource Scarcity', in *Global Environmental Politics* 2:1, February, pp. 1–11.

Haas, Peter M. (2016) *Epistemic Communities, Constructivism, and International Environmental Politics* (Abingdon: Routledge).

Hajjar, R., and J.L. Innes (2009) 'The Evolution of the World Bank's Policy Towards Forestry: Push or Pull?', in *International Forestry Review* 11:1, March, pp. 27–37.

Hall, C. Michael (2010a) 'Tourism and Biodiversity: More Significant than Climate Change?', in *Journal of Heritage Tourism* 5:4, November, pp. 253–66.

Hall, C. Michael (2010b) 'Changing Paradigms and Global Change: From Sustainable to Steady-State Tourism', in *Tourism Recreation Research* 35:2, March, pp. 131–43.

Happaerts, Sander, and Hans Bruyninckx (2014), 'Sustainable Development: The Institutionalization of a Contested Policy Concept', in Michele M. Betsill, Kathryn Hochstetler, and Dimitris Stevis (eds) *Advances in International Environmental Politics*, 2nd edn (Basingstoke: Palgrave Macmillan).

Hardin, Garrett (1968) 'The Tragedy of the Commons', in *Science* 162:3859, 13 December, pp. 1243–48.

Harper, John L., and David L Hawksworth (1994) Preface to Special Issue on Biodiversity Measurement and Estimation, in *Philosophical Transactions: Biological Sciences* 345:1311, 29 July, pp. 5–12.

Harris, Paul G. (2011) 'Climate Change', in Gabriela Kütting (ed) *Global Environmental Politics: Concepts, Theories and Case Studies* (Abingdon: Routledge).

Harris, Paul G. (2013) *What's Wrong with Climate Politics and How to Fix It* (Cambridge: Polity Press).

Harris, Shane (2014) 'Water Wars', in *Foreign Policy*, 18 September.

Harvey, M.W.T. (2005) *Wilderness Forever: Howard Zahniser and the Path to the Wilderness Act* (Seattle: University of Washington Press).

Hausman, Jerry (2012) 'Contingent Valuation: From Dubious to Hopeless', in *Journal of Economic Perspectives* 26:4, Fall, pp. 43–56.

Hay, Bruce L., Robert N. Stavins, and Richard H.K. Vietor, (2005) 'The Four Questions of Corporate Social Responsibility: May They, Can They, Should They, Do They', in Hay, Bruce L., Robert N. Stavins, and Richard H.K. Vietor (eds) *Environmental Protection and the Social Responsibility of Firms* (Washington DC: Resources for the Future).

Hayes, Tanya, and Elinor Ostrom (2005) 'Conserving the World's Forests: Are Protected Areas the Only Way?', in *Indiana Law Review* 38:3, pp. 595–617.

Hayward, Tim (1994) *Ecological Thought: An Introduction* (Cambridge: Polity Press).

Hedden, Steve, and Jakkie Cilliers (2014) 'Parched Prospects: The Emerging Water Crisis in South Africa', African Futures Paper 11, September (Pretoria: Institute for Security Studies).

Hein, James Everett, and J. Craig Jenkins (2017) 'Why Does the United States Lack a Global Warming Policy? The Corporate Inner Circle versus Public Interest Sector Elites', in *Environmental Politics* 26:1, pp. 97–117.

Held, David, Charles Roger, and Eva-Maria Nag (eds) (2013) *Climate Governance in the Developing World* (Cambridge: Polity Press).

Herczeg, Márton (2013) *Municipal Waste Management in Switzerland* (Copenhagen: European Environment Agency).

Heywood Vernon H. (ed) (1996) *Global Biodiversity Assessment* (Cambridge: Cambridge University Press).

Hindmarsh, Richard (ed) (2013) *Nuclear Disaster at Fukushima Daiichi: Social, Political and Environmental Issues* (Abingdon: Routledge).

Hochstetler, Kathryn, and Manjana Milkoreit (2015) 'Responsibilities in Transition: Emerging Powers in the Climate Change Negotiations', in *Global Governance* 21:2, April-June, pp. 205–26.

Hoffman, Andrew J., and Pratima Bansal (2012) Introduction to Pratima Bansal and Andrew J. Hoffman (eds) *The Oxford Handbook of Business and the Natural Environment* (Oxford: Oxford University Press).

Holling, C. S., and Gary K. Meffe (1996) 'Command and Control and the Pathology of Natural Resource Management', in *Conservation Biology* 10:2, April, pp. 328–37.

Homer-Dixon, Thomas F. (2001) *Environment, Scarcity, and Violence* (Princeton, NJ: Princeton University Press).

Hsiang, Solomon M., Marshall Burke, and Edward Miguel (2013) 'Quantifying the Influence of Climate on Human Conflict', in *Science* 341:6151, 13 September.

Hu, Xindi C., David Q. Andrews, Andrew B. Lindstrom, Thomas A. Bruton, Laurel A. Schaider, Philippe Grandjean, Rainer Lohmann, Courtney C. Carignan, Arlene Blum, Simona A. Balan, Christopher P. Higgins, and Elsie M. Sunderland (2016) 'Detection of Poly- and Perfluoroalkyl Substances (PFASs) in U.S. Drinking Water Linked to Industrial Sites, Military Fire Training Areas, and Wastewater Treatment Plants', in *Environmental Science & Technology Letters*, 3:10, August, pp 344–50.

Humphreys, David (1996) *Forest Politics: The Evolution of International Cooperation* (London: Earthscan).

Humphreys, David (2005) 'The Elusive Quest for a Global Forests Convention', in *Review of European Community and International Environmental Law* 14:1, April, pp. 1–10.

Hunter, David, James Salzman and Durwood Zaelke (2010) *International Environmental Law and Policy*, 4th edn (St. Paul, MN: Foundation Press).

Hunter, David (2014) 'International Environmental Law: Sources, Principles, and Innovations', in Paul G. Harris (ed) *Routledge Handbook of Global Environmental Politics* (Abingdon: Routledge).

Indian Express (2016), 'Wastelands of India: Here's How Metros Manage Their Trash', 7 February.

Inglehart, Ronald (1971) 'The Silent Revolution in Europe: Intergenerational Change in Post-Industrial Societies', in *American Political Science Review* 65:4, December, pp. 991–1017.

Inglehart, Ronald (1997) *Modernization and Postmodernization: Cultural, Economic and Social Change in 43 Societies* (Princeton, NJ: Princeton University Press).

Ingraham, Christopher (2015) 'Call Off the Bee-pocalypse: U.S. Honeybee Colonies hit a 20-Year High', in *Washington Post*, 23 July.

Intergovernmental Panel on Climate Change (2013) 'Summary for Policymakers', in *Climate Change 2013: The Physical Science Basis. Contribution of Working Group I to the Fifth Assessment Report of the Intergovernmental Panel on Climate Change* (Cambridge: Cambridge University Press).

International Bottled Water Association (2015) *2014 Market Report Findings* at http://www.bottledwater.org/economics/industry-statistics

International Ecotourism Society (2016). Home page at http://www.ecotourism.org/what-is-ecotourism (retrieved May 2016).

International Energy Agency (2015a) *India Energy Outlook* (Paris: IEA).

International Energy Agency (2015b) *Medium-Term Renewable Energy Market Report 2015* (Paris: OECD/IEA).

International Energy Agency (2015c) *World Energy Outlook 2015* (Paris: IEA, 2015).

International Energy Agency (2016a) *Key World Energy Statistics*, at http://www.iea.org/publications/freepublications/publication/KeyWorld2016.pdf

International Energy Agency (2016b) *Energy Technology Perspectives*, at http://www.iea.org/etp

International Tanker Owners Pollution Federation (2017) *Oil Tanker Spill Statistics* at http://www.itopf.com/knowledge-resources/data-statistics/statistics (retrieved May 2017).

International Union for the Conservation of Nature (2015) *The IUCN Red List of Threatened Species* at http://www.iucnredlist.org (retrieved May 2016).

International Union for the Conservation of Nature (2016). Home page at https://www.iucn.org (retrieved November 2016).

Ivanova, Maria (2010) 'UNEP in Global Environmental Governance: Design, Leadership, Location', in *Global Environmental Politics* 10:1, February, pp. 30–59.

Ivanova, Maria (2012) 'Institutional Design and UNEP Reform: Historical Insights on Form, Function and Financing', in *International Affairs* 88:3, May, pp. 565–84.

Jacques, Peter J., Riley E. Dunlap and Mark Freeman (2008) 'The Organisation of Denial: Conservative Think Tanks and Environmental Scepticism', in *Environmental Politics* 17:3, pp. 349–85.

James, Simon P. (2015) *Environmental Philosophy: An Introduction* (London: Polity Press).

Jenkins, Willis, and Christopher Key Chapple (2011) 'Religion and Environment', in *Annual Review of Environment and Resources* 36, pp. 441–63.

Jinnah, Sikina (2014) *Post-Treaty Politics: Secretariat Influence in Global Environmental Governance* (Cambridge, MA: MIT Press).

Johri, Rakesh (2008) *E-Waste: Implications, Regulations and Management in India and Current Global Best Practices* (New Delhi: The Energy and Resources Institute).

Jordan, Andrew, and Tim O'Riordan (1997) 'Social Institutions and Climate Change'. CSERGE Working Paper, GEC 97–15.

Jordan, Andrew, and Camilla Adele (eds) (2013) *Environmental Policy in the European Union: Actors, Institutions and Processes*, 3rd edn (Abingdon: Routledge).

Josephson, Paul (2012) 'Technology and the Environment', in J. R. McNeill and Erin Stewart Mauldin (eds) *A Companion to Global Environmental History* (Chichester: John Wiley).

Kasperson, Roger E. (2011) 'Characterizing the Science/Practice Gap', in Roger E. Kasperson and Mimi Berberian (eds) *Integrating Science and Policy* (London: Earthscan).

Keleman, R. Daniel (2010) 'Globalizing European Union Environmental Policy', in *Journal of European Public Policy* 17:3, April, 335–49.

Keller, Ann Campbell (2009) *Science in Environmental Policy: The Politics of Objective Advice* (Cambridge, MA: MIT Press).

Kern, Kristine, and Harriet Bulkeley (2009) 'Cities, Europeanization and Multi-level Governance: Governing Climate Change through Transnational Municipal Networks', in *Journal of Common Market Studies* 47:2, March, pp. 309–32.

Kirby, Keith J., and Charles Watkins (2015) 'Overview of Europe's Woods and Forests', in Keith J. Kirby and Charles Watkins (eds) *Europe's Changing Woods and Forests: From Wildwood to Managed Landscapes* (Wallingford: CAB International).

Klimont, Z., S. J. Smith and J. Cofala (2013) 'The Last Decade of Global Anthropogenic Sulfur Dioxide: 2000–2011 Emissions', in *Environmental Research Letters* 8:1.

Knill, Christoph, Daniel Arndt and Stephan Heichel (2011) 'Really a Front-Runner, Really a Straggler? Of Environmental Leaders and Laggards in the European Union and Beyond – A Quantitative Policy Perspective'. Paper given at 6th ECPR General Conference, Reykjavik, Iceland, 25–27 August.

Knill, Christoph, and Jale Tosun (2012) *Public Policy: A New Introduction* (Basingstoke: Palgrave Macmillan).

Kolbert, Elizabeth (2014) *The Sixth Extinction: An Unnatural History* (New York: Henry Holt).

Kraft, Michael E., and Scott R. Furlong (2015) *Public Policy: Politics, Analysis and Alternatives*, 5th edn (Thousand Oaks, CA: Sage).

Krasner, Stephen D. (ed) (1983) *International Regimes* (Ithaca, NY: Cornell University Press).

Kutney, Gerald (2014) *Carbon Politics and the Failure of the Kyoto Protocol* (Abingdon: Routledge).

Kuzemko, Caroline, Andreas Goldthau, and Michael F. Keating (2015) *The Global Energy Challenge: Environment, Development and Security* (London: Palgrave).

Laurance, William F. (2010), in Navjot S. Sodhi and Paul R. Ehrlich (eds) (2010) *Conservation Biology for All* (Oxford: Oxford University Press).

Layzer. Judith A. (2012) *Open for Business: Conservatives' Opposition to Environmental Regulation* (Cambridge, MA: MIT Press).

Le Billon, Philippe (2012) *Wars of Plunder: Conflict, Profits and the Politics of Resources* (London: Hurst).
Lee, William E, Michael I. Ojavan, and Carol M. Jantzen (2013) *Radioactive Waste Management and Contaminated Site Clean-Up* (Cambridge: Woodhead).
Lehmann, Steffen, and Robert Crocker (eds) (2012) *Designing for Zero Waste: Consumption, Technologies and the Built Environment* (Abingdon: Earthscan).
Lenschow, Andrea (2015) 'Environmental Policy: Contending Dynamics of Policy Change', in Helen Wallace, Mark A. Pollack, Alasdair R. Young (eds) *Policy-Making in the European Union*, 7th edn (Oxford: Oxford University Press).
Leopold, Aldo (1968 [1949]) *A Sand County Almanac: And Sketches Here and There* (New York: Oxford University Press).
Lesage, Dries, Thijs Van de Graaf, and Kirsten Westphal (2010) *Global Energy Governance in a Multipolar World* (Farnham: Ashgate).
Lidskog, Rolf, and Göran Sundqvist (eds) (2011a) *Governing the Air: The Dynamics of Science, Policy, and Citizen Interaction* (Cambridge, MA: MIT Press).
Lidskog, Rolf, and Göran Sundqvist (2011b) 'Transboundary Air Pollution Policy in Transition', in Lidskog, Rolf, and Göran Sundqvist (eds) *Governing the Air: The Dynamics of Science, Policy, and Citizen Interaction* (Cambridge, MA: MIT Press).
Lidskog, Rolf, and Göran Sundqvist (2015) 'When Does Science Matter? International Relations Meets Science and Technology Studies', in *Global Environmental Politics* 15:1, February, pp. 1–20.
Lindblom, Charles E. (1979) 'Still Muddling, Not Yet Through', in *Public Administration Review* 39:6, November–December, pp. 517–26.
Linnit, Carol, 'Harper's Attack on Science: No Science, No Evidence, No Truth, No Democracy', in *Academic Matters*, May 2013.
Locey, Kenneth J., and Jay T. Lennon, Jay (2016) 'Scaling Laws Predict Global Microbial Diversity', in *Proceedings of the National Academy of Sciences* 113:21, 24 May, pp. 5970–75.
Lomborg, Bjørn (2001) *The Skeptical Environmentalist: Measuring the Real State of the World* (Cambridge: Cambridge University Press).
Luhn, Alec (2016) 'Anthrax Outbreak Triggered by Climate Change Kills Boy in Arctic Circle', in *The Guardian*, 1 August.
Lytle, Mark Hamilton (2007) *The Gentle Subversive: Rachel Carson, Silent Spring, and the Rise of the Environmental Movement* (New York: Oxford University Press).
McAvoy, Gregory E. (1999) *Controlling Technocracy: Citizen Rationality and the Nimby Syndrome* (Washington DC: Georgetown University Press).
MacBride, Samantha (2012) *Recycling Reconsidered: The Present Failure and Future Promise of Environmental Action in the United States* (Cambridge, MA: MIT Press).
Malthus, Thomas (1798), 'An Essay on the Principle of Population' (London: J. Johnson).
McCormick, John (1995) *The Global Environmental Movement*, 2nd edn (Chichester: John Wiley).
McCormick, John (2001) *Environmental Policy in the European Union* (Basingstoke: Palgrave Macmillan).

McKibben, Warwick J. (2008) 'China and the Global Environment', in Barry Eichengreen, Yung Chul Park, Charles Wyplosz (eds) *China, Asia, and the New World Economy* (Oxford: Oxford University Press).

Manderson, Edward, and Richard Kneller (2012), 'Environmental Regulations, Outward FDI and Heterogeneous Firms: Are Countries Used as Pollution Havens?', in *Environmental and Resource Economics* 51:3, March, pp. 317–52.

Maniates, Michael F. (2001) 'Individualization: Plant a Tree, Buy a Bike, Save the World?', in *Global Environmental Politics* 1:3, August, pp. 31–52.

Markham, William T. (2008) *Environmental Organizations in Modern Germany* (New York: Berhahn).

Markowitz, Gerald, and David Rosner (2013) *Lead Wars: The Politics of Science and the Fate of America's Children* (Berkeley: University of California Press).

Martens, Maria (2008) 'Administrative Integration through the Back Door? The Role and Influence of the European Commission in Transgovernmental Networks within the Environmental Policy Field', in *Journal of European Integration* 30:5, pp. 635–51.

Martens, Pim, Jan Rotmans, and Dolf de Groot, D. (2003) 'Biodiversity: Luxury or Necessity?', in *Global Environmental Change*, 13:2, July, pp. 75–81.

Martin, Claude (2015) *On the Edge: The State and Fate of the World's Tropical Rainforests* (Vancouver: Greystone Books).

Martine, George, Gordon McGranahan, Mark Montgomery, and Rogelio Fernandez-Castilla (eds) (2008) *The New Global Frontier: Urbanization, Poverty and Environment in the 21st Century* (London: Earthscan).

Mathews, Jessica Tuchman (1989) 'Redefining Security', in *Foreign Affairs* 68:2, Spring, pp. 162–77.

Mathews, Jessica Tuchman (1997) 'Power Shift', in *Foreign Affairs* 76:1, January/February, pp. 287–93.

Mayr, Ernst (1942) Systematics and the Origin of Species, from the Viewpoint of a Zoologist (Cambridge, MA: Harvard University Press).

Meadows, Donella H., Dennis L. Meadows, Jørgen Randers, and William W. Behrens III (1972) *The Limits to Growth: A Report for the Club of Rome's Project on the Predicament of Mankind* (New York: Universe).

Mee, Laurence D. (2005) 'The Role of UNEP and UNDP in Multilateral Environmental Agreements', in *International Environmental Agreements: Politics, Law and Economics* 5:3, September, pp. 227–63.

Metz, Bert, Ogunlade R. Davidson, Jan-Willem Martens, Sascha N.M. van Rooijen, and Laura Van Wie McGrory (eds) (2000) *Methodological and Technological Issues in Technology Transfer* (New York: Cambridge University Press).

Miller, Char (2013) *Seeking the Greatest Good: The Conservation Legacy of Gifford Pinchot* (Pittsburgh, PA: University of Pittsburgh Press).

Minogue, Martin, and Ledivina Cariño (eds) (2006) *Regulatory Governance in Developing Countries* (Cheltenham: Edward Elgar).

Mitchell, Ronald B. (2016) *International Environmental Agreements Database Project* at http://iea.uoregon.edu/page.php?query=home-contents.php (retrieved April 2016).

Mol, Arthur P.J. (2016) 'The Environmental Nation State in Decline', in *Environmental Politics* 25:1, pp. 48–68.

Mol, Arthur P.J., David A. Sonnenfeld, and Gert Spaargaren (eds) (2009) *The Ecological Modernization Reader: Environmental Reform in Theory and Practice* (Abingdon: Routledge).

Monbiot, George (2014) 'Put a Price on Nature? We Must Stop this Neoliberal Road to Ruin', in *The Guardian*, 24 July.

Moore, Scott, and Dale Squires (2016) 'Governing the Depths: Conceptualizing the Politics of Deep Sea Resources', in *Global Environmental Politics* 16:2, May, pp. 101–09.

Moosa, Imad A., and Vikash Ramiah (2014) *The Costs and Benefits of Environmental Regulation* (Cheltenham: Edward Elgar).

Mora, Camilo, Derek P. Tittensor, Sina Adl, Alastair G. B. Simpson, and Boris Worm (2011) 'How Many Species are there on Earth and in the Ocean?', in *PLOS Biology* 9:8, August.

Morrisette, Peter M. (1989) 'The Evolution of Policy Responses to Stratospheric Ozone Depletion', in *Natural Resources Journal* 29, pp. 793–820.

Moynihan, Daniel Patrick (1969). Letter to John Ehrlichman, Chief of Staff to President Richard M. Nixon, in Nixon archives at https://www.nixonlibrary.gov/virtuallibrary/releases/jul10/56.pdf

Murphy, Craig N. (2015) 'The Last Two Centuries of Global Governance', in *Global Governance* 21:2, April–June, pp. 189–96.

Naess, Arne (1973) 'The Shallow and the Deep, Long Range Ecology Movement. A Summary', in *Inquiry* 16:1, pp. 95–100.

Nagtzaam, Gerry (2014) 'Into the Woods: Analyzing Normative Evolution and the International Tropical Timber Organization', in *Arts and Social Sciences Journal* 5:2, open access.

Nasr, Seyyed Hossein (1975) *Islam and the Plight of Modern Man* (London: Longman).

Nentjes, Andries, Frans P. de Vries, and Doede Wiersma (2007) 'Technology-Forcing through Environmental Regulation', in *European Journal of Political Economy* 23:4, December, pp. 903–16.

Netherlands Environmental Assessment Agency (2015) *Trends in Global CO_2 Emissions: 2015 Report* (The Hague: Netherlands Environmental Assessment Agency).

Newig, Jens, and Edward Challies (2014) 'Water, Rivers and Wetlands', in Paul G. Harris (ed) *Routledge Handbook of Global Environmental Politics* (Abingdon: Routledge).

Newman, Richard S. (2016) *Love Canal: A Toxic History from Colonial Times to the Present* (New York: Oxford University Press).

Nordhaus, Ted, and Michael Shellenberger (2007) *Break Through: From the Death of Environmentalism to the Politics of Possibility* (New York: Houghton Mifflin).

Norman, Emma S., Christina Cook, and Alice Cohen (2015) (eds) *Negotiating Water Governance: Why the Politics of Scale Matter* (Abingdon: Routledge).

Nuclear Energy Agency (2016). Waste data from web site at https://www.oecd-nea.org/databank (retrieved November 2016)

Nunan, Fiona (2015) *Understanding Poverty and the Environment: Analytical Frameworks and Approaches* (Abingdon: Routledge).

Ohmae, Kenichi (2005) *The Next Global Stage: Challenges and Opportunities in our Borderless World* (Upper Saddle River, NJ: Wharton School Publishing).

Oral, Nilufer (2015) 'Forty years of the UNEP Regional Seas Programme: From Past to Future', in Rosemary Rayfuse (ed) *Research Handbook on International Marine Environmental Law* (Cheltenham: Edward Elgar).

Oreskes, Naomi, and Erik M. Conway (2010) *Merchants of Doubt: How a Handful of Scientists Obscured the Truth on Issues from Tobacco Smoke to Global Warming* (New York: Bloomsbury).

Organization for Economic Cooperation and Development (2011) *Towards Green Growth* (Paris: OECD).

Organization for Economic Cooperation and Development (2015) *Environment at a Glance 2015* (Paris: OECD).

Ostrom, Elinor (1990) *Governing the Commons: The Evolution of Institutions for Collective Action* (Cambridge: Cambridge University Press).

Pahl-Wostl, Claudia, Joyeeta Gupta, and Daniel Petry (2008) 'Governance and the Global Water System: A Theoretical Exploration', in *Global Governance* 14:4, October–December, pp. 419–35.

Panjabi, Ranee Khooshie Lal (2009) 'The Pirates of Somalia: Opportunistic Predators or Environmental Prey?', in *William & Mary Environmental Law and Policy Review* 34:1, Fall, pp. 377–491.

Parker, Laura (2015) 'Ocean Trash: 5.25 Trillion Pieces and Counting, but Big Questions Remain', in *National Geographic*, 11 January.

Parson, Edward A. (2003) *Protecting the Ozone Layer: Science and Strategy* (New York: Oxford University Press).

Partlow, Joshua, and Joby Warrick (2016) 'A Dangerous Export: America's Car-Battery Waste is Making Mexican Communities Sick', in *Washington Post*, 26 February.

Passmore, John (1974) *Man's Responsibility for Nature. Ecological Problems and Western Traditions* (London: Gerald Duckworth).

Pearce, David, Anil Markandya and Edward B. Barbier (1989) *Blueprint for a Green Economy* (London: Earthscan).

Peh, Kelvin S.-H., Richard T. Corlett, and Yves Bergeron (eds) (2015) *Routledge Handbook of Forest Ecology* (Abingdon: Routledge).

Penas Lado, Ernesto (2016) *The Common Fisheries Policy: The Quest for Sustainability* (Chichester: John Wiley).

Peterson del Mar, David (2012) *Environmentalism* (Abingdon: Routledge).

Pierson, Christopher (2011) *The Modern State*, 3rd edn (Abingdon: Routledge).

Pimentel, David, Rodolfo Zuniga, and Doug Morrison (2005) 'Update on the Environmental and Economic Costs Associated with Alien Invasive Species in the United States', in *Ecological Economics* 52:3, 15 February, pp. 273–88.

Piper, Karen (2015) *The Price of Thirst: Global Inequality and the Coming Chaos* (Minneapolis, MN: University of Minnesota Press).

Porritt, Jonathan (1984) *Seeing Green* (Oxford: Basil Blackwell).

Prakash, Aseem (2017) 'The EU Effect: Does Trade with the EU Reduce CO_2 Emissions in the Developing World?', in *Environmental Politics* 26:1, pp. 27–48.

Pratt, Laura A. (2011) 'Decreasing Dirty Dumping? A Reevaluation of Toxic Waste Colonialism and the Global Management of Transboundary Hazardous Waste', in *William & Mary Environmental Law and Policy Review* 35:2, pp. 581–623.

Pring, George, and Catherine Pring (2015) 'Twenty-First Century Environmental Dispute Resolution. Is there an 'ECT' in Your Future?', in *Journal of Energy and Natural Resources Law* 33:1, February, pp. 10–33.

Purdy, Jedediah (2015) *After Nature: A Politics for the Anthropocene* (Cambridge, MA: Harvard University Press).
Ramsar Convention on Wetlands of International Importance (2017). Home page at http://www.ramsar.org (retrieved February 2017).
Rayfuse, Rosemary (2015) 'Regional Fisheries Management Organizations', in Donald Rothwell, Alex Oude Elferink, Karen Scott, and Tim Stephens (eds) *The Oxford Handbook of the Law of the Sea* (Oxford: Oxford University Press).
Redclift, Michael (1987) *Sustainable Development Exploring the Contradictions* (London: Methuen).
Regan, Tom (1985) 'The Case for Animal Rights', in Peter Singer (ed) *In Defense of Animals* (New York: Basil Blackwell).
Reimann, Kim D. (2006) 'A View from the Top: International Politics, Norms and the Worldwide Growth of NGOs', in *International Studies Quarterly* 50:1, March, pp. 45–67.
Revkin, Andrew C., and Katharine Q. Seelye (2003) 'Report by the EPA Leaves out Data on Climate Change', in *New York Times*, 19 June.
Robbins, Paul (2012) *Political Ecology*, 2nd edn (Chichester: John Wiley).
Robinson, Robert A., et al (2009) 'Travelling through a Warming World: Climate Change and Migratory Species', in *Endangered Species Research* 7:2, pp. 87–99.
Rochette, Julien, Sebastian Unger, Dorothée Herr, David Johnson, Takehiro Nakamura, Tim Packeiser, Alexander Proelss, Martin Visbeck, Andrew Wright and Daniel Cebrian (2014) 'The Regional Approach to the Conservation and Sustainable Use of Marine Biodiversity in Areas Beyond National Jurisdiction', in *Marine Policy* 46, November, pp. 109–17.
Rogers, Everett M. (2003) *Diffusion of Innovations*, 5th edn (New York: Free Press).
Rosenbaum, Walter A. (2017) *Environmental Politics and Policy*, 10th edn (Thousand Oaks, CA: Sage).
Rowell, Andrew (1996) *Green Backlash: Global Subversion of the Environment Movement* (Abingdon: Routledge).
Sachs, Jeffrey D. (2016) *The Age of Sustainable Development* (New York: Columbia University Press).
Safi, Michael (2016) 'Indian Government Declares Delhi Air Pollution an Emergency', in *The Guardian*, 6 November.
Saksena, Sumeet, and Kirk R. Smith (2003) 'Indoor Air Pollution', in Gordon McGranahan and Frank Murray (eds) *Air Pollution and Health in Rapidly Developing Countries* (London: Earthscan).
Salman, Salman M.A. (2007) 'The United Nations Watercourses Convention Ten Years Later: Why Has its Entry into Force Proven Difficult?', in *Water International* 32:1, March, pp. 1–15.
Sandford, Rosemary (1994), 'International Environmental Treaty Secretariats: Stage-Hands or Actors?', in Helge Ole Bergesen and Georg Parmann (eds) *Green Globe Yearbook of International Co-operation on Environment and Development 1994* (Oxford: Oxford University Press).
Sandler, Ronald D., and Phaedra C. Pezzullo (eds) (2007) *Environmental Justice and Environmentalism: The Social Justice Challenge to the Environmental Movement* (Cambridge, MA: MIT Press).
Sands, Philippe, Jacqueline Peel, Adriana Fabra, and Ruth MacKenzie (2012) *Principles of International Environmental Law*, 3rd edn (Cambridge: Cambridge University Press).

Sands, Roger, David A. Norton, and Christopher J. Weston (2013) 'The Environmental Value of Forests', in Roger Sands (ed) (2013) *Forestry in a Global Context*, 2nd edn (Wallingford: CAB International).

Schmeier, Susanne (2013) *Governing International Watercourses: River Basin Organizations and the Sustainable Governance of International Shared Rivers and Lakes* (Abingdon: Routledge).

Schmeier, Susanne (2014) 'International River Basin Organizations Lost in Translation? Transboundary River Basin Governance Between Science and Policy', in Anik Bhaduri, Janos Bogardi, Jan Leentvaar, and Sina Marx (eds) *The Global Water System in the Anthropocene* (Bonn: Springer).

Schmidheiny, Stephan (1992) *Changing Course: A Global Business Perspective on Development and the Environment* (Cambridge, MA: MIT Press).

Schnurr, Matthew A., and Larry A. Swatuk (eds) (2012) *Natural Resources and Social Conflict: Towards Critical Environmental Security* (Basingstoke: Palgrave Macmillan).

Schreurs, Miranda A. (2011) 'Climate Change Politics in an Authoritarian State: The Ambivalent Case of China', in John S. Dryzek, Richard B. Norgaard, and David Schlosberg (eds) *The Oxford Handbook of Climate Change and Society* (Oxford: Oxford University Press).

Schubert, Samuel R., Johannes Pollak, and Maren Kreutler (2016) *Energy Policy of the European Union* (London: Palgrave).

Schumacher, E. F. (1973) *Small is Beautiful: Economics as if People Mattered* (London: Blond and Briggs).

Scudder, Thayer (2005) *The Future of Large Dams* (London: Earthscan).

Selin, Henrik (2014) 'Global Environmental Law and Treaty-Making on Hazardous Substances: The Minamata Convention and Mercury Abatement', in *Global Environmental Politics* 14:1, February, pp. 1–19.

Shabecoff, Philip (1988) 'Global Warming Has Begun, Expert Tells Senate', in *New York Times*, 24 June.

Shao, Wanyun (2017) 'Weather, climate, politics, or God? Determinants of American Public Opinions Toward Global Warming', in *Environmental Politics* 26:1, pp. 71–96.

Sharp, Ellis (1998) *The Dump* (London: Zoilus Press).

Shearman, Philip, Jane Bryan, and William F. Laurance (2012) 'Are We Approaching 'Peak Timber' in the Tropics?', in *Biological Conservation* 151:1, July, pp. 17–21.

Shellenberger, Michael, and Ted Nordhaus (2004), 'The Death of Environmentalism: Global Warming Politics in a Post-environmental World', at http://www.thebreakthrough.org/PDF/Death_of_Environmentalism.pdf

Shin, Dong-Chun (2016) *Hazardous Air Pollutants: Case Studies from Asia* (Boca Raton, FL: CRC Press).

Shirani, Fiona, Catherine Butler, Karen Henwood, Karen Parkhill and Nick Pidgeon (2015) '"I'm Not a Tree Hugger, I'm Just Like You". Changing Perceptions of Sustainable Lifestyles', in *Environmental Politics* 24:1, pp. 57–74.

Siebenhüner, Bernd (2015) 'Secretariats', in Morin, Jean-Frédéric, and Amandine Orsini (eds) *Essential Concepts of Global Environmental Governance* (Abingdon: Routledge).

Singer, Peter (1975) *Animal Liberation: A New Ethics for our Treatment of Animals* (New York: HarperCollins).

Skovgaard, Jakob (2014) 'EU Climate Policy after the Crisis', in *Environmental Politics* 23:1, pp. 1–17.

Slaughter, Anne-Marie (2011) 'International Relations: Principal Theories', in Rüdiger Wolfrum (ed) *Max Planck Encyclopedia of Public International Law* (Oxford: Oxford University Press).

Slaughter, Anne-Marie, and Thomas N. Hale (2011) 'Transgovernmental Networks', in Mark Bevir (ed) *The Sage Handbook of Governance* (London: Sage).

Smardon, Richard C. (2009) *Sustaining the World's Wetlands: Setting Policy and Resolving Conflicts* (Dordrecht: Springer).

Smith, Kimberly K. (2012) *Governing Animals: Animal Welfare and the Liberal State* (Oxford: Oxford University Press).

Smith, Robert Angus (1872) *Air and Rain: The Beginnings of a Chemical Climatology* (London: Longmans, Green & Co.).

Smith, S. J., J. van Aardenne, Z. Klimont, R. J. Andres, A. Volke, and S. Delgado Arias (2011) 'Anthropogenic Sulfur Dioxide Emissions: 1850–2005', in *Atmospheric Chemistry and Physics* 11, pp. 1101–16

Spaargaren, Gert, and Arthur P.J. Mol (2008) 'Greening Global Consumption: Redefining Politics and Authority', in *Global Environmental Change* 18:3, August, pp. 350–59.

Steinberg, Paul F., and Stacy D. VanDeveer (eds) (2012) *Comparative Environmental Politics: Theory, Practice, and Prospects* (MIT Press).

Steyn, Phia (2014) 'Oil, Ethnic Minority Groups and Environmental Struggles against Multinational Oil Companies and the Federal Government in the Nigerian Niger Delta since the 1990s', in Marco Armiero and Lise Sedrez (eds) *A History of Environmentalism: Local Struggles, Global Histories* (London: Bloomsbury).

Stoett, Peter (2010) 'Framing Bioinvasion: Biodiversity, Climate Change, Security, Trade, and Global Governance', in *Global Governance* 16:1, January–March, pp. 103–20.

Stokes, Bruce, Richard Wike, and Jill Carle (2015) 'Concern about Climate Change and its Consequences'. Pew Research Centre, 5 November, at http://www.pewglobal.org/2015/11/05/1-concern-about-climate-change-and-its-consequences

Sultana, Farhana, and Alex Loftus (eds) (2012) *The Right to Water: Politics, Governance and Social Struggles* (Abingdon: Earthscan).

Tacconi, Luca (2007) 'Decentralization, Forests and Livelihoods: Theory and Narrative', in *Global Environmental Change* 17, pp. 338–48.

Takao, Yasuo (2012) 'The Transformation of Japan's Environmental Policy', in *Environmental Politics* 21:5, pp. 772–90.

Talus, Kim (2014) *Research Handbook on International Energy Law* (Cheltenham: Edward Elgar).

Tang, Shui-Yan, and Xueyong Zhan (2008) 'Civic Environmental NGOs, Civil Society, and Democratisation in China', in *Journal of Development Studies* 44:3, March, pp. 425–48.

Taylor, Paul (1986) *Respect for Nature: A Theory of Environmental Ethics* (Princeton, NJ: Princeton University Press).

Tews, Kerstin, Per-Olof Busch, and Helge Jörgens (2003) 'The Diffusion of New Environmental Policy Instruments', in *European Journal of Political Research* 42:4, June, pp. 569–600.

Tilt, Bryan (2015) *Dams and Development in China: The Moral Economy of Water and Power* (New York: Columbia University Press).

Tierney, John (2015) 'The Reign of Recycling', in *New York Times*, 3 October.

Tietenberg, Thomas H. (2006) *Emissions Trading: Principle and Practice*, 2nd edn (Washington DC: Resources for the Future).

Tietenberg, Tom, and Lynne Lewis (2016) *Environmental and Natural Resource Economics*, 10th edn (Abingdon: Routledge).

Treves, Tullio (2015) 'Historical Development of the Law of the Sea', in Donald Rothwell, Alex Oude Elferink, Karen Scott, and Tim Stephens (eds) *The Oxford Handbook of the Law of the Sea* (Oxford: Oxford University Press).

Uekötter, Frank (2014) *The Greenest Nation? A New History of German Environmentalism* (Cambridge, MA: MIT Press).

UN Environment Programme (2017). Homepage at http://www.unep.org (retrieved April 2017).

UN Population Fund data at http://www.unfpa.org/world-population-trends (retrieved May 2016).

UN University (2013) *Water Security and the Global Water Agenda*. UN-Water Analytical Brief (Hamilton, Ontario: UN University).

UN World Tourism Organization (2016) *Compendium of Tourism Statistics* at http://statistics.unwto.org/content/compendium-tourism-statistics (retrieved May 2016).

UN World Water Assessment Programme (2015) *World Water Development Report 2015: Water for a Sustainable World* (Paris: UNESCO).

Underdal, Arild (2010) 'Complexity and Challenges of Long-Term Environmental Governance', in *Global Environmental Change* 20:3, August, pp. 386–93.

United Nations Environment Programme (2012) *Global Environment Outlook 5: Environment for the Future We Want* (Nairobi: UNEP).

US Congressional Research Service (2011) *Clean Air Act: A Summary of the Act and its Major Requirements* (Washington DC: Congressional Research Service).

US Energy Information Administration (2016a) 'Waste-to-Energy Electricity Generation Concentrated in Florida', 8 April, at https://www.eia.gov/todayinenergy/detail.php?id=25732

US Energy Information Administration (2016b) 'Changing U.S. Energy Mix Reflects Growing Use of Natural Gas, Petroleum, and Renewables', in *Today in Energy*, 21 July, at https://www.eia.gov/todayinenergy/detail.php?id=27172

US Environmental Protection Agency (1996), 'EPA Takes Final Step in Phase-out of Leaded Gasoline', at https://archive.epa.gov/epa/aboutepa/epa-takes-final-step-phaseout-leaded-gasoline.html https://archive.epa.gov/epa/aboutepa/epa-takes-final-step-phaseout-leaded-gasoline.html

US Environmental Protection Agency (2016) *Light-Duty Automotive Technology, Carbon Dioxide Emissions, and Fuel Economy Trends: 1975 Through 2016* (Washington DC: EPA).

Union of International Associations. Homepage at http://www.uia.org (retrieved July 2016).

Vallero, Daniel A., and Trevor M. Letcher (2012) *Unraveling Environmental Disasters* (Waltham, MA: Elsevier).

Vallero, Daniel A. (2014) *Fundamentals of Air Pollution*, 5th edn (Waltham, MA: Elsevier).

Van Alstine, James, Stavros Afionis and Peter Doran (2013) 'The UN Conference on Sustainable Development (Rio+20): A Sign of the Times or 'Ecology as Spectacle?', in *Environmental Politics* 22:2, pp. 333–38.

Vaughn, Caryn C. (2010) 'Biodiversity Losses and Ecosystem Function in Freshwaters: Emerging Conclusions and Research Directions', in *Bioscience* 60:1, January, pp. 25–35.

Vaughan, Steven (2015) *EU Chemicals Regulation: New Governance, Hybridity and REACH* (Cheltenham: Edward Elgar).

Visgilio, Gerald R., and Diana M. Whitelaw (eds) (2007) *Acid in the Environment: Lessons Learned and Future Prospects* (New York: Springer).

Voelcker, John (2014) '1.2 Billion Vehicles on World's Roads Now, 2 Billion By 2035: Report', in *Green Car Reports*, 29 July, at http://www.greencarreports.com/news/1093560_1-2-billion-vehicles-on-worlds-roads-now-2-billion-by-2035-report

Vogel, David (1995) *Trading Up: Consumer and Environmental Regulation in a Global Economy* (Cambridge, MA: Harvard University Press).

Waldau, Paul (2011) *Animal Rights: What Everyone Needs to Know* (Oxford: Oxford University Press).

Walker, Gabrielle (2007) *An Ocean of Air: Why the Wind Blows and Other Mysteries of the Atmosphere* (London: Bloomsbury).

Walker, Gordon (2012) *Environmental Justice: Concepts, Evidence and Politics* (Abingdon: Routledge).

Wapner, Paul (2014) 'The Changing Nature of Nature: Environmental Politics in the Anthropocene', in *Global Environmental Politics* 14:4. November, pp. 36–54.

Watson, James E.M., Danielle F. Shanahan, Moreno Di Marco, James Allan, William F. Laurance, Eric W. Sanderson, Brendan Mackey, and Oscar Venter (2016) 'Catastrophic Declines in Wilderness Areas Undermine Global Environment Targets', in *Current Biology* 26, November, pp. 1–6.

Watson, Jim, and Raphael Sauter (2011), 'Sustainable Innovation through Leapfrogging: A Review of the Evidence', in *International Journal of Technology and Globalisation* 5:3–4, April, pp. 170–89.

Weale, Albert (1992) *The New Politics of Pollution* (Manchester: Manchester University Press).

White Jr., Lynn (1967) 'The Historical Roots of Our Ecological Crisis', in *Science* 155:3767, 10 March, pp. 1203–07.

Wilson, E.O. (2007) 'My wish: Build the Encyclopedia of Life'. Speech at acceptance of TED Prize, March, at https://www.ted.com/talks/e_o_wilson_on_saving_life_on_earth/transcript?language=en

Wingfield-Hayes, Rupert (2016) 'Japan and the Whale', BBC Online, 8 February.

Witter, Rebecca, Kimberly R. Marion Suiseeya, Rebecca L. Gruby, Sarah Hitchner, Edward M. Maclin, Maggie Bourque, and J. Peter Brosius (2015) 'Moments of Influence in Global Environmental Governance', in *Environmental Politics* 24:6, pp. 894–912.

Wong, Edward (2014) 'China Exports Pollution to US, Study Finds', in *New York Times*, 20 January.

World Bank (2012) *What a Waste: A Global Review of Solid Waste Management* (Washington DC: World Bank).

World Bank (2016) *World Development Indicators: Travel and Tourism* at http://wdi.worldbank.org/table/6.14 (retrieved May 2016).

World Health Organization (2011) *Guidelines for Drinking-Water Quality*, 4th edn (Geneva: WHO).

World Health Organization (2014) '7 Million Premature Deaths Annually Linked to Air Pollution'. News release, 25 March, at http://www.who.int/mediacentre/news/releases/2014/air-pollution/en

World Health Organization (2016) Drinking-Water Fact Sheet at http://www.who.int/mediacentre/factsheets/fs391/en, reviewed November.

World Meteorological Organization *(2014) Assessment for Decision-Makers: Scientific Assessment of Ozone Depletion: 2014* Global Ozone Research and Monitoring Project—Report No. 56 (Geneva: WMO).

World Wildlife Fund US (2016). Home page at http://wwf.panda.org/about_our_earth/biodiversity/biodiversity (retrieved May 2016).

Xu, Y. (2011) 'Improvements in the Operation of SO_2 Scrubbers in China's Coal Power Plants', in *Environmental Science Technology* 45, pp. 380–85.

Young, Oran R. (2002) *The Institutional Dimensions of Environmental Change: Fit, Interplay, and Scale* (Cambridge, MA: MIT Press).

Young, Stephen C. (1993) *The Politics of the Environment* (Manchester: Baseline Books).

Zalasiewicz, Jan, Mark Williams, Will Steffen, and Paul Crutzen (2010) 'The New World of the Anthropocene', in *Environmental Science and Technology* 44:7, 1 April, pp. 2228–31.

Index

accidents *see* environmental accidents
acid pollution   19, 113, 130–3, 228
   and emissions trading   63, 64
   and the policy cycle   49–52
   causes of   119, 120, 130
   Convention on Long-range Transboundary Air Pollution   122, 130–1
   in the North   130–3
   in the South   133
   policy response to   50–2, 130–1, 132–3
   politics of   130–3
   science of   49–50, 130
   solutions to   50–1, 229
   trends   51, 131–2
administrative fragmentation   76
animals and ethics   39
air pollution   8, 31, 55, 63, 112ff, 151, 192
   defining the problem   114–9
   emissions trading   64–5, 243
   in Asia   115–6
   London   15, 16, 56, 115
   long-range transboundary   130–3
   major pollutants   119–24
   See also climate change
Anthropocene   xiv-xv, 203, 205
anthropocentrism   38
anti-environmentalism   3, 12
aquifers   138, 144, 148, 158
Australia   64, 78, 149, 212, 260
authority   7, 20, 52, 59, 93, 96

BP   32, 243
biodiversity   26, 202ff
   charismatic megafauna   216
   Convention on Biological Diversity   20, 104, 105, 110, 165, 166, 209, 218, 220, 221
   defining the problem   204–7
   endangered species   15, 26, 206, 215, 218
   extinctions   xv, 26, 162, 204, 205–6, 218
   megadiversity   55, 204–5
   migratory species   55, 153, 208–9
   poaching   87, 220
   policy   215–18
   protected areas   55, 218–22
   Red List   100, 203, 206
   species   26, 39, 146–7, 168, 174, 203, 204–6, 207, 208, 215, 216–17, 218
   threats to   88, 146, 207–15, 235
   wild genetic resources   209
biofuels   235, 261
biopiracy   209
biosphere   203, 207
   Man and the Biosphere programme   154, 215, 217
Blackstone, William   38
Brazil   153, 154, 212, 256
   tropical rainforests   87, 165, 261
Britain   18, 125, 176, 192, 266
   and acid pollution   131
   and Industrial Revolution   115, 224–5
   London, air pollution   15, 16, 56, 115
Brown, Lester   41
Brundtland Commission   13

built environment   4, 60
bureaucracies   75–7, 103, 104
business and the environment   12, 20, 24, 25, 32–6, 64, 78, 84, 108, 126, 148, 150, 243, 266
bycatch   174

Caldwell, Lynton Keith   3, 37–8
California effect   89, 261
Canada   12, 28, 84, 100, 125, 260, 266
  and acid pollution   115, 132
  Canada's Environmental Choice   35
  Harper, Stephen   28, 260, 266
cap-and-trade *see* emissions trading
carbon capture   229
carbon dioxide   64, 65, 97, 114, 121, 166, 168, 208, 210, 227, 229, 247, 248–9, 254, 257, 265
carbon footprint   252
carbon monoxide   121, 122, 123
carbon sequestration   121
carbon sink   121, 153, 154, 162, 211, 226, 249, 255, 256, 258, 261, 264
carbon tax   64, 65
Carson, Rachel   16, 108
catalytic converters   120–1, 126, 132
charismatic megafauna   216
chemicals   16, 26, 115, 142, 143, 144, 145, 149, 191, 194–7, 228
  See also individual pollutants, air pollution, ozone layer
Chernobyl nuclear accident   56, 196, 241
China   97, 138, 140, 150, 163, 164, 216
  acid/air pollution   55, 121, 133
  and climate change   97, 261, 262, 265
  and energy   226, 228, 230, 231, 236, 241, 243

  and environmental authoritarianism   54–5
  and maritime resources   42–3, 175, 176, 230
  parties and interest groups   82
  waste production/disposal   183, 190–1, 193, 197
Chipko movement   81
chlorofluorocarbons   9–10, 124, 125, 127–9
civil society   69, 80
  global   107
climate change   xiv, 2, 8, 19, 25, 27, 28, 38–9, 55, 95, 113, 242–3, 246ff
  and biodiversity   213
  Climate Change Performance Index   266
  climate refugees   41, 251
  defining the problem   248–53
  doubters and deniers xiv, 20, 28, 154, 247, 253
  effects   208, 210, 250–2
  Framework Convention on Climate Change   20, 60, 101, 104, 166, 247, 258–67
  greenhouse effect   113, 114, 121, 247, 248, 254, 255
  greenhouse gases   xiv, 113, 115, 119, 140, 166, 228, 240, 242, 246, 247, 248–9, 259, 263
  Intergovernmental Panel on Climate Change   94, 95, 101, 243, 250, 258, 259, 264
  Kyoto protocol   247, 259–60
  Paris accord   234, 247, 262–4
  policy   2, 4, 254–8, 266–7
  politics of   129, 253, 254ff
  public opinion   55, 254
  science of   25, 248–52, 254–5, 259
  solutions   89, 153, 255
  trends   264–6
coal   15, 66, 113, 115, 116, 118, 119, 133, 225, 227, 228–30, 240, 243, 252, 264
collective action problem   32, 36

command-and-control 53, 63–4
Commoner, Barry 6, 17, 23, 181
comparative politics xvi, xvii, 53–4, 68, 75, 102
conferences *see* environmental conferences
conservation 13, 16, 139
  wildlife and nature 154, 216, 220, 221
consumer-led solutions 35–6
consumer society 179ff
consumers and the environment 20, 24, 32, 34, 35, 54, 61, 86, 147, 187–9
common pool resources 29–30, 161
  fisheries as 173ff
  oceans as 168ff
contingent valuation 31–2
convention *see* treaty
coral reefs 168, 209–10, 217, 252
courts 62, 75, 77–8
Cornucopian approach to nature 31
corporate environmentalism 108
corporate social responsibility 24, 33–4, 108
cost-benefit analysis 30–1

dams 4, 139, 140, 235, 236
deep ecology 11, 38, 79
Deepwater Horizon oil spill 32, 56, 213, 230
deforestation 55, 81, 82, 86, 161, 162–4, 165, 166, 167
Democracy Index 71–2
dumping 88–9
  of waste 194, 200, 213
Dust Bowl 16, 41

Earth Summit *see* Rio Earth Summit
ecocentrism 38, 79
eco-labelling 35, 82, 84
ecofeminism 38
ecological democracy 73
ecological modernization 14–15

ecological state 74–5
ecologism 79
ecology 5–6
economics and the environment 12, 24, 28–32, 40–2, 189, 237–8
  green economics 18, 79
  natural resource economics 161–2
ecosystems 95, 101, 114, 146, 153, 176, 201, 207, 216, 221
ecotourism 210
Ehrlich, Paul 17
emissions trading 64–5, 243
  and acid pollution 63, 64, 133
  and climate change 261
endangered species 15, 26, 206, 215, 218
  Convention on International Trade in Endangered Species 105, 214–15
  trade in 84, 87, 214, 220
energy 224ff
  and transport 233
  biofuels 235, 261
  defining the problem 226
  fossil fuels 40, 113, 115–19, 159, 224–5, 228–34
  fuelwood 82, 87, 162, 226
  geothermal 237
  hydropower 118, 140, 152, 235–6
  nuclear 56, 83, 196, 225, 230, 234, 240, 241
  ocean power 237
  policy 238–44
  renewable sources 40, 116, 118, 226, 227, 234–8, 241, 242, 261, 266
  solar 236–7
  waste to energy 193
  wind power 237
environment, defined 3–6
  and development 85–9
environmental
  accidents 9, 16, 32, 56–57, 108, 170, 196, 225, 241
  authoritarianism 54–5

environmental (*Continued*)
 conferences   19–20, 60, 61, 99, 104, 106, 149, 258
 citizenship   73, 74
 ethics   36–40
 governance   70–5, 93–6, 101
 justice   39–40, 60, 80, 257–8
 law *see* international law
 peacebuilding   42
 policy   xvi, 8–10
  and business   12, 20, 24, 25, 32–6, 64, 78, 84, 108, 126, 148, 150, 243, 266
  and economics   12, 18, 24, 28–32, 40–2, 79, 161–2, 189, 237–8
  and philosophy   10, 24, 36–40
  and science   9–10, 15, 23–4, 25–8, 95, 128, 204, 248–52, 254–5, 259
  and security   24, 40–3, 140–1, 241
  at the international level   55–61, 92
  at the state level   52–5, 70–5
  convergence/diffusion   69, 82–4, 89, 97, 166, 215
  evolving approaches to   47–9
 policy instruments   61–6
 politics   xvi, 8
 refugees   41
 regulation *see* regulation
 scarcity   40–2
 scepticism   82, 253
 state   73–5
Environmental Performance Index   84–5
environmentalism   10–15, 82, 83
 anti-   3, 12
 corporate   108
 post-   20–21
 radical   10–11, 31
 reformist   10–11
epistemic community   94, 95
European Community *see* European Union

European Environment Agency   99, 100, 103
European Union   4, 33, 103, 126
 and acid pollution   130–2
 and climate change   64–5, 242, 247, 261–1, 264, 265–6
 and NGOs   107
 and ozone layer   127–8
 chemicals policy   103, 195, 197
 Common Fisheries Policy   175–6
 Ecolabel scheme   35
 emissions trading   64–5, 261
 energy policy   116–7, 242
 environmental law/policy   77, 78, 92, 96–7, 103
 forests   161, 163–4
 noise pollution   4–5
 oil consumption   232
 transport   232
 waste   184, 188, 199
 water policy   151–2
eutrophication   122, 142–3, 213
e-waste   188, 191, 199
Exclusive Economic Zone   169–70
Exxon Valdez oil spill   56, 213
extended producer responsibility   188

fisheries   35, 40, 105, 168, 169, 173–7, 214
 North Atlantic   55, 175–6
 Peruvian anchovy industry   174–5
 UN Fish Stocks Agreement   176
forests   162–8
 deforestation   55, 81, 82, 86, 161, 162–4, 165, 166, 167
 forest fires   123
 tropical rainforests   87, 88, 165, 167, 204, 208, 251, 255, 256, 261
fossil fuels   40, 113, 159, 224–5, 228–34
 and air pollution   115–19
fracking   223

Friends of the Earth   18, 109
fuelwood   82, 87, 162, 226
Fukushima Daiichi nuclear accident   56, 196, 230, 234

garbage-can policy model   46, 49
geothermal power   237
Germany   18, 176, 226, 125, 266
  and acid pollution   130–1
  and waste   184, 189, 193
  Blue Angel label   35
  environmental record   83, 89
global civil society   107
Global Environment Facility   89, 100, 107, 109
globalism   97
globalization   xvi, 14, 18, 20, 93, 98, 108
governance   7, 78, 86, 152, 160, 234
  environmental   70–5, 93–6, 101
  global/international   13, 93–7
government   7
  institutions   75–8
Green Belt Movement   82
green economy   14, 21
green growth   13–14, 115
Green parties/politics   18, 38, 78–80, 83, 130–1
green state   73
greenhouse effect   113, 114, 121, 247, 248, 254, 255
greenhouse gases   xiv, 113, 115, 119, 140, 166, 228, 240, 242, 246, 247, 248–9, 259, 263
Greenpeace   18, 32, 109
greenwashing   12
groundwater   137, 138, 139, 142, 144, 146, 153, 158, 234

Hardin, Garrett   30, 79
hazardous waste see waste, toxic and hazardous
heavy metals   123, 130, 131, 143, 186, 191, 228
Holocene extinction   205–6

Hubbert curve   168
human environment   4, 143
hydropower   118, 140, 152, 235–6

Iceland   172, 176, 237
incremental policy model   46
India   55, 71, 83, 97, 138, 145, 163
  acid/air pollution   29, 113, 115–6, 118, 133, 228
  and climate change   97, 261, 266
  Chipko movement   81
  waste   183, 191, 192
indoor pollution   122
Industrial Revolution   xiv, 1, 12, 15, 47, 86, 112, 115, 141, 159, 183, 224, 225, 226, 241
institutions   94
interest groups   6, 12, 17–18, 54, 78, 80–2, 99, 106–7
  See also non-governmental organizations
intergovernmental organizations   99–103
  See also United Nations
Intergovernmental Panel on Climate Change   94, 95, 101, 243, 250, 258, 259, 264
International Joint Commission   99–100
international law   56–60, 92, 97, 98–9
  See also treaties
international non-governmental organizations   99, 106–110
international organizations   98, 99–103
International Organization for Standardization   35
international relations   xvi, 91, 93, 94, 96–9, 141
International Renewable Energy Agency   241
International Tropical Timber Agreement/Organization   100, 167–8

International Union for Conservation of Nature   100, 206, 221
International Whaling Commission   2, 59, 172
invasive species   47, 140, 206, 208, 211–13
issue-attention cycle   50, 130

Japan   83, 193, 230
 air pollution   55, 125
 and whaling   59, 172
 Fukushima Daiichi nuclear accident   56, 196, 230, 234
 Minamata Bay pollution   16

landfill   182, 188–9, 191–2, 195
law, environmental *see* international law *and* treaties
lead, in fuel   117, 123, 124–6
leader-laggard dynamic   83, 84, 97, 218, 219, 260, 261, 262
legislatures   77
Leopold, Aldo   38
liberalism   96–7
limits to growth   11, 20, 79
Lomborg, Bjørn   12
London, air pollution   15, 16, 56, 115
long-range transboundary air pollution   130–3

Malthus, Thomas   17, 31
market-based policy incentives   29, 64–5
maximum sustained yield   174–5
mega-conferences   19–20, 60, 106
megadiversity   55, 204–5
methane   113, 191, 228, 232, 247, 249, 250, 255
Midgley, Thomas   125, 127
migratory species   55, 153, 208–9
models, public policy *see* public policy
Montreal protocol *see* treaties, ozone layer

multinational corporations   20, 32, 108, 168, 243
 See also business and the environment

Naess, Arne   11, 38
national parks *see* protected areas
natural environment   3
natural gas   42, 123, 232–4
natural resource economics   161–2
natural resources   157ff
 defining the problem   159–62
 fisheries   35, 40, 55, 105, 168, 169, 173–7, 214
 forests   162–8
 non-renewable   159
 oceans   168–73
 renewable   159–60
 See also fisheries, forests, oceans
neoliberalism   72
New Zealand   18, 176, 189
Nigeria   88, 108, 198
NIMBY syndrome   192, 193
nitrogen oxides   120–1, 130, 243
noise pollution   5
non-governmental organizations   69, 80, 81, 99, 102, 104, 107, 109, 151, 167, 171–8
 See also interest groups *and* international non-governmental organizations
non-point sources of pollution   142
non-regime   94
North   xvi, 18, 70, 110
 acid pollution   130–3
 energy policy   226, 233
 environmental policy in   74, 75, 83, 86, 87, 115, 142
 forests   166
 protected areas   220
 waste   181, 183, 186, 192, 197
nuclear power   56, 83, 196, 225, 230, 234, 240, 241

ocean power 237–8
oceans 168–73
  marine biodiversity/
    habitats 209–10, 221–2
oil 230–2
oil pollution/spills 56, 88, 170, 213, 230–1
  Deepwater Horizon 32, 56, 213, 230
  Torrey Canyon 16, 170, 213
Organization for Economic Cooperation and Development 33, 82, 228, 240, 256
  waste in member states 183, 184, 189, 190, 192, 198
Ostrom, Elinor 30
ozone (pollutant) 123–4
ozone layer 33, 51, 113, 125
  policy on 127–9
  threats to 9–10, 19, 115, 124, 126–7

paradigm 12–13, 16, 39, 47, 238
particulate matter 115, 122–3, 228
Passmore, John 38
Pinchot, Gifford 13
poaching 87, 220
point sources of pollution 142
policy cycle 49–52
policy convergence/diffusion 69, 82–4, 89, 97, 166, 215
political ecology 6
political parties 78–80
politics 6–10
polluter pays principle 33, 98–9, 118, 200
pollution haven hypothesis 88, 186
population growth 17, 214
post-environmentalism 20–21
post-materialism 18, 54, 83
power 7
precautionary principle 27, 98–9, 176, 200
preservation 16
product stewardship 187–8

protected areas 55, 176, 218–22
  Yellowstone, first national park 16, 217, 219
proximity principle 198
public goods 29, 74, 136, 150
public policy 4, 8–9, 45, 56, 75, 238
  convergence/diffusion 69, 82–4, 89, 97, 166, 215
  models 46
  policy cycle 49–52

radical environmentalism 10–11, 12, 31
rational policy model 46
realism 96, 98, 266
recycling 35, 65, 139, 158, 160, 182, 184, 188–90, 191, 192, 199
Red List 100, 203, 206
reformist environmentalism 10–11, 12
regime 94–5
  biodiversity 215–18
  climate change 256ff
  energy 239–44
  forestry 162, 164–8
  hazardous/toxic waste exports 198–9
  ozone 127–9
  political 70–2
  pollution at sea 170
  tropical timber 167–8
  water 148, 151
regional responses to environmental management 166–7
regional fisheries management organizations 175
UNEP Regional Seas Programme 170–2
See also European Union
regulation 12, 20, 24, 29, 31, 34, 51, 62–3, 73, 76–7, 103, 119, 231, 253
regulatory agencies 62, 76–7
religion and the environment 37

renewable energy 40, 116, 118, 226, 227, 234–8, 241, 242, 261, 266
resource curse 88, 160
Rio Declaration on Environment and Development 19–20, 27, 86–7
Rio Earth Summit 19–20, 33, 101, 105, 106, 107, 109, 110, 164, 166, 258
risk assessment 26
rivers and lakes 152
Russia xiv, 43, 176, 242, 257

Schmidheiny, Stephan 33
Schumacher, E. F. 79
science and the environment 9–10, 15, 23–4, 25–8, 95, 128, 204, 248–52, 254–5, 259
shallow ecology 11, 38
Sierra Club 16, 81
Singer, Peter 39
smog 15, 16, 32, 56, 115, 118, 119
species 26, 39, 146–7, 168, 174, 203, 204–6, 207, 208, 215, 216–17, 218
  See also endangered species, invasive species, migratory species
social movement 10, 78, 80
solar power 236–7
South xvi, 19, 70, 80, 81, 110, 140
  acid/air pollution 118, 122, 133
  energy policy 226, 232, 233, 235
  environmental policy/problems in 85–9, 115
  forests 166
  protected areas 220
  sanitation 145–6
  waste 180, 181, 182, 183, 186, 192, 197
  water quality 143, 146
South Africa 138–9
states 52–5, 70–5
  and international system 96–9
  government institutions 75–8

Stockholm conference (1972) 4, 17, 19, 47, 60, 100, 105, 110
sulphur dioxide 50, 51, 64, 114, 119–20, 130, 228, 243, 261
summitry 105–6
sustainable development 13, 14, 19, 31, 87, 98, 106, 164

technology forcing 119, 231
technology transfer 89, 149
thermal pollution 142
Torrey Canyon oil spill 16, 170, 213
tourism 210, 211
toxic colonialism 197
toxic waste *see* waste, toxic and hazardous
tragedy of the commons 30, 79
transgovernmental network 95–6
treaties 56–60, 102
  Antarctic marine living resources 176
  biological diversity 20, 104, 105, 110, 165, 166, 209, 218, 220, 221
  climate change 20, 60, 101, 104, 166, 247, 258–67
  desertification 166
  law of the sea 42, 52, 169–70, 173, 175, 176
  long-range transboundary air pollution 122, 130–1
  migratory species 154, 208–9
  nuclear energy 241
  ozone layer 104, 127–9
  partial nuclear test ban 16, 19
  prevention of marine pollution 170, 200
  trade in endangered species 105, 214–15
  transboundary movement of hazardous wastes 198–9
  tropical timber 167–8
  wetlands 154
  whaling 2, 172
treaty secretariats 59, 103–6, 110, 264

tropical rainforests 87, 88, 165, 167, 204, 208, 251, 255, 256, 261

umbrella effect 216–17
United Kingdom *see* Britain
United Nations 16, 52, 136
  Conference on Environment and Development *see* Rio Earth Summit
  Conference on Human Environment *see* Stockholm conference
  Convention on the Law of the Sea 42, 52, 169–70, 173, 175, 176
  Economic Commission for Europe 130
  Fish Stocks Agreement 176
  Food and Agriculture Organization 16, 99, 100, 164, 167, 173, 175
  Forum on Forests 164–5
  International Maritime Organization 100, 170, 240
  UN Educational, Scientific, and Cultural Organization 16, 154, 215
  World Bank 99, 100, 101, 140, 150, 151, 164, 240
  World Charter for Nature 217–18
  World Health Organization 114, 143, 149
  World Meteorological Organization 100, 101, 258, 259
United Nations Environment Programme 93, 98, 176, 100–2, 104, 107, 109, 126
  Regional Seas Programme 170–2
United States 5, 16, 35, 78, 80, 81
  air pollution 63, 89, 151
  and acid pollution 64, 132–3
  and climate change 28, 253, 259–60, 264, 265, 266
  and international treaties 166, 218
  and ozone layer 127–8
  Bush, George W. 28, 80, 259, 260
  chemicals policy 26, 194–5
  coal industry 230, 264–5
  emissions trading 63, 64, 133, 243
  environmental scepticism 82, 253
  Environmental Protection Agency 28, 62, 63, 81, 125, 195
  forests 161, 166
  hazardous waste 198, 199
  lead in fuel 124–5, 126
  nuclear waste 196
  oil consumption 231–2
  protected areas 16, 153, 154, 212, 217, 219
  radioactive waste 196
  Trump, Donald 253, 266
  US Forest Service 13, 16, 161
  waste policy 184, 190, 192, 193, 194–5, 198
  water 138, 144–5, 151

Vienna Convention *see* treaties, ozone layer
volatile organic compounds 121–2

waste 179ff
  agricultural 184
  defining the problem 181–6
  disposal of 191–3
  e-waste 188, 191, 199
  exporting and dumping 197–200
  incineration 192–3
  industrial 186
  landfill 182, 188–9, 191–2, 195
  municipal 180, 182–4, 185, 187, 189, 190, 192, 193, 235
  policy 186–93
  prevention of 187–8
  radioactive 196

waste (*Continued*)
  recovery of   188–91
  recycling   188–9
  toxic and hazardous   186, 194–7
  zero waste   187, 189, 190
water   135ff
  and ecology   153–5
  aquifers   138, 144, 148, 158
  bottled   147, 188
  different uses   137
  drinking   143–5
  fluoridation of   145
  groundwater   137, 138, 139, 142, 144, 146, 153, 158, 234
  irrigation   139, 140, 142
  policy   148–53
  pollution   141–8
  quality   136, 141–8
  quantity   135–6, 137–41
  sanitation   145–6
  security   138–9
  World Water Council/Forum   150
wetlands   55, 140, 153–5, 207
  Everglades   153, 154, 212
  Pantanal   153, 154
whaling   2, 59, 172
White, Lynn   37
wild genetic resources   209
wilderness   16, 31, 40, 155, 211, 219
wind power   237
World Environment Day   101
World Resources Institute   41, 109
World Wildlife Fund   18, 109, 216
Worldwatch Institute   41, 81

zero waste   187, 189, 190

Printed in Great Britain
by Amazon